GREECE
ON FOOT

"Trustworthy directions, explicit details, accurate suggestions—the book is chock full of this kind of admirable first-hand information. It conveys a better sense of contemporary culture in Greece than any of the more ambitious guidebooks around."
> —Kevin Kelly, WHOLE EARTH REVIEW

"After reading Dubin's intriguing book, I'll have to take my next trek in Greece!"
> —Hugh Swift, author, *The Trekker's Guide to the Himalaya and Karakoram*

"There is another Greece, away from the fleshpots and all-too-familiar postcard views, and Marc Dubin has discovered it: that wild, beautiful, remote country that sings to you along the old shepherd paths. It is for the curious, the adventurous, the solitaries, and for those who really love Greece. It will always be so."
> —Michael Haag, author, *Guide to Greece;* travel writer, *The Guardian* and *Vogue* (UK)

"By traveling on foot and observing with a fresh eye, Dubin has rediscovered the sense of curiosity and adventure that shone through travel literature of the past. Traveling through Greece at three miles an hour develops your sense of observation and introduces you to a Greece that most recent travel books ignore."
> —Sloane Elliott, publisher, *The Athenian*

GREECE
ON FOOT

Mountain Treks, Island Trails

MARC S. DUBIN

CORDEE
Leicester/London

Copyright © 1986 by The Mountaineers

Published in Great Britain by Cordee
3a DeMontfort St.
Leicester, England LE1 7HD

Published simultaneously:
In the United States by
The Mountaineers, 306 2nd Ave. W.,
Seattle, WA 98119
In Canada by
Douglas & McIntyre Ltd., 1615 Venables St.,
Vancouver, B. C. V5L 2H1

Manufactured in the United States of America

Copy edited by Barbara Chasan
Book design by Marge Mueller
Cover design by Elizabeth Watson
Photos by the author unless otherwise credited
Map art by Marc Dubin and Martha Degasis
Map lettering by Tom Carlyle Graphic Design

Cover photos: (center) southern coast of Crete between Ayía Roúmeli and Loutró; (upper right and clockwise) old woman of Kárpathos, Ólymbos church and village, Ólymbos seamstress, bridge over the Aóös River in Vovoússa, church at Loutró on Crete, Sými fisherman, working windmills of Ólymbos, Cretan priest. (Center photo by Allen Steck, lower right by Marc Dubin, others by Ann Cleeland)
Frontispiece: The peaks Ploskos (right) and Gamíla I reflected in the waters of Dhrakólimni, in the Gamíla range (Hike 15)

British Library Cataloguing in Publication Data

Dubin, Marc S.
Greece on foot.
1. Greece—Description and travel—1981-
I. Title
914.95'0476   DF728

ISBN 0-904405-33-8

Credits

Epigram pp. 11, 205: From *Roumeli* by Patrick Leigh Fermor. © 1966 by Patrick Leigh Fermor. Reprinted by permission of Viking Penguin Inc.
Epigram pp. 41, 56, 117, 135: From *The Flight of Ikaros* by Kevin Andrews (Penguin Books, 1984). © 1984 by Kevin Andrews.
Epigram p. 45: From *Mani* by Patrick Leigh Fermor. © 1958 by Patrick Leigh Fermor. Reprinted by permission of Viking Penguin Inc.
Epigram p. 49: From *The Hill of Kronos*, © 1981 by Peter Levi. Reprinted by permission of the publisher, E.P. Dutton, a division of New American Library.
Epigram p. 77: From *Eleni*, © 1983 by Nicholas Gage. Originally published by Random House.
Epigram p. 149: Reprinted from *Portrait of a Greek Mountain Village* by Juliet Du Boulay (1974) by permission of Oxford University Press.
Epigram p. 158: From *The Colossus of Maroussi* by Henry Miller. © 1941 by Henry Miller. Reprinted by permission of New Directions Publishing Corporation.
Epigram p. 162: From *The Cyclades*, © 1885 by James T. Bent. Reprinted in public domain 1966 by Argonaut Press, Chicago.
Epigram p. 193: From *Journey to a Greek Island*, © 1967 by Elias Kulukundis. Published by Macmillan Publishing Company.

To the shepherds of the Greek mountains,
who have saved my neck more times than I can remember . . .

and to Martha, who walked the last two months with me

Ayía Paraskeví monastery above Víkos, Monodhéndhri (Hike 15)

MAKEDHONIA

⑲ Dhráma

Kaválla ○

THRAKI

Thessaloníki ○

Alexandhroúpoli

⑱

Kónitsa ⑰ ⑯

⑮

Ioánnina ○

IPIROS

⑭

Tríkala ○

Lárissa ○

THESSALIA

Árta ○

⑬

Karpeníssi

②②

②③

MAGNISIA

②④

Vólos ○

②⑥

②⑤

SPORADHES

⑳

②①

Samothráki

Lamía ○

⑫ ⑨

⑪ ⑩ ⑧

Ámfissa

STEREA

Evvia

②⑦

Halkídha ○

Livádhia ○

Pátras ○

⑥ ⑤

PELOPONNISOS

③

Trípoli

④ ○

Kalamáta ○

Spárti

②

③⓪

②⑨

ARGO

SARONIC

⑦

Athens (Athéna) ○

②⑧

②⑨ ③②

③①

KYKLADHES

⑶⑶ ③④

③⑤ ③⑥

(CYCLADES)

③⑦

③⑨ ③⑧

E SAMOS

④①

④⓪

Rhódhos

④②

DHODHEKANISOS

(DODECANESE)

GREECE

Haniá

⑷⑸ ⑷⑷

CRETE (KRITI)

④③ Iráklion

CONTENTS

Safety Considerations

The fact that a trip or area is described in this book is not a representation that it is a safe one for you or your group. This book does not list every hazard that may confront you—and can't, due to changing terrain and weather, and the varying capabilities of different travelers. You assume responsibility for your own safety when you travel, and must exercise your own independent judgment. Political considerations may add to the risks of travel in Europe and Greece in ways that this book cannot predict. When you travel you assume this risk, and should keep informed of political developments that may make safe travel difficult or impossible.

The publisher

Preface

The Greek backcountry offers something—solitude—that has all but vanished from trails in the rest of Europe, the Americas and the Himalaya. This neglect is the result of scant information, not lack of intrinsic merit. Whoever has ventured inland to the fastness of a truly enchanted kingdom can only greet with a skeptical smile the tales of woe from those who have fallen prey to the tourist industry at the beaches or antiquities. Slowly but surely the word is getting out as a handful of the intrepid dust the beach sand off themselves and head for the hills, sometimes in an organized expedition but more often than not as solo travelers.

Ironically, this is occurring just at a point when most Greeks seem to have turned their backs once and for all on their rural patrimony. The bringers of progress, U.S. Army Corps of Engineers style, are hard at work. Roads, ostensibly to benefit shepherds but effectively to service ski lifts, logging operations or military installations, proliferate on many mountainsides and island flanks. A third dam on the Aheloós, below Agrínion, will leave scarcely 50 free-flowing kilometers out of that river's 200-kilometer course; others are planned on the Agrafiótis, where several villages face inundation, and on the Aóös River, of which only 30 kilometers run within Greece. Much of the upper Aóös is white water suitable for rafting; six kilometers are included in the Víkos/Aóös National Park. However, such "protected" status has until now meant relative neglect of a wilderness area rather than sensible development for on-foot visitors, and doesn't necessarily keep the bulldozers at bay. Rarely are the various development projects for the benefit of the adjacent villages, which slowly wither away; instead they promote migration to the towns of an increasingly urbanized, centralized and concretized Greece.

As matters stand, little time—perhaps a generation—remains to enjoy rural Greece as it has been for the past several centuries. Hence this book is as much a memorial and document as a guide, for within the next couple of decades will be completed the unraveling of a cultural fabric that began between the world wars, when the first drastic depopulation of the Greek hinterlands took place. It is romantic fancy to imagine that the hydroelectric barrages will be stopped or that the old villages will ever be revitalized, but judicious use of this book should rescue the old trails that have not yet succumbed to the road builders or expired quietly under a blanket of scree and foliage. To those who know and love them, the old pilgrimage cobbles, shepherds' migratory routes and medieval high roads of backcountry Greece are as valuable a heritage as the Parthenon. The Greeks of the year 2000 will thank you for preserving the abandoned paths, for a Greece that in all likelihood will be half Athenian will never need them so much as then.

Acknowledgments

Although most of this book was researched alone, my steps have been guided by many people, all instrumental in the preparation of this edition.

In California, Marla Kolzamanidhou has remained a friend after my six months in her modern Greek class at the University of California at Berkeley. Paul Young has supplied me with rare books, exquisite Greek music, spirited conversation and many dinners, and he read over the Mt. Athos section. Sandra Klein has shared a love of photographing the disappearing Greece ever since I watched, with growing amazement, her print of Rhódhos old town appear under the enlarger next to mine, where a nearly identical image of old Híos was taking shape. Stephen Pearson of Santa Barbara contributed to and read over the chapter on Sámos, where he lived for six years. Dr. Fred Schwartz has been a friend since we met on Crete in 1978 and is ever willing to field-test my suggestions on his next vacation. Hugh Swift has always been ready with the encouragement and assistance of a colleague in a field where there are few peers.

In England, Mark Ellingham has enthusiastically supported this project, in addition to including other work of mine in his *Rough Guide* series. Michael Haag forwarded updated information on Taïyettos and Kárpathos, and Tim Salmon provided tips on Gkióna and Pílion.

In Athens, I wish to thank John Chapple for favors, introductions and pleasant afternoons too numerous to mention; Nikos Stavroulakis of the Jewish Museum, who gave of his valuable time to fill me in on various Greek minority communities; and Nick and Vicki Lingris, and Ilse Bishop, proprietors of Compendium Books, who always kept a closet free for my use.

On the Pelopónnisos, my successful traverse of Párnon was owed entirely to Hárilaos Kalavrítinos of the Spárti EOS (Greek Alpine Club) chapter; I understand he is a friend to all foreign hikers who meet him. In Ípiros, I wish to express my gratitude to the Délla and Varáka families of Ioánnina, who always had a soft place to land between treks, and to Alékos Goúris and Kóulis Hristodhoúlos, who both freely shared information on Mt. Gamíla. In Thessalía, Mr. and Mrs. Vangelis Doussias furnished valuable intelligence on Mt. Kissávos, and Pavlos Kondopoulos of Dhráma told me much I would have missed about Falakró and other corners of Makedhonía.

On Sámos, the Hadjinikólaou family of Kokkári hosted me for two idyllic sojourns. Thanks are also due the crew of the Dutch yacht *Stressbreaker*, which came through when the ferry *Miaoulis* didn't.

Above all, I wish to express my gratitude to the hundreds of rural Greeks, names never known or unremembered, who offered hospitality, company and directions with no thought of recompense. *Ná zíste pollá hroniá*—may you live full lives.

All hiking times given in this guide exclude rest stops and assume a trail surface unobstructed by snow. We cannot guarantee that paths described might not have been bulldozed in the interval between research and publication. If you know of an instance of this, or are otherwise steered wrongly by this guide, we would appreciate hearing from you. Likewise, if a trail or region deserving coverage has been omitted, we would also like to receive your letter. All correspondence will be taken into consideration when preparing subsequent editions. Quotation of prices has been kept to a minimum, and those that do appear are in dollars, since the dollar equivalent of changing Greek prices tends to change very slowly. Nonetheless, these prices should be used as a rough indicator and not be regarded as absolute.

▢ PART I ▢
Getting Acquainted With Greece

BASICS OF GREEK TRAVEL

Greeks are very conscious of foreign opinion; they tend to shepherd foreigners toward the conventionally acceptable things and away from the backward and the obscure. They need not have these fears. The strangers who form the deepest regard for Greece are not the ones who are bear-led; they are the solitaries whose travels lead them, through chance or poverty or curiosity, along the humble and recondite purlieus of Greek life.

——Patrick Leigh Fermor

According to its National Tourist Organization statistics, Greece is host to roughly five million foreign tourists annually. Ninety-nine percent of them are devotees of a cult, bordering on the fetishistic, which dictates that all of value can be found at selected archaeological zones or island shores. Only a tiny fraction of these visitors are aware that Greece possesses vast tracts of wilderness unequalled, proportionately, in most other European countries; fully 75 percent of the land area is classified as montane, nonarable or otherwise uninhabitable.

While the Greek mountains are not imposingly lofty or perennially snow-clad in the manner of the Alps or the Himalaya, they are graced with a severe, craggy, uniquely Balkan beauty and often riotous vegetation at medial altitudes. The more familiar lower elevations of the islands are no less inviting for foot exploration. These landscapes, together with the remaining examples of village, monastic and pastoral culture, guarantee a satisfying and surprisingly varied hiking experience.

THE LANDSCAPE

Greece, the splintered southeastern tip of the Balkan peninsula, presents a highly convoluted map outline, with a generally rocky coastline equal in length to that of France's, even though that nation is four times larger. What we see today is the result of the primordial flooding of the Mediterranean basin which occurred when a debris dam at the Strait of Gibraltar gave way. Inrushing Atlantic waters inundated most of the mountain ranges that segmented the deep, hot depression. Isolated, exposed summits became the Greek islands, with Crete the highest and largest. More continuous massifs on the new mainland were still joined to the Dinaric Alps of Albania and Yugoslavia, with the important spur of Rhodhópi shared with Bulgaria. If the Mediterranean could be drained, the Yugoslavian systems, the Albano-Greek Píndhos, the Pelopónnisos, Crete and the Turkish Tauros would form one extended, unbroken arc.

Village of Olymbos on the island of Kárpathos (photo by Ann Cleeland)

No point in Greece is more than a hundred-odd kilometers from the sea, and the sierras that crisscross the land steepen the grade over which the various rivers must run. Cultivation is confined to narrow zones on either side of the banks, which were seasonally overflowed until the advent of hydroelectric and flood-control projects. On the west slope of the Píndhos Mountains, which tend from southeast to northwest, rivers flow uniformly and swiftly from northeast to southwest. The only exception is the Aóös which exits northwest to the Adriatic via Albania. On the opposite side of the crest, rivers water fertile plains as they drain east or northeast in a more leisurely fashion. As Greece curls around the north Aegean, the courses of the rivers with their headwaters in Yugoslavia or Bulgaria are deflected to a north-south axis as they meander to the sea through gaps in the east-to-west Balkan ranges. On the Pelopónnisos, most rivers are swift, short torrents, except for the Evrotas and Alfeíos, which flow in opposite southeasterly and northwesterly directions from sources which almost coincide in the center of the peninsula.

On close inspection most Greek rock formations turn out to be limestone or schist, with occasional admixtures of gneiss or fleisch. Sandstones, conglomerates and other sedimentary rocks predominate in alluvial areas. The schists are usually folded and tilted into giant, weathered beds, which crack and rain down the terrible scree that constitutes the hiker's nemesis. Limestone is of the karstic type (named after the Carso region of Italy and Yugoslavia), extremely porous because it's peppered with caves, sinkholes and subterranean rivers. Underground streams often empty some distance out to sea or even channel salt water inland to render springs brackish. The sievelike limestone core of the Greek mountains acts as a giant sponge for precipitation, but unfortunately the extreme steepness of the ranges ensures that springs above 2000 meters are rare. Most of the peaks are not much higher (ca. 2100 to 2400 m), and the sheerness and lack of water can limit camping opportunities, but this is partly mitigated by dramatic, sculpted contours verging on the grotesque. Limestone needles and pinnacles, treacherously brittle and lava-sharp, are best admired from a distance. Not all of these evocative contours are the result of ordinary weathering; the appearances of many summits lend evidence of glacial action as far south as the Gulf of Kórinthos. Large volumes of water are still at work in the mountains, most notably in the wild Ágrafa region where rivers have carved 1700-meter-deep gorges through uplifted strata.

CLIMATE AND BEST SEASONS

Despite its small area, Greece has startling regional variations in climate. Visitors tend to forget that most of the country lies between 36 and 42 degrees north, roughly the same distance from the equator as Japan, the United States, or New Zealand's north island. Therefore, it is the overall mildness of the climate that's surprising, not the well-defined areas and periods of inclement weather.

In the far north and inland locales away from maritime influence, the prevailing climate is termed "modified continental." This is an understated way of designating hot, muggy summers and bitterly cold, snowy winters that call for a Canadian or Siberian wardrobe. Fortunately, there are buffers of moderate, lingering springs and autumns between the two extreme seasons. The entire western coast, from Methóni on the Pelopónnosos to the Albanian frontier, experiences milder but extremely rainy winters that keep the countryside lush year-round, plus the same hothouse summers. Weather rhythms of the central and north Aegean—Magnisía, the Sporádhes, Halkidhikí, Thássos, Samothráki—fall somewhere in between: cold and lightly snowy in winter, more salubrious in summer.

The southern islands, the balance of the Pelopónnisos and the Attic Peninsula enjoy a true Mediterranean climate. This is a convenient description for a pattern repeated in several global zones between 30 and 35 degrees north or south that face a dry, subtropical ocean to the west. Mild and minimally wet winters precede long, hot summers (in Greece, from June to September). Vegetation is almost entirely dependent on ground water accumulated during the winter months; such conditions favor the small-leaved, perennial scrub that makes casual visitors from other "Mediterranean" biomes (California, Australia, South Africa) feel as if they'd never left home. Attikí, the lowlands and most of the islands receive their annual rainfall in sporadic downpours falling at any time between November and March. Only eastern Crete and the southern Dhodhekánisos have really brief (December to February), dryish winters, but even this balmy archipelago may be inaccessible owing to storms between it and Athens' seaports and airports. The prevailing winter winds in most of the islands are the rain-bearing southerlies; for the balance of the year the Aegean is buffeted by high-pressure-fueled north winds, including the infamous summer *meltémi*.

The mountains everywhere—whether Cretan, Peloponnesian or mainland—generate their own microclimates and are pretty much off-limits to nonsnow campers from November to April. No formal rescue service exists and almost every year imprudent and unprepared hikers suffer fatal consequences. Until June you may have to contend with heavy runoff, huge snowbanks or both, depending on the severity of the past winter. Summer alpine thundershowers are inconvenient and common.

This leaves April through June and September and October as the best seasons for hiking. Most, though by no means all, of the famous Greek wildflowers bloom in succession from early to late spring while there is still enough shallow ground water. If you come to see them too early, though, March winds will tear you and the pages of your field guide to shreds. In compensation, the early spring atmosphere attains a lenslike clarity, and photographic opportunities are at their best. Easter week is a movable feast in the Orthodox calendar; it can occur anytime from late March to early May, but it usually falls in mid-April. A Cretan or Peloponnesian Easter festival will not soon be forgotten and coincides with some of the best weather in those areas. The days lengthen and warm up through May, which marks the unofficial beginning of the swimming season. Sensible trekkers or day hikers will move north with the sun as the land behind them dries to a crisp; heatstroke in the south remains a very real danger until fall. By June crampons, gaiters or ice ax are needed nowhere except on Mt. Ólymbos and perhaps two or three other northern peaks.

July is the peak tourist arrival month and that, plus the soaring mercury, frays everyone's nerves. It's a good time to retreat to the alpine redoubts of Ípiros and the Stereá, far from the madding crowds. Insects, especially flies, are present in tropical profusion, and the humidity can be debilitating, but the long summer days permit extended marches, and wild edible fruits abound in many places. In addition, numerous city dwellers rebel against hellish metropolitan conditions and retreat to their ancestral villages, where between mid-July and the end of August the wayfarer can partake in an almost nonstop series of religious festivals. Musical accompaniment is of decidedly mixed quality, but there's no lack of liquid refreshment and shepherd-style barbecues.

The worst of the heat relents by mid-September and the sea is then at its warmest for swimming. Autumn in the mountains is spectacular, with turning leaves and voluminous cloud formations; unhappily, the clouds herald erratic weather, and storms around the equinox are the rule. In the north virtually uninterrupted wetness commences with almost monsoonal regularity around October 1, a date generally referred to as that of the *protovróhia* (first rains). The autumn tramper returns again to the south, keeping in mind that the cheaper types of "rooms" close on November 1 and boats that had hitherto departed on a daily basis now sail only once a week.

BUDGETING

If you live like a shepherd, camping out much of the time, cooking for yourself and shunning all forms of mobility other than your feet and thumb, a $6 daily allowance is still adequate. But if you eat out a lot, even in modest establishments, take a room with a hot shower down the hall and flag the buses and trains regularly, reckon $12 a day for room and board plus $3 more for transport. Frequent ferry boating and domestic plane rides at $5 to $25 a shot put you in another league entirely. Knock off 25 percent if traveling with a companion; that $5 single room becomes a $7 double, a lonesome $4 supper becomes a $6 tête-a-tête.

In summary, a reasonable monthly estimate for a solo tramper is $450, $350 each for a couple. Since Greece's entry into the European Economic Community, grocery prices are rapidly approaching parity with those of other member nations; gone are the early 1960s when, as a friend reports, you could have a fish dinner in Athens for 17 *dhrachmés* when there were roughly that many to the dollar.

HANDLING MONEY

Ordinary banks operate from 8 A.M. to 2 P.M. Monday through Thursday and 8 to 1:30 Fridays, but the following major tourist centers and frontier posts have at least one bank with additional Saturday and evening hours: Athens, Dhelfí, Iráklion, Thessaloníki, Pátras, Córfu, Rhódhos, Skiáthos, Alexandhroúpoli, and any international airport. Note that the frontier posts of Kípi (Turkish border), Promahónas (Bulgarian border), Evzoni and Níki (Yugoslav land crossings) and Igoumenítsa (ferries from Italy and Yugoslavia) seem to keep no extraordinary foreign exchange hours. In the case of Igoumenítsa, you will be offered ruinous rates by money changers if you arrive outside normal banking hours. Also, try not to be caught short by the following bank (and business) holidays: New Year's, January 1; Epiphany, January 6; first Monday of Lent (movable feast, late February to early March); National Day, March 25; Easter weekend, the Friday through the Monday, variable in spring; May Day, May 1; Festival of the Panayía (Virgin), August 15; Óhi Day, October 28; and Christmas, December 25 and 26. Incidentally, if Christmas and New Year's fall on weekends, many weekdays on the previous and following weeks are business holidays.

You will encounter 50-*lépta* pieces worth one-half *dhráchmí* (soon to be phased out), 1-, 2-, 5-, 10-, 20- and 50-*dhráchmí* coins, and 50-, 100-, 500-, 1000- and the recently introduced 5000-*dhráchmí* bills. *Dhrachmés* are often called by the slang term *fránga* ("francs").

Some common terms for denominations you should recognize:

5-*dhráchmí* coin: *táliro*	100-*dhráchmí* bill: *katosáriko*
10-*dhráchmí* coin: *dekáriko*	500-*dhráchmí* bill: *pendekatosáriko*
20-*dhráchmí* coin: *ikosáriko*	1000-*dhráchmí* bill: *hiliáriko*
50-*dhráchmí* coin: *penindáriko*	

ACCOMMODATIONS

There's a proliferation of lodging for every conceivable taste and wallet in Greece, but you'll probably be most interested in *dhomátia*, rented rooms in private houses. On the islands and coasts, they're often clearly marked with tri- or quadri-lingual signs. (The Greek looks like this: ΕΝΟΙΚΙΑΖΩΝΤΑΙ ΔΟΜΑΤΙΑ.) Maximum prices run about $5 single, $9 double, and these are required to be posted on a sign somewhere in the room. The family may or may not live on the premises, but you will very likely first meet them when the boat or bus pulls in.

A good landlord or landlady can make all the difference with respect to how much you get out of your stay in a particular place. Regional pride is highly developed in Greece and a gregarious, sympathetic host(ess) is a veritable storehouse of information on local history, beauty spots, culinary and garden specialties and, yes, walking trails. On the whole, "rooms" proprietors, accustomed as they are to a younger, hardier and less ostentatious clientele, are curious, friendly, helpful and definitely not in awe of their guests. "Curious" and "friendly" can mean that you're subject to interrogation as to your birthplace, marital status, acquaintance with Greeks back home and so on. "Helpfulness" can be a two-edged sword when family and neighbors spend five minutes arguing over how best to answer your request for directions to point A. The quality of being "not in awe" allows your householder to knock and enter simultaneously with a bowl of grapes for your consumption while you're still half-dressed.

Extra amenities such as hot showers, kitchens, verandas, gardens, laundry areas and furniture other than the bed are usually, though not always, present. Often there is an extra charge for showers. Some families entrust you with the workings of the *thermosifono* (water heater); others guard the switch jealously. It's a good idea to ask about doing laundry; in drought-prone areas washing clothes is a rare luxury, and even where there's abundant water you should avoid using bathroom sinks for soaking. Pummeling clothes therein tends to loosen wash basins from the wall; you'll gladly be provided with a *kádos* (wash tub) for the purpose.

Whenever or wherever there are no *dhomátia*, you can make do with D- and E-class hotels of roughly the same price range. These are more impersonal, but single rooms are slightly more common. Nonattached baths are adequate; for baths in rooms and small bars where breakfast may be served, you'll have to move up one notch to C-class hotels.

A *pandhohéio* (inn) is an occasionally encountered class of lodging, a sort of flophouse-cum-Balkan-caravanserai today found principally in Rhódhos, Kalávryta, Karpénissi, Ioánnina and Kónitsa. In a *pandhohéio* the management rents beds, not rooms, and reserves the right to assign anyone it pleases (of the same sex) to any empty beds in your room. My only experience with theft in Greece took place in such an inn, so I recommend patronizing them only in a group or buying up all the extra beds in your room (they're quite cheap—about $2 per person—and at that price you'll never have hot water).

Ksenón neótitos is Greek for "youth hostel" and there are at least 20 official affiliates of the International Youth Hostel Association (IYHA) in Greece. You needn't hold an IYHA card to stay at any of them, except in Thessaloníki, where an International Student Travel Card may be accepted in lieu of the hosteler's card. Hostels are located in: Athens (3), Corfu (2), Crete (Sitía, Áyios Nikólaos, Ierápetra, Iráklion, Mália, Mýrtios, [near Plakiás], Réthimno and Haniá), Dhelfí, Elefsína, Litóhoron, Mykíni, Náfplion, Olympía, Piráeus, Thessaloníki, and Thíra.

The Greek mountains are dotted with numerous (at last count over 40) alpine shelters (*katafýgia*). Unfortunately, few are continually staffed and you must contact the responsible branch of the Hellenic Alpine Club to rent keys for shelter(s) under its control. This is an expensive undertaking—up to $20 a night—and may not be practical unless there are several of you. Some of the mountain huts are wonderful base camps, equipped with stoves, blanketed bunks, meeting-and-eating areas and fully appointed kitchens; others are mean little hovels or glorified saloons for day-trippers with cars. Detailed descriptions and key contacts will be found either in the text or in Appendices C and D.

In extremely isolated areas where there is no lodging whatsoever, it is still not unheard of to be put up for the night by village families. Barring this, you can ask permission to sleep in the school (especially in the summer) or an unused wing of the *kinótiko grafeío* (community records office) and it will usually be granted.

Partly because of sanitation problems and wildfire hazards, and partly to ensure trade for hotels, "free-lance" camping is technically illegal in Greece. This law is rarely enforced as long as you are discreet and exercise a modicum of respect for the local environment and inhabitants, but you must be willing to accept a certain element of risk in case the authorities decide to get strict. Patronage of local groceries and *tavérnes* works wonders in forestalling official harrassment. Where there are no mountain huts, you'll be obliged to camp. Most rural people are tolerant of, or even favorably disposed toward, the practice. After all, the mountain-dwelling guerillas of the independence war are enshrined in the pantheon of national heroes, and every summer an army of shepherds imitates them. Squatting in abandoned monasteries or houses is also popular with Greeks and foreigners alike. First, make sure that your choice is not a protected archaeological site!

Most of the "organized" campgrounds are depressingly regimented, plastic and overpriced for what you get. If you need or choose to use an "approved site," be aware that the use even of a tent, let alone a car or cycle, requires extra payment which brings the cost right up equal with that of a room. Impromptu campgrounds set up by private individuals or a village tend to be less expensive than those run by the National Tourist Organization (NTO, EOT in Greek initials).

TRANSPORTATION

Public transportation of all kinds is alive and well in Greece, and while no longer dirt cheap it's a lot less costly than renting a car or bringing your own. It's also an excellent way to watch, and meet, Greeks. Promptness, vintage of the conveyance and condition of the roads—or seas—are unpredictable, so be prepared for anything. In general, the farther off the beaten track you venture, the more interesting matters become.

Boats (*karávia, vapória*) lend a distinctive romance to travel in Greece; no other country has such an extensive ferry network because no other nation, except Indonesia and the Philippines, has so much territory in insular form. Island steamers are notorious for their erratic scheduling, mechanical glitches and general unreliability. With the exception of the Crete-Piráeus services, I have never boarded an interisland craft that was less than 20 minutes late, and delays of 20 *hours* are not unheard of. If you are planning an "If-this-is-Tuesday-this-must-be-Mýkonos" island-hopping itinerary, you are going to come to grief. Flexibility, a sense of humor and a large backlog of reading or letter-writing should be standard equipment in Greek boat travel (or any other travel, for that matter).

Never buy your ticket until the vessel you intend to board is confirmed to be on its way. Fares once purchased are nonrefundable and usually nontransferable. Always double-check the name of any craft you board; in busy island harbors up to three ships may call in the space of an afternoon. Since two or three are bound to be late, it's easy to get on the wrong boat.

Deck, tourist, third, *gamma* class—whatever the particular company calls it—is adequate for most tastes. If the weather turns bad, you're always allowed in the "low-class" bar or lounge. Boat food, with the exception of the Crete ferries, is usually overpriced so consider bringing your own.

The most authoritative source of arrival/departure information for a given harbor is the *limenarhéio* (port authority). The port police maintain complete, up-to-the-hour schedules (*dhromolóyia*) of *all* craft docking and sailing within their jurisdiction *and* have phone numbers of every other port authority in Greece. Thus you can call ahead from point A to make sure you won't get stranded unwillingly for a week at point B. It helps to know Greek since those on duty cannot be depended on to speak serviceable English; fast-talking travelers may even get port policemen to make pertinent phone calls on their behalf. The next best source of information is a fat paperback publication known as the *Greek Travel Pages*, revised and updated monthly. These invaluable compendia of trivia usually lie about the lobbies of posh hotels and travel agencies. Not only can you obtain a good idea of the schedules (and fares) of virtually any ferry in Greece for that month, but you can also see timetables for many trains, buses and planes moving into, out of and around Greece.

Ferry schedules handed out by the Athens tourist office, covering departures from Piráeus, Lávrio and Rafína, are nearly always incomplete or mistaken and should be viewed with skepticism.

In addition to the big liner services neighboring islands are often connected, especiall in summer, by swarms of 10- to 20 meter *kaíkia* (caiques). A *kaíki* is an informal, one-family entrepreneurial operation where lack of comfort is compensated for by character. Caiques are usually not any less expensive than the big boats, but often they're the only way of moving perpendicularly to the main shipping lines.

Hydrofoils connect Piráeus with the Argo-Saronic islands, Monemvassía, Yíthion and Kíthera; in recent years service has been instituted between certain of the Kykládhes and the Dhodhekánisos. They are twice as fast and twice as costly as conventional steams, but provide a rough ride in heavy seas and are not for the seasick prone.

Trains (*trena*) are administered by the *Organismós Sidherodhrómon tis Elládhos*, widely known as OSE (*oseh*), and serve the hiker's destinations listed below:

Pelopónnisos: Táyettos (Trípoli), Helmós, Párnon, Vassí/Nédhas

Stereá: Párnitha, Parnassós, Oíti, Gkióna (trailhead villages)

Thessalía/Magnisía: Ólymbos, Kissávos, Pílion, Tríkala (east Píndhos)

Sporádhes and Évvia: Vólos and Halkídha (Dhírfis)

Makedhonia and Thráki: Thessaloníki, Falakró, Samothráki (Alexandhróupoli) Trains are cheap (30 percent less than buses, 55 percent on round-trip fares), nearly as fast as road vehicles, depart two to six times daily per route and leave promptly from the *initial* station of the run. On the minus side, cars are often unheated in winter, food service is scarce and costly and as a rule trains are full and invariably half an hour late by the end of the line. OSE also runs a prompter, supplemental coach service between major stops, in effect doubling departure frequencies. But this will not stop at intermediate points and is almost as costly as buses (see below).

Always buy train tickets in advance *and* request a seat reservation, whether you're doing a day or an overnight trip (sleepers available only on the Athens-Thessaloníki-Yugoslavia/Bulgaria/Turkey line). Reservations are free of charge; the car and seat numbers appear on the back of your brown ticket. You must often pay a supplement for express service (your receipt is an extra gray stub), but many express trains do not stop at stations nearest trailheads. (See warnings in individual hike write-ups). There is, as noted above, a substantial discount for booking domestic round-trip fares. Rail-pass holders must secure reservations like everyone else, must pay express supplements and will probably find their passes invalid for the OSE coach service.

Buses (*leioforeia*) serve almost any village, though in some cases you may have to wait awhile. In towns, buy your ticket in advance at the station; on rural lines you pay your fare after boarding. In contrast to boats, buses run on time so be there when they tell you to be. The bus company is universally referred to by the acronym KTEL, which when translated stands for "Joint Administration of Greek Buses" or something to that effect, so if you can't find the stop or the station, ask where the *ktel* is. KTEL is organized by province (i.e., "KTEL Evritanías," with the main station in the provincial capital and substations in the capitals of *eparhies* (counties) if a concentration of villages warrants it (e.g. KTEL in Ioánnina province has two terminals in Ioánnina and a substation in Kónitsa). All villages are served by the KTEL of the province in which they happen to be; if the village you're trying to reach lies in the neighboring province, you'll generally have to use that province's KTEL, even though the hamlet may be just over the border and easier to reach from your side! Hence there are large 10- to 30-kilometer gaps between service in the vicinity of provincial borders, which you have to bridge by walking, taxiing or hitching. As a general rule, buses from province or county capitals tend to follow the school and market day: *from* the village *to* the regional center in the early morning, and *back* to the hamlet after secondary school and morning shopping finish at about 2 P.M. There are, though, numerous exceptions to this; the bus may make only one trip daily or only several weekly, at odd hours. In the more traditional rural areas, Sunday and holiday bus service is severely limited or nonexistent, and some extremely de-populated or isolated villages have no service at all.

In such cases you'll be looking for someone with whom to share a taxi, which may be too expensive otherwise. Country taxis have no meters—you bargain. A reasonable, per vehicle (not per person) charge for a 16-kilometer transfer on a dirt surface would be approximately $7 (U.S.). Occasionally a taxi returning empty from a drop-off will offer you a ride for the equivalent of the bus fare, just to defray gas expenses. Count your blessings.

Hitchhiking ("autostop") is very good if you're only toting a daypack, but I've waited a couple of hours for 70-kilometer rides with a full pack. Although Greek traffic is sparse, much of it is trucks and vans which are good for thumbing. Rides are easiest to come by in remote areas where everyone knows that the bus may not be a viable alternative. Hitching on commercial vehicles is technically illegal, so you may find that, if offered a ride in a large van or semi, especially in the payload space, you'll be left on the outskirts of the upcoming town so as not to be seen at police checkpoints. Don't be offended if set down in this manner, and realize that both you and the driver risk running afoul of the authorities.

If you're in a hurry, you can fly to most corners of the country with Olympic Airways. Flights cost roughly double the ferry passage and more than triple the train fare to the same points. For some reason flights from Athens to Skiáthos, Ioánnina and Sámos—all points of interest to hikers—are less than double the fare of alternate means of conveyance, so you'd do well to consider flying at least one way to these spots if your time is limited. Most of the islands served have flights at least once a day, and in tourist season this may increase as much as fourfold. There are also some off-the-main-line routes between the Dhodhekánisos and Crete and other touristed islands that operate only in summer. If stormy weather keeps ferries in port, and you have a deadline for returning to Athens, you'll make Olympic's acquaintance. Seats are at a premium from May to October and at all holiday seasons, so you'll always need to book two days to two weeks in advance. Other than that, I've heard few substantial complaints about Olympic's service, except that their chaotic Athens domestic-lines terminal merits strict observance of half-hour-prior-to-flight-time check-in rules.

SERVICES

Shops and small businesses other than government and white-collar offices keep hours that may require some adjusting to on your part. Tues, Thurs, Fri hours are 9 A.M. to 1 P.M. and 5 P.M. to 8 P.M. The Mon, Wed, Sat schedule is 9 A.M. to 2:30 P.M. Shopping in Greece is hardly an exact science, and there are more exceptions than rules among different categories of trades, so don't count on getting anything done except in the morning when most everyone is open.

Hiking-Related Commodities

At present there are backpacking stores per se only in Athens and Thessaloníki. Useful establishments in Athens include: Píndhos (4 Leofóros Aléxandhras, in sight of the Mavromatéon bus stop)—state-of-the-art (and costly) packs, stoves, knives, ice axes, foam pads, etc., also Biwell, the Austrian boot conditioner, and pack repairs; Army/Navy, (4 Kynétou, deep in the flea market)—good for mess kits, butane stoves, gadgets; Kázos, in arcade linking Stadhíou 3 and Koraï 4, well-balanced small shop; and Marabóu, Kiáfas 3 behind Akadhimías 78, tents, sleeping bags, and parkas only.

In Thessaloníki Petrídhi (Vas. Iraklíou 43) is a good camping and travel gadget store. Try also stalls near the corner of Monastiríou and Langadhás.

Otherwise, seek out an *eídhe sport* or an *eídhe athletikó* (*eíhde*=shop), where you may find pocketknives, hats, canteens and an assortment of equipment (coolers, lanterns, canvas tents, etc.) oriented toward car campers. In Ioánnina a hunting/woodsmen's shop at Anexartissías 78 stocks some hiking gear; very good boot repairs are available in the old bazaar three blocks east. Klaudátos, a chain department store with branches in Thessaloníki, Athens and Vólos, carries similar gear.

Shoe and boot repairs are inexpensive, high-quality and (usually) easy to come by. Look for a sign reading *Ypodhimatopoeío* but ask for a *tsangáris* (see "Language" for an explanation of the difference). In Athens there are two good cobbler stalls on Platía Avyssinías, the Greek "old things" bazaar. Complete (and expensive) boot overhauls at Voronóf, 28 Menandhrou.

If men's clothes need adjusting, seek out a *ráptis* (tailor). Patches (*balomáta*) are hard to find—bring along some extra scrap material, which can also be used to apply boot seal. Laundries (*plintíria*) are hideously expensive and are apt to shrink all-cotton garments. Most people, tourists and locals, do it themselves.

Writing paper, journals and envelopes can be purchased at a *hartopoléio* (stationer's). A very limited selection of foreign paperbacks is sold on street-corner racks, but you may do better swapping with other travelers, relying on hotel libraries or patronizing proper bookstores in Athens or Thessaloníki.

A *baharikó*, literally "spice shop," is actually a dry-goods store where soap, matches, razor blades, cutlery, plastic ware and camping butane can be bought. These useful, homey establishments offer better prices for these items than the food-oriented, glittery *soupermarkets* [sic] that have appeared of late.

Stove Fuel

Two of the three common types of camp-stove fuels are readily available. Kerosene (*fotístiki parafíni*) is sold at hardware stores (*sidhérika*). Butane, in 190-milliliter cartridges (known as *boutilákia, fiáles* or by the trade name *Camping-gaz*) is widely sold in groceries or *bahariká*. If you own a stove, such as the Bleuet 206, which takes "clic-stop" cartridges, ask for *fiáles méh engopés* (cartridges with grooves) or ones with obviously tapered tops. "*Koffee-gaz*" and certain other kinds intended for blowtorches will *not* fit your stove. Various Italian and Greek *fiáles* perform as well as the French type, for half the price. If your Blue-Gaz needs service or accessories, head for Petrogaz, at Syngróu 174 in Athens. (Don't waste your time elsewhere looking for a windshield, for example.

Camera Repairs

There are only a handful of such shops in Greece:
Athens: Picópoulos, 26 Lekka, 3rd floor. Near tourist office.
Iráklion: Ioánnis Voumvoulakis, Smirnis 8. 200 m from archaeological museum.
Thessaloníki: Damkon, 43 Venezelóu, 2nd floor. Corner Via Egnatía.

LANGUAGE

Traveling in the style advocated by this guide assumes a willingness to acquire at least the rudiments of modern Greek. It can be potentially dangerous to stroll off into the Greek yonder without being able to understand at least the gist of the usually detailed directions being offered you by villagers. The "Greek for Hikers" section of this book is purposely thorough since many readers will not have access to instructional material listed in the Bibliography, let alone formal courses. If you can't make the time to learn Greek systematically, or to commit the "Greek for Hikers" to memory, I strongly urge you to at least master the script transliteration tables below; the majority of rural, business and bus signs are not romanized.

A,α	ah	M,μ	m
B,β	v	N,ν	n
Γ,γ	gh (unique soft palatal), but y before many vowels	Ξ,ξ	ksi
Δ,δ	th as in these—rendered as dh in this book	O,o	o
		Π,π	p
E,ε	eh	P,ρ	r
Z,ζ	z	Σ,σ,ς	s, sometimes z
H,η	ee	T,τ	t
Θ,θ	th as in throw	Y,υ	ee; varies (see next section)
I,ι	ee	Φ,φ	f
K,κ,u	k	X,χ	gutteral h
Λ,λ	l	Ψ,ψ	ps
		Ω,Ω̲,ω,	o

Double letters often have entirely different values.

αι   ay as in *hay*

ει	*ee*
οι	*ee*
ου	*oo*, often rendered on signs as ' Ȣ '
αυ	*av* but often *af* before certain consonants
ευ	*ev* but often *ef* in same conditions as above
ηυ	*eev* or *eef,* as above
γγ	*ng*
γκ	*ng* when medial, *g* otherwise
μπ	*mb* when medial, *b* initial
ντ	*nd* when medial, *d* initial
τζ	*j*

The presence of any of the last three clusters usually indicates a word's Turkish, Italian, Slavic or other foreign origins. Now you are fully equipped to read all signs, menus and phone books.

A Note on Transliteration and Nomenclature

Since many Greek letters have no exact Roman equivalents, the art of transliteration will always be controversial. Some favor an orthographic approach, which dutifully traces the evolution of each Greek letter through the ages and uses its English descendant, despite the fact that the value of the letter has changed completely. Then there is the quasi-phonetic school, which vainly substitutes the nearest "international" equivalent (such as *ch* for letter 'X' the hard *aytch* sound). Spellings used in this book are hopefully those most likely to ensure a comprehensible pronunciation—do not be alarmed if you see other transliteration.

A further source of confusion is the existence of one or more alternate names for many places. Names given on maps are likely to be in *katharévousa* (formal, written language) spelling, with word endings modified from *dhimotikí* (literary, spoken Greek): e.g., *Karyái* in place of *Karyés.* Many locales have an alias of Italian, Turkish, Vlach or Slavic origin. My policy has been to cite first the name best understood in the area and to list important alternatives immediately following in parentheses: e.g., Helmós (Aroánia). In recent decades the Greek government vigorously pursued a Hellenization campaign, promoting classical place names over medieval ones. During the 1930s particularly, the Metaxas dictatorship attempted (unsuccessfully) to suppress the majority of foreign place names north of the Gulf of Kórinthos. It seems that in Greece a rose by any other name is *not* as sweet and might even provoke sedition.

After having spent some time in Greece, you'll begin to recognize a list, as it were, of ecclesiastically as well as bureaucratically "approved" place names, which is not terribly long. When villages aren't named for saints they're apt to be called by certain common geographical or botanical features. Livádhia (meadows), Dháfni (laurel) and Áyios Ioánnis (St. John), of which there must collectively be 300 in Greece, are flagrant examples. Qualify the name of the village you're looking for with the province name if there seems to be any confusion! It took awhile for me to find Poliána (Lakonía), the trailhead for Mt. Taïyettos, because there is a Poliána in Messinía 40 kilometers distant. Nonunique place names in the Index are modified by the appropriate province or island in parentheses.

LOCAL CUISINE

Careful shopping when eating out is rewarded in Greece, where restaurant quality and prices run the gamut from exorbitant oily slop to heavenly delicacies served cheaper than you could make them.

Restaurant menus should be examined closely before seating yourself. Are taxes included in the prices? Designation of an establishment as "Category A" or "B" says

more about the decor and waiters' outfits than about food quality, and guarantees stiff prices. There's a dependable, inverse relationship between swank and excellence; a little *mangáli* (counter barbecue) and rickety tables joint wins every time. Eateries without written menus occasion many misunderstandings and attempted gougings. Settle the price for the most expensive items (entrées, wine) and hope for the best on the small dishes—you'll lose your appetite itemizing charges down to the *koúver* (place-setting fee).

Vegetable fans will be happy in Greece, where produce is regularly transformed into appetizing (lardless) dishes. The seafood also should not be missed. The following menu is discriminating rather than exhaustive.

Vegetables

angináres—artichokes
arakádhes—peas
bámies—okra
dolmádhes—stuffed grape leaves
fasoládha—bean soup
fasolákia—snap beans
horiátiki—olive, cheese, onion, cucumber and tomato salad
hórta—steamed wild greens
koukiá—horse beans
maróuli—lettuce
patzária—beets
yemistés—stuffed tomatoes or peppers
yígantes—giant haricot beans

Dips

melitsánasalata—mild eggplant dip
taramá—fish roe pâté, popular during Lent
tzadíki—yogurt/cucumber spread, heavily garlicked and herbed

Specialties

patsás—tripe stew; a city dish, found at special stalls near the bus stand
salingária—snails, fried whole in oil and herbs
trahanádhes—sourdough dumplings prepared in hot sour milk; an Ipirote specialty

Grilled or Fried Meat

brizóla—pork or beef chop
keftédhes—meatballs
kokorétsi—innards, specifically the gut muscle wall (not tripe) stuffed with anonymous offal
kondosoúvla—essentially same idea as foregoing, but the chunks of meat have a less humble origin
psitó—a portion of sheep or pork spit-roasted whole—may be served cold, bones, eyes, and all.

You may learn to like the above three delicacies if summer trekking in the mountains.

Opposite—top: A typical combination kafnéio-grill-grocery in the mountains; Bottom, left: Making trahanadhes; Bottom, right: typical condition of trailhead placard (if present at all)

païdhákia—lamb chops, often very inexpensive
sikotákia—grilled liver, better than Mom's

Baked or Boiled Meat

kotópoulo—chicken
moussaká—eggplant and ground lamb casserole in white sauce
papoutsáki—variation of moussaká
pastítsio—macaroni pie
stifádho—stew of any kind
tsoudsoukákia—baked meat torpedoes
yiorvoulákia—meat-and-rice balls, often in egg-lemon sauce

Seafood

galéos—shark steak
garídhes—shrimp, fried or blanched
glóssa—sole—tasty
gópes—small but meaty fish, common *kafeneio* (cafe) snack
kalamária—squid, fried
ksifías—swordfish
ktapódhi—octopus, grilled or stewed
péstrofa—trout
sinagrídha—red snapper

Drinks

bíra—beer
bira varelizméno—beer on tap
kokkinélli—rose wine
krasí—wine
levkó áspro—white wine
mávro—red wine
meh to hilkó—bulk wine, *vin du pays*
retsina—pine-resin-flavored wine
oúzo—anise-flavored liqueur
rakí—grape-crushing brandy
tsikoudhiá—Cretan *rakí*
tsípouro—Ipirote, Sterean *rakí*
neró—water

Desserts

The only decadent element of Greek cuisine is the sweets. Many Levantine introductions are tasteless concoctions of sugar and flour, but several desserts are outstanding.

baklavá—*fyllo* dough sheets, honey, nuts
bougátza—Greek eclair
galaktoboúriko—custard pie
kréma—plain custard
loukoúmi—Turkish delight; standard welcome snack at monasteries
moustalevriá—grape pudding; autumn prize in towns of grape regions
rizógalo—rice pudding—world's best

Street Snacks

kalambóki—roast corn on the cob, mainland street corner staple from July to September

kástana—roast chestnuts, sold at street stalls from October through midwinter
souvláki—chunks of pork or lamb, best served in *píta* bread with tomatoes and other garnish
spanakópita—spinach pie
tyrópita—cheese pie

ON THE TRAIL

HIKER'S GROCERY LIST

You will find it unnecessary to weigh down your luggage with packets of expensive, freeze-dried backpacker's food from home, since Greek stores stock a practical and (usually) appetizing array of supplies suitable for trail meals. Food shopping hours are slightly more generous than those for ordinary establishments, being *roughly* from 7:30 A.M. to 2:30 P.M. and from 5 to 9 P.M. As with other shops, Monday, Wednesday and either Friday or Saturday afternoon closure prevails, and it's almost impossible to buy groceries on Sundays except in very large towns or tourist centers or in tiny villages where the *kafeneío* (cafe) doubles as the only store.

In the largest towns, good shops are found in the traditional bazaars. The Athens bazaar centers around the corner of Evripídhou and Athinás streets; a good store is at 34 Evripídhou. Thessaloníki's old market is a warren of alleys bounded by Egnatía, Ermóu, Aristotélous and Karólou Diehl. While shopping try one of the *patsatzádika* (*patsás* kitchens) for which the city is famous.

Following is a list of items grouped by the type of store in which they're most reliably found. *Bakáliko* is the *dhimotikí* (informal) word for grocery store; but the *katharévousa* (formal) sign will read *pandopoleíon*. In *bakálika* you can purchase:

kafés stigmelos—instant coffee in packets or cans—vile
tsaï se sakoulákia—black tea bags, English or Ceylon
votánika tsaï—herbal tea; *hamomíli* (chamomile), *faskómilo* (sage), *tsaï vounou* (mountain tea—in south Greece) are commonest kinds
kakáo skoní hot chocolate powder, imported and local brands; really baking cocoa, needs milk and sweetening
gála skoní—powdered milk; sold in box or bulk
vrómi "Kouaker"—Quaker oats in a can; in some cities, local brands in a bag are adequate
Viamyl—Greek instant mashed-potato mix
marmeládha—jam in assorted flavors; sold in small packets or plastic jars
aláti—salt
ládhi—(olive) oll—in bulk or prepackaged
záhari—sugar; usually sold in bulk
moússa, pudínga—instant mousses that must be beaten for double the stated instruction time; make with cold spring water and let stand 20 minutes

All of the above can also be found at *bahárika* (dry goods stores).

(vrastá) **avgá**—(hard-boiled) eggs
heemí se consérva—miniature (180-milliliter) juices, in cans or cardboard cartons
tyrí—cheese; four most common:
    féta—crumbly, creamy, slightly salty sheep or goat cheese—the cheapest and the
    one most associated with Greece
    kasséri—harder, more delicately flavored than *féta*—also pricier
    goúdha, édam—usually Dutch or German, but reasonable
    graviéra—Swiss-style gruyere—expensive; processed gruyere is also sold in little
    8-pack wheels; not the best but it keeps indefinitely
tsalámi—dry salami
sardhélles—(canned) sardines; not all brands sold with a key
skoumbrí—(canned) mackerel; several brands in tomato sauce
hírino kréas—(canned) pork meat; cook it

Squid, grape leaves, stuffed peppers, beef-and-peas, luncheon meat, etc. are all available in cans and are fine for lunch if purchased on the morning of each hiking day, but they're tiresome to carry until supper. The Greek market is still very weak on dehydrated entrées; you may want to import a few. You can find, however:

sóupa—couple of brands of powdered soups in such flavors as *karóta* (carrot),
    manitára (mushroom), *aspárago* (asparagus)
zymárika—pasta, such as *kritharáki*
fakés—lentils—quick-cooking protein
arakádhes—peas—ditto
fasólia—beans; less practical on small stoves
elyés—olives, salty and delicious; Kalamata variety best
méli—honey; sold in assorted-size containers or in bulk
traganá—"crunchies"—which include:
    stragália—dry chick peas (garbanzos)
    pastéli—sesame/honey and peanut/honey bars
    ksirí kárpi—literally, "dry fruit"—nuts to you, and sold in special shops or off street
    pushcars in big towns—the basis of do-it-yourself trail mix
    síka—(dried) figs—expensive
    stafídhes—seedy black raisins
    sultanínas—small sultanas (seedless, pale raisins), cheaper than figs and no more
    expensive than *stafídhes*
    biskótes—cookies; the biscuit industry has burgeoned in recent years—you can
    now get "organic" cookies as an alternative to the all-chemical, filled-sandwich
    types
    kástana—chestnuts, if boiled, must be split with a knife, scooped with a spoon
Bread is obtained at the *psomádhiko* (bakery), where the sign outside will read *artopoleion.*

psomí—*mávro* (dark) or *starénio* (whole wheat) or *horiátiko* ("country") bread is
    difficult to find; you buy a round loaf (*karvéli*) or long loaf (*frantzóla*) of whatever is
    available. *Misó* means "half."
kouloúria—hard or soft sesame-sprinkled baked goods, in various roll, donut and
    pretzel forms
tsouréki—twisted egg, milk and honey bread, traditional Easter fare
paximádhi—hard bread chunks; soak to resuscitate
friganiés—packaged melba toasts, which keep longer than bread, but roll inside your
    foam pad or you'll end up with croutons

For produce visit the *manáviko*, whose sign reads *oporopoleion.* Eggs are also often sold at *manávika.* In very small towns you'll have to wait for the *manávis* (greengrocer) to appear with his motortrike or pick-up truck. Listed in descending order of portability:

mandarínia—tangerines
portokália—oranges
angoúria—cucumbers
míla—apples
rodhákina—peaches
nektarínes, milorodhákina—nectarines
beríkoka—apricots; often sold dry with *ksíri kárpi*
stafília—grapes
kerásia—cherries
ahládhia—pears
domátes—tomatoes

Dairy products and ready-puddings are usually sold at a *galaktopoleion* (milk shop; *katharévousa* and *dhimotihí* identical) and less often at a *zaharoplasteío* (sweet shop). *Yaoúrti* (yogurt) is sometimes sold at *bakálika* but is easier to find at milk shops. Some brands come in foil-sealed containers that are quite packable; contents can resemble sour cream more than yogurt however. *Próveio* (sheep's milk yogurt) is preferable to *ayelládhos* (cow's milk). If you don't mind risking a mess, the low, flat cartons with pop-lids contain yogurt or pudding from local dairies. These are usually cheaper and better than the foil-sealed products.

An assortment of Nalgene bottles with screw-on lids is useful when collecting bulk items; pop-top honey containers never reclose properly and attract millions of ants.

MAPS

Owing to continued bad relations with Turkey, borders with three non-NATO nations and the resultant security paranoia, it was until recently impossible to obtain maps of Greece up to the standard of USGS topos or British Ordnance Survey quads. The Hellenic Military Geographical Service (HMGS) has long published 387 15-minute sheets covering the whole country at 1:50,000 scale and is in the process of preparing 1291 7-minute 30-second quads (1:25,000), but both series are classified and especially unavailable to foreign civilians. Just why the HMGS should issue an elaborate catalog detailing the two sets of quads is therefore a mystery—at the present it merely serves to make you eat your heart out all the more.

Fortunately for hikers, an intermediary, the Greek mountaineering magazine *Korfés*, has come to the rescue by providing as a centerfold in each issue since number 31 (1981) a 1:50,000 map of some montane area based on the secret army maps. New issues of the bimonthly itself (which I highly recommend to Greek-readers) are available at any *períptero* (street-corner kiosk). Back issues and most of the maps, which are sold separately for about $.50, are obtainable at the *Korfés* office in Aharnés, an Athens suburb at the base of Mt. Párnitha. The address (which is also the Aharnés EOS chapter, see next section) is 16 Platía Ayíou Vlassíou, 136 71 Aharnés; phone (01) 246-1528. You can order by mail from overseas, but enclose $1 per map to cover shipping and any currency exchange problems on their end. As we go to press, *Korfés* maps are known to exist for the following peaks (in addition to those cited in the hike write-ups):

Tymvrlstós— issue 38	Piéria—issues 49, 50
Tringía—issue 42	Mlliá (near Métsovo)—issue 60
Avgó (east Píndhos)—issue 43	Pyrostiá (near Grovená)—issue 61
Kóziakas—issue 44	

Since a new map is circulated every other month, you should visit the *Korfés* office for the most current catalog of their holdings.

Where there is no *Korfés* coverage, you have to make do with the 1:200,000 quads prepared by the Ethnikí Statistikí Ypiresía (ESY, National Statistical Service), 52 sheets gazetting Greece by province and last updated in 1972. In the interim, new roads have been built that play havoc with map accuracy which, according to cynics, was not that great to start with—some allege that small but significant errors were deliberately printed in to confuse invading armies. ESY maps are sold for about $1 apiece at the Athens Statistical Service office at 14 Likourgóu, third floor, near Omónia. The staff there does not seem geared to customer service, and it might be preferable to locate a set of the ESY offerings prior to arrival in Greece. A good university library map room will have a set in captivity—the first, 1963 edition is fine for contours. You can photocopy portions of interest (the sheets are huge) or jot down a list of sheets-by-province to pick up quickly in Athens.

The following retail outlets stock both ESY or *Korfés* maps, and there may of course be other sources.
Stanford's, 12-14 Long Acre, London WC2E 9LP, (near Covent Garden)
Pacific Travelers Supply, 529 State Street, Santa Barbara, CA 93101 (near Highway 101)

For the archipelagos the best choice is to make do with what you can lay hands on after arrival. On nearly all the larger islands, visitor's maps of some sort are on sale, and a dollar investment will often net you something that, with a usual scale range of 1:45,000 to 80,000, looks initially like just what you need. Unfortunately, many of these have adopted a pseudo-topo format, which can be worse than nothing because they report features—beach, trail or hill—that are either 400 meters misplaced or simply imagined. *Toumbis* publishers issue green-covered road maps for most islands and regions, though they are not always the best coverage for a particular spot. These maps show jeep tracks as thin red lines, faint contour shadings, paths on rare occasions and large blank areas where you're left to your own devices.

After each hike write-up, the best map known is cited. *Korfés* and ESY maps are in Greek script—another good reason to master the alphabet.

THE GREEK ALPINE CLUB(S)

Mountaineering and hiking in Greece, like everything else, is factionalized and politicized. The *Ellinikós Orivatikós Sýndesmos* (EOS, the Greek Alpine Club) is the largest and most far-flung organization, but there also exist the *Elliniki* Omospondhía *Hionodhromías kai Orivasías* (EOHO, Greek Mountaineering and Skiing Federation) and the *Sýllogos ton Ellinikón Orivatón* (SEO, Association of Greek Climbers), plus others. The latter two clubs have respective head offices in Athens, at 7 Karayióryi Servías Street (phone 323-4555), near the tourist office and in Thessaloníki; phone (031) 224-719. A complete list of all known branches of the various groups is given in Appendix C.

Local offices of the EOS tend to be receptive to foreign hikers and in general try to make up in enthusiasm for what they lack in funds and political clout. (EOHO is considerably more stand-offish; I've had no contact with SEO.) Very rarely have mountaineers and conservationists in Greece been able to halt construction of high-altitude roads or of several hydroelectric projects planned to disfigure western Greece in the near future. Don't expect branch staff to be well-informed on any mountains except those in the immediate area, though often you will be pleasantly surprised by Greeks who've hiked throughout the country and whose expertise is not limited. Very often good sketch maps of the closest alpine areas(s) are available; also, if you wish to rent keys to the mountain refuge(s) under a particular branch's control, you'll have to apply at the relevant office. Since most staff is volunteer and otherwise employed, EOS locals tend to be open only from noon to 1 P.M., 7 to 9 P.M. and Saturday mornings.

LOST AND FOUND: TRAIL SENSE WHERE THERE ARE NO PATHS

Getting lost is an integral part of the Greek backcountry experience. No matter how good a trail sense you possess, it'll happen to you eventually—it even happens to the Greeks unless they're denizens of the mountain or island in question. Of necessity you become a competent tracker of the correct route after a spell in the Greek woods, but until then (and forever after) mental toughness and a sense of humor will serve you in as good stead as boots and pack. A light attitude sure helps when you're trudging through a drizzle, uncertain whether still on the trail or on a natural rock ledge, with darkness and hostile dogs approaching. At such moments rescuers in the guise of hairy-cloaked shepherds with portable radios(!) and coffee thermoses tend to materialize out of the mist, but it's not good to tempt fate. The following pointers may help you stay on course.

Bona fide trails were originally built, and primarily continue to serve points of economic or religious interest (more recent construction of mountain huts has kept other paths alive). Thus, alpine paths tend to cease at the highest summer pasture; from there on it's usually cross-country scrambling. If a mountain has a summit path, it's probably because of a shrine on top. In the case of two villages on opposite sides of a mountain, a point-to-point foot route generally survives, but it's often badly deteriorated if autos can easily skirt the range. Worse, the old paths were often so well designed that they provided the right-of-way for new roads and now lie bulldozed under tons of rubble. In luckier instances the old trail may persist, paralleling the new road or cutting across its switchbacks. Even where there are no roads, many old paths were dynamited and blocked by the central government during the 1946-49 civil war to hamper the movements of the insurgents.

Trails still regularly used by festival pilgrims or other hikers are frequently marked with red, or more rarely blue or yellow, blazes; the convention of piling rocks to form a cairn is also honored. Cryptic initialings with arrows can be critically important: e.g., ΜΠ and ΠΗ can translate as "Monastíri Prodhromóu" and "Profítis Ilías." Similarly, they can be dangerously meaningless, as is the oft-encountered "K(number)," lumber surveyors' marks signifying "*ktíma* (plot) such-and-such."

Old cobbled trails (*kalderímia*) are usually a safe bet to lead somewhere, though sometimes no further than the nearest hilltop shrine. If you need to know the dedication of a particular rural church (*ksoklísi*), as when matching it to a name on a map, the patron's ikon is usually on a raised platform to the left of the front door, inside. Heavily used dirt trails descending from grazing areas become heavily oxbowed over time, just like old rivers, with multiple, confusing interconnections and shortcuts. Just follow the general bearing of the path.

The unsignposted fork is the perennial hiker's nightmare; you may have to pick among three or four bearings. Goat or sheep traces, studded with their droppings and often crisscrossing a hillside in a fishnet pattern, are usually bad news—there's no guarantee that bipeds have ever been that way. Manure from donkeys or mules is a good sign—these animals rarely march anywhere unaccompanied by humans. A trail with weedy or overgrown sections has not necessarily been abandoned. Conversely, beware of the trail that looks too good to be true—it may merely lead to a chapel, spring or private dwelling and stop there. In today's Greek mountains the correct path is often the one that's visible from afar but seems to vanish under close inspection; that has recent, but not too fresh, candy and cigarette wrappers ground into its surface (you may, for the first time ever, be relieved to see rubbish in the wilderness); and that trundles on meadow after meadow, always seeming to be on the point of expiring in a network of aimless livestock traces but somehow miraculously continuing in the right direction.

On the islands, many trails lie between double walls or alongside a single wall. Many isles, especially in the Kykládhes, have old loop routes for foot circumnavigation which are often located roughly halfway between the shoreline and the island's summit. Convoluted or long islands, logically enough, often have old rights-of-way paralleling watersheds or the long axis, slightly off-center. If gone astray on an island, don't try the old trick of following watercourses downhill; you'll more likely than not end up in a blind cove, with the prospect of a climb back out.

If you plan a cross-country traverse through apparently trailless regions, possession of an ESY or *Korfés* topographical map for the area is imperative. Impassable, yawning chasms and sheer-sided cliffs are common features of Greek topography, and presence of either will obviously add hours to what would seem from a road map to be a relatively straightforward point-to-point trek. Such obstacles are especially common in the south Píndhos and Ágrafa, where your itinerary may be completable only by tiptoeing along, or near, the summits of connecting ridge systems, all the while peering down into fearsome canyons on either side. Western Tayéttos and the summit area of Levká Óri on Crete are also potentially dangerous. All of these areas should be attempted only by experienced cross-country trekkers equipped with map and compass, Greek language skills, and a heavy dose of common sense.

Many locals will express surprise at finding you hiking alone, if that is your preference. Greeks are exceedingly gregarious and to them there is something suspect about people who prefer their own company, but their distress is partly motivated by concern for your safety. The Greek mountains can be lethal—a handful of rock climbers and hikers die each year, though most of the fatalities known to me occurred within a group. If you choose to solo, you should be at least passingly conversant in Greek, have enough prior experience in the type of terrain so that nothing takes you completely by surprise and be conservative in route decisions. The disadvantages of being without a partner are evident; in compensation, though, you have complete freedom, a greater chance of glimpsing wildlife, and more extended interaction with those you meet along the way.

COUNTRY GREEKS AND CITY GREEKS

The overriding demographic trend in Greece for the past 60 years has been massive population movement away from the hinterlands to urban areas. You, as a backcountry tramper, are not only going back in time but bucking the tide as well; my Athens cobbler once introduced me to acquaintances as "the man who's always going up into the mountains we've tried so hard to leave."

As you step off the bus at the end of the line, all eyes may rivet on you and your luggage; the dull roar of *platía* (plaza) discussions and *távli* (backgammon) games subsides. To those assembled you are a marvel, a distinct oddity, but established convention may inhibit them from addressing you. (In Greece the approaching party always greets the stationary group; this custom is still strictly followed in the wilds but is beginning to break down in villages.) Once the ice is broken questions, fueled by roughly equal proportions of good-heartedness, boredom, curiosity and wariness, come back-to-back: "Where are you from?" and "Where are you headed?" are the standard openers, with "Why are you alone?" (if that is the case) as a sequel. A benevolent scrutiny of you and your equipage may follow—walking sticks are invariably conversation pieces, as are high-tech packs and sturdy boots—but such scrutiny is no cause for alarm. Rural Greeks are scrupulously honest and this absence of menace is one of the factors that contributes to the enjoyment of hiking in Greece.

At this point, someone who's visited your hometown as a sailor or who has a close relative there will turn up, lending with his reminiscences a veneer of sophistication to what may be a rustic scene indeed; somebody at the next table may have only a hazy idea of global geography. ("New Zealand? Is that near South Africa?") Certain returned expatriates and pensioners can have overly fond memories of the lands where they made their nest eggs and acquired the rudiments of what they regard as culture, and may wish to bend your ear about how provincial Greece is or their neighbors are; they should be gently but firmly put off. They, or someone of like sentiments, may pop another and more insidious question: "Why do you go on foot when they just built a new road to your destination?"

The query underlines a basic logic prevalent throughout the developing world: namely, that nobody could possibly trek for pleasure. Walking is associated with backwardness and toil, with the hand implements and 12-hour days that were the rule before progress conferred its mixed blessings on the rural populace. In Greece, additionally, the old by-ways seem to bear connotations of shame, as leftovers from the bad old days when the Turks ruled (never mind that some of the finest architectural and engineering feats of medieval Greece—delicate bridges, finely paved *kalderímia*, and handsome mansions—were completed during the supposedly sepulchral *Turkokratía*). Country Greeks, like many peoples eking out a subsistence living, regard their surroundings as a work place and a resource, a repository of water, pasturage, lumber, game, honey and herbs, and usually not something to be enjoyed for its own sake.

These subtle but nonetheless real attitudes may account for any resistance met when asking villagers for directions. On rare occasions you may be told initially that no path exists, and to go use the road. Sometimes this is true; in other cases the native(s) may have sized you up and decided that the route ahead is beyond your capabilities. At such times you may have to deliver an "oral resumé" of your hiking experience, perhaps dwelling on a particularly arduous or faint section of trail that your informant is likely to be familiar with. Or give as "references" friends who successfully did last year what you wish to do now—they may be remembered. This may elicit complete instructions for continuing on your way, delivered, however, with an air of "Since you insist . . . ." Part of this reluctance can be attributed to a Greek host's natural instinct to spare the visitor the unpleasantness of getting lost, but one cannot discount the element of embarrassment over the past. The busybodies of the *kafeneío* committee, like the chorus in ancient Greek drama, will always be ready to offer negative advice or express doubt as to your successful passage, which doesn't help your state of mind as you plunge onward into the little-known. If you find yourself in such a situation, persist until you find a sympathetic villager—there is almost always a way.

Fortunately, such hesitation in giving instructions is rare. A request for assistance, especially if delivered in Greek (however imperfect), is generally met with an elaborate, unequivocal response, assisted by the full repertoire of Greek hand gestures to ensure comprehension. Directions may even be tendered in tandem with hospitality (*filoksenía*); much has been said about this legendary Greek trait, and it generally goes double in rural areas. Fruits of the season are routinely offered to wayfarers passing villagers' front doors; more involved invitations may result in all-day or all-night drinking, eating or even staying sessions. It's always the proper time to be treated to a coffee or an *oúzo*; more elaborate offers may require some discretion or diplomacy. (You should not attempt to reciprocate on the spot, but a letter, or better yet, a post card from your hometown upon return will be hugely appreciated, and pinned on the wall for posterity.)

Extraordinary generosity is deeply rooted in the Greek psyche and goes back thousands of years. In the old days a stranger represented an unknown, possibly hostile power and the bestowal of food and shelter was a method of placation; then again, who could tell if the visitor might not be a god in disguise, come to check on humankind's behavior? Certainly a residue of these sentiments persists, but today the open-handedness is largely an expression of faith and pride. A shepherd may offer you his last bowl of milk, confident that tomorrow will surely bring another. In his capacity to set a table for you, or give you a drink, any Greek is your peer, be you a mule driver or visiting dignitary.

Filoksenía, and that fraction of the naysayers' pessimism that has solid foundation, will be jointly responsible for the 25 percent extra you should routinely add to any estimate of time given to reach a destination. Greeks, up to amazingly advanced ages, cover ground with seven-league strides that will leave you (especially if pack laden) breathless. Even assuming you can match their pace in motion, you will always be delayed by dogs, weather, wildflowers or other chance encounters. You are enjoined by courtesy to chat a bit with any person you meet along the way, and it's the least you can do by way of thanks for the one who gives you supplementary directions or shows you that hidden spring when you're dying of thirst. If they sense they have a willing and interested audience, those left behind in the mad rush to Athens can spin awfully good yarns—anything from a personal history of the last war to the current activities of the Common Market in their area, by way of a local bestiary and catalog of legends. You will have learned far more than from any tourist office or library book, and relieved the monotony of the days that press down on isolated monks, barley threshers or high meadow dwellers who ordinarily have only transistor radios for company.

Town Greeks may already be one or two generations removed from their rural ancestry, and the separation may be sufficient to impart a nostalgia for the country that is usually absent in hard-pressed villagers. You may find carloads of townees, or walking parties, stopping *you*, the seemingly well-equipped foreigner, to ask for directions. Intentions are commendable ("We've never been up here and decided to come look"), but the shepherds' savvy and/or the inclination to meet the mountains on their own terms may be lacking. Every so often you come across an individual, often a village innkeeper or an Alpine Club branch official, in whom the desire and the know-how are happily wedded. Such acquaintances, and the resulting added appreciation of the countryside, are to be treasured.

In the hills the precepts of *filoksenía* overshadow all other considerations, and differences between your hosts and yourself are not dwelt upon; city Greeks in their own environment may be another story. The current nationalist bent of Greek politics and the swarms of foreigners act as irritants to the country's pride; there are small bones, never far out of reach, to pick with natives of several nations. Americans may be taken to task for their government's support of the 1967-74 junta, and for continued perceived interference in local affairs; the behavior of the German occupying forces in the Second World War has not been forgotten; and Anglo-Greek relations have been badly strained by events in Cyprus and within the Greek resistance during the period 1942-47. (Conversely, Canadians, Australians and New Zealanders may find themselves feted almost everywhere they go, especially in Crete.)

Although out-and-out stealing is taboo and considered a serious breach of *filoksenía*, not to mention a sullying of a Greek's *filótimo* (literally, love of honor), the prevailing Levantine fondness for money may lead merchants to squeeze extra *dhráchmes* out of visitors considered easy marks. You are at some disadvantage in efforts to counter this, since as a foreigner your earning power is roughly triple that of a Greek and in all likelihood you're outfitted with an expensive camera, charge cards and hard currency. Obviously it helps to be an inconspicuous consumer and to learn the ropes quickly so that you can request a fair deal. Greeks are not as emotionally invested in their commercial cat-and-mouse game as you may be in your indignation at being initially quoted a ridiculous price, and they'll respect you if you understand when it's appropriate to bargain and proceed to do so. Groceries and produce are almost always a fixed price, although cost may fluctuate wildly from one shop, or region, to the next. Transport fares, taxis excepted, are nationally standardized and don't require any wrangling or undue attention. Fees for special services, such as boot repair, do depend on your bargaining power and facility in Greek—get a general estimate beforehand if it's your first visit to the shop.

ETHNOLOGY OF MINORITIES

There are more minority groups in Greece than is commonly realized, and the backcountry visitor will probably run across at least several of these subcultures. It should also be stressed that a "pure" Greek is a romantic fiction, since centuries of invasion, immigration and subsequent assimilation point to Hellenic cultural durability rather than racial continuity. The average Greek is such a complex amalgam that he probably couldn't dissect his ancestry into its components even if he cared to.

Greece was originally populated from the sixth to the second millennium B.C. by successive waves of settlers from Asia Minor and the Levant. Thereafter, aside from a few citizens of the western Roman Empire, there were not many newcomers until Slavs from the northern Balkans raided the declining Byzantine (eastern Roman) Empire in the seventh to tenth centuries A.D. The Slavs soon lost their separate ethnic identity, leaving only a handful of place names as far south as the Peloponnisos to mark their coming. Shortly after, the less assimilable Vlachs, nomads from present-day Romania (then known as Walachia, hence "Vlach"), appeared and dispersed themselves in Ípiros and parts of Thessalía and Makedhonía. (According to a contending theory, they are descended from Greek natives trained as mountain-pass guards by the Romans; after the empire dissolved, the guards' Latin evolved to a form mutually intelligible with standard Romanian.)

There are two strains of Vlachs, or *Roumanikí* as they prefer to be called. (*"Vláhos"* in the mouths of many Greeks is an insult, equivalent to "bumpkin".) The Koutsovlachs until recently spoke dialectal Romanian (*Roumaniká*) as their first language; their children may still attend Romanian language schools and adults tend to mix *Roumaniká* and Greek in ordinary conversation. They are concentrated in the central Píndhos, from Métsovo to Siráko, and in east Zagória, notably Vovoússa, Láista and Samarína. Koutsovlachs whose villages are above snow line have alternate winter quarters, often near Velestíno in Thessalía or in western Makedhonía. The *Karagounídhes* or Arvanitovlachs are somewhat less prosperous and less settled; until recently they spoke Albanian (hence the prefix "Arvanito") in addition to *Roumaniká* or Greek, but this custom is dying out as this subgroup is steadily absorbed into the Koutsovlach culture.

This brief survey of Ipirote "tribes" is completed with the *Sarakatsáni*, strictly Greek-speaking nomads, possibly of aboriginal or Pelasgian (the first settlers) stock, who formerly wandered through most of northern Greece but whose range is now restricted. Until recently they were true nomads with no fixed address, migrating between summer pastures in the Píndhos and winter grazing in the lowlands. The government has of late required them to establish permanent winter dwellings, but they still return each summer to the mountains, where they rent pastures from the villagers, often the now nearly sedentary Koutsovlachs with whom they are not on good terms. They are quite friendly, though, to outsiders and it is almost impossible to go summer trekking in the Píndhos without happening upon their temporary colonies or meeting them on the trail.

Albanian Christians arrived in Greece around 1300, repopulating the islands of Spétses and Ídhra plus the Argolid mainland opposite, as well as northern Ándhros and portions of adjacent Évvia and Attikí. Albanian and medieval Greek cultures were so alike that assimilation was rapid, although spoken Albanian only disappeared from the areas cited after 1950.

As many visitors will soon be told in an aggrieved tone, the Turks conquered most of the provinces of what is now modern Greece by 1425 and stayed almost 400 years. During that period intermarriage, voluntary or otherwise, was not unheard of and the influence of things Turkish on cuisine, language and music (though *not* religion or folklore) was enormous. After the disastrous Asia Minor war of 1922-23, all remaining Greek Muslims were exchanged for Anatolian Christians, with the exception of the Tsamídhes (Ipirote Muslims, expelled in 1944 for collaboration with the Axis) and the ethnic Turks of western Thráki who today number about 300,000. They maintain their own villages and a way of life largely untouched by the reforms of secular Turkey. In 1948 Greece reclaimed the Dhodhekánisos Islands and inherited a few more Turkish- and Greek-speaking Muslims on Rhódhos and Kos; these communities had been expelled from Crete between 1913 and 1923. If you venture north of Ksánthi toward Ehínos, you may meet the Pomaks, yet another Muslim group speaking a bizarre hybrid of Bulgarian, Turkish and Greek.

Orthodox Christian speakers of Makedhonian, a long-suppressed dialect akin to Bulgarian that is now permitted, live throughout the Yugoslav and Bulgarian border regions. The nationalists' dream of a separate Makedhonian state was a political hot potato until the close of the Greek civil war in 1949; thereafter, the Makedhonian republic of Yugoslavia had to suffice, and all parties concerned lost interest in promoting or squelching secessionist agitation.

Gypsies can be found almost anywhere in Greece (even on ferryboats), although they concentrate in Thessalía, Makedhonía and Thráki, where they may be Muslim rather than Orthodox Christian. They have often traded in their horses-and-carts for pickup trucks and taken up the vocation of fruitseller. Many of the better festival musicians lay claim to gypsy forebears.

Catholics are a holdover from the Genoese and Venetian penetration of the Aegean following the disgraceful Fourth Crusade of 1204. Today they live principally on the islands of Sýros, Thíra and Tínos, and in Athens. Often Italianate last names distinguish them from their neighbors.

The Jewish communities of Ioánnina, Lárissa, Halkídha and Rhódhos are some of the oldest in Europe, dating back to the Roman era. The Sephardic Jews of Thessaloníki, Kaválla and Dhidhimótiho were invited there by the Sultan in 1492 following their expulsion from Spain and Portugal. The Athens enclave is a recent phenomenon, being mostly German Jews who accompanied King Otto from Bavaria to Greece in the 1830s. Although the Nazis decimated 80 percent of Greek Jewry in 1944-45, about 5,000 remain.

Taken together, these various interesting minorities total less than seven percent of the entire Greek population. Nonetheless, they are conspicuous and important out of proportion to their numbers, and any visitor to Greece will derive satisfaction from an informed glimpse of those who would otherwise be mysterious oddities.

It is also sobering to contemplate that at any given moment Greece is engulfed by anywhere from a few thousand to half a million foreigners, mostly concentrated in Athens and the islands. While individually transient, travelers en masse must be considered an important demographic component of the country into the fore-seeable future.

NATURAL HISTORY

Greece has been continuously inhabited for at least 8000 years, and the results have included intense cultivation in the limited arable areas, deforestation by shipbuilders and goats, and increasing population pressure on finite resources.

Expanding urban centers and road networks restrict animal ranges so that wild creatures bigger than a fox are rarely encountered. In addition, Greeks are ruthless and thorough hunters, fishers and woodcutters; conservationist notions were completely foreign to them until after the Second World War.

Since then the *Dhasikí Ypiresía* (Forest Service) has become a powerful entity to contend with, many species of plant and animal are officially protected and a handful of national parks has been set up (though these conform more to the idea of a North American national forest or wildlife sanctuary than a recreational park). Seven reserves—Crete's Samarian gorge, Kefalloniá's Mt. Énos, Attikí's Mt. Párnitha, Mt. Oíti, Mt. Ólymbos, the Víkos/Aóös environs and the Préspa Lakes—are known of, as this volume goes to press. In most there are express prohibitions against picking wildflowers or gathering herbs, and I've personally seen this vigorously enforced by forest rangers. Hikers should refrain from picking plants everywhere, as many Greek wildflowers are endangered species.

In recent years Greece has suffered a rash of summer forest fires, many of them deliberately set. Motives for this arson are unclear and complex, but there seems to be an upsurge of incidents during election years when political extremists of both stripes try to frame their opponents. It is also suggested that agricultural property is torched by speculators to force intransigent owners to sell out at depressed prices. But the foregoing does little to explain the destruction of vast tracts of wilderness; this vandalism seems a protest against the forest service's rigid no-building, no-grazing, no-clearing policies in areas designated as woodland. The firebugs may wish to present the bureaucrats with a *fait accompli* ("no more trees to protect, no more restrictions"), but the authorities have dug in their heels, declaring that land classification is irrevocable and that burnt areas shall be deemed "forest" until doomsday. To aggravate matters, forested tracts are taxed according to their potential value even though the owner is denied income from logging. Some sort of compromise seems in order to prevent the wholesale devastation of Greece's remaining wilderness.

Given this uneven record of resource management, the abundance of smaller mobile and vegetative wildlife may come as a pleasant surprise. Like so many things Greek, the flora is a melange of things African, Asian and south European that meet only here. Some interesting speciations have occurred as a result of the islands' mutual isolation by the Aegean eons ago, and many Greek species are found nowhere else.

Flora of Mediterranean-Influenced Lowlands and Islands

ALEPPO PINE (*Pinus halepensis*); widespread

OLIVE (*Olea*)

CYPRESSES (*Cupressus*); mark chapels, graveyards

KOÚMARO [Gr.] (*Arbutus*); fruit formerly made into *oúzo*

JUNIPER (*Juniperus* [many species]); most common in Crete, Dhodhekánisos, Pelopónnisos

HOLLY OAK, KERMES OAK (*Quercus ilex, Q. coccifera*); thrive in same conditions as above—rocky hillsides

VALONEA OAK (*Q. aegilops*); most common oak

BROOMS (*Spartium and Calycotome*); spring blooming, fragrant

BAY LAUREL (*Laurus*)

HEATH (*Erica*)

TREE-OF-HEAVEN (*Alianthus*); malodorous

OLEANDER (*Nerium*); mark stream beds

WILLOW (*Salix*); prefer running streams

PLANE (*Platanus*); mark springs; become huge

CRETAN PALM (*Phoenix*); select seashore locales only
PRICKLY-PEAR (*Opuntia*); autumn fruit; animal fodder

Low-Altitude Wildflowers

ANEMONE (*Anemone*); spring
IRIS (*Iris*); spring
LILIES (*Lilium*); spring; yellow or white
POPPIES (*Papaver*); spring, fallow fields
ROCK ROSE (*Cistus*); spring; dry sunny slopes
CYCLAMEN (*Cyclamen persicum*); spring, white, part shade
DRAGON AURUM (*Dracunculus*); spring; foul odor attracts pollinators
CYCLAMEN (*Cyclamen graecum*); autumn, pink, widespread
STERNBERGIA (*Sternbergia*); autumn; yellow; loves rock interstices, especially at
    ancient ruins
SEA-SQUILL (*Urginea maritima*); autumn, meter-high white flower spikes, in
    disturbed areas
HERBS; thyme, oregano, basil, mint, sage, "mountain tea" (type of sage), marjoram,
    rosemary

Flora of the Middle Altitudes and Alpine Zones

BEECH (*Fagus*); dominant species in Píndhos, Magnisía, Makedhonía, up to 1900 m
BLACK PINE (*Pinus heldreichii*); highest growing, to 2300 m, in Píndhos, Ólymbos,
    Makedhonía
SILVER FIR (*Abies pectinata*); northern regions
BLACK PINE (*Pinus nigra*); range includes Crete, Pelopónnisos plus bulk of
    mainland
SCOTS PINE (*Pinus silvestris*); small plantations in north
MAPLE (*Acer*); isolated specimens, usually
ASH (*Fraxinus*); isolated specimens
WHITE POPLAR (*Populus alba*); isolated specimens
SWEET CHESTNUT (*Kastanea sativa*); widespread at middle altitudes, especially
    Magnisía
CEPHALLONIAN FIR (*Abies cephalonica*); range includes Evvia, Stereá and
    Pelopónnisos plus namesake island
WILD FRUITS; apple, pear, plum, brambles, wild rose
CLEMATIS (*Clematis*); twining vine; fuzzy seed coat
BRACKEN FERN (*Pteridium*); ubiquitous in forest and pasture

Mid- and High-Altitude Wildflowers

GLADIOLUS (*Gladiolus*); spring
TULIP (*Tulipa*); spring; mostly reddish
VIOLA (*Viola*); spring; lavender to yellow
CROCUS (*Crocus*); spring; few species
BELLFLOWER (*Campanula*); summer; in mountains only
WILD CARNATION (*Dianthus*); as above
RED LILY (*Lilium chalcedonium*); summer; brilliant red; Stereá
(No English common name) (*Carlina*); giant composite; flush with ground in high
    Píndhos, Ólymbos; bracts close in moist conditions
AUTUMN CROCUS (*Colchicum*); autumn; lavender, white, purple
(TRUE) CROCUS (*Crocus*); autumn, most species

Only those species most likely to be encountered have been listed. For thorough
coverage consult one of the field guides recommended in the Bibliography. Some of

the commoner trees are referred to by Greeks when giving directions; the local names for these appear in the "Greek for Hikers" section.

Island Fauna

"KRI-KRI" (CRETAN IBEX) (*Capra aegagrus cretensis*); rare, shy; endemic to Samariá gorge, White Mountains
FRESHWATER CRABS (*Potamon*); streams on Crete, Sérifos, Náxos, Rhódhos, other high-water-table areas
PELICANS; fishing harbor mascots
DOLPHINS (*Delphinus*); often follow boats
PORPOISES (*Phocaena*); as above
MONK SEAL (*Monachus*); killed by fishermen; possibly extinct
GREEN SEA TURTLE (*Chelonia*); found mostly in Ionian Sea, especially Zákinthos
PARROT FISH (*Scarus*); common in Kykládhes

Overfishing and pollution of the Aegean have resulted in the virtual depletion, since World War II, of the breeding stocks of most fish species. Thus deceptively clear waters are often quite sterile.

Endemic Fauna of the Mountains and Inland Regions

EUROPEAN BROWN BEAR (*Ursus arctos*); present range includes the Píndhos and north border regions—avoid overnighting in dense forest
WOLF (*Canis lupus*); very rare
SPANISH LYNX (*Lynx pardellus*); rare; found only in Kará Deré of western Rhodhópi hills
WILD BOAR (*Sus Scrofa*); prolific
ROE DEER (*Capreolus capreolus*); rare
CHAMOIS (*Rupicapra*); inhabit lofty, inaccessible crags and summits of the Píndhos
WEASELS (*Mustela*); favor high-altitude rock piles plus forest habitats
JACKAL (*Canis aureus*); also on larger islands
Other assorted rodents, badgers, foxes
GOLDEN EAGLE (*Aquilus chrysaetos*)
LAMMERGEYER (*Gypaetus barbatus*); also on Crete
GRIFFON VULTURE (*Gyps fulvus*)
EGYPTIAN VULTURE (*Aegypius monachus*)
STORKS (*Ciconia ciconia*); protected in folklore—roost throughout Ípiros, Makedhonia, Thráki, Thessalía

Ubiquitous Species

HARES (*Lepus europaeus*), RABBITS (*Oryctolagus cuniculus*), MOLES (*Talpa europaea*), HEDGEHOGS (*Erinaceus* sp.); roadside animals
RAVENS (*Corvus corax*), ROOK (*Corvus frugilegus*), MAGPIES (*Pica pica*) SWALLOWS (*Hirundo rustica*); commensal with humans
PARTRIDGE (*Perdix perdix*), TURTLE DOVES (*Streptopelia turtur*), QUAIL (*Coturnix coturnix*); game birds, hunted in autumn
FINCHES (*Fringilla* sp.), BEE-EATERS (*Merops apiaster*), HOOPOOES (*Upupa epops*); most colorful avians
EGRETS (*Egretta garzetta*), HERONS (*Ardea cinerea*), BITTERNS (*Botarus* sp. and *Ixobrychus* sp.), MALLARDS (*Anas platyrhynchos*), COOTS (*Fulica atra*); in Greece's extensive wetlands
NIGHT JAR (*Caprimulgus europaeus*), SCOPS OWL (*Otus scops*), LITTLE OWL (*Athene noctua*); night criers
GREEK NEWT (*Trituris*); orange speckles; abroad after rains

GREEK LAND TORTOISE (*Testudo*); widespread; noisy eater
AGAMO LIZARD (*Agama*); medium-size, salt-and-pepper pattern, other types from
 finger to arm size
FROGS (*Rana* sp.); six species

DOG DAYS . . .

Every Eden has its serpents, and in Greece hikers will sooner or later contend with the ferocious *mandhróskilia* (sheepfold watchdogs). They've been bred to intimidate bears, wolves and livestock rustlers so they're unlikely to be impressed by you. In addition, they're often underfed and cuffed by their masters and so have become extra mean. Now that I've frightened you into taking a precautionary three-day rabies series, take heart; there are some things you can do to lessen the chances of chunks being removed from your person.

Avoid turning your back on dogs, if they aren't numerous enough to completely encircle you. Facing your assailants, back away slowly but steadily until enough distance has opened up between you and them to resume normal locomotion. Dogs seem to like nothing better than to sink teeth into fleeing ankles, calves, or buttocks.

Light artillery can be useful. Try shying plum-size rocks toward, but not *at*, the beasts. Best throws are those that bounce once just in front of their snouts; this keeps them distracted and eyes-down, during which time you can sneak a bit further away.

A stout walking stick can double as a club in an emergency—even the most resolutely charging dog will be given pause by a sound whack across the snout. If there are many attacking, though, you'd better be a *kendo* master. Shepherds aren't too thrilled if you abuse their charges—they like to reserve that right for themselves—so it's preferable, if at all possible, to deal with the situation nonviolently.

Avoid traveling in the mountains after dark—canine viciousness increases with the lowering of the sun. Also, never parade through sheepfolds but give flocks a wide berth. If you don't, you may be bitten without so much as a preliminary bark. An Englishman was badly mauled above Tsepélovo (Ípiros) in 1982 because he insisted on photographing a flock closeup.

. . . AND OTHER HEALTH HAZARDS

The primary bogy in Greece is not gastroenteritis, as in more exotic destinations, but overexposure to the elements. Heatstroke, heat exhaustion and simple dehydration are more than conceivable in the south from May to October, and all summer in the mountains. Know how to recognize and treat the various conditions if you or your companion(s) are stricken; religious use of headgear and water container is the best preventative. More insidious but just as dangerous is the threat of hypothermia, which in the Greek mountains can strike anywhere, any time of the year. Never venture into the hills without at least one warm top and raingear; thunderstorms billow out of a clear summer sky on an hour's notice. With thunderheads comes lightning, and the Greek topography is perversely ideal for redistributing air masses so as to threaten hikers. There have been a few fatalities from summit and meadow strikes; seek shelter, if possible, in low-lying wooded areas or *deep*, horizontal caves.

Greeks have an overdeveloped, mostly superstitious fear of snakes (*fídhia*), but I've only seen a handful of snakes in years of tramping and they were all much more frightened of me than vice versa. The only poisonous species is the adder (*Vipera berus, ohiá* in Greek), which has mottled dorsal markings in gray, brown or red. It tends to sunbathe on or near pathside stone walls, so care should be exercised when passing such structures. Scorpions (*skorpií*) are common, especially in arid regions; check your shoes in the morning and don't poke hands under ledges, etc. Body lice (*pséires*) and scabies are endemic in warmer, dryer regions and seasons; avoid groups of schoolchildren (the primary carriers) and suspicious bedding (foam padding comes in handy as a mattress cover). In many lodgings, mosquitos, gnats and other winged pests will torment you all night unless you've lit *fidhákia* or *spéires* (pyrethrin incense coils). Availability at the local stores is a good indication that they'll be needed. The coils are safe for mammals but make a room reek; it's a tough choice between being gassed or bit. Some folks prefer a smear-on topical repellent, which is also your only option when camping in the open.

I have been food-poisoned twice in Greece (both times by bad chicken) but never have suffered from the water, which is in fact world famous for its purity, having usually percolated hundreds of meters down through porous rock. This is essentially the same filtering method used by municipal waterworks engineers and bourbon distilleries so water purification tablets may be redundant. (You may wish to take along some iodine, *not* chlorine [e.g., Halozone], which does not kill amoebic cysts, for other countries visited on your trip.) But even in Greece you should avoid runoff from below a village and springs directly below a *stáni* (shepherd's colony)—grazing animals everywhere in the world harbor *Giardia*. Fountains within a settlement are usually safely positioned, but use your discretion.

The Greek oceans have their own set of annoyances. Armadas of jellyfish (*tsoúktres*) periodically besiege the coasts, making swimming like a dodge game. Suggested sting remedies include a mild ammonia solution, papain meat tenderizer (bring it with you), baking soda or (in a pinch) urine. If you graze against a sea urchin or, worse, step on one, the spines will lodge porcupine-style in your anatomy. If not removed, especially from feet, all but the tiniest fragments will fester or at least make subsequent hiking painful. Set to work with a sewing needle, the finest blade of your pocket knife and olive oil introduced dropwise into the punctures; the oil floats the hollow barbed spines, which can otherwise introduce bacteria deep into the flesh. (Olive oil is also perfect for removing tar from your feet; quite a lot of tar washes up on beaches from time to time.)

In case of more debilitating accidents, remember that emergency-room care at public general hospitals (*yeniká nosokoméia*) and rural clinics is free for Greeks *and* foreigners. Private clinics and extended care are quite costly, however.

⊐ PART II ⊏

The Hikes

THE PELOPÓNNISOS

Once I stayed on the summit [of Táyettos] to watch the sun set . . . and it took five hours to get down to the sheepfold where the shepherds lay wrapped in their goat's hair capes, but the fire was still burning and they had left me a cauldron of milk and some bread. We ate the same thing each morning, watching the shadow of the earth's eastern rim descending the ridge like a curtain as the sun rose.

————Kevin Andrews

The Pelopónnisos—as a glance at the map will confirm—misses being an island by only six kilometers, the breadth of the isthmus of Kórinthos connecting it to the rest of mainland Greece. Today considered isolated and away from the center (politically as well as geographically), it is actually the heart of Greece. There are more ancient ruins and medieval monuments per square kilometer here than in any other region of the country. It was in the Pelopónnisos that the standard of revolution was first raised in 1821, and most of the decisive battles of the War of Independence were fought on the peninsula or just offshore. The scenery, be it the Maniote deserts, the orchards and river valleys of Arkadhía or the sandy Messinían capes, is unsubtle and dramatic, painted in bold swatches always weighted by the mountains that invest the outline of the Moréa (the medieval name) like the bones of a hand. A great wall of consecutive peaks cuts off the center from the Gulf of Kórinthos, with the two great fingers of Taïyettos and Párnon flanked by the lesser hills of Messinía and the Argolíd. Accordingly, the north and west shores of the Pelopónnisos absorb the brunt of winter precipitation; a heaviness and languor in the air suggest correctly that the Adriatic and the softer contours of Italy are not far off. Water becomes more of a preoccupation as one journeys south and east, its extreme lack culminates in the study of austerity provided by Taïyettos and its extension, the Máni.

The Peloponnesians are steady, deeply attached to their villages and lands (which are not languishing as in many other parts of the country) and hold in deepest respect the precepts of *filoksenía* (hospitality).

Opposite—top: The Taïyettos range and Profítis Ilias (extreme left) seen from near Tóriza (Hike 2); Bottom, left: At the pools of the Nédhas river (Hike 4); Bottom, right: The *stómio* (abyss) of the Nédhas river (Hike 4)

1   MT. PÁRNON (PÁRNONAS)

The Párnon massif is a long, low range extending nearly 40 km from the nunnery of Malevís (a.k.a. Melemvís) to a pass near the village of Kosmás, beyond which the mountain gives one last gasp before expiring in the sea of olives on the Evrótas River plain. It has a more montane feeling than its modest (1935 m) elevation would lead you to believe, forming a formidable enough barrier between the high plateaus around Spárti and Trípoli and the lush east coast of Arkadhía. Relative closeness to the Argolíd Gulf gives rise to drifting nocturnal mists and damp rather than dry daytime heat. The humidity promotes thick forests (duly exploited) up to the 1700-m treeline, and riotous spring wildflowers. Most of Párnon is kilometers from anywhere; early in the year Táyettos, hovering like a snowy morning ghost to the west, may be your principal landmark. The north end of the Párnon ridge is the most interesting, featuring as it does a challenging two-day hike from Vamvakóu village to the Malevís convent, but it's also possible to walk the entire crest from Kosmás to Malevís on a forest road.

Getting to the trailhead: There is but one daily bus from Spárti to Vamvakóu, departing around 2 P.M. (not Sun) from the terminal at 47 Agisilaou (across from the produce market and near the Hotel Spárti); ride takes 2 hr.

Vamvakóu to Malevís via Krónio Summit

Route directions: Once in Vamvakóu, start from the church on the central *platía* and find a prominent cement staircase heading up and northeast. Soon the steps metamorphose into a wide mule path that almost immediately crosses a dirt road and then plunges up a chestnut-covered slope. Keep a yawning gulch to your *left* and aim for the ridge above you. This you reach after a half-hour climb, to be rewarded with a

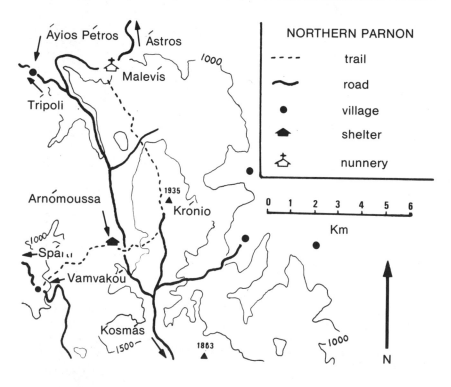

view over a long, fertile valley of potato fields nestled between the north-south longitudinal ridges of Párnon. Your trail drops down, crosses a road, and almost instantly re-intersects it. Amble right about 50 m and again dip down the trail's resumption in the direction of an audible river. About 20 min further along, ford this stream (there's no bridge) and head up a dry gulch on the opposite bank. One hundred m up the gulch, you should see a rusty, jerry-rigged aqueduct just overhead; do *not* go under it, but take a prominent left some 30 m in front of it.

Now there's a 1-hr climb, initially through thick stands of Spanish broom but later through orchards and past a spring. As the path levels out it becomes extremely faint, but even if you lose it, you should intersect a dirt jeep track within the time noted. Turn left onto it and proceed for 10 to 15 min until you reach the high point of the road, on a pine ridge. Make a reckoning of the ridge line (the road crosses it perpendicularly) and plunge right (east); within a moment you'll see red metal arrows (courtesy of EOS Spárti) nailed to trees. There's no distinct trail; the navigational secret lies in keeping exactly to the ridge line without meandering right or left. Two hundred m beyond the last red blaze and a cement benchmark, and 30 min after turning off the *dhimósio* (public road), looms the imposing Arnómoussa alpine shelter. This is superbly sited at 1450 m in a thinning fir and pine forest which allows views of sunsets to the west and the main crest of Párnon to the east. Even if you've not rented the shelter keys, you can still fetch water from a spring 5 min downhill and south (follow a sign *"Piyí, EOS Spárti"* nailed to a tree). The front terrace of the refuge offers some shelter from most night winds. Total walking time from Vamvakóu to Arnómoussa is 2½ hr.

To continue toward the summit, hike down the shelter's driveway past the soccer field until you find another tree-sign; *"Krónion 3 ½ ora."* Head down the path indicated, meeting another road within 100 m. The trail picks up again slightly to the right; 15 min from the refuge, there's a spring at the edge of an orchard alongside the forest road to Áyios Pétros. A red tree marker cues a left turn onto the road; after a few more min you'll see another ambiguously oriented sign on the left: *"Krónion 3 ora."* Take this as the signal to head *right* down a ridgelet covered with Scotch pine; there is no clear trail any longer. Twenty min past the orchard spring, you'll cross a creek; this is the last dependable water until Malevís nunnery! Turn right (south) up an overgrown drover's track on the opposite bank, keeping a sharp eye out for one last *"EOS Spárti"* sign on a tree at the base of a mostly denuded bluff to your left. This is the cue to claw your way up the slope; it's a brutal cross-country exercise, whether you charge straight up or angle around. Moving most directly, it will take you about 45 min to meet the last forest road on the west side of the watershed—and have done with the only unpleasant portion of the trek. Turn left (north) onto this track and follow it for 30 to 40 min until it ends at the base of Krónio (Mégas Toúrlos on some maps) and the head of a valley rising up to the *oropédhio* (high plateau), which is the antechamber to the peak. It's a pleasant 25-min crossing on sheep tracks to a small chapel at the far end of the high meadow. Oddly, there is no spring up here, merely a metal-lidded well between Krónio and the little *ksoklísi*, some 300 m from the latter. However, its water is foul and larvae infested, the only such I've seen in Greece, and can only be recommended boiled for emergency use.

Seen from the Arkadhian coast or the Argolíd to the east, Párnon summit has a symmetrical triple profile, and up close it's obvious why. Beyond the dubious well a low saddle separates the northernmost prominence from the two to the south; the middle knob is the true peak. In spring you may still find patches of snow suitable for melting on the mountain's flanks. To climb Krónio, doff your pack among the saddle boulders and inch up the grade to the altitude marker; this will require an extra hour round trip. Weather permitting, you'll be treated to panoramas of the Argolíd and its gulf to the east, Taïyettos and Lakonía to the west and a large depression to the north beyond the vicinity of Malevís.

To resume course toward Malevís, locate the start of a proper path immediately behind and below the little chapel. Begin in the approximate center of a livestock-frayed trail network. All this soon resolves into one obvious right-of-way—it's sporadically red-blazed, but these are oriented toward uphill hikers. An hour's uneventful descent through a delightful mixed forest is interrupted by a logging road. Go straight across it, continuing along a junipered ridge, before dipping down into an assortment of potato fields. Keep most of these to your left and make for the top of a canyon in the landscape ahead. There's really only one, boulder-flanked "notch" where you can easily leave this plateau; it's red-dashed and a trail of sorts picks up half-heartedly. Initially you face a gradual descent north, with a terraced slope on the left. Soon you must avoid bearing right and uphill in favor of dropping in the opposite direction across a pasture, changing sides of the gully. Presently you'll see a couple of reassuring tree-borne arrows; begin following the actual bottom of the water-course before changing banks again. About 45 min below the lumber road any trace of trail vanishes, as do red marks, and hiking becomes topographic. Keeping clear of dense stands of trees above and below, pick a median course through a vast series of steep terraces belonging to Moní Malevís. The dome of an outlying chapel of the convent tantalizes and guides you. Finally, 2½ hr after quitting the *oropédhio*, you arrive on the grounds of Malevís, a much-rebuilt white-elephantine structure. Weekend visits are inadvisable since religious retreats often fill most available beds. At other times you can request a bed or two (for same-sex duos) from the abbess. No food is available, however, and daylight and stamina permitting, you may prefer to hitch/bus/walk the 8 km west to Áyios Pétros village, which has proper lodgings, eateries and views back at the recently climbed mountain. Alternatively, you can hitch or bus down toward Astros and Paralía Astros, 32 km distant, where you can drown your sundry aches at the beach. However, there is no Sunday bus service, and traffic is patchy on the unpaved road east of Malevís. Westbound buses eventually end up in Trípoli, which can be problematic if you've stored gear in Spárti; if you haven't already passed through, you may prefer to exit from Párnon via the Ástros-Spárti route described below.

Walks Out of Kosmás

Several times daily there are buses down the coast from Ástros as far as Leonídhio, a large market town nestled at the base of reddish cliffs. From Leonídhio *one* bus daily—ca. 1 P.M.—continues up a dizzying road as far as Kosmás (1200 m), the southernmost of the Párnon villages. This is a peaceful, if somewhat chilly place on an exposed pass with tufts of firs and extensive cherry and chestnut orchards. Facilities include two *tavérnes* and an inn, next to which a sign tells you the refuge is 29 km; Áyios Pétros, 50 km; Vamvakóu, 42 km; Paleohóro, 15 km; and Platanáki, 23 km distant, all reachable via detours off the main forest road that begins in Kosmás' *platía* and zigzags along the Párnon crest line.

Traveling from Kosmás to Yeráki, the first town in Lakonía with bus service to Spárti, you need to hitch or walk 16 km down a wretched dirt road which is being improved—stretches of old path still parallel it.

Rating/time course: As noted, the northern trek is meaty, implying familiarity with the vagaries of Greek trails. Long, late-spring/early-summer days are necessary to complete the first leg of the hike in an afternoon. The watershed route from Kosmás to Malevís (or Krónio to Kosmás) should require only an extra day, as one makes good time on the forest road.

Supplies: In Spárti or Leonídhio; Vamvakóu and Kosmás have little to offer in this way.

Map: ESY, Arkadhías.

2   MT. TAÏYETTOS

A wilderness of barren grey spikes shot precipitously from their winding ravines to heights that equalled or overtopped our own; tilted at insane angles, they fell so sheer that it was impossible to see what lay, a world below, at the bottom of our immediate canyon. Except where their cutting edges were blurred by landslides, the mountains looked as harsh as steel. It was a dead, planetary place, a habitat for dragons.

Patrick Leigh Fermor

Despite its savage appearance, the Taïyettos range is possibly the most popular hiking area in Greece, after the Píndhos, western Crete and Mt. Ólymbos. Looking up from the town of Spárti or Byzantine Mistrás, it's hard to resist climbing into the ravines and crags overhead. Once above the Lakonían plain and the foothills you'll find the Taïyettos massif briefly well-watered and forested, but this soon gives way to the arid mineral expanses described by Fermor. The exposed summits of Taïyettos are sedimentary schist rather than limestone; you can see the banding of the tilted beds even when you're a few km away. The gulfs of Messinía and Lakonía, seen from the pyramidal peak of Profítis Ilías, extend in bright ribbons to the west and east respectively. This unusual setting produces striking optical phenomena at sunrise and sunset. In clear weather the sunrise effect is limited to a simple conical shadow projected far out into the Messinian Gulf, but if conditions are correct, you may find yourself the focus of a Brocken bow. In the late afternoon, as the sun lowers into the same gulf, multicolored bands become visible on the water.

The Taïyettos range has figured prominently in Greek religion and folklore over the centuries. Generations of shepherds treated the summits with fearful respect because the *neráïdhes* (forest nymphs) were wont to dance on the heights by moonlight and any luckless mortal who witnessed their revels was hurled to his death. The peaks named Neraïdhovoúna bear witness to this belief. Olympian Apollo was honored on the summit during the Classical era; after the advent of Christianity he became syncretized with Profítis Ilías, and midsummer festivities continue under the new patron.

Getting to the trailhead: The Spárti long-distance bus terminal is located just east of Stadhíou St., two blocks north of the central *platía*. Walk south along Stadhíou to Menaláou St. and the terminal for Paleopanayía, the trailhead village; five to seven departures daily.

Paleopanayía to Profítis Ilías via Ayía Varvára

About 50 m south of the main stop in Paleopanayía there's a large blue placard pointing up a narrow road Erected by EOS Spárti, the sign gives fairly accurate times and distances to various points along the dirt road and trail ahead. However, it's about 10 km along the road to the current trailhead rather than 11, which is the distance to Poliána hamlet proper. There is a slight chance of flagging a truck headed for the villages of Dhipótama or Tóriza—otherwise you've a 2½-hr uphill hike to the first refuge at 9 km. There are some hot, demoralizing switchbacks at the start of the dusty road, and along most of the way the old aqueduct has been replaced by a sealed pipe, so take sufficient water. Pass the turnoff right to Dhipótama at 5 km; at 7 km and the fork left to Tóriza, bear right toward Poliána A dense mixed forest of Cephallonian fir and black pine starts at 8 km (ca. 1000 m).

A German/Greek sign at 9 km announces Nikos' coffeehouse to the right. Food is limited, but you should definitely stop and have a chat and a coffee with Nikos Dousmanis and his wife. Nikos can remember past years when hundreds came July 18 through 20 to climb Profítis Ilías, dance to the strains of the *klaríno* and drink

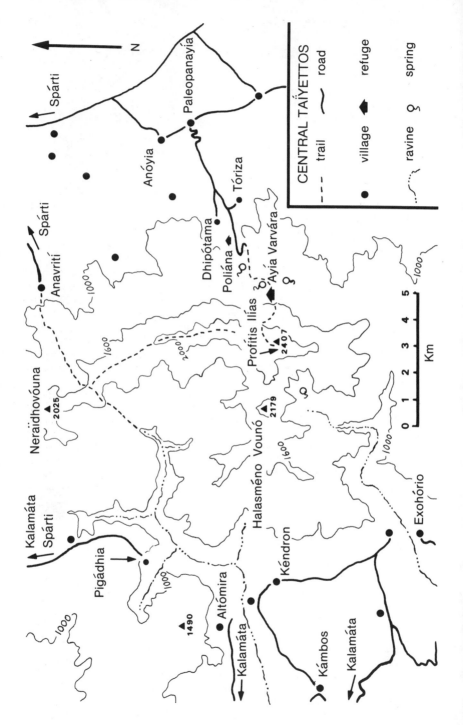

non-stop for the duration of the prophet's feast. Sadly, observance has declined in recent seasons, though Nikos continues to host the *paneyíri* of the Transfiguration in his own yard on August 6. He keeps the mountain house open from May to October, raising rabbits and chickens and allowing hikers to sleep gratis on his front porch.

Beyond Nikos' the road degenerates to a narrow track, which after 10 min reaches a junction with a rusty blue sign (*"Pros katefýgio"*) pointing to the left fork. Five min further, the recent bulldozer track takes a hairpin right, turning away from a capped well and following a tree-arrow. After another 10 min, a defaced sign points to a second hairpin left turn off the track and onto the start of the footpath. Your first water, Piyí Trípolos, lies to the right of the trail at 1390 m, some 80 min above Nikos'. About 30 min higher is the weak (often dry) spring of Ayía Varvára at 1550 m. Two hr above the coffeehouse you'll arrive at the EOS refuge (1690 m), admirably sited on a meadow facing the rising sun.

This hut is likely to be open weekends and holidays from May to October. If you want to hunt down the key, stop at the *kafenéio* on the first floor of the Spárti *dhimarhéio* (town hall); they may refer you to the Kannélo family in Anóyia, the village before Paliopanayía; phone (0731) 26-043. The shelter has a well-equipped kitchen, but with spring water nearby access to the hut is not really essential in good weather; scores of people camp on the front lawn during the July festival.

If both the Ayía Varvára spring and the shelter *stérna* (cistern) run dry (likely in late summer or fall), you'll take a short, pleasant walk to Poulióu tou Vrýssi out of necessity. Descend straight down from the hut along a path that skirts one bracken meadow on its right, and then a second fern dell on its left, passing near a crude *stáni* and corral. At the corral turn right onto a clear path leading to the second meadow's lower right corner. From this spot the trail takes a 45-degree right turn and leads straight south to the spring within 15 min. The fountain waters an attractive hollow with sycamores, a stone-lined irrigation pond, and further down a walnut grove, but it's too damp and steep nearby for camping.

The climb from the hut to Profítis Ilías takes 2 ½ hr on a nominally marked path. However, many of the metal markers have been faded and twisted 90 to 180 degrees by wind and snow, so many unlucky hikers tackle the peak head-on after losing the trail in predawn darkness, only later discovering the entire path—from the top down. The trail surface is decent, but hikers should note that there is *no more* reliable water beyond the hut. The path begins from the left rear corner of the shelter; after 15 min it reaches treeline (1800 m) and bears right (north) across a rocky hillside. Within another 25 min you'll cut through a large, sloping meadow and then abruptly across a tiny gully. A few minutes above the gully, skirt a small bog ringed by ferns; some last straggly pines grow 200 m to the right. For the next 30 min the path picks its way along a hogback heading northwest toward a distinct secondary peak just in front of you. It then worms up a slight crevice before turning abruptly left (south) onto a natural rock ledge on the east face of the ridge leading up to Profítis Ilías. The next 40-min stretch is an easy ascent along this shelf, with the summit cone plainly visible before you. During the last few moments of this leg the path switches back toward the northwest, aiming for a distinct pass at the low point of the saddle between Profítis Ilías and the secondary peak. Just beyond this notch lies a meadow which could serve as a contingency campsite. The final climb to the peak itself, along its northwest slope, takes about 25 min.

On the summit (2407 m) are some sturdy, steel-roofed rock shelters and the chapel of Profítis Ilías, conceivably built from the same stones that once constituted the pagan shrine. The peak marks the border between Lakonía and Messinía provinces. Spárti, the Párnon range and the Évrotas flood plain lie below and to the east; to the west yawn the bare, forbidding Messinian foothills, punctuated by 2179-m Halasméno Vounó (wrecked mountain), joined to Profítis Ilías by a rocky spur.

Beyond Profítis Ilías

Some trekkers may wish to test their mettle and do a complete traverse of the Taïyettos range. An obvious jump-off point would seem to be the head of the canyon enclosed by Profítis Ilías and Halasméno Vounó, but it's not as easy to get down into the gorge as it appears initially. First you must drop for almost 2 hr over loose scree to the vicinity of a small, weak spring, which you should not count on finding—better to bring two to three liters of water per person from Ayía Varvára. Negotiating the floor of the gorge all the way to the village of Exohório requires 9 more hr; the terrain consists mostly of house-size boulders and entire trees strewn matchlike at the bases of great drops, which must be waterfalls in full spate during snowmelt. Only in the last hour or so does a bona fide path begin, leading out of the ravine to Exohório—otherwise there are no signs of human life except for a handful of hunters' or goatherds' shelters wedged under some rock overhangs.

You may correctly gather that, while this downhill traverse is not exceedingly difficult, it *is* dangerous and should not be done alone—a 38-year-old shepherd fell to his death, and was buried, on a slope between Profítis Ilías and the gorge bed in 1982. It is infinitely more prudent to proceed north along the ridge line from Profítis Ilías to a narrow pass before Neraídhovoúna. Turning down and left leads into a gorge similar to the one described above, but far less treacherous, en route to the village of Pigádhia, reached 8 to 9 hr below the pass. Bearing right instead, you should shortly arrive in the high village of Anavrití, with lodging and bus service back to Spárti. If one is leery about the time factor, it is safest to begin in the morning from Anavrití and reach Pigádhia, Altómira or even Kámbos by dark. Patrick Leigh Fermor did this in midsummer and Chapter 2 of his classic *Mani* (see Bibliography) includes an excellent account of the traverse.

Rating/time course: Any excursion on or over Taïyettos requires 36 to 48 hr, which can be allotted in itineraries of varying difficulty, as discussed above.

Supplies: Spárti, near the bus terminals, or Paleopanayía.

Map: ESY, Lakonías; consult the *Korfés* office.

3   ANDHRÍTSENA TO TEMPLE OF VASSÍ

The sanctuary of Apollo Epikóurios at Vassí was probably designed by Iktinos, the same architect who planned the Parthenon, and is one of the most important, and most dramatically situated, surviving classical temples. Its long, unbroken colonnades were erected in the fifth century B.C. by the nearby Figálians to celebrate their deliverance from the plague. Because of its extreme isolation, the sacred precincts have not fallen victim to vandalism or the commercialization typical at other Greek archaeological sites. Admission is free; one caretaker and one post-card vendor make up the entire staff. The shrine itself, now protected by scaffolding until funds for reinforcing and a Mylar roof(!) become available, is built on a north-south axis atop the highest (1200-m) hill in the area. This summit overlooks the valley of the Nédhas River to the south and Mt. Líkaeo (1428 m) to the east; in clear weather the Ionian Sea, 40 km west, is almost visible. Sunrises and sunsets here are impressive and uncrowded—you can be on hand to enjoy both by camping a short distance below the site.

The hike up from, or down to, the village of Andhrítsena is almost as good as the ruin itself. Part of the way is on dirt roads but most of it is by path through forested, rolling hills with ample water and campsites.

Getting to the trailhead: Andhrítsena can be reached either from Pýrgos on the west Peloponnesian coast or from Megalópoli, a town between Trípoli and Kalamáta in the central Peloppónisos. Only one bus daily from either point, in the early afternoon. Andhrítsena is a representative Peloponnesian highland village, dilapidatedly authentic without (yet) being deemed touristically quaint. There are three hotels, ranging from luxury to rustic, several *tavérnes* and a handful of stores. A 14-km road runs direct to Vassí, which is a place name, not a village. Taxis in the Andhrítsena town plaza take a minimum group of three up the hill for about $2 per person. Most choose to ride up and then walk down from the temple; but if you hike up you can simply continue on to the Nédhas River (see Hike 4).

Route directions (temple-Andhrítsena): From the temple grounds, the trail begins descending left (south) from the caretaker's building. Ask him to point the way for you if necessary. After 10 min, you pass a fountain in the wall of a pasture, 500 m below the site. A further 20 min along, a second spring crosses the path as it traverses an oak-shaded hillside; by this point the route has curled around 180 degrees to march north. You can camp nearby on a flagstone-and-grass terrace surrounded by trees. Some 15 min beyond the terrace, ford a large stream and pass some more small campsites under sycamores. In the next 30 min the trail winds past several tiny seeps in the rock strata and one permanent stream before reaching a major creek valley and the last campsites along the way.

The footpath ends 10 min later at a jeep road; one farmhouse and one tin-roofed shed to the west mark the area of the junction. Unfortunately, there's no red dot where it's needed most. Within a few moments the jeep track intersects a larger dirt road; turn right (north), away from the house and shed, to carry on to Andhrítsena. There's another lonely farm, and water, at a bend in the road 20 min further. Shortly past this last farmhouse, the main dirt road intersects the taxi road (here asphalted) going up to Vassí. At the junction a sign ("*Linístena, 7.5*") points up the dirt road you've just quit. Turn down the paved road toward Andhrítsena, and almost immediately cut down and right onto a path passing a stone church; the turnoff is marked by an inconspicuous dot on a roadside rock. Bear right around a cluster of houses and follow the path to its end just past the last house on a grooved-cement street; turn left onto this and descend to its end near the Andhrítsena KTEL office.

For a reverse itinerary starting from the office, take an uphill left onto this street, turn right onto the path after 300 m and invert all subsequent directions.

Rating/time course: The hike, with its moderate grade and usually good trail surface, is an easy 2 ½ hr downhill or just over 3 hr ascending.

Supplies: Andhrítsena.

4 VASSÍ TO THE NÉDHAS RIVER VIA FIGÁLIA

We were down in the gorge of the Neda almost quicker than I wanted.
It was a strange, haunted place . . . . We splashed about, we ate fruit,
we attempted in vain to plumb the Stomio, we explored the chapels and
the waterfalls and the pools, we gazed up at the huge limestone cliffs. I
thought it was the most beautiful place I had ever been in.

——Peter Levi

Visitors to Vassí may wish to budget extra time to visit the idyllic spot described above. A wretched auto road descends a bumpy 6 km from the temple to the village of Dhragoyí (short for Idhragoyío, after the numerous springs that well up in the area). When Professor Levi passed through 20-plus years ago, there was still a faint, disused path between Vassí and Dhragoyí; with luck and the aid of the caretaker, you may find it and save some time over a road walk. Then again you may not, and would be better off accepting a lift or taxi ride the full 11 km to Perivólia village. Here you turn left at a gushing fountain, following signs pointing to Figália. It's 2 km on an increasingly narrow track to a point, just before Figália village, where there are some park-type benches, an *ikonostási* and a sign (*"Perivólia 2"*) pointing back the way you've come. Bear right past the benches rather than entering Figália, which has few facilities, and after 200 m turn right onto a path whose beginning is charmingly strewn with marble artifacts of ancient Figália. Shrubbery to one side almost completely obscures a sign with the legend *"Platánia, 5"* (km). Take the first two possible right forks. Between this pair of ambiguities the Cyclopean walls of ancient Figália almost block the trail, and the proper bearing stays quite close to and just under them. Figália was quite an important town in classical times, but aside from the boundary walls—termed Cyclopean after the only beings who presumably could have maneuvered the giant stones into place—and various marble fragments and statuary unearthed over the years, little remains.

About 25 min out from the *"Platánia, 5"* sign, the trail comes to a stone *ikonostási* (wayside shrine) on a knoll. Step behind it and bear left down a slope and across a dry stream bed; once on the other side the path, partly cobbled and well-shaded now, begins plunging steeply into the Nédhas gorge and the river gradually becomes audible. Twenty min below the *ikónisma* you arrive at a corral just above the river. An inconspicuous trail veers back right (west) at an acute angle; the main path continues another 30 min to Platánia village (rudimentary amenities), where you can catch transport south toward Kiparissía. The little side trail is badly overgrown but well-grooved into a rock ledge overlooking the swirling waters of the Nédhas. Just under an hour below Figália you arrive at the waterfalls and pools at the confluence of two rivers. A few tiny, damp chapels cling to the cliffs beyond the main swimming hole, but they're hardly worth the climb. You can inch out along the outflow of the side stream and peer around a rocky corner at the famous *stómio* (abyss) of the Nédhas, where thousands of gallons of water disappear hourly into a distinctly vaginal tunnel, not to reappear above ground for 10 km.

The site has been holy since before recorded history; it was variously regarded as an entrance to Hades, an oracle of the dead and an appropriate spot for worship of various riparian goddesses. A trace of this ancient worship persists today, in that the *stómio* is considered consecrated to the *Panayía*. On August 15, the modern Platanians and Figalians cast stones into the watery tunnel in lieu of the former vegetable and animal offerings. Currently the vicinity of the swimming hole is still in a pristine state, and villagers are happy to show visitors the way down. Crowds of foreigners strewing garbage or behaving in a manner inimical to the values of the locals could change the present ease of access. Camping at the junction of the rivers is not advised—there's really not enough level space for more than one person anyhow.

5   MT. HELMÓS (AROÁNIA)

The linchpin of the north Peloponnesian barrier mountains is actually a complete minisierra situated exactly halfway across the peninsula. The eastern summits (Krávari, Aetoráhi, Psilí Korfí) and the western ridge (the longer but generally lower Neraïdhórahi) are connected by an intermediate zone called Apáno Lithária. This great U-shaped ensemble encloses a deep, north-flowing canyon rivaling those exiting from Parnassós, Ólymbos and Gkióna and supposed in ancient times to contain the source of the mythical river Styx. It is this defile, plus the wild forests on the north flanks of the Stygian canyon, that distinguishes Helmós from neighboring mountains. In addition to trees—junipers, pines, firs and deciduous species are all jumbled together—Helmós offers seasonal explosions of flowers and reportedly butterflies to aficionados.

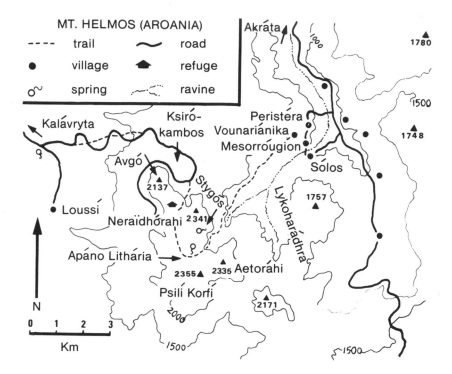

All of the northern Peloponnesian ranges trap moist air from the nearby Gulf of Kórinthos. Hence Helmós is apt to be misty and damp even in summer, and wind soughing in trees and crags creates the illusion of running water where there is none. Most available water is in fact at the bottom of the legendary valley, eventually attaining enough volume to sustain a handful of villages at the margins of the great northern forests. These settlements, plunged in a wilderness even more complete in some ways than the mountain, seem to elude descending hikers like the punishment of Tantalus as they march hour upon hour down the lonely landscapes of the Styx valley. Arrival is sudden, and a lingering isolation is emphasized by the frequent lack of customary signs at the outskirts of each community announcing its identity. The Helmós villages are among the highest in Greece (ca. 1100 m) and the resultant winter cold and snow (1 m) drives the inhabitants down to balmier quarters at Akráta, on the coast.

For such a remote peak, Helmós has been the target of more than its share of development activities. One of the highest forest roads in Greece (ca. 2000 m) passes around Avgó (the westernmost peak) and below the alpine shelter, with a spur up to Loútsa, where a ski lift is planned. In addition there's a direct road from Ksirókambos to Peristéra (one of the northern hamlets), and a waterworks utility track nibbles at the edge of the Styx valley. Probably only its sheer declivities save the inner canyon itself from similar desecration. All this should not deter the tramper, since most of the roads are not in areas of surpassing scenic interest and Helmós' foot routes for the most part run parallel to and out of sight of the automobile age.

Getting to the trailhead: Getting to Helmós is certainly half the fun. Take a train (six daily) from Pátras or Athens that stops in Dhiakoptó, and from there catch one of five daily departures on the famous rack-and-pinion railway up the Vouraïkós river gorge to Kalávryta. This amazing feat of engineering, which climbs over 700 m in 22 km, was designed by an Italian firm in the 1890s. Although the original rolling steam stock is long gone, the ride—with its tunnels, rickety trestles, roaring cataracts and narrow ledges—is not to be missed. The third rail is noisily engaged at the start of each particularly tough grade; passengers bounce from one side of the carriage to another for the views and risk decapitation by sticking their heads out the smudgy windows. Kalávryta has a handful of *pandhohéia* and hotels but they're on the expensive side. You can chat with the local EOS rep at Zaharoplastéio Eremìdhis on 25 Martiou St.; alternatively contact Andhréas Souroúhis, a local alpine guide, by phoning (0692) 22-496 or 22-346. A bus runs daily (not Sun) to the village of Loussí; however, it will only set you down at the turnoff for Ksirókambos, 6 km below it, and will deliver you there too late in the day to make much progress up the mountain except in June or July. You may prefer to ante up for a taxi all the way to Ksirókambos—it's an hr-plus drive. (Purists will note that a trail becomes evident a few km below Ksirókambos meadow; it crosses the road at least twice, well-marked with signs and red blazes. If your transport drops you at the first *pinakidha* [placard], count on an extra 1 ½ hr from there to Ksirókambos.)

Ksirókambos to Peristéra via Apáno Lithária and the Stygós (Styx)

Once up on Ksirókambos, a wide basin covered with scrubby grass, leave the road, crossing it as soon as the track begins veering right toward Avgó peak. Ten min up the base of Neraïdhórahi, just below the last trees and to the left (east) of a gully, find a white and faded-pink sign: *"Pros katafýgio."* The trail should by now be distinguishable on the bare slope. After a 30-min climb you'll reach a second, smaller *kámbos* (clearing), Lóutsa, the planned ski lift site. Ascending past marker poles you should, a bit over 1 hr above Ksirókambos, reach the diminutive Helmós shelter (2100 m, capacity 12 persons), named after the tiny Pouliou tou Výssi (bird spring) a few hundred meters below near the circum-Avgó road. This water source is not reliable in late summer. The hut is a good spot to rest and take in the views over Kalávryta to the west-northwest and Mt. Erýmanthos across the valley to the southwest. Neraïdhórahi looms just overhead to the east—a sign bolted to the refuge window bars gives a reasonably accurate arrival time of 1 hr. Both the Ýdata Stygós (Styx source) and Aetoráhi are correctly adjudged to be 2 hr distant.

To reach Neraïdhórahi and Apáno Lithária, go directly up the hogback behind the shelter; there is no formal trail. Once on the ridge, you can easily pick out Psilí Korfí (2355 m, Helmós's true summit) to the southeast, the Helmós villages huddled in forest to the northeast, the Gulf of Kórinthos to the north-northwest, and Mt. Zíria (Kyllíni) due east. Neraïdhórahi's peak proper (2341 m at the altimeter) is a 15 min stroll north; however, it's a sheer, impassable drop to the Styx directly below 2341, so you must retrace your steps to the lowest point of the western ridge. From there a path leads toward a *stáni* and rock corral wedged in the lee of some giant outcroppings, presumably the Apáno Lithária (upper boulders) themselves. Psilí Korfí is approximately 30 min beyond the *stáni*, but as in the case of Neraïdhórahi, you must return to Apáno Lithária to begin your descent into the Styx valley.

To find the trail down, put your back to the outcrops and point slightly left of dead ahead. You should pass, within 150 m, a reliable pool spring in a patch of green turf; just below this gushes a fountain with a properly fitted spout. Cross to the right (east) bank of the watercourse which can truly be said to be the very head of the Styx canyon. The faint trail next plunges down a rock spine, swerves right past a dripping rock face and crosses a mud bed (possibly a pond in spring). It then slips over the saddle beyond the mudhole and continues down the canyon on its east side for only a few more moments before crossing to the left side of the watercourse just over 30 min from the *stáni*. (Further progress along the east bank is hindered by a nasty drop just beyond a small stone pen). The only possible access to points downstream continues faintly on the west flank of the now-several-hundred-m-wide ravine; turning a corner, the path brings you face-to-face with the 200-m, orange-stained, plant-flecked cliffs of the Styx waterfall. The still-faint trail now switchbacks down the slope southeast of the cataract, reaching the base of the Mavronéri (black waters), as the Styx source is also known, 1 hr from Apáno Lithária. The falls dwindle to a shower in late summer but still administer a mandatory, immortality-conferring (says the myth) ablution to those entering the cave at the base of the cliff. Inside there is year-round water (which you must lap from the rock) and an astonishing amount of greenery and flowers. Do not be lulled, though, by the other-worldly grandeur into forgetting that the falls are quite far up the side of Neraïdhórahi, and half the trek—albeit downhill—lies before you.

Below the cave, and actually a bit above it, the path vanishes under a mess of scree. You slither and slide down this for about 25 min to the canyon bottom, resisting any temptation to cross to the far side. A discernible trail resumes at about the point where the scree-covered hillside dips level to the stream on your right. Ahead on the left lies another forbiddingly eroded slope, but the traverse of this is actually easier than the foregoing, since the surface is more powdery and there's little elevation change. Just under 45 min below the Ýdata Stygós you'll be relieved to see a painted arrow on the first stump at treeline; there's another soon after, and the trail rapidly cleans itself up. Within a few moments more you reach the Dhiásello tou Kinigóu (hunter's pass) from where you can gaze north toward the villages and back at the Stygian cliffs (which from this angle appear stained quite black as well as orange), as well as at the involved banding of the cliffs on the opposite side of the much-widened and deepened valley. From here on, yellow-and-black markers (courtesy of the Égion EOS) are common. In the 50 min below the Dhiásello, there are no complications except several washouts of the path. Then there's a saddle meadow; 15 min beyond you cross a dry gulch and, shortly after, the first permanent stream since the Mavronéri. Here the path regains some altitude, affording your downhill muscles a rest, and good perspectives back on Neraïdhórahi and the new Lykoharádhra (wolf valley) appearing to the east. Two hr below the Styx, oaks begin, and then the path falls victim to an unsightly new bulldozer track constructed to service a water main being brought down from somewhere below the Mavronéri. The trail reappears briefly 20 min later, by a goat pen, and then succumbs for good. Near the highest house of Áno Mesorroúgion (Vounariánika), yet another EOS tree marker reads *"Pros Ýdata Stygó."* Finally, 3¼ hr below the cave, you come to the *platía* of Peristéra, passing one last Ýdata Stygós marker. Thus the total descent from Apáno Lithária is just over 4 hr.

Peristéra is a friendly village with one combo cafo/grill and one comfortable inn, both on the square. Beds are at a premium in summer though; If you have no luck here, you'll have to walk 20 min down-road to Káto Mesourroúgion, where there's another lodging (over a *tavérna*). If this is full, you have one last chance in Sólos, 20 min more by path across the Lykoharádhra stream; walk a few road-paces south of Mosorroúgion, then bear down toward the river just past the town-limit sign. Sólos is graced by no less than two inns (and eateries) as well as the church of Áyios Yiórgos, which sports an inscribed "1806" over the door. Such quasi-Norman rectangular churches are peculiar to the northwestern Moréa. They often, as here, sport a Latin belfry, single-gabled roof and a side door rather than the customary Greek front entrance; only a slightly protruding apse (semicircular recess behind the altar) betrays the Orthodox creed of the faithful. These shrines are probably the only tangible heritage of the Frankish occupation of Aháïa and Ílis during the 1200s.

As of 1984, buses come up from Akráta to the Helmós villages only on Tue, Thur and Sat mornings, returning to the coast immediately. The villages are connected with the main highway by a dirt loop road; if pressed for time, you could always try your luck hitching the 40 km to Akráta. Most will find it no inconvenience to spend a day after their traverse recuperating *in situ* or perhaps taking strolls to the two hamlets not stayed in. The countryside is idyllic, and according to the season you may be plied with apples, walnuts, *óuzo* or tidbits from the grill.

REVERSE ITINERARY

The rail stop for Akráta is called Kráthio—only local trains stop there. The bus to the high villages leaves Akráta early in the morning of the days listed, so you must stay the night. Shopping for supplies the evening before departure is chancy because of traditional business hours. After an assumed 10 A.M. arrival in Peristéra, you will (according to the EOS marker above and behind the *platía* fountain, and my experience) face a 4-hr uphill hike to the Styx, plus another 1½ hr to Apáno Lithária. You might entertain the possibility of picking up the shelter keys at EOS Égion, returning them in Kalávryta. If you elect not to use the shelter, you must collect all water necessary for the night at Apáno Lithária and best plan to camp at Loútsa or Ksirókambos. There is no further dependable water until some distance below the *kámbos*, at the junction of the side road and the main Kalávryta-Loussí route. After descending Neraïdhórahi and crossing Ksirókambos en route to Kalávryta, you may pick up the "real" trail at the lowest, western end of the high plateau, where the path crosses the road obviously just below treeline. You can descend along this trail as long as it lasts before being swallowed by the auto route; there may in fact be no choice as there's little traffic from the mountain down to Kalávryta. The trek from Ksirókambos to Kalávryta should take about 4 hr.

Rating/time course: Done *from* Kalávryta to Peristéra, this is a lengthy though not overly arduous all-day excursion, provided you get an early morning vehicle assist the first few km of forest road above Kalávryta. A reverse itinerary of two days involves the bus schedule into the high villages, the tough ascent beyond the Mavronéri, and the probable absence of any transport from Ksirókambos to Kalávryta.

Supplies: In Kalávryta or Akráta; Helmós villages have little.

Map: ESY, Ahaïas; consult the *Korfés* office.

6   MT. ERÝMANTHOS

This massif dominates the view from the hostel of Helmós and is the westernmost of the mountains that extend from Kórinthos to Pátras. While the average height of the various peaks in this chain does not exceed 2100 m, it is a respectable, underrated range, relatively unmarred by roads or other inappropriate development.

There are five distinguishable summits and four recognized trailhead villages, the latter grouped in two pairs widely separated from each other. However, the villages of each doublet appear close enough together to be end points of two healthy, point-to-point all-day traverses.

At the east end of this east-west chain lie the peaks of Kallifóni and Tris Yinaíkes (ca. 2000 m). You can take a bus from Kalávryta at 6:30 A.M. and 2 P.M. daily (not Sun) to the hamlet of Kértezi, from where it's a 3-hr, 1000-m climb to the saddle joining Tris Yenaíkes and Kallifóni. First you negotiate the length of a long defile, passing one spring en route, and after 2-plus hr you arrive at a saddle somewhat to the south of the peaks, which are another 45 min or so distant. From the peaks you can descend in about 2 hr to the village of Káto Vlassía on the Kalávryta-Pátras bus line. If you reverse this itinerary count on a 3-hr ascent from Vlassía.

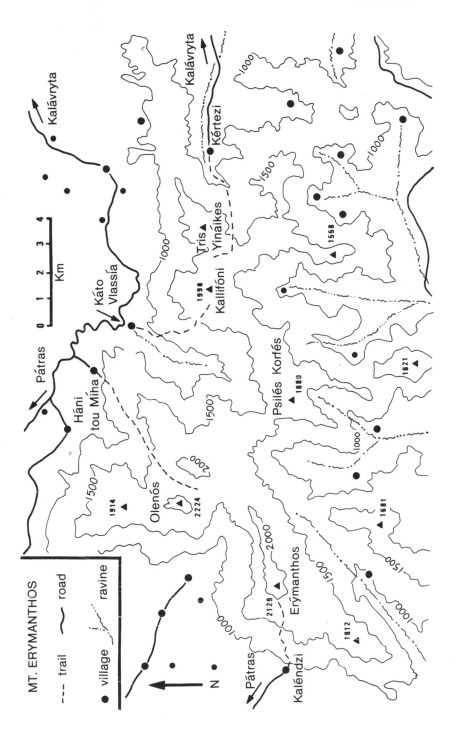

Míhas (Háni tou Míha), a few km west of Káto Vlassía on the Kalávryta-Pátras road, is the takeoff point to the higher, western group of summits. A 5-hr tramp should bring you to Olenós, at 2224 m the highest peak in the range. Continue along this crest to Erýmanthos peak (2129 m). This summit can also be reached from the village of Kaléndzi (bus from Pátras, inns) at 900 m. A good trail partly compensates for the stiff climb (note the 1200-m altitude difference over a small horizontal run). Should you wish to link up the two western ascents, you can anticipate a fairly gruelling all-day traverse between Míhas and Kaléndzi.

A look at the map prompts speculation that a hiker could trek from Kértezi to Kaléndzi via the Psilés Korfés ridge; however, in the absence of hard facts about the availability of water and actual time involved, this route cannot be advised without reservation.

Supplies: In Kalávryta, Pátras or Kaléndzi.

Map: ESY, Ahaḯas or Ilías.

THE STEREÁ

For the next two hours I walked along a path that kept its altitude along the mountain's northern flank a few hundred feet below the ridge, breathing again the crystalline air that poured out of the fir forests over the high fields of limestone.

——Kevin Andrews

"Stereá" is today a quaintly outdated label—literally it means "the mainland" and was more appropriate when most of Greece was insular or Peloponnesian and the territory from Athens to the Amvrakikós Gulf was the full extent of her continental holdings. Of late some have proposed "Róumeli" as a substitute, but this Ottoman Turkish term, signifying "populated with the Rūm (Greek Orthodox)" is even less specific, so Stereá will probably retain its place of honor among such venerable geographical catchalls as Appalachia and the Midlands.

With the exception of Mt. Oíti and the Karpeníssi area, most of the terrain is rocky and dramatic. As you proceed west from the Attic peninsula, communications and settlements grow progressively poorer, so that by the time the vast Vardhoússia and Ágrafa regions are reached many of the villages seem truly forsaken by both God and man. The inhabitants of Kravára, a bleak zone west of the Várdhoussia and south of the Ágrafa ranges, were long famous as caste beggars and itinerant snake-oil peddlers, such was the poverty of their land. Today most Stereans earn a better living, whether from olives, bauxite, sheep, tobacco, grain or lumber, but they are as a rule reserved with outsiders, seeing few of them except in the "little Switzerland" of the Karpenissiótis valley and the major tourist centers near Mt. Parnassós. It would still be safe to say that no actual harm will befall the wayfarer, but in the author's experience the villagers do not always keep the *ksénos'* comfort in mind, as is the case in the rest of Greece, nor are hiking directions received always reliable.

7 MT. PÁRNITHA (PÁRNES)

Among the pines and firs
They told me I'd be cured;
That's why I went to Parnitha,
To heal my pain.

Forever on Mt. Parnitha,
Upon the highest peak.

———Rembetic song from the 1940s

The low but heavily wooded range just to the north of Athens was the hunting forest, military training ground and partial protective barrier for the ancient city; today, with the modern city of three million plus beginning to scale its outriders, it has become Athens' lungs and closest "out" from urban life. Even before smog there was a tuberculosis sanitorium on Mt. Párnitha (which the song alludes to), and recently most of the summit area was declared a national park. Weekend rock climbers besiege the sheerer faces of the peak, but nontechnical hikers will be pleased to learn that Párnitha is endowed with a network of well-maintained trails giving access to an area far wilder and greener than its slight distance from the capital would suggest.

Getting to the trailheads: Line 724 buses depart almost hourly from the corner of Stournári and Aharnón Sts, in Athens, bound for the remote suburb of Thrakomakedhónes. Line 714 departs from the same terminal for the chapel and casino of Ayía Triádha, on the mountain, stopping at Metóhi en route. To approach Mt. Párnitha from the north, take any train (more than 20 daily) to the Sfendháli (Malakássa) station, some four stops out of Athens.

Thrakomakedhónes to Báfi or Flambóuri Hostels

From the last stop of bus 724, walk uphill about 10 min to a stone wall guarding a hairpin right turn. Using a gap at the lower end of the wall, plunge down briefly to the bottom of the Hoúni gully, which exits Párnitha here. The path is clearly visible on the far side of the ravine and is marked along its entire length by a motley array of red or white blazes and paint-can lids. Barely 30 min up the Hoúni canyon the famous fir forest begins, and shortly after you pass a right fork leading to the Kyrá and Katára springs, as well as Flambóuri ridge (1158 m) and its hostel. Continue straight to reach the Báfi hostel (1160 m) some 3 hr out of Thrakomakedhónes.

To pleasantly vary a day-return to Thrakomakedhónes, retrace your steps from Báfi to the above-mentioned fork, cross Hoúni to Flambóuri and from there descend in less than 2 hr to Thrakomakedhónes, ending up only a few hundred meters east-northeast of your original trailhead.

Báfi to Skípiza to Móla

Descend toward Ayía Triádha along the forest road serving the hostel; after a few hundred meters bear right onto a side road, then right again onto the trail which leads within 1 hr to the Skípiza spring, almost in the center of Párnitha. From here a trail leads south in 1 hr to the Ayía Triádha chapel and Paleohóri spring, on the loop road; another leads west within a few min to the Platána spring, at the western extension of the loop road; and most importantly, a third, northeasterly trail skirts the very base of Karambóla summit (1413 m) on its way to the popular recreation area on Móla plateau, which straddles the loop road, and the *ksoklísi* ot Áyios Pétros.

Sfendháli (Malakássa) to Móla

The long (4 ½ hr) but more gradual ascent of Párnitha from the rail line transects the entire rich plant community of the mountain, from the low-altitude *Arbutus* and

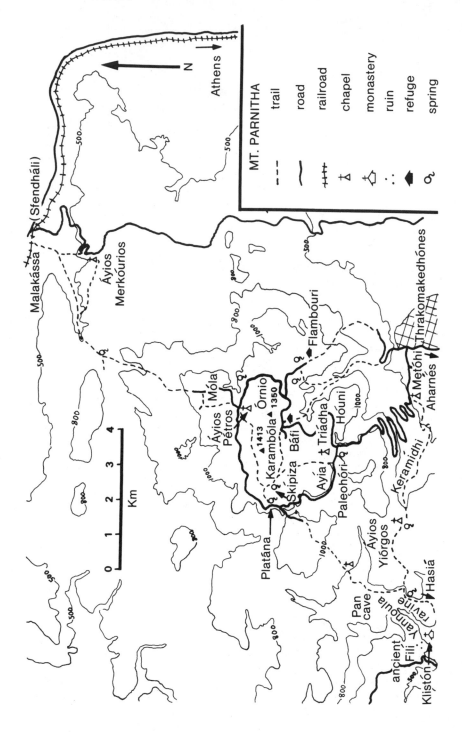

MT. PARNITHA

trail

road

railroad

chapel

monastery

ruin

refuge

spring

Malakássa

(Sfendháli)

Áyios
Merkoúrios

Athens

N

Flambouri

Móla

Áyios
Pétros

Órnio
1350

Karambóla 1413

Skipiza

Báfi

Ayía Triádha

Hóuni

Paleohóri

Metóhi

Thrakomakedhónes

Aharnés

Keramídhi

Platána

Áyios
Yiórgos

Pan
cave

Yambóula
ravine

ancient
Fíli

Hasiá

Klistón

Km

0   1   2   3   4

Aleppo pines to the majestic *Abies cephallonica* of the higher slopes. The trail, on a steady southwest bearing, first closely follows a stream valley, giving the chapel of Áyios Merkoúrios on the left a wide berth (you can detour to visit it), and later climbs almost due south up to Móla. The monstrous telephone tower on Órnio peak (1350 m) is a good landmark for orienting.

Metóhi to Áyios Yiórgos to Klistón to Ancient Filí

Between the base of the Párnitha casino funicular and the start of the hairpin curves leading up to Ayía Triádha, two chapels at Metóhi mark the beginning of a fine, 2-hr trail which follows the Keramídhi gully up to the spring and *ksoklísi* of Áyios Yiórgos. The trail is marked; avoid a nearby forest road. From Áyios Yiórgos head west on more trails to the vicinity of the Tamílthi spring, overlooking the Yannoúla ravine, and then either bear right to visit a cave sacred to Pan in ancient times or left toward the monastery of Klistón, ancient Filí and the village of Hasiá (modern Filí).

The 14th-century monastery of Klistón (Our Lady of the Closed-In Places) dominates the Yannoúla gorge and is arguably the most beautiful in Attikí. Clamber 20 to 30 min up the hill to the northwest to visit the well-preserved remains of the fourth-century-B.C. fortress of Filí, built to defend the narrowest spot on the ancient Thíva-Athens road. From Hasiá, a 30 to 40 min walk down-track from Klistón, there are regular buses down to the Stournári-Aharnón terminal.

Time courses: All the outings described are designed to be completed in one (full) day. Staying at the Báfi hostel may greatly extend your range.

Map: *Korfés*, issue 54.

8 MT. PARNASSÓS

With any number of Parnassus or Montparnasse streets, districts, bars and parks as namesakes throughout the world, Parnassós is perhaps the most famous peak in Greece after Mt. Ólymbos. Since earliest history the mountain itself was sacred to Diónysos, as well as Pan; later the peak, and the Delphic oracle at its base, also became associated with Apollo and the Muses.

Geologically, Parnassós is a jagged and complex limestone massif a few km north of the Gulf of Kórinthos. Its contours resemble a great bird with outstretched wings and upward-pointing neck; hikers "wing walk" to visit the peak on the "neck." The south abutment drops sharply into the gorge of Pléistos—about three-fourths of the way down lies the Dhelfí archaeological zone. The north flank, indented by the Velítsa canyon, descends more gradually toward the Kifissós and Sperhiós river valleys. Most sources counsel an ascent from the south or west flanks of Parnassós, and by implication a retracing of steps for the descent. Those who follow this advice are bound to be disappointed, since the mountain shows its full majestic character only from the northeast face; thus you are wise to include the length of the Velítsa ravine as one leg of your journey.

Though not the highest peak in the Stereá—Gkióna, some 60 m loftier, cops that honor—Parnassós, at 2457 m, is uniquely situated to provide a giant-relief-map perspective of Greece from its summit. However, this 360-degree panorama is dependable only in summer, and occasionally not even then. Weather near the peak is consistently wet or blustery from the end of September to the start of June.

Getting to the trailhead: For the south side of Parnassós, take a bus from Athens direct to Aráhova, or from Pátras in stages, with potential changes at Río/Andírio, Návpaktos, Itéa and Hrissó (below Dhelfí). Train users should alight at Livádhia and continue by KTEL to Aráhova, which is infinitely preferable as a mountaineer's base to the tourist circus at Dhelfí 11 km west. The village is famous for its yogurt, grilled meats and handcrafts (nowadays mostly imported from northern Greece and Albania). Groceries are plentiful, and two modest hotels at the east end of town are more than adequate. Despite being washed by the fringes of the tide of visitors to Dhelfí, the Arahovans are friendly (in the reserved Viotian manner) and Aráhova itself remarkably unspoiled away from the main highway; a day spent exploring the steep, narrow alleys between the 19th-century dwellings, before or after mountain-climbing, will not be misspent.

The designated Parnassós guide, Níkos Yiorgákos, lives in Aráhova, phone (0267) 31-391, but his large-capacity van may interest you more than his expertise. The fee for a shuttle to the Yerondóvrahos trailhead above Aráhova is about $15. For solo climbers and others who may not wish to tender this sum, the only alternative is hitchhiking up the mountain road which begins at the large blue ski center sign just west of Aráhova. Traffic is sparse and you can anticipate a long wait. The tiny hamlet of Kalívia, 7 km up, huddles at the northeast edge of the vast, bleak Livádhi plateau, used for growing livestock fodder. From Kalívia (one newish hotel) an extremely faint trail purportedly threads its way through vast stands of fir to the "official" trailhead, but I've never found it and the intrepid are advised to check carefully with the Kalivians before setting out. Most riders will be set down 4 km beyond Kalívia, at a right fork marked by another Athens Ski Club placard. From here it's a rather demoralizing 14-km, uphill, asphalt-road walk to Yerondóvrahos. Halfway, take another right fork, following a third ski club sign. The small EOS shelter at Sarandári, just at treeline, heralds imminent arrival at the three-building ski complex on the west foot of Yerondóvrahos peak.

Access to the northeast of Parnassós is via Tithoréa, reached by train four times daily from Athens or northern Greece (caution—some eight trains pass the rail terminal at Kato Tithoréa, but only the four locals stop). Ano Tithoréa is a pleasant Viotian hill town 4 km above the train station; a $2 taxi fare is well-spent. The village's medieval name of Velítsa is often heard, though supposedly consigned to oblivion by the government Hellenization campaign of the 1930s; it is still the name of choice for the giant ravine just to the east. Ancient Tithoréa was in fact important enough to merit a mention in Pausanias, and you can still see stretches of vine-cloaked classical-era wall below the platía. A handful of stores and tavérnes provide for the hiker, but there is presently only one lodging, in the pleasant ground-floor apartment of Ioánnis Mintzas 300 m west of the plaza. Capacity is six persons, best booked for two days at $4 per person; beds are not available during the school year, when the teacher rents the entire flat.

Yerondóvrahos to Liákoura Summit

Begin between the fourth and fifth pylons of the ski lift. The trail, marked by a red schematic peak-and-arrow painted on a rock, heads left (northwest) past a stunted tree and continues toward a second small tree on a ridge 400 m distant. Just past the latter tree, the path veers right and sharply up toward a large cairn liberally splashed with red paint. Beyond this landmark the way continues through a gulch between two ridgelets. As you climb out of this trough, note a cairn on the left and another red dot to the right; Yerondóvrahos looms above. The greater part of the ski resort, forlorn and unsightly in summer, sprawls to your left; keep well clear of the twin lift areas for now. After a brief level interval the trail descends to the first of four pastoral colonies, a collection of stone huts and a corral, and shortly after disappears under the ski-run surface. When this happens, march straight up a bulldozer track to the top of the graded ridge in front of you, until reaching a distinctive right-angle junction. Do not continue toward Yerondóvrahos, but bear left onto the wide livestock track that heads toward the last pylon of one of the ski lifts. Soon the path acquires a neat stone edging

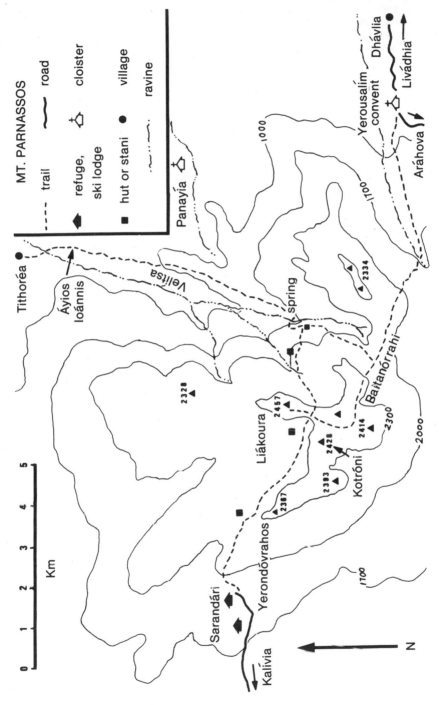

MT. PARNASSOS

- - - trail
———— road
🔺 refuge, ski lodge
⌂ cloister
■ hut or stani
● village
·-·-· ravine

and occasional red dots on its clear way to a second shelter some 2½ hr above the ski center. This conveniently located stone hut sleeps three on a raised platform and normally stands with its loose beam-and-sheet steel roof stacked to one side. Be sure to redismantle it after use so that the weight of winter snow doesn't damage it.

From this shelter the path climbs abruptly via a rock stairway splattered with red arrows, coming out on a low spur of Yerondóvrahos. You can leave the main trail here for the easy, 30-min climb up to this secondary summit (2367 m). Returning to the main route, follow it down toward two consecutive meadows, skirting the first and cutting through the second. Just the other side of the far meadow, an enormous, vertical rock pinnacle provides support for a cluster of crude shelters. The route bends left, paralleling the ridge line above, drops into yet a third pasture, and climbs out of it at the far end.

From this small saddle you face Liákoura peak directly to the northeast. At its base, at the edge of the highest *stáni* on Parnassós, a final shepherd's cottage with a mortared roof seems more often used than previous ones, but in all likelihood any tenants will share the shelter for the night.

Beyond the hut a jeep road runs along the base of Liákoura; cross the track, keeping a lookout for faint red dots on the rocks opposite, and aim for the low point in the ridge running down from the summit. Here the trail divides; the right-hand, downhill choice is discussed in the next section. The Liákoura altimeter is a 20-min scramble up and left, bringing the total hiking time from the Yerondóvrahos ski center to nearly 5 hr.

A compass is handy to identify features of the "living map" that surrounds you upon reaching the benchmark. All of the landmarks listed below will, of course, be visible only in optimal conditions.

NW to NE: Timvristós (Veloúhi) peak is a bald, almost cylindrical knob; Mounts Ólymbos, Kissávos and Pílion merge to the northeast.

NE to SE: The Pagassitic Gulf shines in front of Mt. Pílion; the Maliakós Gulf (left) and that of Évvia (right) merge and are the closest bodies of water; beyond long, skinny Évvia Island float the Sporádhes Islands; Mt. Párnitha hides Athens to the southeast.

SE to SW: The Gulf of Kórinthos basks in the foreground of the northern Peloponnesian ranges Zíria, Helmós and Panahaïkó (east to west).

SW to NW: Returning to the mainland, the prospect west is truncated by the peaks of Vardhoússia and Gkióna, both actually higher than Liákoura.

Tithoréa to Liákoura

Leave town from the *platía*, heading southwest on various narrow driveways. The foot trail proper begins by the waterfall (really a leak in an aqueduct) and some park benches overlooking the Velítsa ravine which borders Tithoréa to the southeast. A partly covered cement *idhragoyeío* (aqueduct) crosses the trail a few min past the waterfall, and 100 m beyond the water channel you bear left into the canyon, following some orange dots on trailside rocks. Do not proceed further up the wider, apparently main path—despite anything else you may hear in the village, the following route is the *only* way up to Liákoura.

Here in its lower reaches the Velítsa ravine, cited in some sources as the Kakórevma, is interesting but not breath-taking. After a 10- to 15-min descent to its usually dry bed, change sides where the aqueduct (also usually dry) spans it. Natural rock steps worm up the opposite bank, roughly following the course of the *idhragoyeío*, and finish their climb right next to the watercourse at the edge of a large plateau. Follow the waterworks for 20 more min to the unsightly cement *ksoklísi* of Áyios Ioánnis. (Note that below this chapel the aqueduct divides, water being diverted on a day-by-day basis to either of the two branches. If you're coming down

Looking down the Velítsa ravine from Liákoura saddle

from Liákoura, be sure to follow the left bifurcation.) About 300 m uphill from Áyios Ioánnis, the foot trail resumes among some firs just uphill from a bulldozer-scraped area and the aqueduct, which is the last dependable water supply for some time. Count on a 1-hr march from Tithoréa to the start of the alpine trail, and don't be overly dismayed by the initial condition of the route; matters improve dramatically above Áyios Ioánnis.

After a stiff 30-min climb through thick forest, the grade lessens and the trees thin out to permit views of one Parnassian peak after another filing by in stately review on the far (northwest) side of the now-magnificent chasm. Some 2 hrs above Tithoréa, a high waterfall at the base of the crags opposite contributes to the perennial sound of rushing water. Twenty min further, the path scales a sparsely treed ridge and briefly runs along the crest; you have perspectives east (left) over the Ayía Marína valley and the isolated monastery of the Virgin, and straight up toward the eastern "wing" of the massif. Soon the dry ridge widens into a high stony pasture; when trees recommence, some 2¾ hr out, the trail dips inconspicuously to the right—do *not* go steeply up from the pasture. After quitting the pasture, the route runs levelly for a spell along the gorge and then gradually dips further into the Velítsa canyon, which has narrowed considerably and rises to meet the trail just below treeline, approximately 3½ hr along. Cross the ravine where a permanent spring gushes—this is the last reliable water on Parnassós! Bear left, not right, on the opposite bank and climb 30 min more up scree-laden switchbacks to a small (two huts, corrals) *stáni* just at treeline. You must bear right here, going straight up the hill across from the second corral, and begin a cruel 30-min climb up to another *stáni* perched on the southeast slope of the main defile leading down from the Liákoura saddle. The grandeur of the escarpments that loom on all sides offers some compensation for slow, painful progress on this stretch. After this last *stáni*, the valley to the right, a tributary of the Velítsa, closes, the grade becomes gentler and the trail crosses to the right (northwest) side of the couloir, where it stays for the final hour up to the saddle. Total elapsed hiking time from Tithoréa up to the ridgetop junction with the paths to Yerondóvrahos and the peak is 5½ hr; from Liákoura saddle downhill, count on 1 hr less. Note that orange blazes on this trail are primarily for descending.

Other Routes on Parnassós . . .

If you accidentally or deliberately miss the right (westerly) turning at the Velítsa *stáni*, you end up within 1 hr at a pass known as Baïtanórrahi. Here trails go southeast or left to Yerousalím convent within 4 hr, and northwest or right to the meadow at the foot of Liákoura, beyond Kotróni peak. There is also said to exist a route southwest to Aráhova, but this would be along the sheerest face of Parnassós and a hiker reportedly fell to his death in this area in 1980.

From the nunnery of Yerousalím, where people camp among the trees near the front gate, the village of Dhávlia (rooms) is a mere 1-hr walk east. It is dominated by a medieval castle built directly atop the ruined acropolis of ancient Daulis, whose inhabitants were reputed to be of prodigious strength and size. Dhávlia has bus service from Livádhia, and its own rail station (local trains only) lies 8½ road km below the village. Alternatively, you can somehow cover the 11 road km from the nunnery to the main Livádhia-Aráhova road—the junction is within sight of the turnoff for Dhístomo and hence a recognized bus stop.

. . . And Below

For years I have heard persistent reports of a trail from the Filomelos fort, beyond the stadium in the Dhelfí archaeological site, to the Korýkion Ándhron, a grotto sacred to Pan and his Bacchantes, at the southwestern rim of the Livádhi plateau. The outing is reputed to take 3 hr on foot—first on an ancient trail known as Kakí Skála, later on an assortment of farmers' tracks. The tourist police in Dhelfí, and probably a fair number of the archaeological-site employees, know about the route, and just because I've been unable to find it doesn't mean you can't. However, it would be a ghastly piece of work in midsummer, when the western flanks of Parnassós shimmer in heat.

Many visitors to Dhelfí can't help but notice the wide *kalderími* that zigzags obviously up the far side of the olive-swathed Pléistos gorge. This in fact leads over Mt. Kírfis to the little-visited village of Dhesfína, from which there are occasional buses the 16 km back to Itéa, the major transport hub of the Gulf of Kórinthos. First, of course, you must descend 1 hr to the floor of the Pleístos, intersecting the main Hrissó—Dhesfína route. The visible switchbacks take up another hour, with the third and final hour spent crossing flat-topped Kírfis to Dhesfína.

Rating/time course: There is much to recommend a single day's outing on Parnassós, especially during the long days of June and July. With a timely departure from Aráhova, you could leave Yerondóvrahos at 9 A.M., climb the summit by 2 and be safely down in Tithoréa by sunset. Alternatively, you could schedule an out-and-back day hike from Tithoréa of about the same duration but without the necessity of lugging a full pack from the south of Parnassós to the north. You're virtually obligated to use the Tithoréa-Liákoura path at least once, as much because of the location of the single spring as the beauty of the scenery. Ascending from Tithoréa and coming down to Yerondóvrahos with a full kit is less than ideal; the steep slope above the Velítsa *stáni* would be brutal, and in all probability you'd have to walk the entire 14 km down from Yerondóvrahos to the main trans-Parnassós road. If you are intent on crossing the mountain from Tithoréa, you're advised to complete the traverse by descending from Sídheres Pórtes to Dhávlia, where it's easiest to arrange mobility to Aráhova or Dhelfí.

The best campsites on the mountain, should you wish to apportion the crossing over two days, are the two shelters west of Liákoura and the spring at the head of the Velítsa ravine, though there is precious little level ground near the latter. A compass is recommended not only for orienting at the summit but along the way; it's easy to get lost among the peaks to the south and east of Liákoura, many of which look alarmingly similar.

Supplies: Aráhova, Tithoréa and Dhávlia.

Maps: Parnassós lies at the triple juncture of Fokídhos, Fthiótidhos and Viotías ESY sheets; hence coverage on none of the three is entirely satisfactory. For example, contour shading on the Fokídhos quad is superior to that of the other two but only Viotías covers the Dhávlia side of the range.

9   MT. OÍTI (OETA)

This often-ignored mountain is blessed with far more meadowlands, forests and springs than the rocky norm for central Greece and actually displays most characteristics of the Makedhonian ranges; in recognition of this, much of Oíti has been set aside as a national forest. In fact, Oíti marks the southeastern tip of the rainy climatological belt extending south from the Albanian frontier through the Píndhos and Ágrafa; the lushest territory, and the best hiking, is found on the abrupt north side of the massif. Most of the summit area consists of rolling meadows, and the peak itself is not striking; however, a secondary summit was in mythology the site of Hercules' self-immolation and accordingly has been dubbed Pyrá (the pyre). From the heights you continue south over a variety of surfaces toward a handful of villages between Oíti and Gkióna, the next Sterean peak.

Getting to the trailhead: The best path begins in the village of Ypáti, reached almost hourly by buses from Lamía. However, it's not necessary to catch the bus in town; hikers coming from Parnassós or northern Greece should take a train to Lianokládhi, the station halfway between Lamía and Ypáti. Walk east from the terminal (take a right out the station door) to the crossing guard's booth by the tracks—this is an official stop for Ypáti-bound coaches.

In Lamía proper there are three separate bus stands: one for long-distance coaches of the Athens-Thessaloníki line, one for service west to Karpeníssi and south to Ámfissa and one for service to local villages, Ypáti being one of these. By the time you locate the appropriate terminal you'll probably agree it's a good deal easier to take the train. Once on the bus make sure that you're set down at the end of the line, the pleasant hill town of Ypáti, and not at the malodorous sulfur spa just before. Upper Ypáti was sufficiently important to give rise to a small castle in the Middle Ages, when it was known as Pátrai; today it attracts enough Greek vacationers to support a couple of hotels and eateries.

Ypáti to Trapezítsa Shelter

From the spring on the central *platía*, start up the steep paved street heading south. This snakes through the highest houses of Ypáti; adhere always to the principal cemented right-of-way. Some 7 m past the highest point in the road, turn left onto a prominent mule track; after another 200 m, turn right opposite a final, rustic house with a water tap in its front corral. Initially the climb is severe, but an aqueduct running alongside the path provides coolant for baked heads. Soon the *idhragoyeío* meanders off to the left, and shortly after you must take a narrower, right fork. Confidence is restored by the sighting of a few red dots as the trail plunges onward,

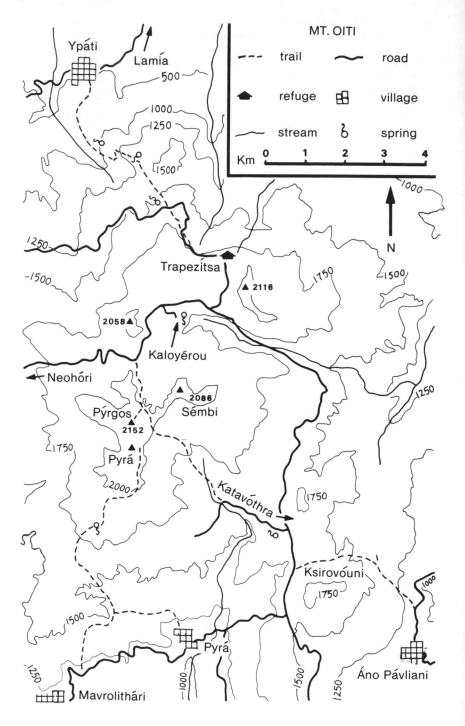

deeply grooved into the terrain by generations of livestock. Owing to hoof action, the path is usually bifid, even trifid—try to maintain a median bearing.

The first fringes of Oíti's fir groves offer valuable shade about an hour above Ypáti, and some 15 min beyond the beginning of the trees you'll reach a meadow with a vigorous stream and the ruins of an old mill or farm. From these, bear off across a denuded hillside toward the resumption of the trail among some trees; don't dip into the stream valley to the south. After another 1½ hr of steady climbing through stately firs, a marshy spot heralds the Amalióvrysi spring near the top of the ridge separating Oíti from the Sperhiós river valley. A rusty blue sign just to the right points along the path continuing to Trapezítsa.

Immediately above Amalióvryssi you could camp quite satisfactorily in a large meadow; the trail itself skirts the south edge of the turf and veers off across the top of a gully to begin a stiff, 30-min climb up to Perdhikóvryssi spring. The way is often obscured by the wildflowers that grow in profusion, as late as midsummer, at the base of firs draped suggestively with moss. Perdhikóvryssi (unmarked) is a muddy, stomped-about place with none of the masonry or charm of its lower neighbor; it lies just below a forest road which you cross, oriented by red dots. The trail resumes feebly on the far side, recrossing the road again instantly and twisting steadily up through more firs on a carpet of midaltitude turf and blossoms.

About 30 min beyond your first encounter with the road, the path is often imaginary and walkers are heavily dependent on red blazes. Once again that old nemesis, the road, does its best to submerge the trail with multiple switchbacks, and after a few min the red blazes—and your patience—give out. Resign yourself to following the road the final 10 min to the 300-m-long driveway leading to the alpine hut, strikingly situated on a canyon-bound plateaulet (*trapezítsa*, little table) with views of the setting and rising sun. About 300 m west of the hostel a slow (ca. 2 lit/min) spring offers water to those who wish to camp under the trees by the refuge. A sign ("*piyí*") tacked to one of these is nearly wrecked but a well-worn trail betrays the location of the fountain. The total hiking time from Ypáti is 4 hr, but you should allow more leeway than usual since the steep grade prompts longer rests.

Trapezítsa to Pýrgos, and Beyond

From Trapezítsa walk 25 min uproad to the Livadhíes tableland that surrounds most of the major peaks of Oíti, keeping a stream to your left. Bear right at a crossroads in the vicinity of two weedy ponds. Pýrgos, the official 2152-m summit of Oíti, is sandwiched by two lesser heights directly in front of you but still some km distant. Some 20 min past the little ponds a sign marks a side road going left to the Kaloyérou spring and picnic area (camping feasible); after pausing for water continue along the main track, in the signposted direction of Neohóri. Thirty min beyond Kaloyérou the road broaches a high saddle, from which a small *stáni* is seen below and to the left; Pýrgos, with its attendants, hovers just to the south. Leave the road here for an easy, 45-min cross-country lope, occasionally on shepherds' trails, to the base of the peak; there's one last puddle-spring about 15 min past the saddle. Fifteen min of scrambling covers the distance from the foot of Pýrgos to the altimeter, which you should reach no more than 2½ hr after leaving the hostel. In clear weather you can see many of the important peaks of the Stereá arrayed from the southeast to southwest, but under most circumstances the distinctive cone of Gkióna and the jagged crenelations of Vardhoússia further west are the most prominent.

Pyrá, Hercules' final resting place, is the next peak south of Pýrgos, from there it's a 3-hr walk to Pyrá village at the southern base of the range. Keep to the faint rights-of-way just below the ridge line and resist the temptation to plunge into the tempting valleys to the left (east) of the summit zone. Pyrá has marginal facilities but there is bus service some days of the week to Pávliani (see below).

Most trampers will in fact drop down into the territory east of Pýrgos, using the saddle between Sémbi and the peak. A steep, virtually trailless drop leads to a meadow with some tracks plainly visible from the peak. One hr below Pýrgos, you should pass a *stáni* tenanted by some men from Mavrolithári, an isolated hamlet west of Pyrá village. You will probably make their acquaintance, as their dogs are not easily deterred. Just below the *stáni*, a bigger road and a watercourse intersect your track; turn left. Tramping 45 min further brings you to a vast, flat expanse enlivened only by a trough spring on the right. An incline on the left slopes down to Katavóthra, "the drain," a deep maw at the base of a prominent cliff and the exit point of all water on this plain. The Katavóthra lies just the other side of an important forest road, in fact the left fork not taken just above Trapezítsa. From the track leading down from the *stáni*, turn right onto this road and proceed about 10 min to its highest point in the area. To the left (east) you'll see the faint beginnings of a trail which threads its way between the bulk sheltering the Katavóthra and Ksirovoúni (dry mountain), so named because of its bare western flank. After a 1½-hr descent through forest, which dispels any negative impressions left by the previous half-day's road walking, you arrive in Áno Pávliani, an attractive village set among firs and apple orchards. Unhappily, most of the inhabitants seem strangely indifferent to outsiders, and any amount of cajolery may only yield somewhat expensive lodgings above Grill Morgonis in Káto Pávliani, 1 km below. Totting up the elapsed walking time from Trapezítsa to Pávliani gives a sum of just over 6 hr.

Rating/time course: Allow at least a day and a half to cross the range from north to south. Oíti's springs run even in summer, which offers balmy nights and only some daytime discomfort on the initial ascent. Good orienting skills necessary for the territory south of Pýrgos.

Supplies: Ypáti or Lamía.

Map: *Korfés*, issues 31 and 67.

10   MT. GKIÓNA

The name of the highest point in the Stereá is related to the Greek word for the scops owl (*gkiónis*), and indeed the pyramidal summit does seem to perch alertly, surveying the positively savage topography on all sides. Gkióna is certainly the wildest and most unspoiled of the central Greek mountains. Although the local bauxite company has thoroughly disfigured the northeast quadrant of the range, none of this activity has spilled over into the premier hiking areas and little trace of the industry is visible from the routes described. The highlights of any traverse must include the view west from the crest line over the valley of the Mórnos River, which supplies Athens with most of its water, and a passage in some direction through the village of Sikiá, from where you can gape at the 1300-m Pláka cliff which falls abruptly away from the 2510-m peak. From the other side of Gkióna, access to the alpine zone is via the Rekká ravine, a 13-km gravel-floored gallery set between beetling cliffs and a respectable third to the canyons of Samária and Víkos. In an inverse of the usual Greek conditions, spring water here is more plentiful in the alpine zones than lower down, but with moistureless air at all altitudes, expenditure of half a stick of lip balm is routine.

Getting to the trailhead: Trekkers continuing from Oíti and Pávliani village must somehow cover the 10 road km between Pávliani and Kaloskopí, and if possible a bit beyond. There is no bus service between the two communities, but three times a week (Mon, Thur, Sat in 1984) the bus that runs between Pávliani, Pyrá and Mavrolithári can take you halfway, to the left turnoff for Kaloskopí. In the early morning you can often successfully beg a lift from the bauxite ore trucks that rumble up Gkióna to within a reasonable distance of the actual trailhead above Kaloskopí. In any case try to avoid

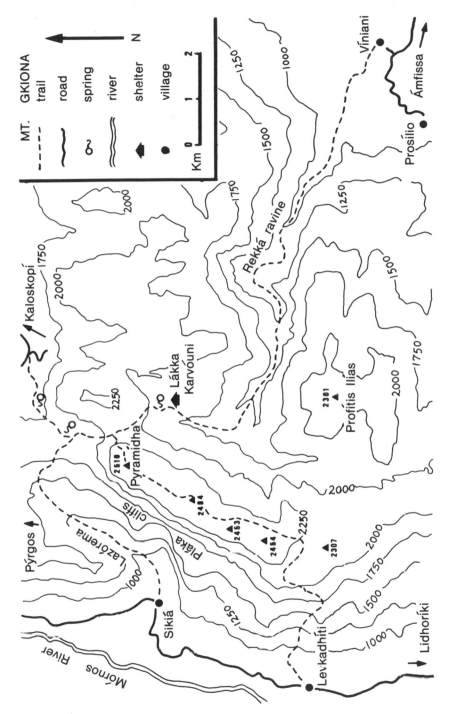

the hot, dusty and fly-infested 2 ½-hr walk between the two villages—money for a taxi is well-spent. Kaloskopí, with a couple of stores but no conventional eatery or lodging, is no great shakes as a mountain village and you'll have little regret in bypassing it.

Víniani (Káto Prosílio) is the closest settlement to the mouth of the Rekká ravine but from the trekker's point of view is not terribly well-appointed; no formal restaurant or lodging, and mediocre bus connections (7 A.M. outbound to Ámfissa, 1:15 P.M. return). You can certainly request space to camp in or near the *kafenéio*, where limited canned supplies are available, or you may even be hosted by one of the village families, most of whom work for the bauxite company. Those interested in hiking *up* Rekká should hire a taxi in Ámfissa for the 17-km trip, since arrival with the afternoon bus will not allow you enough time to reach the alpine zone and the best campsites before dark.

Sikiá, with its setting plus a handful of *tavérnes* and "rooms" establishments, is easily the most appealing jump-off or landing point for excursions on Gkióna. There is daily bus service from Lidhoríki, 17 km down the Mórnos valley, which in turn is reached two to three times a day from Ámfissa or Eratiní on the Kórinthos Gulf.

Kaloskopí to Pyramídha Peak

These directions begin with the assumption that you have ridden or walked only as far as Kaloskopí. Take the main *dhimósio* leading south out of the village; after about 30 min you'll reach a triple junction. Shun the options bearing hard left or doubling back to the right—on a placard erected by the bauxite company, a rusty, barely discernable arrow, accompanied by the legend "*Gkionas*," points toward the correct turning at about "two o'clock." If you manage to hitch with an ore truck, you'll probably be set down here. An hour and a quarter past this sign, or just under 2 hr out of Kaloskopí, the forest road becomes impassable to vehicles in the neighborhood of a cement trough-spring (usually dry). A taxi would leave you at a turnaround just before the dry spring, near some bee-hives—the locale is called Mnímata. Five min after the trough, a healthy spring burbles out onto the track, which dwindles hereafter to a chaos of boulders, twigs and animal tracks and excreta until, 2½ hr above Kaloskopí, you come upon a giant *lákkos* (pit) in which snow persists until late summer. A few minutes above the *lákkos*, do not follow a switchback left or east but bear right onto an apparent dead end. Almost immediately, red dashes in the trees above you to the left mark the start of the footpath. The worst climbing is over 30 min along the trail, and Pyramídha comes into sight. Next you negotiate an inclined pasture crisscrossed by rivulets, and a bit less than 4 hr from Kaloskopí, you'll pass the last spring on the north face of Gkióna, just to the left of the route. Within another 15 min you arrive at a high, level pasture at the base of Pyramídha, suitable for camping but bespattered with sheep droppings from the two local *stánes*. From the ridge that closes off the plateau to the west you can watch moody, primordial sunsets and sunrises on the jagged contours of Vardhoússia across the Mórnos valley.

Facing the peak from the high pasture, you'll notice a saddle to the left (east); it takes about 45 min, assisted by blazes on a faint trail, to cover the distance to this pass. From it, you can spy the head of the Rekká canyon and the Gkióna hostel (Lákka Karvoúni) hundreds of meters below; beyond them, the outline of semi-forested Profítis Ilías (2307 m) defines the southern horizon. To the right the main crest of Gkióna, a half-dozen peaks in all, culminates in Pyramídha, the northernmost and closest to your vantage point. Another 45-min trailless scramble takes you to the grafitti-embellished 2510-m altimeter. Beyond the peak, the west escarpment of Gkióna forms a sheer wall that drops dizzyingly into the canyon carved by the Mórnos; in contrast Vardhoússia, on the far side, slopes up far more gradually. Sikiá village is tucked out of sight unless you move slightly south along the crest.

Pyramídha to the Mórnos Valley and Vice Versa

It is possible to pick your way south along the entire Gkióna ridge within a couple of hours to a point where you can drop down and right to the village of Levkadhiti (5 km south of Sikiá), but the grade from the southernmost summit on the crest (ca. 2300 m) down to Levkadhiti (ca. 800 m) is unresearched and you should allow a minimum total of 5 hr for this descent.

From Sikiá a well-known ascent aims initially northeast up the Lazórema, comes out on a saddle joining the high *stánes* to the secondary peak Pýrgos (2066 m) and then bears southwest toward the pasture itself. The climb takes 3¾ hr with a daypack but closer to 5 hr with complete gear. There are few if any well-demarcated trails in the Lazórema after the first 30 min out of Sikiá, but the chances of making a wrong turn are considerably lessened by the severe topography. If you elect to descend toward Sikiá—a 4-hr undertaking—you can view virtually the entire route from Pyramídha.

Pyramídha to Viniáni via Rekká

From the east end of the saddle at the foot of Pyramídha, a faint but occasionally marked trail curls down to the level of the mountain refuge at Lákka Karvoúni. Twenty min down, scree and steepness lessen as the route curves onto the edge of a high meadow above the valley at the foot of Pyramídha. The red legend *"Katafýgio"* appears on a rock outcrop, followed by red dots. A powerful spring surges out of a long steel pipe 10 min below—this is the last dependable water until Víniani. The shelter lies some 45 min below the watershed, but its sponsor, the Athens Hiking Club, has let it slip into a state of disrepair; for emergencies a side stable, often used by local shepherds, is permanently open. Ascending from the hostel to the watershed, count on at least a 1-hr climb; it's best to curl right, then left, in the inverse of the directions just given, rather than charging up the steep grade directly below the saddle.

With your back to the front door of the hostel, point to the last handful of firs at treeline on the slopes to the right; the path to Víniani continues there. You face a 1-hr descent to the bed of the Rekká; the first 20 min across the split upper reach of the canyon uses an adequate trail, but the balance of the hour is spent wrestling with faint bifid and trifid parallel livestock traces laden with scree. Just as you emerge onto the Rekká at the point where it divides, you'll notice a couple of cairns beckoning to those souls hardy enough to tackle the gorge uphill. After about a 15-min march on the bone-dry gravel bed of the watercourse, a bona fide trail cuts in on the left (north) bank of the canyon at the point where the bed turns jumbly and impassable. Soon it's apparent that the path was once an excellent *kalderími*, now much deteriorated in the wake of slides and tree falls but still generous by Greek montane standards. Just over 1½ hr after quitting the shelter, you cross to the right (south) bank of the Rekká—only stumps of a bridge remain but the drop to the ravine floor is slight. The 2-hr mark in the descent finds you recrossing to the left or north side, and within another 30 min the built-up *kalderími* ends just before a thick water pipe sallies into the Rekká from a side canyon.

The confluence of the two gorges was the site of a bloody ambush of occupation forces by ELAS (Greek Popular Liberation Army) guerrillas in 1942 or 1943. A company of 33 Italian soldiers had been ordered to march from the east to the west side of Gkióna. A shepherd, seeing the party proceeding up the Rekká, sped up the mountain to tip off the *andártes* (rebels), who fell on the Italians at dawn while they were still asleep. In reprisal the Italian command ordered the burning of Segdítsa (Prosílio), at the mouth of the Rekká, thus according it the dubious distinction of being one of the first of several hundred Greek villages to be vengefully destroyed during the Second World War. Rather than rebuild in Prosílio—which remains half-occupied today—many of the inhabitants relocated three kilometers downhill at Víniani, which had been relatively unimportant until then.

Follow the water main down the Rekká away from this haunted spot; 20 to 25 min along the gravel bank, or 3 hr below the refuge, oak and other deciduous trees supplant fir as the primary species. Twenty min further, a sharp drop in the ravine bed is marked by a rusty sign announcing a bauxite tailings dump—danger—and the preferred trail bears slightly uphill and right, following the water pipe. After skirting the tailings you redescend to the gully bed; the walls of the Rekká dwindle steadily on both sides, ore cable cars swing in the distance and 4 full hr below the Lákka Karvóuni shelter the Rekká ravine can be said to terminate—or begin—near a stock trough and a path on the left (north) which leads within 15 min to Víniani.

Note again that there is *no* available water in the ravine; the source of the sealed aqueduct leading from the side canyon is quite inaccessible. Hiking up the Rekká from Víniani is certainly not out of the question, but the canyon seems to extend forever in its most majestic moments and the monotony of its lower reaches will be telling on morale. At least 6 daylit hr should be budgeted for reaching Lákka Karvóuni.

Rating/time course: Extremely motivated individuals could cross the range from Sikiá or Kaloskopí to Víniani in one long summer day, but this would neither be particularly enjoyable nor permit time to linger on the peak. Those headed the opposite direction must plan on overnighting in the alpine zone. Although not technically difficult, the traverse of the Rekká in either direction will test the fit of your boots, and the ravine is subject to possible flash flooding in spring.

Supplies: Kaloskopí, Ámfissa or Sikiá

Map: *Korfés*, issues 32, 63-64.

11   MT. VARDHOÚSSIA

The most severe and barren of the Sterean ranges primarily attracts rock climbers and winter alpinists, but the cross-country tramper can still make a pleasant traverse of the mountain through its high pastures, rarely climbing above 2100 m unless desired. An east-to-west crossing of Vardhoússia can easily be added to a ramble through Gkióna, provided you descend that peak in the direction of Sikiá or Levkadhíti villages.

Getting to the trailhead: If you are not already in Sikiá, take a bus from Ámfissa to Lidhoríki and from there another as far up the Mórnos valley, upstream from Sikiá, as possible. The ideal destination is the village of Áno Moussounítsa (alias Athanásios Dhiákos, after a revolutionary hero).

Áno Moussounítsa to Artotína

Two alpine huts at Pittimáliko lie 4 hiking hr above Áno Moussounítsa. From the hostel area you can accomplish a nontechnical ascent of Kórakas summit (2495 m). Heading west via the Meterízia pass or the Moussounitsiótiki saddle, one comes to the Artotína Livádhia, a meadowland at the head of a watered canyon running down to the village of the same name. You should plan to spend at least one night on the mountain.

From Artotína there is at least one daily bus, probably in the morning, to the coastal town of Náfpaktos; service up from Náfpaktos, at around noon, may be useful to those interested in reversing the above itinerary.

Supplies: Ámfissa, Lidhoríki or Sikiá.

Map: ESY, Fokídhos or Fthiótidhos, Korfés, issues 65-66.

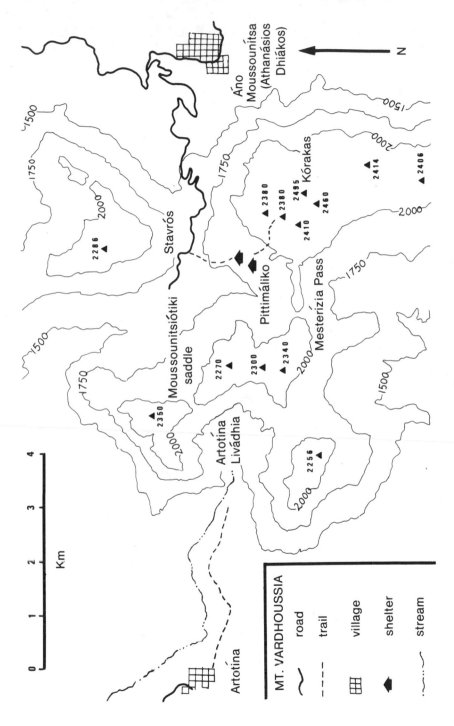

MT. VARDHOUSSIA

—— road
---- trail
village
shelter
—··— stream

12   DAY HIKES IN THE KARPENISSIÓTIS RIVER VALLEY (AND BEYOND)

After the often bare marches of Vardhouśsia, the green and forested valley south of the town of Karpeníssi presents the most opposite vision imaginable. The area is often compared in beauty to the high valleys of the Tyrol or Switzerland and for once the tourist-office hype is not an exaggeration. At the head of the vale, and the base of the road- and ski-lift-scarred, unattractive Mt. Timvristós, Karpeníssi offers an assortment of cheap hotels and *tavérnes*. The town was razed first by the Germans during World War II and again during the civil war, so no architectural treasures induce you to linger during daylight hours. Better to head 15 km downstream along the Karpenissiótis to the twin traditional villages of Mikró Horió and Megálo Horió, which face each other on the west and east banks, respectively, of the river. Thickly firred Mt. Helidhóna (1975 m) presides over Mikró Horió, from where a path leads to the summit in just under 4 hr. Across the Karpenissiótis, Mt. Kalliakóudha dominates Megálo Horió, and another half-day's climb on a good path brings you to the 2100-m summit. There are inns in both communities, so a three-night stay would give you the opportunity to enjoy the best of the valley in two consecutive all-day hikes.

Beyond the two villages the auto road deteriorates as it enters the savage Proussós gorge, and 22 km below Karpeníssi it passes the meeting of the Krikelliótis and Karpenissiótis rivers. The combined stream, the Trikeriótis, curls completely back on itself within the space of a few kilometers and flows into the giant Kremastón reservoir which is visible from the top of Helidhóna. The Krikelliótis takes its name from Kríkello, a high village directly east of Kalliakóudha; the well-equipped could attempt a 7-hr traverse of the peak from Megálo Horió to Kríkello, which as a summer resort of some repute has adequate lodging. It may even be possible to continue hiking over Mt. Oxiá (1926 m) from Kríkello to the village of Gardhíki, as there is a trail from the peak to Gardhíki via the alpine hostel, but the Krikelliótis River or its tributaries may present an impassable barrier.

Getting to the valley: Two daily buses connect Lamía and Karpeníssi; one runs between Agrínion and Karpeníssi—a real mud wallow. Local services include one daily coach from Karpeníssi to Megálo Horió and Krikello. There is also daily seasonal service between Gramméni Oxiá and the main Lamia/Karpenissi highway, which will be welcome news for trekkers coming down from Mt. Oxia or north from Artotína.

Rating/season: The "twin" day hikes are ideal late-spring to late-summer outings with moderate 1000-m elevation changes. Exploring the territory east of Kalliakóudha peak is in another category, requiring considerable experience in the Greek mountains.

Supplies: Karpeníssi.

Map: ESY, Evritanías, especially for any prolonged adventures.

13   THE ÁGRAFA

Opinion differs on how the high valleys of the Ahelóös, Agrafiótis and Mégdovas rivers came to be called *ágrafa* (unwritten), but the most accepted version holds that during Ottoman times the area remained a blank on the Sultan's records because census takers and tax collectors were apt to be ejected at sword point from the high villages. The peaks between Karpeníssi and the south Píndhos are not surpassingly high—maximum elevation is a mere 2164 m—but they are shapely and the local rivers

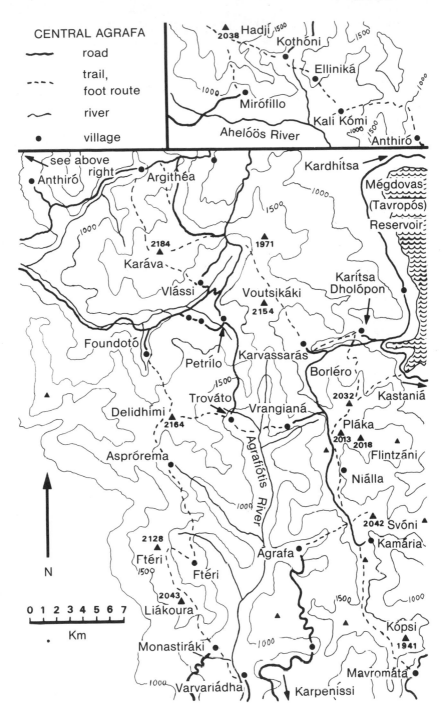

CENTRAL AGRAFA

~~~ road

- - - trail, foot route

~ river

● village

2038 ▲ Hadjí 1500
Kothóni ●
1500
Elliniká ●
1000
Mirófillo ●
Kalí Kómi ●
Ahelóös River
Anthiró ●

see above right
● Anthiró
Argithéa ●
Kardhítsa
Mégdovas (Tavropós) Reservoir
1000
1500
1000
2184 ▲
Karáva
1971 ▲
Vlássi
Voutsikáki ●
2154 ▲
Karítsa Dholópon ●
Foundotó ●
Petrílo
Karvassarás ●
Borléro ●
1500
Trováto
Vrangianá
2032 ▲ Kastaniá
Delidhími ●
2164 ▲
Pláka ●
2013 ▲ 2018 ▲ ▲
Flintzáni
Asprórema ●
Niálla ●
Agrafiótis River
1000
N
2128 ▲
2042 ▲ Svóni ▲
Kamária ●
Ftéri ●
1500
Ágrafa ●
Ftéri ●
2043 ▲
Liákoura
1500
1000
Monastiráki ●
1000
Kópsi
1941 ▲
0 1 2 3 4 5 6 7
Km
●
Mavromáta ●
Varvariádha
Karpeníssi

have carved tremendous, 1700-m deep gorges which the Greek equivalent of the Army Corps of Engineers has set its sights on for hydroelectric projects.

Getting into Ágrafa: There is daily bus service from Kardhítsa at least as far as Kastaniá. The turnoff for Kerasohóri is the closest point to the Agrafiótis River on the Karpeníssi-Agrínion road; inquire in Karpeníssi for bus service up the river, and to Mavromáta. There will be bus service from Kardhítsa, past Mouzáki, as far as Argithéa and Anthiró. Theodhóriana is served once daily from Árta.

Route directions: Ágrafa can be approached from the north, as an add-on leg to a south Píndhos traverse (see Hike 14). From Theodóriana, walk a full day across the Ahelóös River to Korifí. Mt. Hadjí (2038 m) can be traversed in another day, the hike ending in either the village of Mirófillo or Polynéri (Kothóni). A third day's walk takes you first through the hamlets of Elliniká and Kalí Kómi, a prelude to crossing a ridge separating you from Anthiró. There a bus takes you to Argithéa village and the trailhead for the ascent of Mt. Karáva (2184 m). From its summit descend to Vlássi village and continue briefly by road to Petrílo, the starting point for further explorations of central Ágrafa.

South of Petrílo the Agrafiótis River intrudes into the topography, splitting the central Agrafan summits into a west wing centered around Delidhími, Ftéri and Liákoura (all ca. 2100 m), and an eastern ridge consisting most importantly of Borléro, Pláka and Svóni peaks (all ca. 2000 m). From Petrílo, transfer to the nearby village of Foundotó, from where there is a recognized route up Delidhími, or take the Petrílo-Trováto road and make an ascent from Trováto village. Delidhími (2164 m) is the beginning of a longitudinal traverse of the western massif, stopping in the hamlets of Asprórema, Ftéri and Monastiráki en route to Varvariádha, the first village on the Agrafiótis River with sure road access to the Karpénissi-Agrínion highway.

Alternatively, you can veer east from Petrílo, skirting the northeast flank of Voutsikáki (2154 m) en route to Karvassarás village, from where you trail-walk to the oddly named village of Karítsa Dholópon for the conquest of Borléro (2032 m) and Pláka (2013 m). Note also that from Trováto you can climb east to Vrangianá hamlet and then Pláka peak, assuming there's a healthy bridge over the Agrafiótis. From Pláka you could bear northeast toward the Mégdovas (Tavropós) Dam (see below), descend west to Vrangianá if you haven't already come that way—there are early Byzantine churches in that village—or turn south toward Svóni, reachable via Niálla hamlet. From Svóni (2042 m) you can descend west to Ágrafa village (road connection to Kerasohóri) or opt for another long day via Kamária village and the west flank of Kópsi (1941 m) to Mavromáta village (bus to Karpeníssi).

You may not be willing to devote eight to ten days tramping through this problematic territory. A shortcut from the village of Kastaniá, near the Mégdovas Dam, allows a briefer two- to three-day excursion through the best of southeastern Ágrafa. Proceed approximately 10 km west of Kastaniá on the dirt road that loops around Mégdovas Reservoir; on the far side of the Mégdovas River, as it exits from the dam, a trail begins which takes you within 5 hr to the summit of Borléro peak. Late starters can camp on the plateau between Borléro and Pláka; early birds can continue, on long summer days, a further 5 hr to 6 hr, first along the ridge south of Pláka and then down a stream valley where the ridge divides, to Ágrafa village.

Anyone planning an expedition into this area—for such it must be reckoned—should understand that most of the Ágrafa villages are exceedingly poor, and the trekker must be self-sufficient as well as hardy; you cannot expect more than the coffee, canned meat and occasional egg which are the staples of the all-in-one store/*kafenéio*/phone booth found in the mountains. Many of the settlements just barely have two-digit populations and outsiders are a distinct rarity; to my knowledge only an occasional British group trek has brought anything resembling tourist trade to Ágrafa. For all that, the adventurous should not be disappointed by their sojourn in perhaps the most isolated corner of Greece.

Supplies: Dependable only in Kardhítsa, Karpeníssi or Árta.

Maps: *Korfés*, topo maps originally appearing in issues 34, 35, 36; sketch map, issue 37. If additional coverage is needed, try (from south to north) ESY, Evritanías, Kardhítsis and Trikálon.

ÍPIROS

It was an isolated and magnificent world that every villager saw from his window . . . tucked into folds of the mountain and out of sight, were ten more villages strung along the timberline, without even a road to connect them to the rest of the world . . . . The isolation and cruelty of the landscape, especially in winter, made the peasants short-tempered and sometimes drove them mad, but those who managed to escape from these mountains would never find any other place as beautiful.

———Nicholas Gage

The character of Ípiros (Epirus) is determined by the rugged, thinly populated Píndhos range which, together with its extension, the Ágrafa, makes up nearly a fourth of the Greek mainland (excluding the Pelopónnisos). In antiquity mountainous Ípiros was considered the bourne of the civilized world; few traces of ancient culture have been unearthed aside from the shadowy oracles at Dodóna and Aherón. The Romans and their heirs the Byzantines had little use for the rugged province lying to one side of the Via Egnatía, which linked the Eastern and Western empires. During late Ottoman times it was the lair of the colorful Ali Pasha, who governed a quasi-autonomous domain centered on Ioánnina, which after the fall of Constantinople had become a refuge and showcase of medieval Greek culture. Union with Greece came late—1913—and shortly after was put to the test by the Italian invasion from Albania on October 28, 1940. The Greeks astounded Allies and Axis alike by soundly thrashing Mussolini's legions, and only irresolution, a Píndhos winter and Hitler's subsequent blitzkreig prevented them from annexing the long-coveted, ethnic Greek area of Voraía Ípiros (northern Ípiros), which today remains Albanian.

From the 15th through the 19th centuries the isolating Píndhos fostered the growth of a fabulously wealthy and cultured society of semiautonomous villages in the district of Zagória, whose traders, weavers, woodworkers, jewelers and masons were famous beyond the borders of the Ottoman Empire. The inaccessibility of the heights simultaneously discouraged depredations by the Turks, who preferred to leave the prickly mountaineers alone in exchange for nominal tribute. In recent years the montane barrier has worked against the vigor of the Zagorian communities (and indeed all Greek alpine villages); poor communications, lack of livelihood and wartime destruction have rendered many moribund. Attempts to reverse this decline have focused on touristic development of the 46 traditional Zagorian villages, still architecturally intriguing though otherwise left desolate by the lapse of Ottoman political and economic privileges. An abundance of local limestone and oak has been transformed into Hansel-and-Gretel housing that is all of a piece; street paving, walls and roofs blend together in a uniform gray which, rather than being depressing, is an example of perfect adaptation to environment.

Alpine Ípiros is no less impressive. Wild rivers such as the Aóös, the Thíamis, the Aherón and the Árachthos furrow the terrain, often separating densely forested peaks towering hundreds of meters above the water. The Víkos gorge, a 17-kilometer cleft in the flank of Mt. Astrákas that compares favorably with the more publicized Samarian canyon of Crete, slices through the heart of Zagória. Where there are no forests—a common condition on west-facing slopes—the limestone skeleton of the mountains protrudes in various uncompromising forms.

Nor are the people to be trifled with; *Ipirotikó kefáli* (Ipirote skull) has long been synonymous with stubbornness and fanatic (even suicidal) resistance to outsiders bent on harm (or even subtler change), as generations of occupiers discovered to their sorrow. But Ipirotes honor the peaceable stranger to sometimes inconvenient degrees; indigestion and biliousness are often the consequences of accepting invitations to village bacchanalia. Ipirote dairy and meat products (in moderate quantities) are the best in Greece, produced by the pastoral Vlachs and *Sarakatsáni* who tenant the high meadows.

14   SOUTH PÍNDHOS TRAVERSE

The Katára Pass (1705 m), just east of the Koutsovlach town of Métsovo, was the first (and still one of the few) in the Píndhos to have a road built through it; since the late Byzantine era, the road has separated Zagória and the north Píndhos on one side from the south Píndhos and Ágrafa on the other. The territory to the south of Katára is starker, wilder and less developed than the country to the north; and the three main peaks of the south Píndhos, Peristéri, Kakardhítsa and Tzoumérka, on average are nearly as high as their counterparts nearer Albania. They're certainly steeper and more forbidding, forming an uninterrupted wall approximately 30 km long. Most of the western slopes are barren, but the impression still left is that of a wilderness on a scale rarely associated with Europe. Four- to seven-hour stretches without encountering another human can be expected, and even then the shepherd family or members of a work crew will be dwarfed by the desolate grandeur surrounding them. As a rule, villages on the three-to-four-day route are, if more prosperous than those of west Stereá and Ágrafa, equally unequipped to handle outsiders; foreign tourists are virtually unknown.

The terrain covered on this trek is varied, except for a somewhat monotonous stretch on the afternoon of the first day. Almost immediately you're vaulted into the high fastness of Mt. Peristéri (Lákmos), 2295 m, whose serrated crest line makes it seem higher. Avoiding the sheer bony ridge that connects it to Mt. Kakardhítsa, you descend gradually across high meadows until a gorge opens up and leads down to the Hroússias River, which has cleft an even larger defile into the local strata. This canyon is flanked by the two southernmost Koutsovlach villages of Siráko and Kallarítes, from which it's a short walk to the Kipína monastery, wedged into a cliff face like a swallow's nest. Unhappily, the bulldozers have been at work hereabouts and it's a while before good trails resume. Fragments of foot routes continue onward to Hristí, Prámanda and Ágnanda, but from the last-named village a respectable path with a front-seat view of Tzoumérka proceeds to Kataráktis and a little way into the Tzoumerkan foothills. From the hard-won summit (2399 m) multiple parallel ridges threaten from every direction, but the village of Theodhóriana and hike's end is also in sight. Theodhóriana is a good base for ascents up the more moderately pitched south slope of Kakardhítsa and onward tramps into the Ágrafa, across the Aheloös River.

Getting to the trailhead: For an early morning start up Peristéri, you'll need to reach Métsovo or the nearby village of Votonóssi the previous afternoon. From Ioánnina to Métsovo, via Votonóssi, there are four or five daily departures; from Tríkala, east of Katára, there are perhaps three buses daily. Métsovo boasts nearly a dozen hotels, most overpriced because of the town's reputation as a ski resort and center of folk culture; lodging in Votonóssi, a few km west of Métsovo and just opposite the side road to Anthohóri, is limited to one inn. However, staying there would give you a considerable head start the next day; otherwise, in Métsovo you must catch a 6:30 A.M. bus which passes through Votonóssi. Hitchhiking the 6-km dirt road up to Anthohóri is a possibility, as there is only one bus from Ioánnina a day (ca. 2:30 P.M.). I would recommend this afternoon bus rather than any others, except that there seems to be no lodging in Anthohóri, so you'd have to camp out in a meadow an hour or so above the village.

Anthohóri to Siráko

Once in Anthohóri, take the ascending jeep track starting at the junction with a school and a large new *kafenéio*. Two hundred m up the hill, cross a stream. Just the other side, in front of the highest house in town (a modern concrete structure), the path proper starts on your right. It snakes up a ridge and almost immediately passes a spring and a stock trough, then skirts a fenced tree plantation on your right. With the help of occasional red blazes, follow the path to the other side of a bulldozer track, and then charge up a ridge looming to the left. About 45 min into the day, you'll recross the service road and maintain a straight bearing along the long axis of the ridge. The path now broadens briefly before dropping sharply to the left and entering the lowest *stáni* of Mt. Peristéri. Just before a low stone hut, the correct trail turns left toward a lone tree and a stock watering trough, which you'll reach about 1 hr above Anthohóri. This is also the best campsite for those who've left Anthohóri in midafternoon.

The route continues with a gradual cliimb along the hillside, curving around it just below a second trough some 20 min past the first. Don't drop too low into the valley on the left, but climbing up high on the spur above the troughs garners you no advantage either. Still on the west bank of the big vale, keep veering toward a very broad couloir running between two series of bony peaks which become more and more visible to the south (right). At the point where the main shepherds' path crosses to the east side of the valley to your left, it's of no more use—bear sharply right up into the alpine "gallery." At the beginning of your second hour of walking red arrows reappear among the rocks, directing you along an extremely faint right-of-way. After another 30 min of careful progress, the "path" worms right, up a series of rock shelves. The red marks are difficult to follow in this jumble; if you lose them, simply keep high and to the right, away from the central gully draining north off the high walls of Peristéri. About 3½ hr above Anthohóri the 2295-m summit, Tsoukarélla, pops into view, hovering just beyond a stone-lined collecting pond. It's the rightmost peak of an imposing line of needles which has provided a backdrop for your ramblings since leaving the lower shepherds' trail. By the fourth hour of march you should arrive at the highest Peristéri *stáni*, just at the foot of Tsoukarélla. This sheepfold is memorable for some of the most vicious dogs, and best cheese, in the Píndhos, so if you can avoid becoming lunch for the former you may get to sample some of the latter for *your* midday meal.

The trail, much clearer now, meanders uphill from the *stáni* and almost immediately passes a slow, cement-improved spring that's an ideal place to lunch if neither dogs nor cheese makers are about. Here a final red arrow points left toward the 45-min detour up Tsoukarélla peak, but unless you camped above Anthohóri, or it's a long midsummer day, you probably won't have time to make this side trip and arrive in Siráko before dark. Detour or no, you continue 15 more min straight up to the saddle just in front of you. Follow the trail over the pass—which has sweeping views down the long axis of Peristéri to both the southwest and northeast—and slip down the other side. Avoid a beguiling right turn onto the path coming up from the two villages

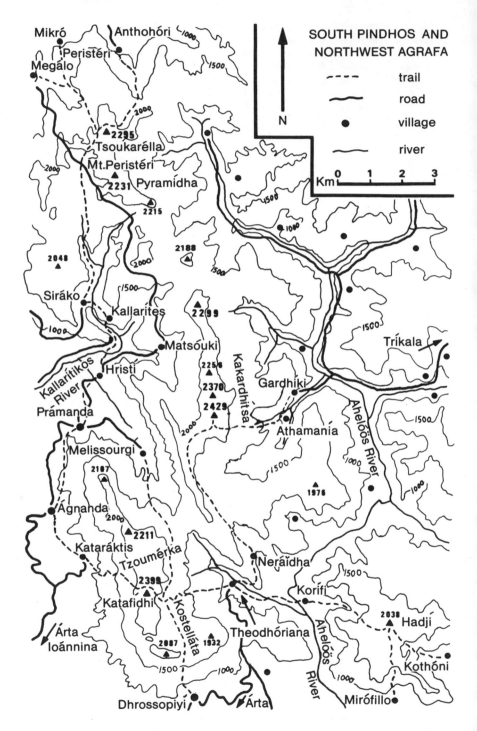

SOUTH PINDHOS AND
NORTHWEST AGRAFA

- - - - - trail
——— road
● village
——— river

Km 0   1   2   3

of Megálo and Mikró Peristéri; instead hug the base of Tsoukarélla peak on a southerly course. The path becomes exceedingly faint but suffices to lead you onto the next low ridge overlooking a giant expanse of high pasture and knolls to the south. In this vicinity you'll meet a brand-new *dhimósio* linking Matsóuki village with the two Peristéri communities. An on-and-off trail descends, following the course of least resistance and passing Pyramídha peak (2231 m), seen to your left, just over 1 hr below the *stáni*. The only major landmark in these featureless downs is a stone-lined livestock pond; from it a clear path picks up and aims down toward a sturdy stone-and-cement cottage. Just beyond this, almost 2 hr past Tsoukarélla, a long tongue of land splits the upper reach of the Hroússias River ravine leading down to Siráko. Do not venture out onto it—it's sheer on three sides—but instead angle down and left into the easterly gully which has a stream running through it. This is the first permanent, potable water since the Tsoukarélla spring. The trail resurrects itself yet again in tentative but traceable guise, snaking down the left (east) bank of the canyon, which deepens rapidly after absorbing the western tributary. A bit over 3 hr beyond Tsoukarélla, and shortly after a crude gate on the trail (which you should close to keep the local cattle from straying), the gorge and surrounding countryside open out noticeably. Still on the east slope, the path crosses a manure-laden hillside, quickly dips down to the right past a recently renovated fountain and then changes over to the west bank. It crosses yet another, usually dry stream bed draining off a sierra further to the west, and then metamorphoses into an excellent, heavily used trail leading steadily down the gorge. Four hr below Tsoukarélla the countryside opens out toward the left (northeast) as the main gorge running due south from Pyramídha peak joins your branch; you can see the two watercourses mingle below the trail on the left. At the start of the fifth hour of march from Peristéri, a *kalderími* takes over and quickly steps up to a fine viewpoint—turn around and watch the various peaks glimmer in the late afternoon light to the north.

Within another 20 min, entrance to Siráko is marked by a church and a loud spring to the right and a few ruined foundations lower down on the left. There's much more to come, as Siráko-on-the-Hroússias is much the most beautiful settlement of the South Píndhos. The well-preserved mansions, archways and churches bear a strong resemblance to those of Zagória, but the barren, cliffside, almost fortresslike setting of Siráko hardly recalls the gentle slopes and greenery of the realm west of the Aóös. The village is also the birthplace of many national heroes, statesmen and poets; in several spots there are statues of the hometown boys who made good, and any older local will be pleased to show them to you. Cultural sightseeing may be the last thing on your mind after 9-plus hr of walking; unfortunately, you may be obliged to continue on to Kallarítes, since while Siráko has a couple of *kafenéia* and a *tavérna*, there was no inn as of 1983. If you're benighted, you should ask to sleep in the school, especially in summer; a bed and a blanket in a turn-of-the-century classroom will seem like heaven after the day's trek.

Siráko to Hristí via Kallarítes

Partially retracing your entry into Siráko, follow the single streetlighted walkway east out of town. Just past the next-to-last inhabited house on the cliff face overlooking the Hroússias gorge, and just before a grove of three or four walnut trees, bear right onto a path passing just under the last, small occupied house of Siráko. A 20-min descent along a progressively clearer stair-trail brings you level with the river, right by an abandoned mill and a new metal bridge. The scenery is riveting and the cool depths of the gorge are balm on a summer day. As you begin your climb up the opposite cliff face you'll catch sight of another, much larger empty mill a few hundred meters upstream. Part of the 50-min ascent to Kallarítes is via a ladderway hewn out of the rock face, a bit of engineering the locals are justly proud of. Once through this stone gallery you'll have an all-encompassing view back over Siráko.

Kallarítes is less closed in and greener than Siráko, facing south over the gorge of the river which from here on is known logically enough as the Kallarítikos. There's quite a good *psistariá* on the main square here, and Filippas Kotsia, the village phone operator, has around 10 beds to let; you can find him during working hours in the little booth just off the *platía*; phone (0659) 61-251.

To move on toward Hristí, descend southeast from the *platía* via the street leading away from the Pandopoléio I Mélissa. The cobbled way zigzags down for 30 min to a spring, and 20 min more to a fine old bridge over the river. Sadly, 20 min beyond the bridge, you'll stumble upon the leading edge of an ugly new road, which threatens to wipe out all of the preceding—be prepared to find most of the *kalderími* badly chewed up or even obliterated. Within a few moments the Kipína monastery, parts of which date from 1381, peeks out from its perch some yards up the cliff face. Just below it, by the side of the road, lies a peculiar cave concealing an icy river running through and down to unplumbed depths. This is the point on the route closest to Mt. Kakardhítsa, which looms above the dense forests on the far side of the Kallarítikos. About 15 min past the cave and a full 1½ hr out of Kallarítes, you should leave the road just shy of a shed/haystack/terrace garden in favor of a new path switchbacking down a scree slope to a grove of plane trees. A full 15 min below the road, you'll cross an appealing stone bridge which no bulldozer will ever molest. Once on the opposite bank, climb 30 min up an old wagon road to a modern chapel on a knoll overlooking Hristí; just before reaching this *ksoklísi* you'll notice the Hristí-Matsoúki road above and to the left. From Kipína on, the landscape is more open and less dramatic; fern, oak and *plátanos* comprise the main vegetation of the flood plain of the Kallarítikos. Beyond the plain assorted outriders of Kakardhítsa and Tzoumérka dominate Hristí, huddled down by the river. From the chapel, a 15-min downhill scramble along the degenerated trail lands you on a rockslide spilling onto a road junction just above the church and *platía* of Hristí, a dull, modern village with a single store and *kafenéio*.

Hristí to Prámanda

Since the extension of the road beyond Prámanda to Hristí and Matsoúki, the trail in this sector has fallen into disrepair, but it's still possible to follow much of it and this will save you considerable time. Cross the river bridge just outside Hristí; the path begins with a sharp left uphill, just above the irrigation ditch and a bit to the left of the power poles. It's 20 min of hot work, snaking up through semicultivated terraces and fernbrakes, until you reach the *dhimósio*. Follow this for another 20 min until reaching an *ikonostási* and a cement (KTEL?) booth on the right. The trail reappears some 15 m behind these landmarks, climbing up the ridge with the aid of intermittent cobbling. It quickly mounts above the road, permitting a good look at the northwest wall of Tzoumérka towering above Prámanda, some of which is already visible. After yet another 20 min the old trail is ignominiously swallowed by the road just about 2 km shy of Prámanda; however, 10 min further along, the path revives to the left. A mostly dirt surface leads within 30 min directly into Prámanda, through a mixed biome of open scrub and fir. At the outskirts of town there's a drop to a stream bed and a bridge, then a gradual uphill past backyards and chicken shacks until your path merges with the cement street (21 Fevrouaríou) leading up to the *platía*.

An inn, with about 15 beds, is on your right just before two barbershops north of and below the square. The proprietor is Hrístos Papatheodorou; phone (0659) 61-393. You can eat fairly well, albeit carniverously, at a handful of *psistariés*, and a good grocery and a *galaktopoléio* are found south of the *platía*, past the bus stop. Prámanda is the main market center for the Kallarítikos valley and is large enough to warrant the detailed directions given—the town is spread over several ridges, each with its own view of the others and the canyons below.

Prámanda to Kataráktis via Ágnanda

A direct 3-hr path from Prámanda to Ágnanda exists, but I didn't use it and many hikers will appreciate a vehicular assist. The bus situation hereabouts is enlivened by the fact that Melissourgí, a village 6 km uphill from Prámanda, lies in Árta province while Prámanda is squarely within the *nomós* of Ioánnina. Hence you have double coverage, the Árta KTEL running to Ágnanda in the early morning and afternoon, and Ioánnina KTEL offering service at dawn and in the evening. If you need to stay in Ágnanda, Theofanes Kapelis (phone 31-476) has rooms but only in midsummer—the rest of the year he may be absent. Given the uncertainty of accommodation, it's advisable to plan on immediate departure for Kataráktis.

Ágnanda, nearly as large as Prámanda, is divided into a lower town (in whose plaza the bus halts) and an upper borough, where a plaza abuts the municipal offices and the primary school. Leave this *platía* via Napoleon Zervas St. in the direction of the large church visible to the south. Rather than pass the church, turn left and pass behind a lone, modern, yellowish-tan house. Just above this building, bear right onto an ample trail which snakes up the scrubby slope between fenced corrals and past a ruined house. About 30 min along, your path is subsumed into an even bigger donkey track coming up on the right. Within 10 min you top the ridge you've been climbing and come out onto a wide jeep track—the junction's marked by a white *ikonostási*. Turn left, and this track ends almost immediately; however, the footpath jumps down to the right and presses steadily on. Cross the first stream bed encountered perpendicularly rather than veering left. In contrast to some of the hot, exposed terrain of the previous day, this is superb walking country alive with oak, juniper and fir. The apparently sheer walls of Tzoumérka, framed by peak "2211" (m) on the left and the main Katafídhi summit (2399 m) on the distant right, menacingly dominate the scenery. As you complete an hour's march out of Ágnanda, the landscape flattens and the forest opens onto an expanse of sandy meadows and flat rocks where the trail becomes hesitant. Suddenly the houses of Kataráktis come into sight, resolving any doubts about orientation as the right-of-way begins to descend. Soon you're free of an occasionally wet creek bed and should pass another *ikonostási* 15 min downhill from the meadow. The montane vegetation ends abruptly and you begin crossing badly eroded hillsides, passing many damlets which under the circumstances must be considered too little too late. You'll cross a running stream on the rim of one flood-control device, just upstream from the ruined supports of a bridge long since swept away. After traversing the last few moments of scree slope, dip down to a cement bridge over the principal local watercourse. From here on it's apparent how Kataráktis (waterfalls) got its name—running sluices and gushing springs are heard, if not seen, on all sides, and if you look carefully at the cliff walls higher up, you can count several cascading torrents. Finally, 2 hr after leaving Ágnanda, you should arrive in the grassy, informal *platía* of Kataráktis, a village blessed with good orchard land and an open, plateau top setting in addition to its noted hydraulics. Dhimitrios Panoutsis runs an inn with 10 beds a block west of the plaza—it's advisable to write ahead if in a large group, since many city Greeks with distant relations here take summer holidays in the village. If you're completely done in and not up to tackling the territory described below, there is a daily bus to Árta.

Kataráktis to Theodhóriana over Tzoumérka

Leave the Kataráktis *platía* from its southeast corner and head south through a maze of path-streets until you reach the edge of the inhabited plateau and are able to overlook a sizable stream canyon. With the water on your right, descend to the bridge at the bottom, first noting a lone house on the wooded ridge above the far bank. A few moments above the bridge, an *ikonostási* marks a fork—make a hard left onto a narrow path which passes just a few yards to the left of the solitary dwelling as it climbs the ridge. Within 45 min of crossing the river, low scrubby bushes give way to terraced pasture. The trail is faint and hard to trace—as a guide, do not meander right but keep to the line of this ridge forming the south wall of the canyon on your left. There are occasional red dots but these are less helpful than a small church and an outbuilding atop a small knoll, at the end of some bulldozed S-curves. The *ksoklísi* marks the end of the first hour of climbing.

Line up the chapel and the outbuilding for the next leg of the journey; your preliminary goal is the gap in the peak line ahead, the river's point of exit into the gorge and also where the "proper" trail begins its way to Katafídhi summit. The next 30 min involve a tough climb up the ridge line, whose pitch has greatly steepened. During the following 30 min up to the 2-hr mark, the grade lessens and you get an assist from an old disused aqueduct, which directs you through the many turfy pastures here even if you don't choose to actually walk in or on it. The high pastures end at a *stáni* consisting of two huts, one strong and well-roofed, the other crude. To their left (north) you should see the waterfall at the head of the gully; more importantly, you must also find the initially faint trail starting just above the aqueduct as it loops off toward the falls. During its first 30 min, this path is clearly marked with red blazes as it zigzags up the right side of the watered ravine, but as the route levels out into a boggy meadow, the path disappears and blazes become rare. Halfway up the grassy slope to the right (south) of the meadow, a pile of boulders marks the entrance to a grotto spring. This is the only dependable water on the way—the waterfall is too difficult to get to—so you should budget adequate water for the 3 hr that it takes to reach the grotto from Kataráktis.

From here on it's line-of-sight to the saddle just to the left of Katafídhi peak, which is at long last visible. The next 1½ hr is spent in a grueling climb up the only partly grassy ridge pointing to the base of the peak. Keep a large *stáni* well to your right—there is no easier way up from its stone pens. The last 20 min of the scramble are truly hair-raising, as you toil on all fours up miserable piles of scree which end only upon reaching a tiny ridge joining the two points of Katafídhi peak. The western (rightmost) knob is a tad lower than the true summit, which offers some comfort in the form of alpine grass with good footing. The turfy spot is your base for the final few moment's push up to the top, but if you merely wish to continue (and it's not a spot for acrophobics to linger), veer away from a small natural arch and round the north side of the summit, using little goat walkways in the grass. A generous 4 hr after leaving Kataráktis, you'll come out onto the main north-south ridge of Tzoumérka to catch tremendous views over Ágrafa to the south and east, Kakardhítsa to the northeast, and much of Ioánnina province to the west. The red roofs of Theodhóriana peek reassuringly from out of the gray rockscape some kilometers down the mountain. Immediately below you stretches the Kostelláta plateau, which supports two *stánes* separated by a nasty-looking gully. You will be aiming for the right-hand one.

Clamber down the rockslides on the east flank of Katafídhi any way convenient and direct your steps toward the southern *stáni*. Faint trails furrow the turf of Kostelláta, starting especially from the vicinity of the left-hand sheepfold, but you should link up, no more than 1 hr down the mountain, with a clear trail crossing the head of the above-mentioned gully. This is the only safe way to get to the appropriate *stáni*; further up Katafídhi, the slopes are too steep, and below the trail crossing, the gully quickly becomes impassable. Less than 30 min from the top of the gully you'll reach the stock trough of the sheepfold; the water is potable, and the first since the cave spring. Once clear of the shepherd's colony, the path widens a bit before starting to switchback down toward the base of the ravine. It doesn't quite make it, instead flattening and straightening out as it passes yet another *stáni* 300 m to the left in the canyon bed itself. Theodhóriana has plunged out of sight; all that's visible to indicate settlement are some fir trees ahead and a *ksoklísi* or two. One hr or so below the stock trough, the ridge whose crest you've been following since passing the valley-bottom *stáni* ends abruptly. About 300 m beyond the last traces that could definitely be ascribed to humans rather than animals, watch for a rock with a red "K40" painted on it. This marks the spot where the trail from the canyon-bed *stáni* comes up to round the "snout" at the end of the ridge—thorny groundcover blocks further straight progress, so the new path is hard to miss. Turn right onto it; as it wiggles down through abandoned terrace lands, Theodhóriana pops into view once again. Forty-five min below the meeting with the new trail, a copse of willows shades a good spring and a hairpin left turn; just after, the trail crosses the runoff from the fountain to be on the same bank as Theodhóriana. Your south Píndhos itinerary finishes just over 3 hr below Katafídhi, and 7 or more hr from Kataráktis, a little below the village *platía*.

Theodhóriana is a friendly community with a couple of stores and an abundance of *psistariés*, including one specializing in roast chicken. Hrístos Papadzíkos, phone (0689) 73-402, runs the central *kafenéio* and lets eight beds upstairs; conditions are spartan but at least the quilts are warm. There is a 6:15 A.M. bus to Árta, which returns in the afternoon.

Alternative and Onward Routes

There are two other routes for Mt. Tzoumérka. Once on Kostelláta, a 90-degree turn south should enable you to pick up a right-of-way going down to Dhrossopiyí (Voulgaréli), but this is an appreciably longer (ca. 4½ hr) descent than that to Theodhóriana and should only be attempted with an early start out of Kataráktis. There are several hotels in Dhrossopiyí, which is visited (at 7:15 A.M. and early afternoon) by the same bus that serves Theodhóriana.

Mt. Tzoumérka is separated from the Kakardhítsa massif by a high, broad saddle locally known as Avtí (the ear), whose southern extension assumes the identity of the Kostelláta plateau. From the village of Melissourgí (one seven-bed inn, one *tavérna*) a trail crosses this upland, but a tramp from Melissourgí up to the Kostelláta *stánes* would take the better part of a day, even though the grade is the most moderate of the four paths up the mountain. You should be prepared to camp on the highlands in lieu of arriving in Theodhóriana, and a Melissourgí-Dhrossopiyí traverse (or vice versa) would almost certainly require a 1½-day trek.

From Theodhóriana, a good trail leads northeast to the village of Neráïdha, from which the ascent of Kakardhítsa on its more reasonable south face takes 6 hr. From the 2429-m summit, you will prefer to bear east for the 3- to 4-hr drop to the adjacent villages of Gardhíki and Athamanía, since return to Neráïdha is hardly possible in one day and camping conditions on the mountain are uncertain. Both villages have bus service to Tríkala; on the way you can alight to explore the reportedly delightful alpine country of east Píndhos, centered around the villages of Pertoúli, Eláti and Neráïdhohóri.

Access to Ágrafa from Theodhóriana is discussed in Hike 13.

Rating/time course: This is a tough, demanding trek best done—despite summer heat—during the long-day period on either side of the solstice; if you get lost, you'll definitely appreciate the extra light. The itinerary takes three to four-and-a-half days, depending on whether or not you make an afternoon start out of Anthohóri and camp above the village, and whether or not you walk the stretch between Prámanda and Ágnanda.

Supplies: Specialty or luxury items, plus enough staple meals for the first half of the trek, should be gotten in Ioánnina. Prámanda has a good grocery, but siesta hours may deprive you of its services. The Ágnanda store may do in a pinch.

Maps: ESY, Trikálon; although most of the hike falls within Ioánnina and Árta provinces, contour shadings are superior on this sheet. *Korfés* covers Kakardhítsa in issue 40, Peristéri in issue 41.

15 NORTH PÍNDHOS CIRCUIT

No discussion of hiking in Greece would be complete without the inclusion of this itinerary. Not only do several of the highest Greek summits lie along the way, but their foothills are largely unspoiled and the surrounding villages are conveniently spaced so that you may sleep in a bed most nights and avoid the necessity of lugging a tent or three days' worth of supplies most of the way. Most of the villages are also distinguished architecturally (those of Zagória), or they are home to Vlachs or *Sarakatsáni* (see "Ethnology of Minorities"). Progressive depopulation of the various communities, which began after the end of Turkish rule in 1913, has slowed or halted as a lumber industry has developed, government and EEC subsidies have trickled down to shepherds and (most importantly) Greek and foreign tourists have found their way into this surpassingly scenic corner of Greece.

The long, serrated crest of Mt. Gamíla (Týmfi) forms a barrier between the two main plant communities of the north Píndhos. A usually dense mixture of black pine, Balkan pine, and beech thrives in the fleisch and serpentine to the north and east of the palisades, but to the south and west, in central Zagória, only scrubby oaks and low shrubs grow, evidence of more porous limestone soil. Many edible fruits—wild plums, arbutus, brambles, strawberries—and fleetingly glimpsed animals complement the usual array of wildflowers. Water along the way is rarely a problem and, except in July and August, temperatures are moderate.

Getting to the trailhead: Once daily (not Sun), at roughly 4 P.M., there's bus service from Ioánnina to Monodhéndri, one of the more attractive and strikingly situated Zagorian villages. The bus takes about 1½ hr to cover the 37 km from Ioánnina, since it detours to the villages of Asprángeli, Káto and Áno Pedhiná and Elafótopos, giving you a willy-nilly tour of west Zagória. If you arrive on the afternoon bus, you can overnight at a single rooms establishment, (0653) 61-240, or in Vítsa, the village 3 km below, where Ioánnis Papahristos has a 15-bed inn. Both hamlets have *psistariés* with limited menus, but the Monodhéndhri establishment enjoys an incomparable ridgetop setting and the breakfasts served are more than adequate to chase away the dawn-bus blues and ready you for the stomp ahead. Allow some time to explore the two neighboring communities, which are protected national monuments.

Monodhéndhri to the Pápingo Villages via the Víkos gorge

From Áyios Athanásios, the newly restored main church of Monodhéndhri, leave the village to the north on a downhill dirt driveway; a small sign, *"Pros Víkon,"* points the way. The road ends at the uninhabited monastery of Ayía Paraskeví, which like Áyios Athanásios has recently been refurbished. This eyrie, constructed in the regional style, overlooks the south end of the gorge 500-odd m below; for the dedicated acrophile, a trail creeps 400 m beyond the cloister, along a hair-raisingly sheer plummet, to caves used in centuries past by hermits and persecuted Christians.

The trail into the gorge proper begins off the monastery driveway, about 300 m before the gate; you need to keep a sharp eye out for red dots marking its start, as recent bulldozing has buried many traces of the trailhead.

Initially the path descends steeply for 40 min into a tributary canyon of Víkos; surfaces are apt to be damp and slippery owing to a lack of morning sun, promoting intensive study of feet and footholds to the exclusion of all else. Near the end of the drop, the route winds out into daylight and onto the left (west) bank of the actual gorge. Red dots are plentiful from here on; as the first hour's hike ends, you touch bottom, having passed through a stand of beeches, rosemary bushes and cyclamens. The trail immediately rebounds up and to the left, but 15 min later it's temporarily

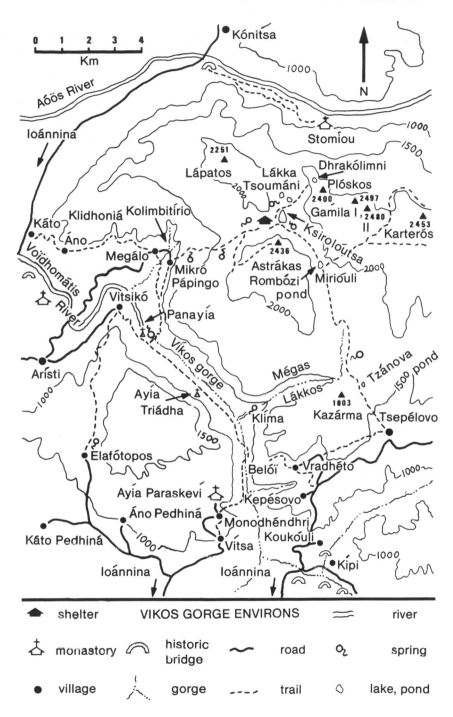

shelter   VIKOS GORGE ENVIRONS   river

monastery   historic bridge   road   spring

village   gorge   trail   lake, pond

obliterated by a rock slide; it resumes on a ledge 200 m to the north. After 30 min of level progress, the path plunges again and crosses the bed of Víkos on giant, red-blazed boulders. Once on the far bank, don't venture up onto the east slopes of the gorge, but stay within the watercourse. Some 200 m further an important arrow on another boulder points back across the wash to the left (west) side. Upon completing this strenuous, ankle-threatening crossing, you'll be about 2 hr into the hike with the worst behind you. Be cautious about your choice of foot- and handholds when boulder-hopping, since snakes love to bask here in the morning sun. Another 30-min hiking takes you to the top of a grassy hill with superb views up, down and across the gorge—an ideal lunch stop.

A few moments below this knoll the trail barely avoids another crossing, heading left up a rock face instead, where branches lashed together form a crude but serviceable ladder. Once past this tight spot the path threads through dense growths of maple, beech and chestnut, staying within 15 m of the canyon bed; resist any enticements to veer uphill during the next hour. Some 3 hr out of Monodhéndhri, the route wends through a dank, sunless zone where moss festoons branches, ferns carpet the forest floor and frogs hop across slimy rocks. Nearby a major side canyon, the Mégas Lákkos, intersects the Víkos gorge on its east side, and a gushing stream (Klíma) at the junction provides the only dependable fresh water en route. Past Mégas Lákkos, the path closely parallels the gorge bed, and after another 45 min past clumps of ivy, blackberries and currants, it reaches a small, grassy meadow and full sun once more. Cued by the timely red dot, leave the meadow at its far end. The fourth hour of hiking should see you pass, in rapid succession, a corral, the white *ikonostási* of Ayía Triádha on the right and a recessed well to the left. The previously listed shade-loving flora is here supplemented by rhododendron and assorted fungi. During the next hour's march the gorge gradually opens out, the landscape becomes more arid and pastures appear more frequently.

Just over 5 hr from Monodhéndri there is an important but obscure forking. Proceeding straight on the best-defined trail brings you close to the large *ksoklísi* of the Panayía on the right with an excellent paddock for camping, past which the increasingly well-demarcated path becomes an engineered *kalderími* that climbs up and left to the hamlet of Vitsikó (Víkos). However, this would put an abrupt end to any circuit through the Píndhos, so you're urged to locate the initially arduous but eventually more rewarding path that detours right a few hundred meters south of the church.

In the moments prior to charging uphill and left, the path traverses a large pasture bounded on the north by a stick fence and a rude hut built of the same material. Just past the fence, bear immediately right, clamber down into the bed of the gorge, and hunt for a blue "*Pros Pápingo*" sign on the opposite (east) bank of the gorge, some 30 m above the level of the watercourse. The marker is rusty and inconspicuous, but once you spot traces of the ruined masonry that formerly buttressed the bottom of this deteriorating trail, the sign is just to the right. It is in the vicinity of this sign that the Voïdhomátis River, which drains the north end of the gorge, has its source. However, the spot where the water erupts form the bed of Víkos is not a reliable landmark; early in the year it is somewhat to the right of the tiny blue sign, and as the summer progresses the springs bubble up further and further downstream (left of the sign) as the water table lowers. Upon locating the sign, note that the seven switchbacks painted on it are schematic, not literal. There are at least twice that number during the first 30 min along this initially overgrown and scree-laden path. In the next 30 min you aim above and to the right of individual and clustered, slightly phallic pinnacles. These wind- and water-eroded artifacts effectively mark the end of the Víkos gorge; the trail improves noticeably approaching them, at times even reacquiring a masoned border. Approximately 50 min above the gorge bottom, another, more obvious sign indicates a down-and-left turnoff to Megálo Pápingo.

Hillside Junction to Megálo Pápingo

The path, initially very faint and narrow, wades through some knee-high grass, next crosses the bottom of an enormous rock slide, and then rounds the corner formed by a rocky promontory. A brief descent, sheltered by an overhanging cliff face, follows, after which the trail skirts the edge of some small pastures. From the rock slide onward the route is intermittently marked with reddened paint-can lids kindly installed by Kóulis Hristodhóulos, proprietor of the Megálo Pápingo lodge. You'll continue slightly downhill from the pasture area through vegetation choking the damp, at times soggy, trail, until reaching a stream with a beautifully sculpted (and slick) rock bottom. This should occur about 45 min past the fork; it's another 20 uphill min to the Megálo Pápingo church, which makes for a total hike (assuming no straying from the route) of just under 2 hr from the bed of Víkos. This compares to just over 2 hr for the march up to Mikró Pápingo, so plan accordingly if darkness is approaching.

Hillside Junction to Mikró Pápingo

Beyond the sign, the right-hand bearing crosses the infamous rock slide, then angles up to a gap in the tree-tufted ridge in front of you. Once through this pass the trail levels out and widens, and progress toward the now-visible village of Mikró Pápingo is relatively uncomplicated provided you do not wander off onto one of many parallel livestock traces. About 2¼ hr above the canyon bottom, two springs on its outskirts mark your entrance to the village.

Elafótopos to Vitsikó (Bypass of Víkos gorge)

Those daunted by the prospect of an all-day-and-then-some trek through the problematical gorge might well consider this shortcut start for a Píndhos loop. While not in the same league scenically as the canyon, its trail surface is excellent and you do at least get to visit the north end of Víkos, as well as the source of the Voïdhomátis River.

The same early morning and late afternoon buses serving Vítsa and Monodhéndhri stop at Elafótopos, an underrated and well-preserved Zagorian village. Two adjacent *kafenéia* can whip up Spam and eggs on short notice, and one functions as a *psistariá* on summer evenings, but overnight housing may be impromptu at best.

To get underway, first find a peculiar church northeast of Elafótopos, set apart from the town at the base of a hillock covered with roofless walls and small, low stone huts. The church gate, inscribed "*Pazedros*" (presumably the family that donated it), opens onto a courtyard with a curious fountain; a hole in the wall "weeps" continuously, and beside it is a plunger-spigot that you have to work to fill canteens for the 2½-hr walk to the next water. The trail begins just to the left of the chapel, and passes, within a 10-min climb, a shaded wall fountain, a covered reservoir and a masonry-lined livestock wallow. This route is heavily used by drovers and at the outset consists of many parallel traces, but after a good 30 min the way becomes much more discrete, giving weedy hollows below and to the left a wide berth. There's a crest of sorts about 45 min above Elafótopos, and after a last backward look at the village rooftops, you proceed more or less levelly across consecutive, high, fly-infested meadows. Descending from these pastures, the path is a bit ambiguous; a little over 1 hr along, you must take two successive left forks in the once again well-grooved right-of-way. Soon you negotiate a brief series of switchbacks dipping down into a patch of Zagorian oaks. By the 2¼-hr mark the trail has settled down into a steady north-northeast bearing through stunted oaks and pumpkin-size boulders toward not-yet-visible Vitsikó. The route continues to drop gradually through another meadow, meeting a lone tree and an *ikonostási* on the ridge directly above Vitsikó, 2 ¾ hour out of Elafótopos. From this vantage the two Pápingo villages and the hoodoo spires above them are plain to see, as of course is Vitsikó (Víkos). It's perhaps another 20-min downhill scramble to the niche fountain at the outskirts of the village; this spring is also just opposite the top of the fancy *kalderími* leading down to the source of the Voïdhomátis River.

Vitsikó to Voïdhomátis Springs

To continue on to the two Pápingos, proceed down the handsome stair-trail (which soon reverts to a dirt surface) and begin looking for the junction near the source of the Voïdhomátis, just as you would if you'd hiked the entire gorge from the south. Recall that the source of the river is movable—the later in the year, the further downstream—and is not an infallible device for finding the blue sign and ruined buttressing described in "Monodhéndhri to the Pápingo villages via the Víkos gorge." Locate instead the ramshackle hut and fence, turn left across the pasture and proceed as in the section just mentioned.

The Voïdhomátis (the ox-eyed one) merits a further word. The springs that well up at the base of the northeast cliffs of Víkos are among the coldest in Greece, and reputedly a tonic for the digestion. Further downstream, near the bridge on the auto road to Pápingo, anglers try their luck in the river's mineral-green depths. (Tracing the Voïdhomátis' course on foot is next to impossible owing to sheer walls before the bridge—try a rubber raft.) Upstream from the springs, the boulder bed of Víkos is generally dry except for the vicinity of Mégas Lákkos; however, from April to June snowmelt from the cliffs overhead adds to the volume of the Voïdhomátis and slows hiking progress.

The Pápingo Villages

The two Pápingos (Mikró to the east, Megálo to the west, not vice versa as stated on many maps) are if anything more impressively situated than Monodhéndri or Vitsikó, and their superlative beauty has earned them as well the status of protected traditional communities. Mikró musters some 30 houses huddled at the base of the weird limestone bulwarks known locally as the 'Pýrgi' (towers). There's one inn with beds and meals, run by Kléarhos Stáras—(0653) 41-230—but no store; in an emergency you could camp on the lawn of Mikró's church which, with its water spigot hidden behind the apse and outhouses just to the north, is a well-appointed unofficial campsite. Megálo, cheerier and roughly twice the size of Mikró, sprawls on the opposite side of a tributary of the Voïdhomátis. It offers a unique, if not luxurious 17-bed lodge managed by the Hristodhoúlou family, which also runs the combination cafe/grill/store adjacent. Koúlis Hristodhoúlos speaks a bit of German and English, is quite knowledgeable about trails in the area and also rents out the keys to the alpine shelter on Astrákas saddle. Fee for these is approximately $20 for parties of two to nine persons; the keys may be returned either in Pápingo or Tsepélovo. Both the Pápingo lodge and the refuge may be booked on certain dates from May to September by British trekking companies, so it's a good idea to phone Koúlis, (0653) 41-238, in advance to reserve beds. If he is full, there is another inn run by Kalliópi Ránga (41-081) with seven beds.

While in the area, don't miss the *kolimbitírio* (natural swimming hole), roughly halfway between the two Pápingos and slowly becoming west Zagória's worst-kept secret. From Megálo's church, graced with an unusual hexagonal belfry, walk up the dirt *dhimósio* toward Mikró Pápingo; after about 10 min follow the blue sign ("*Kolimbitírio*") left off the road and up a stream. A 2-min walk brings you to a deep,

The "Pýrgi" (Towers) dwarf Mikró Pápingo

though not overly wide, pool whose natural level has been augmented by a skillfully constructed rock dam. The water is brisk and best-savored at midday.

If you need to finish your trekking in Pápingo, buses in and out tend to be elusive. Most (but not all) days of the week a coach leaves Ioánnina in midafternoon, arriving in Pápingo and returning immediately at around 5 P.M.; some days departure from Ioánnina takes place at about 9 A.M., arrival at Pápingo (with instant turnaround) by 11. In the past, Wed, Fri and Sun have been the days with the most unpredictable or absent service, and summer schedules vary from those of fall and spring, so check for current information at the Ioánnina KTEL station.

The bus passes through Arísti on its way down to the main Kónitsa-Ioánnina highway, so if you finish a walk in Vítsikó, you can easily walk down the 4-km dirt drive from that hamlet to Arísti. Though by no means as well-preserved as the two Pápingos, this is a pleasant village with lodging and an outstanding festival of scholarly lectures, music, dance and puppetry during August.

Pápingo to the Main Highway via Áno Klidhoniá

If you are marooned in Pápingo by uncooperative bus schedules, a reasonable trail leads west and down to the main Ioánnina-Kónitsa highway in considerably less time than it would take to hike down the auto road via Arísti. The route includes the now almost completely desolate village of Áno Klidhoniá, one of the remaining few in Zagória without automobile access.

Leave Pápingo by the street running west below the Hristodhoúlou cafe terrace. After passing a small *ksoklísi*, you dip into two consecutive stream beds; avoid little goat paths to the left when climbing out of the second creek gully. Thirty min beyond Pápingo, you'll come to an *ikónisma* of Áyios Trífonos on a ridge. Here bear right and uphill; the trail becomes untidy, then levels out and neatens and finally tilts downhill past a lone, five-meter plane tree which stands out in the scrubby vegetation. An hour's hiking should suffice to complete the descent into, and quick crossing of, the largest ravine met with en route. The path again deteriorates as it climbs out of this gully, on its way to an as-yet-unseen pass. Beyond this next saddle, reached 1½ hrs out of Pápingo, the trail surface again improves and Áno Klidhoniá comes into view. You can choose either the right or left of an impending fork. The left-hand alternative passes a substantial *ksoklísi* shaded by some tall oaks, but shortly after the path gives out completely and you cover the last 20 min cross-country to Áno Klidhoniá, a virtual ghost town of some 25 crumbling houses. It is not a terribly uplifting sight: most roofs are collapsed, and springs are dry or capped except for the inevitable *plátanos*-shaded one in the central *platía*. The village was fully exposed to the elements summer and winter, the climate congenial only for the vineyards still tended; perhaps three families remain living here.

From the *platía*, continue west, paralleling the phone lines of the lone subscriber toward a little chapel on the edge of the plateau ahead. Pass under the *ksoklísi* as you stumble upon a grand view over the valleys of both the Voïdhomátis and the Aóös rivers, which mingle some kilometers west of the Ioánnina-Kónitsa road which is also laid at your feet. Mt. Nemértska, in Albania, towers beyond the flood plain west of the road. From the *ksoklísi* you've an hour-plus descent, on a well-defined but often steep and uneven *kalderími*, to the thriving village of Káto Klidhoniá. Ioánnina lies 52 km to the south, Kónitsa 11 km to the north; the bus stops for both directions are within sight of the Mamadhákis gas station.

Pápingo to Astrákas Hut

The direct trail between Megálo and Mikró Pápingo has almost disappeared over the years; the only conspicuous remnant is the footbridge you espy in the deep canyon between the two villages, 400 m downstream from the *kolimbitírio*. Just less than 3 km of dirt road separates the villages, and without shortcuts this will take 45 min. Once in Mikró Pápingo, make your way to a large, blue placard at a three-way fork in its cobbled streets. The sign, pointing up and left (northeast), gives these fairly accurate estimates to popular destinations:

Refuge	3 hr	Provatína cave	3 ½ hr
Dhrakólimni	4 hr	Gamíla peak	5 ½ hr

Ten min beyond the junction the shrine of Áyios Pantelímon surmounts an alcove with a couple of jets of water; the requisite plane tree shades a flat, grassy festival terrace which could serve as an emergency campsite. Just past Áyios Pantelímon a sign ("*Katafýgio 2³⁰˝*") points to the right of a fork. After a 40-min hike through a mixed forest of birch, oak and two kinds of juniper, you arrive at Antálki spring. Some goat-eroded switchbacks above the fountain are perhaps the hardest portion of the demanding climb to Astrákas col. Beyond Antálki the forest thins out gradually to the treeline at about 1800 m; keep your eyes peeled for hand-sized chunks of jet scattered on the path. The weak Tráfos spring lies 1 hr above Antálki; the featureless ridge of Lápatos (2251 m) extends to the north, while the infinitely more compelling "Towers" of Pápingo loom in the opposite direction. Tucked between certain of the tower summits is the mouth of the Provatína cave, 405 m deep and the second longest straight-drop sinkhole in the world; only a *cenote* in Yucatán beats it. The nearby Épous Cave is more than 447 m deep but its drop occurs in several stages.

Some 20 min above Tráfos spring, ignore for now the red arrows pointing right to the Astrákas peak trail and instead proceed straight toward the refuge. The strong spring of Kroúna burbles 15 min beyond the junction, and 20 min further, a total of 2¾ hr above Mikró Pápingo, the EOS hut perches strategically on the saddle joining Lápatos and Astrákas. If you haven't rented the keys in Pápingo, you can still camp on the flat stone porch; when the hut is occupied by Greek or foreign trekking parties, you can often beg a spare bunk—if you don't mind the enforced sociability.

Megálo Pápingo has finally hove into view to the west, but Astrákas to the south, Gamíla to the east and the Lákka Tsoumáni valley with the seasonal pond of Ksiroloútsa at the base of the two peaks are much more immediate. A small conical rise on a green ridge beyond the Tsoumáni *stáni* marks the direction of Dhrakólimni, the famous round, luminous lake of the Gamíla range.

Astrákas Col to Dhrakólimni of Gamíla

Make the 25-min descent to the north end of Ksiroloútsa pond; the trail ends there within a stone's throw of the huts and corrals of the *stáni* itself. A giant bog below and north of the shepherds' colony literally crawls with hundreds of newts, frogs and insects; several springs, arranged in an arc, feed the marsh. The closest to the trail's end trickles from the base of Lápatos, west of the *stáni*; the easternmost springs, at the foot of the grassy ridge 400 m on the other side of the bog, mark the start of the easiest ascent to Dhrakólimni. These two adjacent springs, probably the lake's drainage, discolor the turf about 200 m to the right of a furrow in the hillside. Atop the ridge you'll notice five stone cairns which seem decidedly barrellike from a distance; these constructions form a rough ring around the sparkling gem of Dhrakólimni, scooped out like an oversize baptismal font at the edge of a 600-m drop into the Aóös River basin. You can tease your stomach by peering over this abrupt edge, reached about 1¾ hr after quitting the EOS shelter. Below the watershed a profusion of firs and deciduous trees extends to the Aóös and beyond to the base of Mt. Smólikas, 10 km away.

Dhrakólimni supports a large population of amphibians; still the water appears potable, but there are no level campsites on the nearby slopes. The lake also reflects two peaks, arranged like sawteeth to the southeast: Ploskos (2400 m), and Gamíla (2497 m), the highest point in Zagória. If you wish to climb the latter, the only nontechnical route up it involves a side trip off the Astrákas-Tsepélovo trail (see below).

Astrákas Col to Astrákas Peak

Backtrack toward Pápingo approximately 20 min until reaching the fork below Kroúna spring. Turn left and follow the marked side trail for about 45 min, then leave it where red arrows deviate across a rocky area. From a small green hollow just beyond the rocks, follow a hogback another 30 min up to the main ridge line, marked by a row of barrelish cairns. The apparent ridge turns out to be the edge of a vast hummocky upland which culminates, some distance to the left, in Astrákas peak. Bear left and follow random red arrows toward the highest visible cairn, which is still a bit below the summit. The 50-min climb is rather uneventful until you approach another line of cairns perched on the brink of Astrákas, from which you can contemplate the abysmal drop-off to Lákka Tsoumáni. The hiking surface here is Zagória roof shingles in the raw: acres of reef limestone beds which are easy going when dry but treacherous if wet. From the pinnacle of Astrákas ridge (2436 m), Dhrakólimni is just visible. In clear weather the Albanian Píndhos and Smólikas close off the horizon, while Gamíla (the camel) hunches just across the way. The climb from the fork below Kroúna should take 2 hr, the return 30 min less.

Astrákas Col to Tsepélovo

Begin the descent from the hut toward Lákka Tsoumáni just as you would to reach Dhrakólimni, but in this case make a sharp, right, downhill turn (marked by a red blaze) barely 10 min below the shelter. After crossing the usually dry, turfy south end of the pond at the base of Astrákas, start climbing the lowest point in the slope ahead. If you glance over your shoulder, you'll see a line of red blazes intended for hikers coming from the opposite direction. About 50 m beyond the edge of the level turf, there's a variable spring (the Romióvryssi) which moves from year to year and seasonally but generally pours out from under some of the many rocks studding this hillside. The trail is just visible without blazes, being conspicuous as worn places in the turf between the numerous boulders; 30 min past the hut, the grade lessens and red blazes cease. Astrákas looms just to the right, while Gamíla slopes more gently up on the left (northeast). Traces on the hill to the right merge into a natural path along the west side of a gully—natural in the sense that the flat, seemingly man-made surface is eroded from limestone strata. One hr along, after traversing the multi-branched upper reach of this gully, you come to the large Rombózi pond, buttressed by a stone dam and set squarely in the middle of the high plateau linking Astrákas and Gamíla; ahead and behind are broad vistas of the territory covered and yet to come. To the left lie some hillocks which are convenient start points for side trips up Gamíla. Seen from these slight elevations, Plóskos presents its profile of banded rock, while the next peak to the right, Gamíla I (2497 m), appears lower than Gamíla II (2480 m), to which it's joined by a saddle, because it's further away. At the south end of the pond is a little "notch"—slip through this to descend a natural staircase down to the next *stáni*, Mirióuli. The canine welcoming committee will probably be out in force, so steer clear of the buildings until the last possible moment, when you'll have to pass within a few meters of them. Here is another gap and a second, even more distinct natural stairway which drops over limestone badlands. After a few hops and jumps between sheer gullies on either side, the countryside flattens out a bit and the trail continues just under the shadow of a low limestone bluff to the right. The descending gully on your left begins to drop off more and more sharply, and about 1 hr past the saddle pond, your path plunges left and within 15 min has switchbacked down to the bottom of a dry wash and the lowest point on the route. From the ravine bed climb about 20 min until meeting, on the left, a very weak spring oozing out from a tiny, maidenhair-garnished crevice protected by an overhanging rock. This spot, shaded until past midday by high cliffs to the east, is an excellent lunch stop and place to survey the beginnings of the Mégas Lákkos in front of you. Trails down this largest tributary of the Víkos gorge are said to exist, ending eventually at the Klíma springs at its mouth.

From the maidenhair spring the path begins climbing in earnest, rounding a corner with the best views of the Lákkos and then switchbacking up the mountainside before you to a small pass some 30 min above the spring. Mégas Lákkos recedes from view, and after a few moments clambering up and down through a patch of dirt, you meet another pond, that of Tzánova. Skirt it and proceed until, about 45 min past the grotto, you come out on a crest overlooking the ravine leading down to Tsepélovo. Do not bear right onto an obvious trail leading past Kazárma hill toward Vradhéto, but plunge doggedly straight downhill; it's a quite nasty 1¼ hr down scree slopes to Tsepélovo. Sometimes there's a clear right-of-way, sometimes not; initially you can use many parallel tracks in a grassy hillside, but eventually you'll find yourself at the top of a juniper-studded rock pile flanked by two concavities. Begin zigzagging carefully down this to the canyon bed, where a legitimate jeep track picks up on the Tsepélovo side. At the top of this last grade, a lone fir tree stands guard over a *ksoklísi*—just before, turn right onto the cobbly way that skirts the edge of the ravine as it heads downstream into town. You should arrive about 5 hr after leaving Astrákas hut.

In Tsepélovo Alékos Goúris, phone (0653) 81-214, has an inn, a store and prepares simple suppers. He speaks good English (learned via the BBC, he claims) and is the resident expert on the nearby mountains. When trek groups fill his lodge you can stay at the Ksenónas Aléxandhros, run by his cousin Faní Tsiavalia. Tsepélovo itself will be the last central Zagorian village on your route and suffers in no way from comparison with Monodhéndhri, Elafótopos or Pápingo. It has become something of a regional center since the atrophy of surrounding settlements, boasting a secondary school and a stable population of about 600. Plans are afoot to run a road up the mountain, one ridge over from the trail just described, to the highest *stáni* to facilitate transfer of dairy products to market. But until then, Tsepélovo should remain a sleepy community whose quiet is disturbed only by the mutterings of summer thunder and the tolling of the hours from the church clock tower. Two buses run daily to and from Ioánnina; this frequency is halved on Sun or festivals.

Side Trip to the Kípi Bridges, Return via Vradhéto

From Tsepélovo, you might break the loop for an all-day visit to the famous bridges below the village of Kípi—they are the best surviving examples of a craft that flourished throughout northern Greece during Ottoman rule. Until very recently the tiny hamlet of Vradhéto was accessible only via an ingenious *kalderími* of successive hairpin turns hacked out of a steep cliff.

The first bridge, a graceful single-arch structure, is right next to the modern asphalt Ioánnina-Tsepélovo road, 12 km below the latter. Pass under the span and walk up the ravine for 20 min until you reach the second wonder, a unique three-chambered bridge just below the village of Kípi. Kípi, interesting in its own right, is located at the merging of the main ravine with another, over which there is yet a third bridge, carrying a now badly overgrown trail up to Koukoúli. A km or so east of Kípi lurks still a fourth span over the major stream bed.

From Kípi return to the main road and walk, hitch or bus up it 4½ km, past Kepésovo, to a junction marked *"Vradhéto 6 km."* Bear left onto a path about 30 m down this vehicular side road. The initial 15 min involves a descent to the bottom of a canyon, where you cross a tiny bridge; from there it's 45 min up to Vradhéto, 30 min of this along the above mentioned *kalderími*. This snaky, paved-and-bannistered stair-path, which skillfully conquers a palisade, is one of the premier engineering feats of Zagória. In the last 15 min the grade moderates and the path dims. Vradhéto is tiny—one *kafenéio*, seven winter inhabitants—and distinguished mainly by its unusual church; the belfry is short and rectangular, contrary to the slender, tall hexagons favored elsewhere in Zagória. A 40-min walk beyond Vradhéto will take you to the site Beloï, an overlook of the Víkos gorge's south end. A livestock track heading first west and then north out of the hamlet ends within 15 min, after which you should bear left (west) across pastureland, being careful to not lose altitude in numerous small gullies.

To return to Tsepélovo from Vradhéto, walk east about 1 hr on the auto road serving the latter village. At the point where the road bears straight down and right (south) toward the main highway, turn left onto a trail heading east. After another 30 min, you'll see a rocky crag ahead crowned by a cross and an isolated belfry, associated with a tin-roofed *ksoklísi* at the base of the knob. By the chapel, the trail veers left briefly, then plunges right along the opposite side of a gully; in this vicinity it was once a well-maintained *kalderími* but is now much crumbled. Tsepélovo, a difficult village to photograph except from this perspective, comes into view, and the path, deteriorating by the minute, begins manouvering down the slope toward a walnut grove near the floor of the same ravine in which ends the Astrákas-Tsepélovo trail. You enter Tsepélovo about 200 m downgully from that route, in the vicinity of house No. 86 (should you wish to walk *to* Vradhéto).

Top, left: Goatherd and flock; Top, right: Leader of the flock (photo by Ann Cleeland); River of goats on the triple-arched bridge at Kipi

Sarakatsános Goatherd at the Triple Bridge

A Sarakatsános shepherd drives his flock across the famous triple-arched bridge below Kípi. He spends the four warmest months of the year in Zagória, rather than six as in years past, and winters near the Thesprotian village of Mazarakiá, south of Igoumenítsa. He and his fellow shepherds live there in permanent houses on land to which they have title; their former existence in *barángas* or *konákia* (reed huts) is fast dying out. In recent years many Sarakatsani have begun to cultivate olives and other crops in the lowlands from Messolóngi to the Albanian border, to tide them over the winter and spring.

Other details of Sarakatsan transhumancy have changed in the last 30 years. Most Sarakatsani appear on the voter registration rolls only in their winter villages and have no political rights in Zagória as in the past. Their summer pastures change yearly, since many villages now auction off grazing rights, for goats only, to the various bidding flock-owners. A family with 500 goats could expect to pay about 60,000 *dhrachmés* or $500 for four months' grazing rights on the commons of a summer village. This substantial sum must be defrayed by income from cheese-making, the occasional butchered animal and winter crops.

In some Zagorian communities Sarakatsáni have managed to preserve their presence on the voter rolls and thus their political rights, and have to pay only a per-animal (sheep or goat) fee for the period May to October. A flock of 500 would cost 8 *dhrachmés* x 500 head x 5 months, or 20,000 *dhrachmés*, which is a far cry from the 40,000 to 60,000 commanded by those villages auctioning off their commons.

The triple bridge is a marvel because the stones support each other with no cement, just a bit of mortar. One or two villages were responsible for the bridge that served as their lifeline to Ioánnina in the old days. Hence, the triple span was built and maintained by Koukoúli an hour north, and not by Kípi, just a shout away, which sponsored a bridge still further upstream. The large single span by the auto road was the responsibility of Vradhéto and Kepésovo. A blue placard near the bridge informs passers-by that the triple-arched Kaloyeriko or Plakidha bridge was dedicated 15 July 1866 at the expense of the brothers Alex and Andreas Plakidha, (and) restored in 1912 by Evyenios Plakidha in memory of his father Andreas. If this is accurate, the present stonework is relatively new, possibly the last great Zagorian civic works project before the end of the Turkish era.

Tsepélovo to Vovoússa via Mórfas Ridge

The next leg of the loop begins, unavoidably, with a vehicle ride. Three days a week (usually Mon, Wed, Fri, but these vary with the year and season—check in Ioánnina) a midmorning bus plies between Tsepélovo and Vrissohóri, passing the desired trailhead 17 km above Tsepélovo at Yiftókambos. Yiftókambos, "the hobo's field," is so named after a crafty sheep-stealing vagrant who according to local legend escaped from his Turkish jailers at this site. Today the plot is devoted to beekeeping and potatoes and is the high point on the road continuing down to Vrissohóri in the Aóös valley. The amiable Bárba (uncle) Yiórgo runs a lone cafe, but stock is limited to soft drinks, cookies and sardines in addition to the coffee.

Barely 100 m north of Bárba Yiórgo's, a green sign points to the right of a fork,

Amazing cliff-scaling path to Vradhéto, Zagória

reading "*Dhasiki Odhos—Paparouna—9 km.*" The narrow road climbs gently through fine stands of pine for the first 25 min; traffic is light, never amounting to more than one or two logging trucks per morning. Avoid all subsequent forks right! From the top of the first rise there's a steady descent into the valley containing Láista village; its buildings are visible below and to your left as you wind through the trees. The imposing bulk of Gamíla to the west slowly recedes, and some 45 min past Bárba Yiórgo's you get your first comprehensive look at Mórfas, straight ahead to the southeast. The lumber track straightens and levels out, and soon Láista slips behind you to the left. About 1½ hr above Yiftókambos, take a fork right to "*Tsoukan.*" The first water en route is on the right about 15 min beyond the junction. The grade stiffens and, some 2 hr past Yiftókambos, small grassy meadows to the right adorn the flanks of 1727-m Tzouka hill, each with little trickles of potable water. Despite the description of the right-of-way as a lumber track, it should not be despised. The alpine scenery is commendable, and you can gorge yourself on berries four months of the year; wild raspberries from late spring to early summer, strawberries in midsummer and blackberries thereafter. About 2½ hr past Yiftókambos, a strong spring sprays into a roadslide cleft and immediately after, you come to a wood cottage with a cement veranda. Unfortunately, the interior has been thoroughly vandalized, but it makes a satisfactory lunch stop or emergency shelter.

Right past the hut you must make a right turn uphill; the left option leads down to Láista. In the next 45 min you cross the heads of two streams which drain down through a meadow extending to the hut, and then you snake about toward Mórfas watershed. Some distance below the crest you reach a *stáni* by a spring, occupied in summer by a friendly family from Ioánnina. This seems more of a poor man's summer home than a typical sheepfold; sheep there are in plenty, but well-dressed women, proper furniture, crockery and silverware as well. According to them, an elderly Englishman returns periodically to the vicinity to search for a small fortune in gold sovereigns buried hastily during the Second World War—unfortunately, senility threatens to befuddle already hazy recollection of where the cache was secreted. (Ípiros abounds in such tales, and Ioánnina metal-detector vendors do a brisk trade.)

Mórfas crest is not as close as it seems—the track curves northeast for another 30 min past piles of cut beech wood to the actual watershed. To the north-northeast and northwest, Vassilítsa and Smólikas rear their respective heads; to the east you've a panorama over part of the Vália Kálda ("warm valley" in Latinate Vlach), partial source of the Aóös. The *dhasikó*, which has carried you faithfully the 3¾ hr from Yiftókambos, expires at last. A path, just visible in the high weeds on the slope to your left, takes off in the general direction of a prominent, white, vane-style altimeter marking Mórfas' highest point, 1785-m Koukouroútzos summit. Keep this well to your right, as your barely perceptible trail follows a gradual grade, skirting a line of trees at the top of a bare, scooped-out zone to the left (west) of the altimeter. On the far side of this eroded basin, some 400 m west of the marker, a path resumes, heading north-northwest through beech thickets. You can reduce chances of getting lost here by keeping just to the right of the ridge once on the trail; don't make the mistake of plunging into the dense foliage on either side. After 1000 m the path arrives at the head of a broad, eroded gully running down to a visible jeep track; descend this wash as best you can, although with some perseverance you may find a worn trail on the right (south) side. Assuming no involuntary detours, it's about 1 hr from the end of the forest road until you tumble out of the badlands onto the new jeep track.

Mt. Avgó looms dead ahead and its distinctive egglike summit helps you fix a bearing on Vovoússa, out of sight at its base. A small summer farm huddles just to the right along the newly met track; you should turn left. At about the 5-hr mark in the day's march, you pass a small puddle-spring to the right of the road, just next to the turnoff down to a second *stáni*. Its tenants can fetch you more water from another, well-concealed spring. The *stáni* is also the start of the final descent to Vovoússa along an attractive, bona fide trail.

Begin by dropping below the *stáni*, a bit to the left of a line of trees tufting a slight rise. Just at the point where ferns begin to overrun the lowest margin of the pasture, bear left. A trail should be distinct by now; the locals occasionally tie blue plastic strips or bags to shrubs on either side of the route. Twenty min after crossing the foot of the pasture, take a left fork on a scalped, exposed hillside; the right-hand bearing is more scenic but longer and harder to follow. The left route crosses a plummeting ridge to its north side, joining the Láista-Vovoússa *dhimósio* after 40 min. Walk east (right) 10 min down this road until meeting an *ikónisma*, and immediately after a red "K1" on a rock just as Vouvoússa comes into sight. The "K1" is your cue to plunge down a clear path through a ravine to the right of the road. This shortcut reintersects the road barely 70 m from the debouchment of the long, scenic route (for details on that, see Reverse North Pindhos Loop, "Vovoússa to Mórtas." The descent from Mórfas via the short route should take no more than 80 min.

Within a few minutes of the sixth hour of hiking, the thick mud of the *dhimósio* is transformed into the cobble of the last street in Vovoússa, the only Píndhos village built directly on the Aóös. Low enough not to be completely snowed in during winter, it enjoys a modicum of prosperity by virtue of the sawmill a few kilometers upstream. You enter town over a fine medieval bridge, though it's not nearly so large as those at Kípi or Kónitsa. Many foreign visitors refer to these graceful spans as Turkish, at which most locals bristle and correct that label to *Romaíki* (medieval Greek). Foundation plaques (such as the one at Kípi) tend to support the theory of Greek construction, as does the plain fact that the Zagorian bridges differ sharply in design from the famous Ottoman bridges of Anatolia and Yugoslavia.

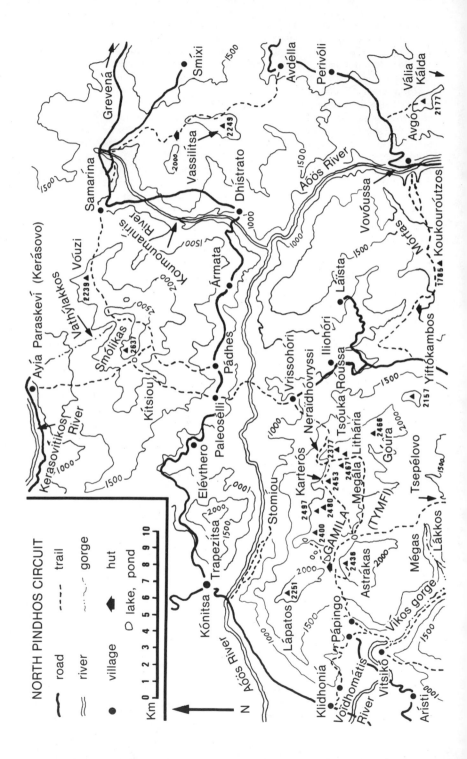

Unhappily, its bridge is essentially the full inventory of Vovoússa's architectural charms, since most of the village was burnt by the Germans in 1944 in reprisal for resistance activities. Only one house was left intact, and it's now maintained, with its interior trappings, as an informal museum. Vovoússa is also the last Zagorian, and first Koutsovlach village on your loop; most inhabitants are bilingual in Greek and *Romaniká*, and there are still commercial, cultural and sentimental ties with Romania, including partial funding of standard Romanian classes for the young. Many Vovoussans have emigrated to America, especially Texas and Georgia, but in summer the population swells as long-lost relations return to visit their roots. There are several eateries but really only one place to stay: Tó Oráío Perivóli, a giant, rambling hotel overhanging the river.

If you've had enough walking, there are five or six buses weekly (at 6:30 A.M.) to Ioánnina—a horrendous 4-hr ride that will probably leave you wishing you'd kept trekking. Better to spend a half-day enjoying the sumer pleasures of the Aóös valley; the river, although green and murky, makes for surprisingly warm swimming. Afterward, snack on wild plums (*korómila*)—they're best when yellow, insipid at the red stage. It is also possible to walk along the river some distance downstream from Vovoússa.

Vovoússa to Perivóli via Mt. Avgó

A tedious, 3-hr uphill walk on the *dhimósio* leads from Vovoússa to the saddle marking the boundary between Ioánnina province and Grevená *nomós*. Get a taxi or hitch to this point, the start for any ascent up Mt. Avgó. (Rumors of a direct trail from Vovoússa have yet to be substantiated.) If you end up having to walk, know that there's only one spring along the road, roughly halfway. From the pass, an unwanted track leads down in the direction of Dhístrato; the main way continues to Perivóli; and a prominent bulldozer track charges hard right and uphill. Follow this for 15 min as it snakes around and up before fading away. Next follow the ridge line—in fact a main spur of Avgó—through heavily grazed meadows toward a jagged outcrop that greatly resembles a ruined fort. Many parallel livestock traces and some red dots herald the beginning of a proper path at the base of this optical illusion. Just past the "rock fort," the now-distinct trail plunges through a young beech thicket to emerge on a pebbly hillside; Avgó summit, crowned by its shelter, hunkers down before you. Once off this slippery slope, avoid the boggy meadow on your left, but keep a moderate course to the right through a venerable stand of trees; occasional red bark blazes keep you from straying too far uphill and right. After crossing a couple of ditches you must charge cross-country up a steep, trailless, 200-m slope; once on top you're rewarded with an opportunity to rest at a beautiful, flat, round meadow where strewn logs offer some shelter. At the southwest corner of the meadow, where a gap affords a view of the Aóös valley, a tiny spring bubbles out of a sandy pothole hidden from view by overhanging boulders With a full pack, you'll need just over 1 hr to hike from the saddle crossroads to here—it's suggested you park your luggage now for the next stage.

From the meadow the ascent of Avgó that best balances ease with speed is one that starts straight up through the gnarled trees on the left, almost but not quite on the hogback that drops steeply off to the north. If you begin too far to the right, you must contend with a gully, or worse, an initially easy grade that soon sharpens to over 45 degrees. When 30 min above the meadow, you should cross a long, skinny pasture like a bowling alley leading up to the base of Avgó proper, which closeup resembles more the tip of an American football than an egg (*avgo*). An obvious trail winds its way up to the 2177-m summit, which seems much higher than it really is and is quite dramatic because it's completely isolated from any other mountain. The peak's refuge, apparently never finished, has collapsed under the ministrations of vandals and the elements. It would never have performed its office very well, as it's an ideal target for lightning, and two Greek youths were killed here during a summer storm in 1982. If big clouds are brewing, you're advised to run, not walk, down to the meadow or beyond. In fair weather the peak is an excellent observatory for reflecting on points of your trek already covered and yet to come. Vovoússa is miniaturized at your feet, while the giant escarpment of Gamíla hovers in the west. The Aóös separates the latter from the twin "horns" of Smólikas, second highest Greek peak, to the northwest. Vassilítsa seems from here a perfect pyramid, dominating Avdélla village to the north, which in contrast to Perivóli is visible. Minor ridges in Grevená province dissolve into the haze to the east and northeast, while to the south the densely forested Vália Kálda harbors some of the headwaters of the Aóös.

From the province-border crossroads it's about 1 hr down to Perivóli via the *dhimósio*—scraggly trails in the bare creek valley southeast of the road are hardly worth following. This second Romanic-Vlach village on your route was, like Vovoússa, completely razed during the last war. Unlike the Vovoussans, the Perivolítes practice true transhumance, moving lock, stock and barrel down to Velestíno, Tírnavos and other towns on the Thessalian plain during the winter. The lumber trucks cease rolling for the year and one guard keeps a lonely vigil over acres of snowed-under vacation chalets, for such is the post-war architecture of Perivóli. In summer a half-dozen *psistariés* satisfy the most carniverous appetite in the enormous *platía*, and a handful of stores make this an excellent provision stop, but as in Vovoússa there's only one place to stay. The Hotel Perdhíki, phone (0462) 24-110, is the large, three-story lodge on a knoll at the west edge of town. Buses run to Grevená, which is of little solace if you've stored things in Ioánnina—better to backtrack to Vovoússa.

Perivóli to Mt. Vassilítsa via Avdélla

The old footpath between Perivóli and Avdélla was overgrown or bulldozed years ago, and the best counsel is to take the 1¼-hr stretch of nearly level road connecting the two villages. It's not all that unpleasant and the forest is as dense and cool as any met with thus far. Avdélla, small with no hotel, has much the same history and life cycle as Perivóli and is the perfect spot for a midmorning coffee before tackling the flank of Vassilítsa, a red-dirt mountain with a healthy admixture of oaks interspersed among the usual beeches.

Leave the Avdélla *platía* by the winding cement drive that climbs west through the village; continue to its highest point, passing the last few houses and a knolltop church. In the flat, grassy meadow beyond the church, find a small cement-faced spring at the edge of a large stand of bracken—here the trail up Vassilítsa begins. After 10 min through the ferns, you intersect a recent lumber road; walk uphill on it for about 20 m to where the trail resumes on the far side. A 45-min steady climb on a fairly distinct, lightly shaded path brings you to another fern-speckled meadow in a cul-de-sac just below Vassilítsa's lowest spur. A year-round creek, the last water for another hour-plus, flows just to the right of the trail, which soon fizzles out, necessitating a 20-min confrontation with a steep, goat-eroded hill. Keep a deep gully well to your right and aim for three massive oaks atop the ridge in front of you; just to the left of these trees the legitimate path picks up again—don't stray too far beyond the crest into the valley behind. The trail is clearly grooved into the turf, with the exception of a dubious stretch on a skittery, eroded grade. About 20 min along the ridge you pass a goat pen, and past it the way becomes ambiguous. Stick closely to the ridge crest as it begins to slowly curve left toward the primary summit of Vassilítsa; with a sharp eye or binoculars you can just make out the bent, three-meter altimeter (2249 m). Soon the ridge you're on is oriented almost at a right angle to the apparent long axis of Vassilítsa, though the trail is intermittent at best. Treeline is imminent, and upon seeing the last twisted black pines, some 2¼ hr above Avdélla, you begin to veer to the right (north) flank of the ridge away from these specimens, toward an inconspicuous but helpful spring. You're likely to meet shepherds in this area, who will be more than happy to elaborate fine nuances of the route or help you find the spring (otherwise betrayed only by a lushness of turf and the sun-glint of sardine cans used as cups).

From the spring it's easy to hook up with remnants of the once-ample direct trail between Avdélla and Samarína; you can see the initially straight, level right-of-way against the mountainside from a hundred meters off. After traversing a couple of gulches and topping a rise, you must tackle a sizable stream canyon; cross this just above treeline. The path is nonexistent from the rise onward, but all is well as long as you don't climb unnecessarily or dip down into the impenetrable forests above Smíxi hamlet. The path revives on the opposite bank, among a cluster of pines; continue rounding the mountain, without changing altitude, for some 10 min before dropping gradually down to a delightful meadow with another spring. This is perhaps the most appealing site on Vassilítsa. Above it, two ridges merge; to the right (northwest) of the junction, and below the peak, nestles a small, potable lake. The side trip up takes 20 min from the meadow, itself 3 hr above Avdélla.

Near this second and final spring of Vassilítsa, the path resurges again at the base of the ridge leading up to the lakelet. Head slightly downhill through the black pines, parallel to the ridge, and once among the trees all duplicate, misleading traces disappear in favor of the primary trail. As you slip over this ridge, about 400 m along, you should see a few pylons of the Vassilítsa ski lift visible on the mountainside before you. Descend further, heading virtually due west, pass a dry lake, and then keep an even altitude on goat tracks. Don't veer right onto a jeep track that curves by at this point, but stay slightly left as the trail re-emerges again. Now a surface of tree roots and badly disrupted cobbles leads through a dense beech grove, and some 45 min past the last spring you'll reach in quick succession a long, narrow pasture and two *stánes*. The shelter is now visible, straight ahead; it's most practical to leave the trail and use jeep tracks for the final 30 min over open meadowland to the hut.

There is also a new hotel being built in this area and in fact two refuges, all some 400 m away from the base of the ski lift strung up the northwest face of Vassilítsa. One is generally locked and intended for winter use; the other is public, permanently open and has 12 comfortable bunks. Most nights you will share it with a local shepherd or the fire lookout; water is available from a tap by the front porch. Camping is not an attractive alternative, as level ground is at a premium and Vassilítsa is much frequented by bears. Count on 6 hr in motion from Perivóli to the shelter(s), which with the ski-lift control kiosk sit on a broad saddle. To the north and east the Píndhos foothills fall away in low parallel ridges, and the little gap to the south allows a glimpse of Gamíla and the Aóös basin from yet another angle. Dhístrato village lies out of sight down the stream valley draining off the gap; a jeep track leads to it.

Vassilítsa to Samarína

Begin on the uphill jeep track winding west behind the two shelters; this soon rounds a bend for a first overlook of Samarína in the distance. Next drop down to a chaos of mud, weeds and bulldozer patterns, from where you veer right into the handsome stand of beech slightly downhill. It's tempting to proceed straight onto open pastures which appear to extend uninterruptedly to Samarína, but they are in fact deeply cleft by the Koumoumanírls River valley. The correct track heads steadily north under the beeches until meeting the Samarína-Smíxi *dhimósio* just under 1 hr from the shelters; a white *ikonostási* marks the junction. Downhill to the west, a stock trough provides drinking water and also marks the resumption of the old trade route to Samarína, which though fragmented is still preferable to the tedious *dhimósio*. The narrow dirt track leading away from the trough switchbacks twice as it descends and abruptly meets a section of old *kalderími*. You can follow this or the more comfortable surface of the newer drovers' track that runs in rough tandem with the cobbles across a small stream, past a tiny *stáni*, and then over a second, larger ravine, where the *kalderími* expires for good. The caravan track continues another few hundred meters before meeting a lumber road; it resumes on the far side but carries on only 600 m further before colliding with a tributary of the Koumoumaníris and the Samarína-Smíxi road. You're forced to head up the road a km or two, but at the next crest, the old path again emerges a few paces to your left. It parallels power lines before disappearing forever at the junction marked "*Smíxi 6*," where the Smíxi-Samarína road and the Grevená-Samarína *dhimósio* link up for the final 45-min downhill march into town.

An acquaintance with little tolerance for road-tramping notes that if you bear left and downhill early enough—before intersecting the lumber road—you can safely arrive in Samarína going cross-country. If you try this, be sure not to angle too far down toward the Koumoumaníris River, a good 250 m below Samarína. In any event, this is an easy leg of the circuit, the downhill distance from the *ikónisma* to Samarína being coverable in 3 hr or less.

Samarína claims to be the highest (ca. 1450 m) village in Greece and excluding Métsovo is the largest Koutsovlach community in the country. Like Perivóli and Avdélla, it's occupied only from mid-May to mid-October, but many inhabitants overwinter in Makedhonian Árgos Orestiádha as well as Thessalía. The town suffered the same pyromaniac vengeance at the hands of the Wehrmacht as did the other Vlach settlements, so there remains little to see aside from the church (spared) at the base of the village. Inside, an intricately carved ikon screen and lurid frescoes of the Last Judgment (a favorite didactic subject of medieval muralists) compete for your attention. Outside, a husky black pine has planted itself, and flourishes, in the roof of the apse! However, Samarína, even more than Perivóli or Vovoússa, is principally a social phenomenon; on any given summer evening up to 4,000 people stroll and frolic in the central square and the half-dozen *tavérnes* giving on to it. The local pastoral economy produces fine cheese (though, strangely, not yogurt) and any cut of grilled meat imaginable. The village also boasts a legitimate OTE office capable of making good connections internationally and locally. There are supposedly three places to stay in Samarína: the big *ksenónas* high above town, some rooms just above the *tavérna* on the east side of the *platía*, and the Hotel Kiparíssi, way down the hill near the old church; but the first two are booked months in advance until mid-September, at which time the *Ksenónas* closes. If bad weather or contingencies do not allow you to complete the upcoming portion of the loop, the most sensible strategy is to take an early (6 A.M.) taxi to Dhístrato, 17 km down the Koumoumaníris in Ioánnina province, and from there the 7 A.M. bus to Kónitsa.

Over Mt. Smólikas from Samarína

Mt. Smólikas (2637 m), Greece's second highest summit, is also one of the most imposing and has lately become relatively popular with Greeks and foreigners alike. Tucked in the heart of its lunar, limestone-and-serpentine grandeur are two lakes: one easily accessible and favored by campers, the other isolated and frequented only by shepherds watering their flocks. The range is quite massive—a good 70 km^2 of territory above 1700 m—and is home to numbers of small wildlife: field mice, hares, chamois, raptorial birds, plus the occasional bear or wolf. The two-day trek across is the longest, and one of the most difficult, on the nine- to eleven-day loop but is also among the most rewarding in terms of scenery, campsites and chances for side trips.

Starting in Samarína, find the aforementioned *ksenónas*, a solid hewn-stone structure west of town. Head up the slope just past the big soccer field behind the hotel, keeping to the left of a flat-roofed water-pumping station which protrudes bunkerlike from the ground. Just below the edge of the forest, join a prominent livestock trace looping around and up into the outermost trees, on one of which is a red metal arrow. For the first hour the path winds steeply up through a thick stand of young black pines until these begin to thin out in anticipation of a turfy meadow with a strong spring almost right on the trail. During the next 30 min the grade lessens, and as most trees are left behind, Smólikas' metamorphic character becomes evident from the glistening serpentine surfaces all around. A small rivulet in the rocks at the 1½-hr mark makes a good rest stop; beyond this the route flattens for 30 min as you traverse a windswept meadow just to the south of Mt. Voúzi, whose altimeter (2239 m) is clearly visible. In the lee of this peak the wind relents and some massive gnarled specimens of black pine have taken root. The temporary respite ends at treeline, 2¼ hr out of Samarína, where the trail begins climbing sharply up the ridge line from another exposed pasture. As you switchback laboriously up this bare hogback, a green tarn pops into view on the left, just east of Smólikas' secondary peak which is also now in sight. At first this body of water seems just a pond, but as you mount higher it shows itself to be a lake of almost a hectare. There's no side trail to it, though, and it would be a difficult though by no means impossible scramble there. Soon the lake disappears from view as you devote all available energy to a steep portion of path penetrating a "notch" in the rocks ahead. Suddenly, just 3 hr above Samarína, you're onto a curious tableland, offering the best views yet over the lake.

Continuing, the trail seems to have disappeared in a boneyard of evenly spaced, football-size rocks, but a kindly hand has actually arranged some of these stones into a line of cairns leading up and right. Red blazes still surface now and then, but as you reach the top of this tilted plateau, yellow markings supersede the red convention. The point of color change over is also the watershed between the eastern, Samarína side of the range and the northwestern flank facing Ayía Paraskeví. But topographical details cannot do justice to the awesome and forbidding overlook of the entire spine of the Smólikas range unfurling east to west up to the primary peak (2637 m). This ridge drops off precipitously to the north into the nasty, trailless Vathýlakkos chasm where pines struggle for a toehold; Ayía Paraskeví lies visible to the northwest.

As yellow blazes commence, the route drops steeply; here is the most dangerous footing on the mountain, so don't mix gaping and walking. Ten min below the pass, a tiny trickle oozes out of the rocks—barely an emergency supply for thirsty humans, but enough for wild animals whom you may see sipping if you approach quietly. The next downhill 20 min remains slow going but happily for your knees the path levels out again and then, climbing a bit, makes up for lost altitude in the next 15 min, eventually ending up just below a saddle-pass in the east-west Smólikas crest. The north-facing cirque here often retains a sizable patch of year-round snow, but cleaner and more reliable water is found in a tiny spring in the center of this bleak zone. It's welled in by rocks and is about a half-meter across—if you don't spot it right off continue a bit toward the pass and look back. Camping here is conceivable, but even in the absence of the usual howling winds the northern exposure makes the place frigid.

The pass, which you clear a little over 4 hr out of Samarína, is the highest point on the route. A few minutes beyond there's some possibility of losing the way when a ravine opens up in the tundra ahead of you. Keep to its right, following yellow blazes; the overly inviting, cairned trail on the left leads to Ármata. From the saddle it's just under 1 hr down to the main *stáni* on the south flank of Smólikas, with the entire time spent at eyeball level with the full length of Gamíla across the Aoös valley. After leaving the barren ravine behind, the path becomes indistinct as it marches across flat turf to an obvious "notch" in the terrain just ahead. From this gap there's a healthy drop into the first pines below treeline; shortly after entering the forest even yellow

Dhrakólimni of Smólikas at sunset

blazes become a chore to find, but just descend slowly to the right and cross the stream that flows down the valley draining from Smólikas peak, plainly visible to the northwest. Corrals and huts of the *stáni* cluster atop the opposite bank of the creek; yellow blazes return some 50 m upstream from it, but it's not a bad idea to stop here and check your bearings.

This *mándhra* (synonymous with *stáni*) is fairly typical of most such in the Píndhos. The two shepherds have their wives and children in Samarína from May to October and manage to visit them every four to five days during that season. When the first snow flies the flocks are herded under their own power all the way to Thessalía, but the livestock is brought back in spring by the more prosaic means of pickup trucks. Technology has similarly invaded the daily life of the *stáni*; the shepherds are more likely to while away long evenings listening to portable radios than playing the *floyéras* (end-blown flutes) or *klarína* (clarinets) of yore.

Leaving the sheepfold, the path curls left for the first time since the watershed, describing a gentle arc along the top of a lush meadow before turning abruptly right down another grassy patch. After one last glimpse of the Gamíla range the route dips down through more trees and heads west-northwest up one of the major drainages on Smólikas, south flank. A half hour below the *stáni*, a brook gushing over the trail is a tributary of the sizable river 5 min ahead.

Side Trip to Dhrakólimni of Smólikas

Memorize the location of the river crossing and leave the marked trail, electing instead to follow the stream up to a bare saddle at the top of the valley. The rocky surface leaves something to be desired but the steady grade is initially gentle, and it's difficult to get lost since topography and running water dictate your footsteps. Resist temptations to crawl up on the grassy banks, because about 1 hr after leaving the path the valley closes off first to the left, then to the right. Here you're forced to leave the impossibly narrowed canyon, charging up a steep, grass-slick hillside on the left toward a relatively flat plateau on top. The lake itself is right behind the low point of a second saddle some 400 m to the left of the ridge originally used for orienting when you left the marked route. Not more than 1 ½ hr after starting the detour, and some 7 ½ hr beyond Samarína, you top this ridge overlooking the pristine, heart-shaped

Dhrakólimni of Smólikas, the rival in every respect of the more famous Dhrakólimni of Gamíla across the Aóös basin.

There's better-than-average camping on the gradual slopes of the natural depression here which, once submerged below the lake's surface, plunge swiftly down to uncertain depths. Smólikas' Dhrakólimni (dragon lake) is so named, as is Gamíla's, because according to legend, the guardian spirit dwells at the bottom in the form of a dragon. From the top of the slopes enclosing the lake you can take in alpine sunsets during which the adjacent peak and canyons below are bathed in a vivid light that dies away to an orange streak in the Albanian west. At dusk the wind dies (fortunately, since this is one of the coldest bivouacs in the Píndhos), and the only ripples on the lake surface are those made by surfacing salamanders (dragon spawn?). After dark the only sound, until late summer, is that of the snowmelt cascading from the base of Smólikas peak to the northeast. In the morning, climb a nearby ridge (all ca. 2200 m) to glimpse the wall of Gamíla glowing in the sunrise. By noon the salamanders have retired to the dragon's realm, and in midsummer a hasty swim in the frigid, clear waters could be recommended, but remember that the lake is the sole convenient water source here and you will have probably been preceded by sheep and dogs (if not dragons), so boil or purify water for drinking.

Speaking of sheep and dogs, there is a *stáni* downhill and north from the lake which is also the start of the trail down to Ayía Paraskeví. The tenants are friendly and if you choose to descend from Dhrakólimni in the early morning in this direction you may have company. It's just under 3 hr, through fine forests and beginning in the rivulet-laced meadow below the *mándhra*, to Ayía Paraskeví (Kerásovo). (The dual name dates from the Metaxas era when Vlach and Slavic place names—most of the latter ended in "ovo"—were suppressed as un-Hellenic manifestations of those minorities.) The descent will now be reversed in some detail.

Ayía Paraskeví to Dhrakólimni

Ayía Paraskeví is a friendly village with a handful of *tavérnes* and a new inn set on a bluff overlooking the Kerasovítikos River. There's one daily bus from Kónitsa, at 2:30 P.M., which returns the next morning at 6:30.

From the top of the community, take the path leading right off the road just past the chapel of Ayía Paraskeví and an *exóhiko kéndro* (rural restaurant). If you again bear right at an immediate fork you'll be rewarded with red dots. After crossing the last fields of Kerásovo and a damp meadow, the trail broaches a pine forest about 45 min along. It's another 30-min march to a stream crossing the trail, and within 15 more min you should pass the spring feeding this stream. Just under 2 hr out of the village, the path veers abruptly right across a grassy slope, forsaking what appears to be the main track in favor of a narrower right-of-way. Within 20 min of this turning a mixed forest of beech, fir and pine begins; the trail shifts gradually right to follow a watered canyon upstream toward a bare ridge just ahead. You reach treeline after slightly less than a 3-hr climb, and just beyond a potable stream licks the base of the last meadow before the lake, which is tucked out of sight among the bare spurs above you. The Kerasovotes' *stáni* huddles by a final spring almost exactly 3 hr above the village. From the sheep pens you've a 20-min trailless clamber up to the lake, which is just to the right (southwest) of the long gully draining off the low point in the saddle abutting Smólikas on its south face.

The Ayía Paraskeví trail is shorter, easier and arguably more attractive than the route beginning or ending in Pádhes (see "Dhrakólimni to Pádhes below). A moderately difficult ascent of Smólikas summit can be accomplished by leaving the red-dotted route at treeline where the stream borders the meadow, going up the gradual grade of the stream canyon and then following the northwest-to-southeast ridge up to the 2637-m altimeter.

Other Routes up Smólikas Summit

The most direct ascent of the peak begins from Dhrakólimni, but it's also the most difficult—you're tackling a 500-m elevation change over about 400 m in horizontal distance. Just take off on the slope to the right of the lake's overflow outlet (the point of the "heart") and sink your teeth into it for 1 hr. The least strenuous route up to the peak, from where there are magnificent views over Mt. Grámmos and Albania to the west and all Ípiros and the Píndhos to the south, begins at the *stáni* of the Samarinotes and basically involves following the creek passing it to its source. In all cases, moving around the peak with a full pack is inadvisable, so most trekkers will content themselves with a short, sharp climb.

Dhrakólimni to Pádhes

After finishing an hour-plus easterly descent from the lake, it's easy to miss the turnoff from the riverbed back onto the southbound yellow-blazed trail, even if you've been by the previous day. If the river does a quick S-bend and plummets suddenly, back up about 400 m. Once comfortably underway, the trail actually follows the dipping river gorge fairly closely. Some 15 min after quitting the riverbed, take an important left fork marked by a prominent blaze. A few minutes later a spring dampens the trail, which takes this as a signal to veer away from the canyon on the left and descend to an enormous meadow on a wide but slick surface. The clearing is quite suitable for camping, although the insects agree, especially in midsummer. Potable water is supplied by a nearby rivulet. The path remains unusually broad for a Greek mountain thoroughfare, but beyond the meadow, it drops sharply to a capped well that fortunately has an overflow tap for filling canteens. A few meters past the well you twist across a small, dry ravine; soon after, the dense forest that cloaks this flank of Smólikas is more drastically interrupted by a deeply eroded badland of serpentine scree which you're obliged to traverse. Twenty min below the big pasture, you'll pass an *ikonostási* on the right and start the final descent, on a surface slippery with pine droppings, to Pádhes. Keep a lookout for luridly colored red and yellow mushrooms in this area. An orchard at the foot of a giant outcropping announces your return to civilization; the track curls around this and enters Pádhes, passing a niche fountain and a ruined stone hut, about 3 hr after setting out from Dhrakólimni.

Pádhes is a sleepy, though not necessarily dull village in which all tourist activity centers around the combination innkeeper/restauranteur/grocer Vassílis Kourtínos, in "downtown Pádhes" near the bus stop, church, phone booth and beer cooler. You can camp gratis in his backyard if you're not enthusiastic about his spartan indoor accommodations. There's a bus to Kónitsa via Paleosélli and Elévthero each morning at 8:00 (some variation Sun and holidays).

So ends a taxing, though rewarding circuit of several hundred square kilometers of fine Greek alpine lands. Voluptuaries may retire to the hot springs at Amárandos, 35 km north of Kónitsa by bus (one a day, at 2 P.M.). The section below and Hikes 16 and 17 detail the merits of a backward north Píndhos loop, abbreviating it with shortcuts out of Vrissohóri and a day trip in the Aóös River gorge.

Rating/time course: Whether you plan on the full nine- to eleven-day loop described or opt for the high points only (see shortcut under Hike 16), this is a strenuous (though not torturous) tramp that presupposes good physical condition and ability to cope with boulder-strewn stream beds, torrential cloudbursts, menacing dogs, slippery slopes and the like.

Seasonal limitations: Snow is a factor to contend with on the peaks until the end of May. Summer fruits partly compensate for midaltitude flies and crowded village accommodations. The *protovróhia* (first rains) arrive with watch-setting regularity the last week of September, so don't plan your trek after the equinox. Early June and early September are the best times.

Supplies: Two day's worth of meals should be purchased at the outset in Ioánnina. Pápingo's range of groceries is spotty; Tsepélovo's is better, but Vovoússa's is nonexistent. Perivóli and Samarína have much the best *bakálika* en route. Ayía Paraskeví is on par with Pápingo, with Pádhes being more basic.

Maps: *Korfés*, issues 55 (Víkos and west Gamíla), 56 (Tsóuka Roússa to Mórfas), 57 (Smólikas range), 58 (Vassilítsa) and 59 (Avgó).

REVERSE NORTH PÍNDHOS LOOP

The counterclockwise circuit described above is superior in terms of panoramas, grades and ease of orientation, but since you may have a compelling reason to reverse the itinerary, I include brief instructions for finding trailheads and junctions going clockwise.

Pádhes to Samarína

A bus leaves Kónitsa for Pádhes daily in midafternoon (ca. 3 P.M.); except in summer you'll make little headway up Smólikas before dark. Starting on the narrow lane just to the left of the Kourtinou lodge, proceed up stone steps and bear left at house No. 83. Follow the jeep track to the footpath taking off to the left, cross a stream and pass the ruined cottage. Approximately 45 min uphill, you'll reach the *ikónisma* on a hillock left of the trail; 200 m beyond is a critical right fork. The left-hand turning, actually broader, leads only to some logging and grazing tracts. Allow a generous 4 hr from Pádhes up to Dhrakólimni.

Ascending from the Samarinote *mándhra*, most yellow blazes face you. Once out of the last trees curve gently right along the base of Smólikas' primary crest to the pass. A 2½-hr stretch should bring you from the *stáni* to where blazes change to red. The contours of the high, rock-studded plateau just beyond help determine where to dip down into the "notch"; keep the green tarn below and right, perpendicular to your course. From here on the route presents no special problems; total walking time from the *stáni* to Samarína will amount to 6 hr or slightly less.

Samarína to Vassilítsa

Coming uphill it's almost impossible to find the point at which the old trail sneaks away from the Samarína-Smíxi road; your best strategy is to hitch or taxi up to the *ikonostási*. If you can't find a ride, it's a tedious 2 ½-hr uproad walk from Samarína. From the *ikónisma* allow 1 ¼ hr up to the public shelter; on a long summer day you could conceivably reach Avdélla over the balance of the afternoon, but best plan this as a short trekking day.

Vassilítsa to Avdélla and Perivóli

As in coming from the opposite direction, the main danger lies in going too low on the flank of the mountain and becoming entangled in the impenetrable beech forests to the northeast. Landmarks are much the same up to the goat pen on the ridge above Avdélla; shortly thereafter the fern-speckled valley to the left, leading down to Avdélla, is also marked by a corral or two not evident to hikers approaching from below. Again avoid falling off toward the deep valley between your ridge and Vassilítsa proper; by various convolutions of topography this is on the Dhístrato side of the watershed. Count on a 5-hr trek downhill off Vassilítsa rather than the 6 quoted for uphill.

Perivóli to Vovoússa

Leave Perivóli on the high road to the southeast, subsequently taking the left, right and left of forks as met. After your excursion on Mt. Avgó, bear down and southwest at the saddle crossroads. After 45 min, pass a right fork toward Baïtáni Falls on the Aóös; 30 min further lies the only roadside fountain on this stretch. During the last 20 min of the 2-plus-hr descent to Vovoússa, the *dhimósio* switchbacks wildly and a few paths shortcut the hairpin bends.

Vovóussa to Mórfas

Leave town by the old stone bridge and follow the cobbled street uphill to the last, highest house. Leave the now-dirt road (start of the *dhimósio* to Láïsta) and find an overgrown path on the hillside taking off from the corral of the last house, above and to the left. Do not pass the damp gully where the *dhimósio* veers sharply right. Once on the path, keep to the left at every option and avoid various fence rails spanning the gulch on the right. After 25 min of uphill progress, the dense woods thin out to a grassy meadow; the trail renews more distinctly at the upper left corner of this expanse. Now the route, heading west, keeps a bit to the left of the crest of this ridge that runs perpendicular to Mórfas. The next hour is one of the most pleasant on the clockwise circuit, as you traipse through alternating forest and meadow, with views south over a wooded vale. Tortoises are particularly common here; the reptiles seem to congregate near numerous muddy seeps by the trail but the first potable, running water comes from an all-year brook reached 1 hr above Vovóussa.

The path charges from the stream bed up a dusty hill and then promptly dissipates among the ferns and pines up the slope, often being nothing more than worn spots where livestock have rampaged through the bushes. Keep slightly left until, near the summit of the ridge, you reach a clearing at whose far end the trail resumes on a west-southwest bearing; you shouldn't be without a clear trail for more than 25 min. After another 30-min of well-defined, gently graded trail through steadily thinning forest, you arrive at the base of the *stáni*; turn right, meet the ridge-top track and proceed to the foot of the dry wash described above in "Tsepélovo to Vovoússa via Mórfas Ridge." Allow a bit over 2 hr for the climb from Vovóussa to the *stáni*.

Tsepélovo to Astrákas Saddle

Exit Tsepélovo to the west, passing the clock tower and the post office, and turn right at the edge of the ravine. Follow the cobbled street up to the lone fir tree and small chapel, where you descend the now-dirt track into the watercourse. Head up the hillside before you on the initially clear trail, and then negotiate the purgatorial terrain described in the last paragraphs of "Astrákas Col to Tsepélovo" above, being sure to stay on the west bank of the gully and to not lose altitude. Just shy of 2 hr out of Tsepélovo, pass first a barrel cairn on the right at the top of the slope, and then link up with the trail coming in on the left—proceed straight ahead on it to the small Tzánova pond. After the descent past Mégas Lákkos and the grotto spring, it's easy, 3 hr along, to miss a switchback on the ascent to Mirioúli *stáni* and get stranded on a dead-end meadow. Shortly beyond the *stáni* itself lies the high point of the trail, the gap overlooking the giant Rombózi pond in the uplands between Astrákas to the west and Gamíla (2497 m) to the northeast. Within another hour you should be picking your way down the boulder-studded slope above Ksiroloútsa, with the Astráka shelter in plain view before you. If you overshoot this natural stairway, you may not be able to leave the high plateau, as it drops off sharply into Ksiroloútsa at most other points. The uphill trek from Tsepélovo to Astrákas takes 6-plus hr, as opposed to the 5 required for the downhill.

16   SHORTCUTS OUT OF VRISSOHÓRI

You may not have the time or inclination to complete the entire north Píndhos loop in either direction, but may be intrigued by the descriptions of Gamíla and Smólikas.

Conveniently, there exist two routes starting in Vrissohóri, one across the Aóös toward Smólikas, the other back up the wooded northeast face of Gamíla toward Astrákas.

Getting to the trailhead: After finishing an Astrákas-Tsepélovo trek, take the same thrice-weekly bus that you would to Yiftókambos, except to the end of the line in Vrissohóri, a village pleasantly nestled among beech forests facing north across the Aóös. The peaks of Gamíla loom to the southwest, Tsoúka Róussa (2377 m) being especially prominent. Vrissohóri has a rather skeletal combination cafe/store/grill, and reports of a bed or two for late arrivals.

Vrissohóri to Paleosélli

Leave the village, heading north, on the road passing the cafe on the left and the old church to the right. Continue straight until the track curves back on itself; a prominent mule track takes off from this bend on a direct bearing for Paleosélli, visible ahead. The mule track soon dwindles to a well-defined trail which roughly follows power lines downhill and passes an unused medieval bridge and a stream some 20 min below Vrissohóri; this is your last potable water en route. In the next 10 min the path traverses a succession of weedy pastures. Slightly over 1 hr along, you cross the Aóös on a post-war cement-and-stone bridge; finally there's the partly shaded, 1½-hr ascent to Paleosélli. Here there are two *kafeneía* with the usual offerings of canned goods and *mezédhes* (appetizers), and rooms (0655-22-040); Padhes is still a 3-km road walk east. In sum this is a worthwhile, but seasonally hot and dusty hike of 2½ hr; Paleosélli to Vrissohóri is slightly lengthier and more difficult.

It's worth noting that you need not go to Pádhes to climb Smólikas; from Paleosélli a partly marked path leads within 4 hr to its Dhrakólimni. After a 1-hr climb you'll come to the Toúrkou spring and the *ksoklísi* of Ayía Paraskeví. Thirty min above this is the Kitsiou *stáni*, and next a more difficult 30 min on the fainter trail to Náne spring just below which is a new wooden shelter (keys and info in Paleosélli). Between Náne and Dhrakólimni lies one more *stáni*, approximately 1½ hr beyond the former.

Vrissohóri to Lákka Tsoumáni, via Tsoúka Roússa-Karterós Pass

This attractive but challenging trail is the preferred method of climbing Gamíla directly after Smólikas or of returning to Pápingo from central and east Zagória without entirely repeating the Tsepélovo-Astrákas trail.

Leave Vrissohóri's main *platía* going southwest on a path-street which first descends to a bridge, a spring and a sign inscribed "*Pros Ayía Paraskeví.*" After leaving behind the last metal-roofed structures of the village, the trail begins to climb, passing after 10 min the *ksoklísi* of Ayía Paraskeví. A few moments later, a torrent splashes over the path, and shortly after that you take a right fork leading to a minibadlands of schist slopes where the trail is faint. Just under 45 min out of Vrissohóri, the erosion zone stops and you cross a forest road; there's a spring on the roadside a few paces right. One hr along, bear right at the base of a series of terraces that seem out of place in the midst of thick woods; ¼ hr beyond the terraces, you'll top a saddle from which the needle of Tsoúka Róussa is seen overhead and slightly to the left. Once over this little pass there follows 45 min of enchanting, level progress through the forests that line the base of the Gamíla escarpment to your left. Two hr above Vrissohóri you'll reach the Neraïdhóvryssi spring gushing out from under a rock overhang flecked with damp-loving flora—this is the last dependable water source for the next 7 to 8 hr! In the ¼ hr past the spring, vegetation thins enough to allow glimpses north to Paleosélli village and the cone of Smólikas behind it. Thirty min after the fountain, the route rounds the plunging tip of a ridge and begins an earnest ascent up a broad couloir (Goustéra) toward the *stáni* dubbed Loútsa, but more properly known as Kátsanos, 3½ hr from the village.

From the shepherds' huts the trail, such as remains of it, bears left—do not continue straight toward the base of the sheer walls of Karterós peak. Your goal, reached after a 1-hr stiff climb, is a false summit marked by three cairns off to the left. The worst of the ascent over, you find yourself at the margin of a high cirque ringed by jagged peaks. Tsoúka Roússa lies off to the left, the crenelations of Karterós considerably to the right and the peaks of Megála Lithária stand athwart the rear of this high, gloomy moor used to graze cattle. The low spot in the alpine wall ahead is the principal pass between Tsoúka Roússa and Karterós, reached 1½ hr beyond Loútsa via a faint trail etched in the scree above the cirque. There appear to be two saddles, but the left-hand one only looks over the sheer drop into the blind valley hemmed in by Tsoúka Roússa and Góura peaks; the right-hand gap gives out on a much more manageable descent into a high plateau.

From the col plunge straight down for 30 min, then begin bearing right to follow livestock trails and gullies heading west. You should see some caves in the mountainside to your right; do not continue straight south from the pass for too long, as this will only put you in Skamnélli. At 90 min below Megála Lithária, you'll see on the left the end of a dirt road coming up from Skamnélli (possibly the one built for the benefit of local shepherds with EEC funds). Ahead, in the flank of a very long spur extending down from Karterós, is a prominent lone cave just large enough to shelter one or two persons.

From the cave do not head back north along the spur toward Karterós, but continue behind it toward the west for a little over 1 hr to reach the potholed eastern slopes of the downs between Astrákas and Tsepélovo. Once over the top of the bluff in which the cave is lodged, Astrákas peak to the west-northwest will guide you. After sighting this height you can anticipate 3 more hr of cross-country march through the limestone dells, which become grassier and flatter as you approach the main Tsepélovo-Astrákas trail in the vicinity of the Rombózi pond.

The various legs of this transect of Gamíla add up to 11 hr of hiking, no mean feat and possible as a unit only in midsummer. Start from Vrissohóri in the early morning so as to reach Lákka Tsoumáni by dark, or failing that spend the night at or near the Loútsa *stáni*.

Another, hard-to-find pass exists, threading between Karterós peak and Gamíla II, to the left (south) of a ridge named Liméria Kleftón (the bandits' lair). To reach this saddle, bear hard right (west) just above Kátsanos/Loútsa rather than heading straight toward the obvious gap between Karterós and Tsoúka Roússa. After Liméria Kleftón, the route descends slightly to Kopánes cirque—where you can camp, getting water from a year-round snowbank—before tackling the 2350-m pass. This route to Astrákas is a good 3 hr shorter than the other, but possession of *Korfés* issue 55 is essential to locate it.

17 AÓÖS RIVER GORGE

A little downstream from the bridge noted on the Vrissohóri-Paleosélli shortcut (see Hike 16), the Aóös (pronounced ah-ohs) River squeezes between the sheer bases of Mts. Gamíla and Trapezítsa in a tight gorge about 10 km long. The upstream 4 km are inaccessible to all but the occasional river rafter, but the lower 6 are served by good paths leading from the Kónitsa-Ioánnina road up to the clifftop monastery of Stomíou which overlooks the narrows. The Aóös gorge is part of the same national park that includes the Víkos canyon, Mégas Lákkos, the environs of Pápingo, and Astrákas; the dense forests clinging to the precipitous palisades above the river furnish safe habitats for various endangered species, among them lynx, roe deer, chamois and raptorial birds. Unhappily, poaching, aggravated by proximity to

Looking up the Aóös river gorge through the old medieval bridge

Kónitsa and Ioánnina, is a problem and we can only hope that a dam slated for construction somewhere between Vovóussa and Stomíou falls well outside the park boundaries.

Route directions: From the Kónitsa bus stand, walk south and downhill on the main road through town, leaving the central business district behind. The vast flood plain of the Aóös extends to the right, and an old residential district with several ruined Turkish-era buildings huddles on the left at the base of Mt. Trapezítsa. Cut through this neighborhood rather than winding along the main highway, and presently you'll see the famous medieval stone bridge, the largest such in Greece, spanning the Aóös where it exits from the confines of the ravine. You can cross the river either on the old span (pedestrians only) or on the more modern wood-and-iron cart bridge just downstream. Once on the south bank, a bumpy dirt and cobble road begins running parallel to the river, which is quite popular with Greek weekenders and small boys of all ages who fish, wade or play on inner tubes in the river here. Fifteen min upstream from the two bridges, watch for a wood cross on the right side of the track marking the beginning of the old, roller-coaster *kalderími* up to Stomíou. It's 1½ hr on a variable surface to the monastery, with one small but vigorous waterfall about 20 min below it for filling canteens. The trail, despite not being terribly efficient about where it's going, is replete with views of the palisades of Mt. Trapezítsa opposite and deserves a try, at least outbound if not round-trip.

Stomíou is visible almost from the moment you've turned off the riverbank track; upon arrival it proves to be improbably perched on a high but fertile bluff surrounded on three sides by air and the river. Until recently many young Greeks and foreigners were wont to tote groceries up here and squat for days or weeks on end, but in 1983 the monastery was renovated in preparation for reoccupation by monks of a recognized order and overnighting is likely to be at least regulated, if not forbidden, in the future. Until the remodeling, Stomíou—dating from 1774—was of architectural interest as one of the few monasteries in Ípiros to escape war damage or corrugated metal roofing; it remains to be seen whether or not the refurbishers have respected at least its exterior appearance. In any event, you can still camp just outside the monastery's front gate in the flat space newly planted with fruit trees. The little path that runs along the wire fence to the southeast leads within 5 min to a shady grove and a good spring. From there the trail continues, within 4 hr, up to either Kopánes cirque or Lákka Tsoumáni, but the way is choked by some of the densest vegetation in Greece and you are certain to get lost without a guide.

To return to the mouth of the gorge, retrace your steps 15 min downhill, passing the little waterfall, but instead of veering left onto the old path, continue right on the wide downhill track to the Aóös. At the base of this grade you find some of the more secluded swimming spots on the river. Besides proximity to the Aóös there's not a whole lot to recommend what could be called the "waterworks" track, which is disrupted by mains supplying Kónitsa, cement retaining walls and weirs as opposed to the nice old stairways and flagstones on the upper route. It is, however, quicker, being only about 70 min total from Stomíou down to the bridges. There is a spot, some 35 min below the monastery, where the two trails come within 5 m of each other—lots of red dots and arrows flash back and forth—and since the downstream end of the high path is in less than ideal condition, the best combination of speed and aesthetics would be to pick your way along the riverbank for the first 45 min beyond the bridges and then switch over to the more interesting *kalderími* for part of the final 30 min up to the monastery.

Rating/time course: The foregoing should provide sufficient enticement to schedule an easy 3- to 4-hr day hike in the Aóös ravine, which includes time for a dip in the river's deeper spots (watch for submerged rocks in the opaque greenish water). Readers who arrive in Kónitsa on a morning bus after finishing a north Píndhos loop will find an afternoon at the Aóös "icing on the cake."

Seasonal note: In late summer and early fall, wild cherry and *kóumara* (arbutus) ripen and shower the walker with ripe fruit. Edible arbutus tastes something like a ripe strawberry and is eaten when strawberry red. Of course the river is warmest for swimming from July through September.

18 MT. GRÁMMOS

The melancholia of this high, bare mountain is magnified by its historical and political associations. It marks the frontier with mysterious Albania and was the last stronghold of the leftist *andártes* (rebels) from 1947 to 1949. Appropriately for a

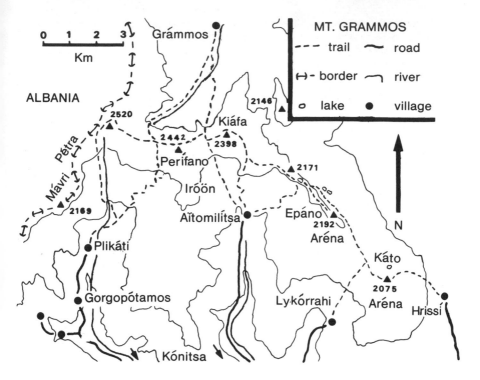

border range, Grámmos as seen from the south forms a sheer, even-topped wall separating Ípiros from Makedhonía as well as *Shqiperia* (Albania); it also has the dubious distinction of having been the first testing ground for napalm during the Greek civil war. Only recently has the turf on the highest ridges regenerated, and any climber will stumble upon cartridge cases and other rusty paraphernalia among the crumbling rebel bunkers near the summit.

Despite its grim past a foot tour of Grámmos makes a rewarding all-day hike, especially in early summer when wildflowers outnumber flies, rather than later in the season when the ratio is reversed. Not the least of the peak's attractions is the opportunity to set one foot (but not two, if you're prudent) into Albania or at least get a good look at that shadowy realm.

Getting to the trailhead: Buses run from Kónitsa to Plikáti at 2 P.M. daily except Sun. If you descend Smólikas via Ayía Paraskeví, 10 km from the Kónitsa-Plikáti road, and plan to climb Grámmos next, bear this in mind. From Ioánnina there are at least seven coaches daily to Kónitsa, but only three or four arrive by 2 P.M. If you miss this departure for the villages of Pirsóyanni, Vóurbiani, Gorgopótamos and Plikáti, it's a simple matter to get a bus or a lift to the turnoff below Pirsóyanni, but you'll stand a good chance of walking most of the 20 km from the junction to Plikáti.

Plikáti itself is a friendly village of mostly old stone houses and traditionally attired womenfolk. There are two inexpensive inns on the main *platía* and rooms at the Agápi store. Agápi also fixes simple meals on short notice; more substantial fare, e.g. a post-hike chicken dinner, can be ordered in advance. This is the last village on the Greek side of the Mávri Pétra ridge, and a remote, end-of-the-world feeling is accentuated by panoramas over a river valley (the Gorgopótamos) of Asiatic grandeur, closed off at its head by the bald barrier of Grámmos that glows orange in the twilight. Each year an Albanian or two still slips across the nearby frontier, a considerable reduction from the voluminous clandestine movement in both directions during the 1950s, but there is little palpable Iron Curtain paranoia in the village. A handful of army conscripts loll about in a state of bored indiscipline, and the bush telegraph suffices to inform the gendarmerie that yet another foreigner has come to make a curious pilgrimage up the mountain.

Route directions: Proceed north out of Plikáti on the principal jeep track; 10 to 15 min out of the village, just after crossing a small brook, bear left onto a narrower path. After another 5 min take a second left onto a *kalderími* that threads through well-irrigated fields and orchards; the cobbles are in fact often ankle-deep in water. Mávri Pétra ridge, extending from peak 2169 to 2431, roughly parallels the way to your left. Thirty min beyond Plikáti, cross from the left (west) bank of the river to the east side and begin climbing steadily through lightly wooded meadows. The assymetrical summit of Grámmos—formerly called Tsóuka Pétsik, but known by the pedestrian moniker of "2520"—looms before you. About 1¼ hr beyond the river crossing, the trail steepens markedly, begins switchbacking up a grassy hillside devoid of trees and reaches a beech grove watered by a powerful spring at its high end. A little over 2 hr above Plikáti, you'll come to a *stáni*, after which the trail deteriorates markedly. Angle up the ridge behind the shepherds' colony, passing a cairn a bit above and to the right, and then bear left (north) toward the primary Grámmos watershed. The secondary peak of Perífano (2442) and the *Iróön* (a large, white memorial, presumably to the central government troops fallen in battle here) are clearly visible to the right. Twenty min above the *stáni* a spring feeds a sizable pond, and 15 min higher the last water on the Plikáti side of Grámmos surfaces as a trickle in a sheltered spot of turf that makes a good lunch halt. A bit further, roughly 3 hr from Plikáti, is the pass in the crest line connecting 2520 and Perífano. To the south you can pick out the peaks of Smólikas and Gamíla and, of course, Plikatí village; to the north, for those with a full pack and no further interest in Ípiros, an obvious trail leads down in 3½ hr to the just-discernable hamlet of Grámmos, where public transport (if any) would take you to Kastoriá and Makedhonía.

A good, plain trail runs much of the way along the watershed, connecting various points of interest. Perífano summit is reached by a 30-min detour east of the pass, 15 min of it on the path and the rest a cross-country scramble over packed scree and turf. Perífano, scarred by a handful of caved-in bunkers, gives you a new perspective on 2520 off to the west and your first good look at some minor peaks of the massif to the east. Continuing in that direction along the ridge trail leads, with an appropriate down-turning into the large valley beyond Iróön, to the summer pastoral hamlet of Aïtomilítsa. Two to three hr distant, it's considerably more primitive than Plikáti, almost as far (17 km) from the main road and served by no public transport.

Most dayhikers will return from Perífano to the saddle above the pond, from where you can hike 45 min on a westerly bearing to the base of 2520. The ridgetop track adheres closely to the crest except for a stretch, 15 to 25 min along, where it swings south, and then north again above a catastrophic landslide area. Twenty min more walking just north of the watershed brings you to the 2520 altimeter, etched with the initials of hundreds of climbers and surrounded by stove-in bunkers, cartridge cases and dozens of radio or ammo boxes and machine-gun mounts which garnish the entire range but nowhere in such profusion as here. The watershed running north-south perpendicular to the Kiáfa-2520 ridge is in effect the Greek-Albanian frontier, and the dirt road visible just to the west lies well within Albanian territory. This road was originally built by the Italians to facilitate their bungled 1940 invasion of Ípiros and was later used by the Albanians to supply the *andártes* during 1948-49. The fertile, intensely cultivated valley to the west, with its rivers, ponds and giant functional buildings, provides a striking contrast to the wilderness on the Greek side. The border zone may appear deserted, but don't let that fool you into attempting extended forays into *Shqiperia*; should you cross the dirt road, which some sources call the legal border, armed guards would appear in a twinkling. While stationed primarily to keep Albanians from escaping, they would probably have little compunction about firing on *you*.

To return to Plikáti, descend south along the frontier ridge through the wildflower-studded (mostly violas and gentians) turf that has overgrown various gun emplacements and dugouts. To your left the south flank of 2520 drops off sheerly—heavy erosion is possibly the result of wartime bombardment—and the steepness compels you to remain on the watershed for some 20 min until reaching a saddle where the grade allows veering left further into Greek territory. It's fully 1¾ hr down miserable slopes with no sign of a trail, along the west bank of the headwaters of the Gorgopótamos, before a *stáni* and the first beeches show themselves. After another 40 min hiking, virtually in the riverbed, change sides where a jeep track erupts on the opposite bank. Follow this east for 20 min until you meet the trail used in the ascent. Descent from the peak to Plikáti by this route takes 3½ hr; ascent is *not* recommended.

Rating/time course: The detailed itinerary is an easy full-day outing, except for the moderately difficult descent from 2520 m. Most of the trails in the Grámmos area are in reasonable condition, being old rights-of-way connecting settlements on different sides of the mountain. Note that times given for the various portions of the hike were logged with a daypack; add 25 percent if hauling a full pack.

Supplies: Kónitsa or Plíkati.

Map: *Korfés*, issue 62.

MAKEDHONÍA AND THRÁKI

I was laying out my sleeping bag when from the forest above came a rushing sound of bells and the dry clatter of innumerable hoofs grating over the stony slope . . . . For some time I could hear the herdsmen milking and the barking of the dogs and the voices of the women . . . . Down the hill someone put out the fire, then all was quiet.

——Kevin Andrews

Makedhonía and Thráki are the borderlands of Greece, the until recently expendable or moot buffer zone; only between 1913 and 1920 were the two provinces annexed to the Greek state. They have served as a corridor for every group bent on Balkan settlement or conquest, from the Dorians, Persians and Makedhonians themselves up to the Germans and Bulgarians of this century. The receding tides of empire have left a patchwork of religious, ethnic and linguistic minorities that have long since vanished from southern Greece. Today it's still useful to think of the north of Greece as Byzantine, rather than Hellenic, with all the attendant connotations of imperial intrigue, subject tribes and atavistic holdovers.

In the lowlands the usual Greek rocks defer to hummocky hills and straight roads lined with poplars. It is by and large productive real estate, which partly explains why it has been fought over so often. As a rule there is more than enough water, often too much; lakes, rivers and swamps speckle the landscape. Corn, tobacco and fruit trees

are king, encouraged by muggy summers of almost narcotic intensity. Mountains are sometimes densely forested and always carpeted with thick turf, a legacy of heavy winter snowfalls. Here it hits home that Greece is, after all, a Balkan nation.

19 MT. FALAKRÓ(N)

This massif in eastern Makedhonía forms the heart of the province of Dhráma and is also the most northerly of the Greek mountains. "*Falakró*" (bald) is something of a misnomer, since where not forested the slopes here are carpeted with luxuriant grass, flowers and herbs all the way up to the 2232-m summit. The upper pastures are even lush enough to support that Greek highland rarity, cattle. Many of the place names in the range are Turkish or Bulgarian, a reminder that this area was securely wedded to Greece only after the First World War. That, proximity to Bulgaria, and the haze that frequently obscures the Makedhonian plains below, combine to leave an impression of Falakró as an eerily beautiful if somewhat moody mountain at the threshold of Eastern Europe.

Getting to the trailheads: From the KTEL stand in the town of Dhráma there are two daily buses (early morning and afternoon, except weekends) to Vólakas, a village on the northwest flank of Falakró. Otherwise you can take an *agoráio* (collective taxi), of which there are two; these charge the same fare as the bus, and they leave in the morning and at midday except on Sun. The *agoráia* are usually parked in Dhráma bazaar, in front of Proïnó Patsás restaurant, 300 m north of the Néa Zoí hotel. This in turn is not far from the central bus terminal, and if Pávlos Kondópoulos is still the night clerk there, he is one of the best sources of information on the mountain (for Greek speakers). Failing either of the above you should take any bus toward Nevrokópi and descend at crossroads "*Km 27*." From this fork it's a 6-km hitchhike to Vólakas, but slightly less on foot since you can shortcut several of the road's switchbacks.

Vólakas, surrounded by a quiltwork of fallow and productive fields, is a large community of decidedly un-Greek appearance. This is not surprising since the inhabitants, many towheaded and freckled, are offspring of Greek Orthodox Bulgarians relocated here early in this century. There is no proper hotel in the village, but if benighted, you can ask at one of the two *kafenéia* about renting a bed.

There are also two daily departures, except weekends, from Dhráma to the village of Pýrgi on the southwest flank of Falakró. Trails beginning and ending in Pýrgi are more challenging but also more scenic than those linking Vólakas to the peak.

Vólakas to Áyio Pnévma

Almost any trail heading southeast (but not due south) out of the village will do, but try to start on the prominent one beginning between the grammar school and the secondary school (*yimnásio*), both just off the main *platía*. After 1 hr of gradual climbing through fields, pine patches and then thick beech, it joins what appears to be a more important trail coming up from the north. The beeches disperse a bit and soon give way to more numerous, loftier black pines, and after another 30 min these thin out as you arrive on the bare Kourí ridge. A recent road winds its way past the tiny locked shelter here, on its way up to the Falakró ski center.

Opposite—top: Grigoriou monastery from the path descending from Símonos Pétras, on the Athos peninsula (Hike 20); Bottom: Kartálka seen across Naskvítsa from summit 2232 (Hike 19)

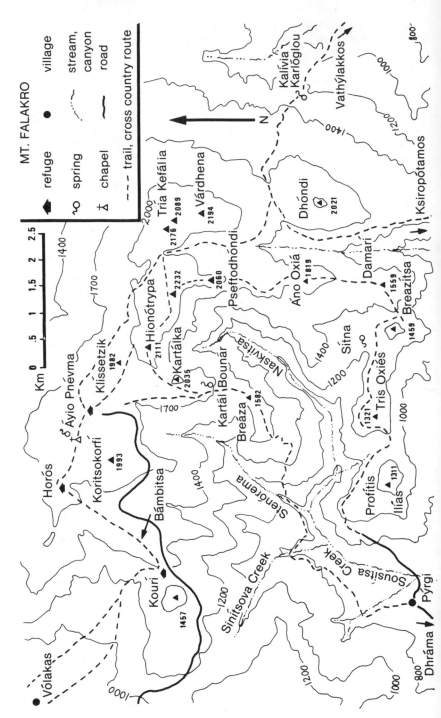

MT. FALAKRO

refuge
● village
♀ spring
stream, canyon
♁ chapel
road
--- trail, cross country route

The path now switchbacks up the slope just above the roadcut, doubling back on itself as it adopts a northeast bearing. This delightful way through alternating stands of pine and slopy meadows is marked with occasional *blue* dashes on tree trunks and rocks; the grade is gentler than the slopes below Kourí. The area is known locally as Bámbitsa, and once you've cleared treeline (quite low, at ca. 1700 m) you can enjoy views west over the way you've come; to your right (east) the road makes a prominent hairpin turn. A large hotel is scheduled to be built here, though financing has not yet been forthcoming; still, hikers should not be surprised in the coming years to find the trail in this area disrupted or even destroyed.

Soon the orange Horós refuge (also locked) appears; you should pass it about 1 hr after leaving Kourí. From Horós the trail, faint in spots, turns sharply above and behind the hut to continue roughly east. Pylons of the ski lift should now be visible and they make good orientation points—keep them slightly to your right. The path attains its highest point on a flat, spongy meadowlet and then begins the descent into the Áyio Pnévma plateau, now at your feet. The first prominent landmark is the chapel of Áyio Pnévma, lying a bit below and to the left of the apparent trail bearing; a spring, the only one on the route, issues from beneath its foundations. Next you meet cattle sheds, stock troughs and finally, 45 min above Horós, the giant shelter at the base of the ski run. Total tramping time from Vólakas should not exceed 3½ hr.

Falakró is slated within the near future to be the Greek ski resort third only to those on Parnassós and Vérmio. The lodge being prepared to this end is eventually supposed to be open year-round, catering to automobile day-trippers and hikers as well as skiers; but if it's closed, you can try to shelter in the small cottage near the big cattle sheds by Áyio Pnévma chapel. For more information call (0521) 23-954, Mr. Kanarás.

Áyio Pnévma to Summit 2232

It's 1¾ hr cross-country to the peak, ignoring for now the trail described under the next heading and relying instead on a more southerly route closely hugging the main peak line. After scaling Klíssetzik slightly to the right of its actual tip, follow the ridge line fairly closely, pausing to admire the precipitous drops into the chasm to the south, and also the odd Hionótrypa, a double-barreled sinkhole full of ice. This is located between the peak of the same name and summit 2232. In preelectricity days Hionótrypa was a perennial source of refrigeration for hospitals and banquets; the ice gatherers were lowered the necessary 30 m on ropes. Your hiking surface here is both enchanting and tiring, consisting as it does of a dense turf in which you sink up to your shins. From the top of 2232 you have, as expected, commanding lookouts south over the Naskvítsa (Bulgarian for "washtub") ravine, north (haze permitting) over the Néstos River valley into Bulgaria, and west over Makedhonía; to the east your panorama is abbreviated by the secondary peaks Tría Kefália and Várdhena (both under 2200 m).

Southeast Traverse or Descent to Áyio Pnévma

Scamper down the grassy, flowered slope northeast of the peak to the trail visible below, between 2232 and peak 2176 of Tría Kefália. By turning right, you can hike within an hour to the saddle between the peaks Várdhena and Dhóndi, the next summit south. From there you can continue south along the west flank of Dhóndi, avoiding excessive descent into the Damarí ravine to your right, and thus arrive after 5 more hr of hiking in the village of Ksiropótamos, 8 km from Dhráma. Or you can slip through the Várdhena-Dhóndi saddle and descend toward the locale known as Kalívia Karlóglou (springs but no longer any cottages). From here bear right to follow the Blátsista stream downhill to Vathýlakkos village, also 8 km from Dhráma and a 4-hr march from the Várdhena-Dhóndi pass.

Others will want to turn left (west) on the trail encountered at the base of 2232 and begin heading back toward the Áyio Pnévma plateau. The path is initially véry faint and clogged with vegetation, but after dropping down through a gully it becomes more noticeably grooved into the turf and there are even occasional orange blazes. The margin of extensive beech forests, and bear country, lies 100 m below and to the right. Soon a large patch of herbs graces a slight, east-facing rise; once atop this spur of Klíssetzik, you round a bend and the ski lodge appears. The way is orange-blazed through cow pastures for a short time longer, but soon the blazes disappear and it's strictly line-of-sight down to the building.

Loop Hike out of Pýrgi

Leave Pýrgi by the recently built forest road heading northeast toward the Sítna meadows; soon this fizzles out and a path begins, skirting the north feet of the low peaks Profítis Ilías and Trís Oxiés and arriving at the spring of Sítna some 2½ hr out of Pýrgi. Another 30 min suffice to take you from the meadowland up to the 1450-m ridge just to the west of Breazítsa peak. Next bear sharply north toward Áno Oxiá summit and then negotiate the edge of the peak line up to Pseftodhóndi (2060 m) and 2232, which falls off sharply to the left into the Naskvítsa canyon. From 2232, which you reach some 6 hr after quitting Pýrgi, wade west-northwest through the trackless turf past Hionótrypa to the eponymous peak. Then follow the brink of the Naskvítsa as it winds south past 2035-m Kartálka peak, and finally plunge swiftly down to the Kartál Bounár, a corruption of the Turkish *kartal pınar* or "eagle spring." Here you meet up with a faint trail linking the spring to Áyio Pnévma (a 2-hr trip either direction). The augmented path presses onward along the thin neck of land joining Kartálka peak with Breáza summit (1582 m). This ridge is one of the most beautiful spots on the mountain, perfectly positioned for the best perspectives on 2232 and Naskvítsa. Just below Breáza there's a *dexamení* (water tank); the trail now switches to the south slope of Breáza and begins to curl west down toward the Stenórema gully draining off Koritsokorfí and Kartálka peaks. Follow the Stenórema briefly, bear right before its junction with Sousítsa Creek and change over to the vale of Sinítsova Creek, on whose west bank you descend into Pýrgi.

From Kartál Bounár you should allow just over 4 hr to arrive in Pýrgi, bringing the total elapsed time for the circuit to 12 hr—best divided over two days. An Áyio Pnévma-Kartál Bounár-Pýrgi itinerary can be expected to consume just over 6 hr.

Rating/time course: A point-to-point outing from Vólakas to Vathýlakkos or Ksiropótamos via Áyio Pnévma and 2232, or to Pýrgi via Kartál Bounár, is a moderate two-day undertaking, implying an early start out of Vólakas. More difficult excursions from Pýrgi toward the summit assume your willingness to overnight in the peak area, not at Áyio Pnévma, and mean a second strenuous day back down to Pýrgi. Late starters out of Vólakas can still see Falakró in two (full!) days if on the second day they ascend 2232 fully equipped and continue on to Ksiropótamos or Vathýlakkos.

Seasonal note: Snowpack is liable to be heavy in spring; wild strawberries await the summer hiker in the meadows near Bámbitsa; and beeches are ablaze with fall foliage color.

Supplies: Dhráma
Map:*Korfés*, issue 52.

20   ÁTHOS PENINSULA: MONASTERIES OF THE HOLY MOUNTAIN

On the easternmost of the three peninsulas of Halkidhikí, which dangle south of Makedhonía, a fragment of Byzantium and the Middle Ages persists. The roughly rectangular, 400-km² territory of Athos is to Greece today what the Vatican is to Italy, except on a much grander scale.

The history of Áthos extends back to the 9th century A.D., when the first Christian hermits settled at present-day Karoúlia. In 963, St. Athanásios founded the first group-living arrangement, the monastery of Meyísti Lávra. Matters snowballed from then on and soon the Áyion Óros (Holy Mountain) became a powerful religious and political entity which most Byzantine and later Slavic rulers subsidized, courted and in some cases retired to in old age. At the height of its power in the 15th and 16th centuries, after the final demise of the Byzantine Empire, Áthos supported a population of some 20,000 monks. They were citizens of the parliamentary monastic republic of Áthos; each of the "ruling monasteries," whose number was fixed early on at 20, had a representative at the central council where all policy matters were deliberated.

Internal dissension between Slavic and Greek monks often threatened to tear the republic apart. But Áthos was adroit in its dealings with the outside world and managed to preserve a measure of autonomy during centuries when the rest of the Levant was under stricter Ottoman rule. Turkish Istanbul was as assiduous in paying respects to the Mountain—thus defusing a potential hotbed of Greek nationalist sentiment—as Orthodox Constantinople had been. In 1926, Áthos finally assumed its present status as a state-within-the-Greek-state.

In recent decades the Mountain's chief enemy has been a growing conviction among outsiders that it's an anachronism, and increasing materialism and rationalism steadily reduces the number of new novices. (It is difficult to say whether growing numbers at some Athonite institutions reflect a reversal in the decline or merely relocation of monks from monasteries closed elsewhere in Greece.) Nowhere is Áthos' obsolescence more evident to some than in the survival of an 11th century edict, the "*avaton*," which forbids access to Áthos for all females of species more highly evolved than a bird. Supposedly the law was laid down after a period of famine, when women and children came to beg and camp in the fields of the comparatively wealthy monasteries. The more theologically-minded point out that the ban is consistent with the Christian view of a monk as "married" to the "Queen of Heaven" (the *Panayía*). The revisionist view, asserting that the riot act was read after a major scandal involving nomadic shepherds renting their female relatives to needy monks, is less popular but perhaps closer to the truth. Whatever the exact motives for its inception, the *ávaton* remains in effect by virtue of inertia if nothing else, causing hardship for inseparable heterosexual couples.

In Greece one comes to expect monasteries in stark, forbidding, inaccessible settings relieved only by the fountain that keeps the cloister alive. Therefore it's something of a shock to tramp through the copses and thickets, often bordering on jungle, that festoon southern Áthos. The streams, vines, flowers and ferns that run riot here seem to mock the austerity of monkish life and reintroduce an element of the feminine principle that the ascetics sought to cast out. The monks are not insensible to this beauty and often refer to Áthos as the Garden of Eden—perhaps voicing a wish to return to the times before the Fall and the appearance of duality, sexual and otherwise. While many of the monasteries are stereotypic rock-bound citadels, some, especially those built inland, are almost obscured by lush greenery. Nearly all of them are outstanding examples of an architectural and artistic genius that will not be seen again.

In midsummer lugging a full pack the considerable distances between each religious community must be reckoned a new form of religious penance, but then and in other seasons the stunning landscape, largely unplowed, ungrazed and unlogged until recent years, provides ample distraction. The gray, bony peak of Áthos (2030 m) towers above the dense growth at the southern tip of the peninsula like a cassocked

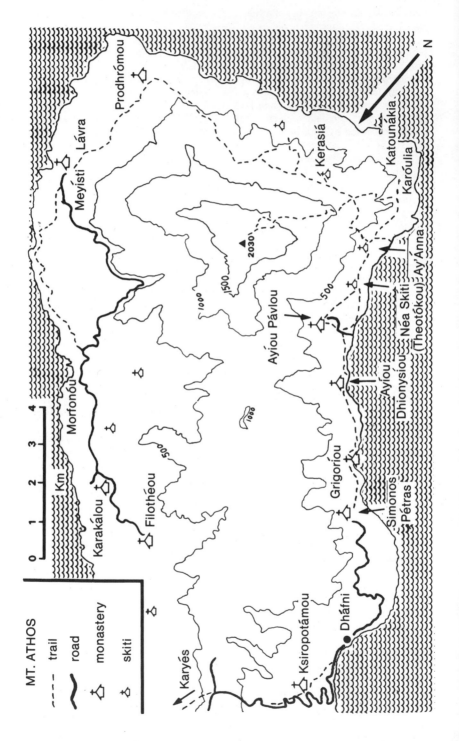

monk aloof from the secular hothouse. It's a magnificent climb up to the summit, though it will use up a day of the four usually allotted on Áthos. The peninsula is enormous, and even if you make use of the caiques that sail along its southwest and northeast shores, you'll be obliged to scale down overambitious sightseeing plans. In addition to the time factor, most monasteries furnish meals and quarters separately to monks and the non-Orthodox. These two limitations make it difficult for most guests to garner more than an inkling of monastic life. Much of your day will be taken up in moving from one community to the next, with some time left over to discreetly eavesdrop on the lives of your hosts.

Numerous lumber and utility roads in central Áthos confuse hikers looking for the medieval byways and are depressing reminders of our century. Thus the mostly roadless, southern route described is the most rewarding for men seeking communion with rocks, creepers, crystal water and even a hermit or two. The vegetation along this itinerary changes gradually. The arid scrub on the southwest coast blends subtly with the oak groves near Kerasiá. This is in turn succeeded by the ash, chestnut and fir forest near Prodhrómou. Between Meyísti Lávra and the trail's end sprawls the "jungle": chestnut overgrown with ivy, orchids, brambles and other hanging vines. Butterflies, as well as less pleasant biting flies, abound.

Securing the Permit to Visit Mt. Áthos

You can apply for entry to Áthos in Athens or Thessaloníki, though it's easier in the latter city. First you should consult your embassy or consulate to see if a letter of introduction is required. Foreigners beginning the application process in Athens will find a list of embassies in the "Organizer" pages of *The Athenian* magazine. Next take the letter, for which there may be a charge, to the Ministry of Foreign Affairs at Zalakósta 2 (Mon through Fri, 11 to 2), and finally to the Aliens' Bureau at Halkondili 9 (Mon through Fri, 8 to 1). In Thessaloníki, take consular letters first to the Ministry of Northern Greece, Diikitriou Square, Room 218 (Mon through Fri, 8 to 2), where you exchange it for another, to be further processed at the Aliens' Police (41 Polytehníou or 25 Megálou Aléxandhrou, some confusion on exact address). The final product in either case is your entrance visa to the Áyion Óros. It's smartest to start and finish the application process in the same city—I have heard that, for instance, you cannot take an introductory letter from your embassy in Athens and expect it to be worked with in Thessaloníki.

The number of foreigners admitted to Áthos is limited to 10 daily, so you should be prepared to wait a couple of days in or around Thessaloníki until the entry day assigned to you comes round. In summer, entrance can be deferred as much as two weeks, so if you must go then, it's highly advisable to get paperwork started in Athens comfortably in advance. The permit issued is for a maximum of four days at the outset, but you can get extensions in Karyés on Mt. Áthos. Letters of recommendation are no longer handed out to the merely curious or those with blatantly frivolous motives. Present yourself as a student or a professional ("man of letters" was my classification) with some interest or proficiency in art, architecture, theology, music, etc. Jesus-length hair and beards, presumably considered a disrespectful mimicry of the monks who wear the same, are reportedly not allowed on the Mountain (though the ávaton stipulates that one cannot be "beardless"—presumably this means no eunuchs or boys as well as women).

Getting to Áthos

Once in Thessaloníki, take a No. 10 bus from city center to the Halkidhikí KTEL terminal at 68 Karakási. There are several daily departures for Ouranópoli and Ierissós, the two villages closest to the Athonite border, but only if you catch the earliest (ca. 6 A.M.) bus are you assured of getting to Áthos the same day. In any event you face a stomach-churning, 3-hr ride to the base of the Áthos peninsula. From Ierissós a caique runs at around noon to Ivíron, 3 km below the official Athonite capital of Karyés. From Ouranópoli skiffs sail to Dháfni harbor, 8 km below Karyés; outside of summer there is only one daily departure, around 10 A.M. For more information call the Ouranópoli port police, (0377) 71-248. Most visitors embark from Ouranópoli; both villages have nice beaches (and accommodations) so if you miss your boat, things could be worse.

When you board your skiff, the captain will collect your passport and triple-stamped letter and send them from the dock at Dháfni up to Karyés. When you yourself finally arrive in Karyés, you fetch them from the Holy Epistasía or Church Authority, housed in a yellow building on the main square. Upon payment of an $8 fee ($5 for students) you at last exchange the remaining letter(s) for a *dhiamonitírion*. This document entitles you to board and lodging, without any further donations, at any of the 20 monasteries and a half-dozen *skítes* (see "Glossary of Athonite Terms"). Have a student ID handy to qualify for the reduction if your letter of introduction doesn't specifically state that you're a full-time student.

Entering and Leaving Karyés

If you've taken a caique from Ierissós to Ivíron, you'll be able to get a ride, if you wish, up to Karyés on a monastery service vehicle—it's a relatively busy route. Otherwise you can walk (45 min) or wait for the exorbitantly priced bus which plies midmorning and midafternoon between Ivíron and Karyés.

For a Dháfni-Karyés shuttle, the rattletrap bus costs $2 a head for the 8-km ride and frequently fails to complete the distance under its own power. Much better, and shorter, is a *kalderími* which starts on the right of the road, immediately past the bridge 500 m out of Dháfni. This quickly climbs to Ksiropotámou monastery, passes it and cuts across some switchbacks in the road up to Karyés before fizzling out, like so many trails in central Áthos. You then follow the road, which has obliterated all but a few traces of the old right-of-way, until 2 hr above Dháfni you reach a saddle marked by a wrought-iron cross. Immediately to its left begins the trail descending within 30 min to Karyés.

The second oldest church on Áthos, the Prótaton dating from 965, dominates the center of Karyés. Rectangular and dull-looking from the outside, its interior boasts some of the finest frescoes on the Mountain. Since it stands directly in front of the Holy Epistasía, it's difficult to miss. If you haven't done so in Ierissós or Ouranópoli, visit one of Karyés' shops and stock up on chocolate, sesame *pastéli*, dried fruit and nuts, or quince paste. Sweets and trail gorp are entirely absent from monastic diets and are badly needed along the trail. Breakfasts are often nonexistent, so biscuits, cereal and eggs are also wise purchases.

After completing paperwork, grocery shopping and church visiting it will be midafternoon. The safest and quickest way to the starting point of the recommended itinerary as described is to retrace your steps to Dháfni and thence take a coastal trail or road to the monastery of Símonos Pétras. I attempted to find a route from the iron-cross ridge toward Ayíou Dhionysíou, and spent three-and-a-half hours lost on lumber roads until a truck en route to Símonos Pétras rescued me. The tourist maps sold in Ouranópoli are unreliable, failing to show trails accurately or roads at all, and getting lost can have unpleasant consequences, since all the religious communities lock their front gates at sunset.

Before you rely on any clock towers on Áthos, remember that most run on Byzantine time, which fixes "12 o'clock" at the hour of sunset. So the sun may be overhead and the dial will correctly read "five o'clock." Only Vatopédhi and Ivíron deviate from this standard. With the limited amount of daylight available at most times of the year, it may be wisest to head for Filothéou monastery from Karyés (see "Rating/time course").

GLOSSARY OF ATHONITE TERMS

cenobitic—The class of monastery where property is held in common, meals are shared in the refectory and daily life is rigidly scheduled. These communities best exemplify the Orthodox monastic ideal as formulated by St. Basil.

idhiorhythmatic—In this type of cloister monks are permitted to manipulate their own property for gain (e.g., sell ikons), eat in their own quarters and study or pray at will.

skíti—A satellite community of a monastery. The number of "ruling" monasteries with a vote in the council at Karyés has long been limited to 20 but no ceiling was set on the number of dependencies. Cenobitic *skítes* resemble miniature monasteries both in their life style and fortified, compact architecture. The scattered dwellings of idhiorhythmatic *skítes* surround a *kyriakón* (chapel), and the monks in these groups spend much of their time painting ikons and crafting other religious articles for sale.

kelliá—Small agricultural colonies of monasteries, manned by three or four monks who've sought a compromise between solitude and the regimentation of the monasteries. Few restrictions, dietary or otherwise, are placed on these farmer-monks, and hikers arriving at nightfall may be treated to a comparatively luxurious table.

arhondáriki—The guest quarters of any monastery or *skíti*; similarly, *arhondáris*, the guestmaster.

trapezaría—The refectory of an Athonite monastery. Often painted with lurid frescoes to keep monks from paying more attention to their food than their salvation.

katholikón—The central church of a monastery.

arsanás—The harbor annex of each monastery, usually guarded by a fortified tower. Even coastal monasteries have one, since they too were built a little out of reach of marauding medieval corsairs. Today the inter-monastery caiques call at the *arsanádhes*.

evlóyite—"Your blessing," the proper greeting of a trekker to monks met on the trail. The reply will most likely be "*O Kýrios*"—"The Lord" (blesses you).

Símonos Pétras to Filothéou

Route directions: Símonos Pétras, Grigoríou and Ayíou Dhionysíou are the three "hanging monasteries" that cling like Tibetan lamaseries to the rocky southwest coast of Áthos.

Símonos Pétras (Símopetra), the most spectacular of the group, is taller than it is wide and visible from as far away as 10 km. Its original walls were destroyed in an 1893 conflagration but the plaster-and-cement replacement still manages to attract a deserved share of visitors. Forty-five monks glide up and down echoing, winding passages and the creaking wooden balconies which girdle the top four floors of the ten-story structure. This is a dizzying perspective, for directly beneath the balcony floorboards lie 300 m of thin air.

Símonos Pétras is also one of the few communities where non-Orthodox guests may be invited to services. In a cenobitic monastery such as this, all monks are required to attend liturgies, which entails standing for hours with only an armrest for support. Orthodox canons forbid instrumental accompaniment of sacred music, so the brothers have perfected four-part chanting which is hauntingly beautiful and takes your mind off the standing vigil.

Grigoríou, the next community, is most easily reached by going 20 min down a cobble path toward the *arsanás* of Símonos Pétras, turning left through a gate, and passing a sheet-metal chapel before joining the main coastal trail. It's a 1 hr walk to Grigoríou, whose buildings date from the 18th century. Very few relics or works of art are housed here but the monastery, perhaps the most nautical of the 20, juts out into the sapphire-blue water of its own harbor. The comfortable guest study contains a small collection of English books on Orthodoxy and the monastic life, which you can read while watching the north Aegean just outside the windows.

A Day in the Life

If you're thinking of converting, know that a monk's life at a cenobitic institution is highly ordered, to put it mildly. "Lights out" occurs between 7 and 9 P.M., depending on the season. The brothers awake sometime between midnight and 3:30 A.M. for solitary study and meditation. Matins is chanted between 3:30 and 4 A.M.; you'll know it's the small hours from the (un)godly racket of bells and *símandra* (wooden or iron gongs struck with a mallet). The noise seems calculated to wake the dead and metaphorically that's what it does. In the Orthodox cosmology the monastery is a Noah's Ark of Salvation from the Flood of Sin, and the mallet and plank of the *símandro* are the tools of Noah the carpenter calling all creatures to come seek eternal safety. The morning liturgy follows directly (4 to 6 A.M.) on matins; from 6 to 8 A.M. the monks catch up on sleep. Between 8 and 9 A.M. the first common meal of the day is served in the refectory. Afterward the community exits to the fields, sawmills or workshops and works until 5 P.M., with a brief rest at midday. Between 5 and 6 P.M. the second daily meal, about the same size and constitution as the first, is served in the *trapezaría*.

Monks eat in silence except for the voice of one of their number reading a chapter from the Gospel. If you've been invited to share table, eat as quickly as you politely can, because on cue everyone rises in unison, there's a closing invocation and the group files out, leaving any uneaten food. At such moments you understand why it's easier on guests to have a separate, leisurely meal hour. Unfortunately, there can be glaring discrepancies between the quality of the monks' fare and visitors' food, with visitors given the leavings. Good food, and where you can get some to sustain the pace of hiking on Áthos, becomes a conversational preoccupation among all guests on the Mountain. If you want to eat relatively well, stay at inland monasteries, such as Filothéou and Hilandharíou, away from the tourist caique routes. Everywhere, the monastic cuisine is mostly vegetarian: cheese (presumably imported), legumes, coarse bread, eggs, produce from kitchen gardens and foraged greens are the staples. Fish may be served on Fridays or Sundays. The year is punctuated by numerous fasts, which spell complete absence of the heartier foodstuffs (oil, cheese, eggs) from the monks' tables.

Smoking, wearing hats or shorts, loud conversation, whistling and singing are forbidden on Áthos and will earn you a quick reprimand from the monks. Standing with your hands behind your back, or sitting with crossed legs, is also considered bad form. Full-body washing is frowned on as self-indulgent and anyway there are no showers in the monasteries—take a sea bath if you want. You should be fully clothed when not actually in the guest quarters, even on the way to the toilet.

The 90 min path to Ayíou Dhionysíou starts on the stairs ascending to the left just outside the main gate of Grigoríou.

Ayíou Dhionysíou resembles a truncated Símonos Pétras, but it has largely been spared the fires that periodically devastate most of the rickety Athonite cloisters. The majority of the buildings date from the 16th century, and the frescoes in the *trapezaría* of this austerely cenobitic monastery are considered among the best on the Holy Mountain. The Monoksilitikós wine produced by the brothers here is also counted as the best on the peninsula, although wine of varied quality is served with meals almost everywhere on Áthos.

A further 45 min along the coastal trail, the crenelated castle-type monastery of Ayíou Pávlou lurks at the mouth of a ravine more than a km from shore. Though differing in visual impact from the preceding three, this community is not numerically on the decline like so many others, owing to the charismatic personality of its *igoúmenos* (abbot).

The idhiorhythmatic Néa Skíti (Theotókou) lies another hour beyond Ayíou Pávlou. Forty min later you arrive at the *skíti* of Ay'Ánna, known for the fine chanting voice of the monk Pantelímon. Relatively good food is served here—something to keep in mind since this is the "base camp" for ascending Áthos peak. Kerasiá *skíti* is actually closer to the side trail up the peak, but monastic hospitality there is limited.

The caique from Ouranópoli to Dháfni continues past the "hanging monasteries," stopping at each on its way to the *arsanás* of Ay'Ánna. From the dock it's a 40-min walk to a signposted fork; Ay'Ánna lies 10 min to the left. The right fork leads to Karoúlia and Katounákia, the dwelling places of most Áthos hermits.

The name Karoúlia (pulleys) refers to the former method of transferring provisions and offerings from fishing boats below to the rock-bound hermitages; access trails are a relatively recent addition. The few ascetics who live in these nearly inaccessible cliffs at the extreme south tip of the peninsula subsist on wild plants, seafood and bread. The stronger ones, including perhaps a saint or two in the making, spend their lives crafting devotional articles, studying, praying and meditating intensively. Others may simply be crazed by a surfeit of weather, hardship and loneliness. A few of the anchorites are Russians who arrived shortly after the 1917 revolution and so may speak some French or English. The hermits are not necessarily inclined or obligated to offer the hospitality of Áthos, but many Greeks and foreigners, some seeking spiritual guidance, are received graciously.

From Ay'Ánna you have a demanding 1-hr climb up to the high point on the circum-Áthos trail, marked by a splintery wood cross. From this saddle you can gaze up the southwest coast of the peninsula as far as just-visible Símonos Pétras. About 80 min above Ay'Ánna a water tap presides over a sizable junction. To the right a trail descends to Katounákia and Karoúlia, and from there back to Ay'Ánna. On your left is the start of the trail to Áthos summit. The peak, with its boulders piled in eerie arrangements, is a 4-hr one-way climb from this junction; some 45 min below the top, you pass the chapel of the Panayía.

Proceeding straight through the above junction, you then take two successive left forks in order to bypass Kerasiá and continue toward Meyísti Lávra. After a level stretch and a third turnoff to Kerasiá, there's a 1-hr interval when the trail is marked by numerous springs and jungly patches. About 3½ hr out of Ay'Ánna you'll pass the fork for Kapsokalívia, the last idhiorhythmatic *skíti* on the southeast end of Áthos. Thereafter the way descends sharply to the *skíti* of Prodhrómou.

More the dimensions of a monastery than a dependency, Prodhrómou is a cenobitic Romanian annex of Meyísti Lávra. Its 12 elderly tenants rattle around inside the enormous rectangular compound; they are as friendly as the community is poor. They communicate with the outside world in imperfect French or English, as do most of the Slavic Orthodox establishments on Áthos.

The fifth hour of the leg Ay'Ánna-Meyísti Lávra follows the cobbled way between Prodhrómou and Meyísti Lávra. This, the largest, oldest and most famous of the Athonite monasteries, is decorated with some of the finest frescoes on the Holy Mountain. The *narthex* (portico) of the red, 10th-century *katholikón* features vivid scenes from the Last Judgment. The sanctuary itself may not be open but contains more images. In the refectory by the church, the mural "The Saints Marching into Paradise" covers all available wall space; the classical Athonite seating plan of round, square and rectangular marble tables and benches sprouting out of the floor seems oddly modern.

If you've had enough walking or are short on time, a caique bound for Ivíron and Ierissós departs from Meyísti Lávra daily at about 6 A.M. To continue the itinerary on foot, leave Meyísti Lávra on the service road leading straight out the main gate. After some 700 m a path, initially well-maintained, veers off at a 70-degree angle toward the sea. After 10 min the way is nearly blocked by overgrowth, but you're not lost; within another ¼ hr the trail comes to a fine old stone fountain in a patch of jungle. Once past the fountain, the forest thins enough to permit some of the best views of Áthos peak along the way. A little over 1 hr beyond Meyísti Lávra the path skirts the seashore and crosses the mouth of a creek over an old bridge. The 90 min beyond the bridge is an up-and-down exercise through creek valleys where "jungle" alternates with scrub. Finally, just under 3 hr out of Meyísti Lávra, the trail passes a cave spring and widens into a jeep track. Take the next two forks to the right; between the two junctions, Morfonoú Bay has a gravelly beach where you can swim.

Beyond Morfonoú the footpath has deteriorated or become overgrown, making it more trouble than it's worth to follow any remnants. An easy but tedious 3-hr walk from the beach along signposted roads brings you first to Karakálou monastery and shortly thereafter to Filothéou.

This physically small but numerically vigorous cloister on a lush hillside overlooks the coast and Stavronikíta monastery in the distance. Filothéou, founded in the 10th century, is one of the best institutions at which to stay. Most of the monks are young and educated, and as an indication of their commitment, they have recently reverted to the cenobitic mode after centuries as an idhiorrhythmic house (the reverse transition is not permitted). Meals are appetizing preparations from the garden rather than the usual cold soup and bread; beds are set up in double rooms rather than the dormitory-style found elsewhere. Such considerations may sound trivial on reading, but after three to four days' walking in the broiling Áthos sun, with mortification diets of 1500 daily calories and occasionally surly guestmasters to look forward to, even minimal creature comforts assume enormous importance if you are to remain in any condition to enjoy the less mundane aspects of Áthos.

From Filothéou a 2½-hr trail leads to Karyés, but you may have to rise at dawn, and miss breakfast, in order to reach Dháfni in time for the early afternoon caique to Ouranópoli. Ask if there's a truck going to Karyés via Ivíron. Of course, if you are returning to Karyés only to get a visa extension (required on the fourth day), enjoy the path.

Alternate Routes North of Karyés

A group of monasteries on the northwest half of the peninsula has been recommended by Greeks and foreigners alike as an equally fascinating alternative or add-on to the southern circuit.

Doheiaríou or Vatopédhi, both with exceptional architecture, would be the logical starting monasteries for a northern trek. On the long, second day you would proceed to Esfigménou, a strict cenobitic community, and from there on the third day to Hilandharíou, a hospitable Serbian idhiorrhythmic group with high morale. From Hilandharíou you would return to Esfigménou to catch a *kaḯki* to Ierissós or walk a full day to Ouranópoli through mostly uninhabited country.

Rating/time course: As hinted above, conditions met with in certain monasteries may make essentially moderate hiking days seem difficult. You will have an easier time of it if you bring along morale-boosting foodstuffs missing from the proffered meals and remember that two or three visits to the Holy Mountain would be required to do a "once-over-lightly" of its scattered treasures. Assuming a willingness to apply for an extension of the *dhiamonitírion*, you could spend your first night at Símonos Pétras; the second at Ay'Ánna; pass the third day climbing Áthos peak or visiting the hermits, staying overnight at Prodhrómou or Meyísti Lávra; reaching Filothéou by the fourth evening; and presenting yourself in Karyés the following morning. Several correspondents have reported it much easier to reverse the itinerary as set forth, i.e., reach Filothéou the first night, Meyísti Lávra or Prodhrómou the second, spend the third day en route to Ay'Ánna or Ayíou Pávlou, and pass the fourth and final night on Áthos at Áyiou Dhionysíou or Símonos Pétra. Note that most monasteries require you to move on after a single night's stay, and if you don't observe bureaucratic formalities in Karyés—such as timely application for extensions and returning of "landing card" before departure—you may be barred from reentry to Áthos.

Except for one long climb, most of the southern circuit is nearly flat. If you choose to detour up Áthos peak, considerably more stamina is called for.

Seasonal note: In spring Áthos summit sports a few attractive snow patches and the heat near sea level is tropical only at midday. There are no restrictions on Greek Orthodox pilgrims, who arrive in biblical hordes during summer and on weekends, along with a generous leavening of foreign tourists—whom many monks contemptuously despise as such. Autumn is once again a good season for a visit.

Supplies: Ierissos or Ouranópoli.

Map: *Korfés*, issue 51.

21   SAMOTHRÁKI ISLAND

Since this island belongs to no archipelago, and has been linked throughout history with the mainland opposite, we shall consider it as part of Thráki. The "Sámos of Thráki" is earning a reputation among lovers of striking natural beauty throughout Europe. No other Greek island is as dramatic seen from the sea; the enormous mass of Mt. Fengári (Sáos) looms over your approaching ferryboat like some higher, celestial ship. The north face of Samothráki resembles the Thrakian mainland across the water: a broad coastal plain, furrowed by streams and burgeoning with planes and oaks, precedes the sudden eruption of Fengári. The south flanks of Fengári drop steeply, at times even sheerly, from Lákoma to Cape Kípos, but heavily cultivated flatlands occupy the entire southwest extreme of the island. The area south of the mountain is warmer and dryer, with primarily evergreen vegetation in untilled regions.

Samothráki has been a place of pilgrimage for millenia. Supplicants were initiated into a mystery religion at the Sanctuary of the Great Gods, tucked into a small valley just above the north shore. These Great Gods or *Kabíri* were pre-Olympian, Thrakian or possibly local chthonic deities, and little is known today about them, the cult, or the initiation ceremonies.

Worthwhile hikes—the following four by no means exhaust all possibilities—are scattered throughout this 30-by-15-km island, and it's probable that you'll want to change your base of operations at least once. At present short-term accommodations are available in Thermá, Paleópoli, Kamariótissa and Hóra, with advantages and drawbacks to staying at each. The shady groves and hot springs of Thermá constitute an undeniable lure, but facilities change with the seasons. Beds are scarce in July and August, and both lodgings and eateries tend to open late in spring and close early in fall. A new campground has been built about 3 km away on the seashore. Kamariótissa is unprepossessing, but it does have a good selection of eateries and

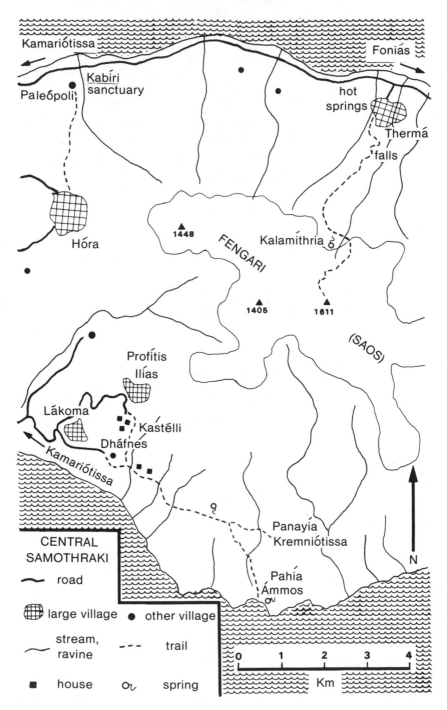

Kamariótissa

Foniás

Paleópoli

Kabíri sanctuary

hot springs

Thermá

falls

Hóra

▲ 1448

FENGARI

Kalamithria ○

(SAOS)

▲ 1405   ▲ 1611

Profítis Ilías

Lákoma

Kastélli

Dháfnes

Kamariótissa

○

Panayía
Kremniótissa

CENTRAL
SAMOTHRAKI

Pahía
Ámmos
○

N

— road

⊞ large village   ● other village

stream,
ravine

- - - trail

■ house   ○ spring

0   1   2   3   4

Km

groceries. Hóra is attractive, but often windswept and cold. Paleópoli has little to offer in the way of food and is convenient to only one of the hikes described.

Getting to Samothráki: From Alexandhroúpoli on the Thrakian mainland, the *Sáos* sails six days a week, usually at around 10 A.M. Once a week (Wed?) there is service from Kaválla and onward to Límnos and Lésvos.

Buses, or getting to various trailheads: Upon disembarking you should check out the current bus schedule, posted on a sign in the little waterfront park in Kamariótissa. As of 1983, departures were as follows: Harbor-Thermá, 6:30 A.M. and 1:30 P.M. weekdays, slight variation weekends, with return 30 min later; Harbor-Hóra, five times daily from 8:30 A.M. to 3:30 P.M., three on Sun, with return 15 min later; Harbor-Lákoma-Profítis Ilías, three times daily from 6 A.M. to 2 P.M., return 30 min later, twice Sun.

Climbing Fengári

This is most quickly and safely done from Thermá (Loutrá). From the bus turnaround plaza, proceed up the muddy street paralleling the stream; this soon narrows to a donkey track. Do not pass a large cement water tank, but instead turn left just before—the path up the mountain starts behind a huge, open-boled plane tree close to the overflow outlet of the cement cistern. Toil uphill through a big fern brake until you find an old roofless stone chapel—the very clear trail picks up just to its left. For the next hour the route wends its obvious way through arbutus and heather; about 30 min along you can see and hear giant waterfalls in a canyon to your left. The arbutus-heather biome transits fairly suddenly to an oak community on a ridge devoid of underbrush; it's important during this second hour to keep an eye peeled for piled stone cairns, since the path is no longer hemmed in by shrubs and is none too easy to pick out in the forest gloom. After about a 2-hr march the trail veers off this ridge and crosses a gully just a few m east of the spot where the Kalamíthria spring gurgles over the path. From the bed of this ravine you've a 20-min climb to a knoll-meadow just at treeline. Rock cairns, and with a stretched imagination a trail, continue a little further up the peak, but in all honesty it's an hour-plus cross-country scramble through bracken and boulders up the ridge hovering just ahead of you to the southwest.

Once up on the watershed, you should see two altitude markers to your left. The nearer column (1600 m) was erected in 1942 by the Bulgarian occupation force; however, the true (1611-m) peak is indicated by the Greek survey marker a little beyond. Fengári, "moon," lives up to its name—great crags and boulder slides subdivide a barren landscape in all directions. To the west, Mt. Áthos and the top of Thássos Island ride above mists kicked up from the ocean's surface, and the mainland peaks of Pangéo (left) and Falakró (right) flank Thássos to either side. Swinging north, Rhodhópi huddles beyond Komotiní, marking the boundary with Bulgaria, and Ulu Dağ above Turkish Bursa is sometimes visible to the east. If Poseidon of old did in fact watch the progress of the Trojan war from this peak, he couldn't have picked a better vantage point.

It's well over 3 hr up the mountain, slightly less coming down; allow at least 5½ hr for tramping, plus time for rests, lunch and gaping. Fengári's igneous heart pumps out a steady flow of just-right hot water in the rickety old public bathhouse just around the bend in Thermá from the fancy, sterile new spa by the bus stop. If the bathhouse is too hot (ca. 42 degrees C) or occupied, there's a cooler (ca. 37 degrees) open-air tub about 50 m past the enclosed one, and a soak in either makes a perfect reward for the completion of the trek.

Waterfalls above Foniás

Walk down from Thermá to the coast road, turn right, and continue 4.3 km (about 1 hr unless you hitch) to the vicinity of the medieval tower of Foniás. There's a bridge on the road, just before the tower, over the stream flowing down from the cataracts. Find a red "B" (for German *baden*?) and a green splotch, which together mark the beginning of the right-of-way up to the falls. Sporadic red dots guide you all along the essentially pathless left (east) bank of the stream for the entire 40-min duration of the walk; if you lose sight of them, don't despair, it's not possible to miss the falls as long as you stay by the water. At the end of the route, 12-meter falls plunge into a large, deep swimming hole that's more like an abandoned quarry than the catch basin of a cataract. The absolutely frigid water can only be appreciated in warm weather. Further progress up this valley is made difficult by towering rock walls on three sides of you.

Valley of the Kabíri to Hóra

Kabíri sanctuary can be done from any of the four villages mentioned. Only five columns of the main temple remain standing in the sanctuary of the Great Gods, but the site, poised between the plunging, northeasternmost ridge of the Sáos range and the sea, is pregnant with the rustling of leaves and flitting ghosts. This and the Vassí temple are probably the most isolated and savage sacred precincts in Greece, and the sense of mystery is heightened by the antiquity of the Kabíri cult and our lack of secure knowledge as to what exactly took place here.

To move from Paleópoli to Hóra, begin on the track leading uphill from the museum past the uppermost four houses of the village. Take the first two lefts encountered, and you're on your way. The surface is a 1950s-era jeep track, but a much older mule path parallels it most of the way where it hasn't been obliterated by bulldozing. First it's above (east of) the newer route, and after the first false summit, below (west of) it.

This route is in fact much easier to see if descending from Hóra to the Sanctuary. In Hóra, the old track begins at the medieval citadel that curiously envelops the police station at the top of the village. It initially winds above the newer road, then crosses it and dips below it until the above-mentioned false summit. The walk takes about 1 hr in either direction; besides the end points, the scenery consists principally of views of the final descending ridge of Fengári (Sáos).

Hóra is the most interesting and largest village on Samothráki. Simple-gable, tile-roof houses in the Thrakian style, vaguely reminiscent of architecture in the Argo-Saronic gulf, are arranged ingeniously in the form of two amphitheaters facing each other. The town is refreshingly unspoilt and free of concrete atrocities; many of the buildings date back to Turkish days. In addition to grocery stores there are three *kafenéia*, two *tavérnes* and "rooms" at your disposal.

The South Shore, to Pahía Ámmos

To begin hiking on this side of Samothráki, you should take an early-morning bus from Kamariótissa to either Lákoma or Profítis Ilías—this presupposes that you have spent the previous night in either Kamariótissa or Hóra. If you start at dawn from Thermá, you will have to hitch or taxi from the harbor to Lákoma and all the way back to Thermá to complete the itinerary in one day, or stay overnight at Pahía Ámmos.

If you get off the bus at Lákoma, it's a pretty straightforward matter to walk east along the dirt track to Dháfnes hamlet and then beyond on the narrower mule track toward Pahía Ámmos. However, you may elect to continue to the end of the line at Profítis Ilías; the walk is no longer if begun from there and the scenery is rewarding. The higher village, alive with the sound of running fountains, also has two *psistariés* (but no rooms) and is one of the best places on Samothráki to watch the sunset.

From Profítis Ilías, follow the asphalt road to its end in Kastélli, 5 min below. From the uppermost three houses of this hamlet, point "10 o'clock" to a good mule trail threading its way down the ridge toward the Lákoma-Dháfnes-Pahía Ámmos track. Your path links up with the latter just east of Dháfnes after about 20 min. Much of this road hardly merits the label, being barely passable to most four-wheel vehicles—it's more of a glorified donkey track through peaceful, olive-mantled countryside.

About 45 min beyond the Kastélli trailhead, a spring feeds a trough on the left (north) side of the track; 20 min later is an important fork. The left option leads up, within 30 min, to Panayía Kremniótissa chapel, perched atop one of a group of pinnacles. Outriders of Sáos stand guard behind and to the northwest, and there are sweeping prospects over the entire south coast. In clear weather you can glimpse the formerly Greek (Turkish since 1923) island of Ímbros a bit to the southeast—on calm mornings you can reportedly even hear its roosters crowing. The chapel itself is of no great antiquity or architectural interest, and there's no water nearby.

The right fork of the crossroads leads, also within 30 min, to the justly famous bay of Pahía Ámmos (broad sand). Olives yield to a landscape of stunted oaks, wild apples, sumac and aloe, and the last dependable water on the trail lies about 10 min past the junction in the form of a tiny creek.

The paradise-like beach itself extends for 700 m, closed off at either end by two gaunt headlands and lapped by crystal water. It's much frequented in summer, and if you decide to camp here, remember that Lákoma is the last outpost of civilization, so plan groceries accordingly. Some visitors never find the tiny fresh-water spring in the cleft in the rocks at the beach's eastern extreme. Here water trickles from the strata to fill two potholes about half a meter above sea level!

Seasonal note: Samothráki is surprisingly crowded (mostly with Greeks, Germans and Italians) at the height of summer, and Thermá closes down after October 1, leaving June and September as the best months for a visit.

Map: Rékos' "Touristic Map" (1:50,000) is good enough but often sold out on the island, so buy it in Alexandhroúpoli if possible. ESY's Évrou is useless.

THESSALÍA AND MAGNISÍA

At three [in the] afternoon the fog floated up in small, white puffs like water-lilies through the ravine . . . the sky became hazy and more and more white clouds floated upward from the sea . . . in a matter of minutes everything around me was invisible . . . then a dim pyramidal shape loomed through the mist . . . so I crossed to (it) along the edge of a precipice and there waited for Olympos to reveal itself . . . .

——Kevin Andrews

Mt. Ólymbos, often considered a Makedhonian mountain, has been included in this section because the geologic record shows that it, like its neighbor peaks to the south, is a product of a single surge of mountain-building activity that took place during the Eocene epoch, some 70 to 80 million years ago. Much later, the inland sea that inundated the Thessalian plain finally succeeded in boring a way through to the Aegean, thus creating the celebrated vale of Témbi and forever separating Mts. Pílion and Kissávos from their massive brother to the northeast.

Further south, the Pagasitic plains at the base of Mt. Pílion were host to the earliest humans to settle in present-day Greece. Looking at the rich agricultural lowlands

west of the so-called Pelagonic arc of mountains, it's easy to see what induced those bygone Neolithic pioneers to homestead, but equally obvious that there is little to detain the mountaineer or tramper. Your attention is more profitably directed back to the slopes of Pílion and Kissávos, many of them still as thickly mantled with primeval vegetation as they were in the days when the centaurs were said to dwell there. These horse-men are probably a mythologization of an aboriginal tribe that retreated to the hills after the invasions of the Dorians, and were reputed by the latter to be adept at all manner of earth magic and sorcery, including the ability to change shape. Hikers caught in the elemental force of a storm on a forested flank of Pílion or Kissávos will find it easy to believe that every rustling branch hides a lurking character out of a Rousseau painting, watching them with the same eyes that gaze half-comprehendingly, and perhaps jealously, at the peaks of Ólymbos to the north.

22 MT. ÓLYMBOS (OLYMPUS)

The mythological abode of the ancient Greek pantheon is today still outstanding among the Greek mountains in almost any category you could care to list. Ólymbos is first in the number of both Greek and foreign visitors and in the quantity, color and variety of wildflowers in a country which overall is distinguished with respect to alpine flora. It possesses far and away the best trail system in Greece and the most sumptuous alpine refuges. The range constitutes the core of one of the first national parks to be established in Greece and—more ominously—is the number-one killer of mountaineers who fail to respect the peak's idiosyncracies.

Ólymbos is actually a complex massif of a half-dozen summits culminating in 2917-m Mýtikas (the beak), the second highest peak in the Balkans between Austria and Turkey. It marks the border between Thessalía and Makedhonía, and leaves a strong impression on the visitor due to its abrupt rise from a narrow coastal plain and the rugged beauty of the numerous limestone pinnacles, saddles and walls above treeline. Proximity to the Thermaic Gulf means that Ólymbos acts as a trap for moist air masses; thus Olympian weather is fickle even by Greek standards and can change with a rapidity usually associated with the climate of tropical volcanos. Blinding mists which boil up to the crests from the deep canyons to the east and west are a particular specialty, so a compass could save you from aimless wandering if you're caught in a white-out.

On its lower slopes, especially in the occasionally precipitous canyon of Mavrólongos, Ólymbos is blanketed with a dense mixed forest, mostly of beech, black pine and Balkan pine; above 1900 m there are few deciduous specimens. The best meadowlands lie between 1800- and 2200-m elevations, with treeline at about 2300 m. Good campsites and permanent springs are rare owing to the steepness and porosity of the mountainside. A handful of refuges scattered through the range, staffed and sponsored by a variety of organizations, partly fill the need for protected overnighting spots. You may, however, want to bring extra supplies to free you from complete dependency on the huts.

Getting to the trailhead: Litóhoro(n), a gritty army town on the coastal plain, is the base for most excursions. It's linked by rail to both Athens and Thessaloníki, but the station is 9 km out of town (hourly bus service). There are also direct buses from Kateríni and Thessaloníki. The cheapest place to stay is the youth hostel, near the town park; hotels start at about $6 single, the most inexpensive being the Park. The EOS information booth (rarely open) is on the main square next to the church; SEO's office is nearby, below the bus station. Grocery stores line the street heading southwest and uphill from the *platía*.

Opposite: Skolio looms over the Kazánia chasm beyond Skala saddle

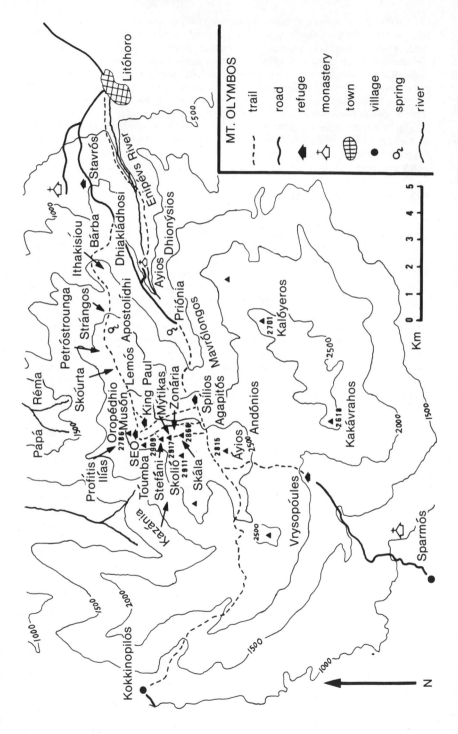

MT. OLYMBOS

- - - - trail
───── road
◄ refuge
⌂ monastery
⊕ town
● village
ᥩ spring
~~~ river

Km

0 1 2 3 4 5

N

Litóhoro
Stavrós
Enipévs River
Bárba
Ithakisíou
Dhiakládhosi
Ayios Dhionýsios
Petróstrounga
Strángos
Lemós Apostolídhi
Priónia
Skóurta
Mavrólongos
Papá Réma
Oropédhio
Musón
King Paul
Mýtikas
Zonária
Spílios Agapitós
Andónios
Profítis Ilías
SEO
Toúmba
Stefáni
Skolió
Skála
Ayios
Kalóyeros
Kakávrahos
Kazánia
Vrysopóules
Kokkinopilós
Sparmós

2701
2500
2618
2815
2785
2905
2917
2911
2866
2000
1500
1900
1000
500
2500
1500
2000
1000

A mostly unpaved road leads 18 ½ km out of Litóhoro past the national park boundary to the two principal trailheads, starting from a sign by the police station. Try if at all possible to get a ride up to the trailhead area—phone the various alpine-club numbers listed to find out about car-pooling if hitching or taxiing does not appeal to you. Most people are aware that there is no bus service up the hill, so rides are usually forthcoming. Do not spurn the offer of a late-afternoon lift—you can stay at the Stavrós mountain lodge or at an abandoned monastery, both within striking distance of the two trailheads. Above all do not waste your stamina walking up the roads— you'll need it on the trail. If desperate, there is reportedly an abandoned trail straight up the Mavrólongos gorge, paralleling the Enipévs River from Litóhoro to the old monastery, but it's badly overgrown.

Approximately 10 km above Litóhoro, the Stavrós refuge (also known as Hostel "D", phone [0352] 81-867) offers meals and bunks to those who want a good jump on the mountain the following morning. Four km further, a trailhead known variously as Dhiakládhosi or Gortsiá, and marked by a defaced placard, takes off to the right. Roughly halfway between this trailhead and road's end at Priónia, a 1-km driveway descends to the half-ruined monastery of Áyios Dhionýsios, where a sign in English, Greek and German tersely states that the central shrine was blown up by Nazi troops in April 1943. Intact it must have been an architectural gem, since even half-destroyed it is one of the finest monasteries outside of Áthos. Fortunately the monks' living quarters were unharmed, and several cells, all with fireplaces and some with cots and blankets, are kept open for the benefit of passers-by. There's plenty of water, but you should leave an offering in the chapel(s) for candles taken for secular purposes. A monk-caretaker is in full-time residence from June to October to minimize the appalling vandalism perpetrated on the premises; after the war most of the brothers were moved to a new monastery just outside of Litóhoro.

Priónia itself has in recent years acquired a *kafenéio* constructed of crude branches, manned in season only, and a mule-team station for supplying the most popular Olympian hostel. With prearrangement you may get your baggage sent up the trail along with the normal load of foodstuffs.

Dhiakládhosi to Oropédhio Musón

The most direct route to the SEO (Apostolídhis) and EOS "C" (Vasilévs Pávlos, or King Paul) shelters begins at the 11-km trailhead. Here the reasonably accurate, if dilapidated placard indicates points of interest and walking time to them.

Bárba meadow, 40 min uphill, is the first stop; camping is possible here and at a smaller grassy spot just beyond, but there's no water. In spring there's a good concentration of wildflowers here. Having kept well to the right of the ridgetop, you reach, after 1¼ hr, a saddle with a good view down into the Mavrólongos valley; there's one campsite here. Shortly afterward a side trail leads left within 10 min to the Ithakisíou cave, a rock overhang which was walled in as a rustic studio by the eccentric painter Vasílis Ithakísios in the 1920s.

Strángos, 2 hr out, is a small, slopy meadow with poor camping, but 5 min off the main trail to the left lies the Apostolídhi spring, the only reliable water on the trail—however, the slopes at the spring do not permit camping. Some 45 min beyond Strángos, Petróstrounga meadow (ca. 2000 m) has the best wildflower displays and campsites on this side of the Mavrólongos. Next the trail keeps mostly to the north face of the ridge until Skoúrta, an exposed knoll just beyond treeline and 4 hr above the trailhead. From the altimeter here you get (weather permitting) your first complete view of the peaks Profítis Ilías, Stefáni and Mýtikas.

For the next 45 min the trail negotiates, without gaining much altitude, the length of the Lemós (neck) which, as the name suggests, is a long, narrow ridge joining Skoúrta and Pérasma Yiósou, a pass named after Yiósos Apostolídhis (former

Stefáni ("Throne of Zeus"), with typical afternoon mist (left) rising out of Mavrólongos

president of SEO). The Enipévs River canyon yawns to the left, while a more gentle grade slopes down the opposite side toward the Papá Réma ravine. A few short, sharp switchbacks put you over Yiósou and onto the Oropédhio Musón (plateau of the Muses). Twenty min from the bottom of the pass is a well-signed fork, where two colored placards point the respective ways to the King Paul ("C") shelter, 15 min left, and the SEO Apostolídhi hut, 20 min straight on. The path across the plateau to the SEO establishment is well-marked with red flags and is in fact part of the main route looping through the entire massif in snow-free seasons (see "Spílios Agapitós to Oropédhio Musón indirectly, via Zonária").

Both shelters enjoy unparalleled ringside views of Stefáni, aptly nicknamed the "Throne of Zeus," with Skála hovering just behind. If you haven't made prior arrangements with the EOS office in Litóhoro, their King Paul shelter will be shut tight. The outhouses, water room and glassed-in porch of the SEO shelter are kept open year-round as a favor to climbers; the interior is manned only from mid-June through August—for exact dates dial (0352) 82-300. Beds and meals cost about $2 apiece, and this hostel has an enormous capacity (ca. 80 bunks), so don't despair if Spílios Agapitós is booked. During the day, the greenhouse effect created by the front porch makes this a wonderful spot to gape at the peaks even on windy afternoons when the mist is starting to boil up out of the Mavrólongos. Water, which comes from a cistern, is in short supply late in the year, as signs over the sink duly warn. If it's all gone, you *may* be able to tap a pair of cement reservoirs sighted in the gulch at the very base of Stefáni; to be on the safe side, collect a couple of liters per person when passing Apostolídhi spring 3 hr previously.

From the SEO hut it's 1½ hr via Lóuki to either Stefáni or Mýtikas summit. Stow full packs at the shelter—you'll need all four limbs and perhaps an ax on the pinnacles.

There are some stomach-twitching 500-m drops on either side of the peaks, and this approach is much more dangerous than the classic route via Skála—only experienced Class 3 climbers need apply. All times were logged with a daypack; with a full pack, count on 6 to 7 hr from Dhiakládhosi to the SEO refuge. If you're hiking downhill from either the King Paul or Apostolídhi shelters, subtract 1½ hr from this figure.

Prióna to Spílios Agapitós Hut

The Prióna trailhead, 18½ km above Litóhoro and about 3 km west of Áyios Dhionýsios monastery, is the start of the very popular ascent to EOS shelter "A" (Spílios Agapitós). This is the only Greek trail besides the one through the Samarian gorge in Crete that could be described as habitually crowded. The waterfall just above Prióna is the sole source of water along the way, so fill up for the steady, 3-hr climb through a mildly gloomy forest to Spílios Agapitós. This lodge is continuously staffed from May 15 to October 15, and it's a good idea to reserve a bunk by phone, (0352) 81-800, since "A" is apt to be full nightly from June through August. Beds (bring your own sleeping bag) are about $3 a head, meals slightly less. The current refuge warden is Kóstas Zolótas; when he's not at the hostel he lives in Litóhoro (phone 81-329). Mr. Zolótas is trilingual in Greek, German and English, has a set of keys on hand for the "C" shelter (18 beds) and has been known to lend ice axes in spring.

Spílios Agapitós to Mýtikas or Skolió

Above the shelter the trail continues, with two important forks, to Mýtikas summit via Skála peak. Beyond Spílios Agapitós, 45 to 60 min (depending on snowpack), the cutoff for the Zonária trail to Oropédhio Musón is marked by a sign on a tall iron pole (see "Spílios Agapitós to Oropédhio Musón Indirectly . . ."). About 15 min further the second fork is also marked by a pole; it's just visible from the first. Proceeding straight takes you over the ridge separating Skolió peak from Áyios Andónios, and then you veer south around the latter's west face and down to Refuge "B" (Vrysopóules); it's 3½ hr one way from the pole to "B." In spring, snowfields on the eastern flanks of Skolió and Áyios Andónios are eerily lifeless and silent, except for the occasional rumble of an avalanche.

Bearing right and following the red arrows and dots on the rock leads you toward Mýtikas. One hr above the junction the trail reaches Skála peak and deteriorates to a series of dots, dashes and arrows in the scree and crags. During snowmelt the way is slippery and dangerous, making an ice ax mandatory before June. Finally, 3 hr after leaving Spílios Agapitós (slightly less if there's no snow), you arrive at Mýtikas summit (2917 m), whose first recorded ascent, by a Swiss-Greek team, took place only in 1913. A metal Greek flag planted in a cairn marks the spot, from where you have a 200-km view in every direction. It is arguably certain that nobody had enjoyed this panorama prior to the liberation of Makedhonía, though Sultan Mehmet IV made an unsuccessful attempt on the peak in 1669.

Spílios Agapitós to Oropédhio Musón, Direct Route

Two red arrows adorn the main trail toward Skála and Zonária about 200 m above Refuge "A." One, accompanied by the legend "9," points left; the other points right with the same numerical designation. Bear right; a faint and narrow (though not impossibly so) path winds up, steeply at times, to the Plateau of the Muses and huts King Paul and Apostolídhi. This should take about 1 ¾ hr, at least 30 min more with a full pack (*not* recommended). The way first crosses forested hillsides, then a scree-littered gully (which presents snow problems in spring) and then climbs steeply up, along the base of the Zonária, to a pass. Finally it threads across the north end of the

Oropédhio to the two shelters, which are about 10 min apart though within sight of each other. From the pass, the briefest way to King Paul, just out of view over the brow of a ridgelet, is an uphill, scuffed-out way in the dirt to your right. If it's the SEO hut you want, follow the red numbers up to "72" and continue from there by line of sight. These numbers on the rocks, which guide you the entire way, are supposed to be the serial order of curves in a proper, regraded, trail, but they correspond almost exactly to minutes in the supposed ideal course of 90 min. However, funding is not forthcoming to improve what is currently little better than a surveyed goat path, so for the forseeable future the shortcut described must remain just that rather than a full-fledged trail for those with full packs.

Spílios Agapitós to Oropédhio Musón Indirectly via Zonária

Follow the route described in "Spílios Agapitós to Mýtikas or Skolió" until the first iron-poled junction, and turn right toward the Zonária (stripes), the banded layers of rock that give the area its name. Hiking distance from the turnoff to the Oropédhio is merely 1 hr, but the trail is only open after snowmelt, usually by July. Just over 30 min along is the well-marked detour for climbing Mýtikas via the couloir Loúki—look for the legend "MYTIKAS" and red arrows on the rocks just after a sign announcing that the SEO shelter is 20 min away. This extremely dangerous route—which seems to claim the life of at least one climber annually—runs right up amongst the goblin needles that are a big attraction on the Zonária traverse. Shortly after, there's another turnoff to climb Stefáni—watch for this name written in Greek characters on the rocks, followed by red dots. Like the Mýtikas "ladder," this ascent takes about 1 hr but is even steeper and definitely not for acrophobics or the timid. In its last moments the main trail snakes along the base of the magnificent fan-shaped Stefáni and then past Toúmba, a mere lump in comparison, until ending at the front steps of the SEO lodge.

Western Approaches

Though the scenery on the Thessalian side of Ólymbos is rather bleak compared to the fine forests and meadows of the Mavrólongos flank, you may wish to undertake a straight traverse of the range. From Elassóna, a town on the main Lárissa-Kozáni highway, take a bus passing through the villages of Kalithéa and Olimbiádha—if possible up to the hamlet of Sparmós, below the eponymous monastery. If you're obliged to hitchhike, the right fork for the communities listed is 8 km north of Elassóna. From the vicinity of Sparmós you must thumb a further 29 km to the "B" refuge at Vrysopoúles, which seems often partly or completely occupied by soldiers. For more information contact either the Elassóna branch of EOHO, phone (0493) 22-261, or the ski lift near the refuge, (041) 228-915—a Lárissa number which might answer year-round. There is no meal service at the Vrysopoúles hut.

A trail climbs from the refuge up Áyios Andónios, slipping through a pass to the left of the peak and meeting a disused trail coming up from the village of Kokkinopilós. Next it traverses the ridge between Áyios Andónios and Skolió before slipping over the watershed to within striking distance of Spílios Agapitós.

Rating/time course: Hiking Ólymbos is moderately strenuous to difficult but should not be too daunting to anyone in good physical condition. With few exceptions trails climb relentlessly, often over less than ideal surfaces. Expect giant snowbanks above 2200 m before June 1 and bring along needed equipment. Obviously, if you were to explore in detail every trail mentioned, you could spend an enjoyable week on the mountain; the minimum time counseled is three days, excluding any period spent in Litóhoro.

Seasonal note: Alpine refuge schedules have been noted and should be super-imposed on the following considerations. The annual Olympic wildflower explosion commences in mid-May, but many of the high-altitude trails do not come out from under snowpack until late June. Weather remains relatively stable until late September, and many Greeks declare October the finest month for a hike. **Supplies:** Litóhoro or Elassóna. **Maps:** *Korfés* has gazetted the entire range on four sheets (issues 45-48). Also, EOS produces a very useful color pamphlet with a sketch map.

23 MT. KÍSSAVOS (ÓSSA)

Kíssavos has always suffered in comparison with its five-star neighbor Ólymbos, starting in mythological days when the Titans reputedly used the peak as a doormat and front step on their way to the latter mountain to do unsuccessful battle with the Olympian gods. The denigration continued in medieval Greek folk literature, in which a personified Ólymbos disparages Kíssavos as *"Turkopatiméni"* ("Turk-trampled"), in contrast to itself teeming with freedom fighters. Today's hikers are likely to whiz past it through the vale of Témbi, on their way to the greater charms of Ólymbos, or if they do stop and climb 1978-m Kíssavos, it's only to get an unusual look at the high summits to the north. While this is certainly a reason to make the ascent, it is by no means the only one, and Kíssavos, with its dense eastern forests, startling ocean overlook and network of trails (some albeit in poor condition) again demonstrates that in the Greek mountains altitude is not the only criterion of quality.

Getting to the trailheads: From Lárissa on the Thessalian plain there are two daily buses to Spiliá (early morning and midafternoon); two to Anatolí; three to Ambelákia; and three (oddly spaced) to Stómio.

Spiliá to Kánalos Shelter

Spiliá, elevation 800 m, is a tiny village at the headwaters of the Sikouriou River. There are a handful of *psistariés*, but the only conventional accommodation is booked continually by OTE (phone company) workers. You may obtain permission to sleep on the second floor of the *kinótiko grafeío*.

Leave Spiliá on the road heading northeast, which after 15 min bears a sign pointing right—"*Poréia óres 2 ½. EOS Lárissa*"—and directing you to a shelter 2 ½ hr away. Red arrows and a trail begin climbing through sturdy oaks; turn right at the top of the first rise, marked by a crumbled *ikónisma*. Bear right a second time upon reaching the first meadow; you must look carefully to spot a small arrow nailed halfway up a tree on the upper margin of the pasture. The path becomes distinct once again as it ascends through more oaks to a chapel and a hairpin left turn about 30 min above Spiliá. About 45 min out of the village, the route emerges from the oak groves and begins switchbacking up a bare hogback on an at first faint but eventually well-engineered path. Káto Ólymbos and various river valleys running parallel to Témbi appear to the northwest; the cone of Kíssavos itself, with the summit proper still hidden, looms just to the southeast.

Approximately 2 hr beyond Spiliá, you'll cross the forest road that serves the hostel; you should follow red blazes along a rock shelf on the other side. Soon you recross the road, and the trail, by now very haphazard, goes directly up a moderate, sparsely wooded hillside. Within another 30 min a drippy spring inside a cement pavilion (courtesy of EOS Lárissa) marks Tésseres Vrýsses—no sign of the other three springs. The placard on the outskirts of Spiliá is a tribute to Greek unladen quick-marching, since it takes almost 3 hr with a full pack to reach the EOS hostel; for the last 10 min the trail ceases to exist, having been plowed under the roadway.

The alpine shelter is an appealing, rambling structure at Kánalos (1600 m). A handful of dependable springs dampen the pasture land immediately around it, and you could camp, if necessary, under various protecting overhangs of the refuge. It's usually in use on weekends, though, and you might wish to phone ahead, (0495)

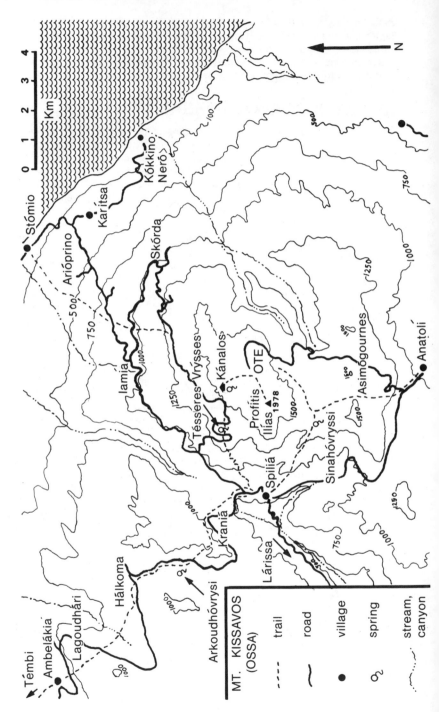

MT. KISSAVOS
(OSSA)

- - - - trail
——— road
● village
♀ spring
.... stream, canyon

51-485, to see if anyone will be on hand. The interior is well-appointed and there may be a fire going on chilly spring or fall days.

(Speaking of cold, Kíssavos is an uncommonly frigid mountain outside of summer—3- to 4-m snowpack and winter temperatures of -10 degrees C are the rule, and climbs in poor visibility are, as anywhere else in Greece, not advised. There is a very prominent memorial below the hostel to two local youths who froze to death in the snow here in 1983, and another accident was narrowly avoided in 1984.)

Kánalos to the Peak

Follow the rather hopeful, too-short ski tow rope, and then power poles, 30 min up to the OTE antenna relay station on the brow of the ridge above the hostel. The OTE staff is friendly and hospitable but unfortunately, since most of them hail from other provinces, know little about the mountain or its environs. From OTE hang a right and proceed west-southwest another 30 min up the summit ridge on a path well-grooved into the soft turf. Profítis Ilías peak (1978 m) features, besides the inevitable altimeter, an isolated belfry (difficult to resist ringing it) and an odd subterranean chapel with a burrowlike entrance. To the north the serrated crest of high Ólymbos rears up in miniature; to the right of the Témbi gorge the channels of the Pineiós River delta meander along, and to the northeast the triple prong of the Halkidhikí peninsula is just discernible. Closer in, the wave patterns of the crystal blue north Aegean apparently lapping at your feet make it seem deceptively close, and the dense beech forests to the east and south seem a continuation of the surf line. (A radius of about 2 km from the summit describes a roughly circular area once dense with fir trees—these were logged off centuries ago.) Finally, the north flank of Mt. Pílion rides above the hazy hills to the southeast.

Spiliá to Ambelákia or Vice Versa

This 5- to 6-hr, up-and-down route connects the two villages via Kraniá, Arkoudhóvrysi (the only water en route), Hálkoma meadow and Lagoudhári ridge. Beginning from Spiliá the trail follows the new road as far as Hálkoma, where it leaves the auto right-of-way and shortcuts to the ridge overlooking Ambelákia. The path traverses mostly open country and is still in fair condition where it has not been chewed up by the road.

Ambelákia was once a prodigiously wealthy, cultured village, this prosperity being confined mostly to a 50-year period immediately before the Napoleonic wars when the locals had a monopoly on various natural dyes extracted from wild plants growing on Kíssavos. The industry was organized along the lines of a cooperative, the world's first, with participant benefits including schooling, free medical care and performances of drama and opera. The insolvency of the cooperative's bank in Vienna, plus the depredations of Ali Pasha of Ioánnina, brought about the organization's untimely collapse in 1812. The last president of the cooperative, Yiórgos Mávros (known as Schwartz to the Austrians) died while undeservedly in debtor's prison, but you can still see his partly restored, fairy-tale mansion, of a decidedly Turkish style, from 9 A.M. to 3:30 P.M. except Tue. As many as 600 similar villas graced Ambelákia at one time, but the majority were burned by the Germans in 1941 in reprisal for the villagers having helped retreating ANZAC stragglers escape south and for subsequent resistance activities. Most of the 36 remaining arhondiká (lordly houses), including that of Yiórgos' brother Dhimítri, are in deplorable condition.

When in Ambelákia try to also see the 350-year-old church of Áyios Yiórgos, with striking frescoes and a peculiar design, 500m northeast of town. As of 1984 there was no overnight accommodation, but this may change soon—ask in the platía.

If you're bound from Ambelákia down to the main highway or beyond to the Témbi train station, there's an old trail which will save you at least 30 min. It begins behind

Áyios Athanásios church at the south end of the village, but it's almost impossible to find coming up from Témbi.

Anatolí to Profítis Ilías

Although Anatolí is almost 200 m higher than Spiliá, this ascent of 4½ to 5 hr is a bit longer because of the greater horizontal distance covered and an altitude loss coming off the first ridge encountered. It takes 1½ hr to climb the thickly wooded Asimógournes spur (1400 m) and a similar period of time to descend to the meadows (ca. 1100 m) at the south side of Profítis Ilías and reach Sinahóvryssi spring, where you meet a disused trail coming up from Spiliá. The balance of the route is your choice of 700-m grades from the spring to the summit. Lodging in Anatolí is uncertain, but certainly no worse than Spiliá's.

Kánalos to Stómio

This trail does exist but has fallen into horrendous condition since a network of forest roads was built. It's a minimum 6-hr descent, and the trail is visible nowhere near the hostel. The stubborn can best try to pick up the path by taking the forest road 6 km downhill and east to the first big junction sign (which points back uphill). The trail or remnant thereof heads down and left from the left fork; many red markers are said to be lost and the right-of-way has been overgrown by one of the densest forests in Magnisía. EOS Lárissa plans to reblaze the trail in the future.

In the meantime, forest road-walking (24 km) instructions are as follows: take the left of the fork 6 km below Kánalos; another left 3 km below this, at Skórda; make a right at the signed junction of Iamía; straight on to the "pik-nik" grounds at Arióprino, where you can camp; and finally, upon meeting asphalt, a left for Stómio, a low-key resort popular with Yugoslavs. The very good beach here is the main draw, but Stómio feels like a mountain village because of its moderate distance from the shore and the overhanging forest. Amenities include two tavérnes and a range of accommodations, including a well-equipped campground behind the beach. There are few mosquitos, but many rays inhabit the warm, sandy water at the mouth of the Pineiós estuary. The delta is also something of a sanctuary for birds attracted by the same waterlife that sustains the locals who fish, and it's an altogether enchanting place to end a Kíssavos traverse (except in peak season).

Rating/time course: Hiking western Kíssavos is only moderately difficult, though a traverse through the dense forests of its east flank is an altogether different exercise, enlivened by both the distance involved and the rudimentary trail. Overnighting facilities at the various trailhead villages are also less than optimal; you might consider leaving Lárissa for Anatolí or Spiliá on the earliest morning bus and plan to overnight at the hostel or, if trekking in the long summer days, leave Spiliá in the afternoon in time to reach Kánalos by dark.

Supplies: These must be gotten in Lárissa.

Maps: The Lárissa chapter of EOS puts out an excellent pamphlet on Kíssavos (Greek text), with a good 1:100,000 sketch map showing roads and trails on the mountain. Korfés published a map in issue 37.

24   MT PÍLION: MAKRINÍTSA TO SOURVIÁS MONASTERY VIA LESKANÍ

The villages of Mt. Pílion, along with those of the Máni and Zagória, comprise the third nucleus of traditional settlements in Greece. Makrinítsa, the showcase of the Magnisian communities, was founded in 1204 by refugees from the Latin sack of Constantinople and is to this day crowned by six architecturally notable churches and several dozen mansions in assorted states of repair.

From Makrinítsa you do not climb Mt. Pílion so much as hike parallel to the long axis of the summit ridge (1651 m), which is cloaked in both the impossibly thick Magnisian forests and a variety of military installations. From the right-of-way, a comfortable distance west of the watershed, you first enjoy comprehensive views of the Pagasitic Gulf. A subsequent section over mediocre terrain is redeemed by sweeping vistas west over Thessalía, including the seasonal lake of Voïvís; returning through here, the generous foliage of high Pílion glows in the fading light. The remoteness and wildness of the landscape, relieved only by an occasional goatherd, is heightened and deepened (literally, too) as you negotiate the gorge of Leskaní. Beyond the hamlet of the same name, occupied in summer only, the tree-shrouded countryside becomes haunted, preparatory to arrival at the semiruined cloister of Sourviás. When glimpsed from a distance in wet weather, lonely Sourviás may begin casting its spell on you, with only the sound of raindrops on beech leaves to interrupt your reverie.

Getting to the trailhead: From Vólos, an important port just off the main Athens-Thessaloníki route, at least eight coaches a day run the 17 steep km up to Makrinítsa, perched on a south-facing slope 950 m above sea level. There are a handful of *Tavérnes,* two groceries and several inns, though these last tend to be overpriced because of Makrinítsa's designation as a historical monument.

Route directions: Leave Makrinítsa on the road passing the convent of Áyios Yerásimos; this auto track snakes up the ridge dividing the lush canyon in which much of the village nestles from the bare canyon to the west. Makrinítsa slips out of sight behind you near a blue, spindly *ikónisma* where the road changes sides of the ridge. From this point it bears generally north as the arid canyon to your left (west) comes up to meet you. A small vineyard with a low, damaged fence just to the left of the road marks the easiest spot to pick up the foot trail, which actually begins near the blue *ikonostási;* it's heavily traveled and you may notice and adopt it long before the fence.

Cross the head of the canyon, usually a dry watercourse with a few plane trees, and begin climbing on the hillside opposite to complete your first 30 min of walking. Fifteen min past the stream bed you'll top a ridge near an iron cross embedded in a cairn. Approximately 1 hr above Makrinítsa you should see a corral to the left and a

Sourviás monastery in the Mt. Pilion forest

stock-watering pond and a meadow straight ahead. Here the trail becomes ambiguous; veer left, passing between the corral and the pond, and find an initially faint continuation which marches more and more steadily over the low ridge beyond the corral. Aim for the barest spot on the ridge. Soon there's a descent to a rough but double-treaded track which must carry pickup trucks at some point in the year; this takes you to a giant cement trough-spring about 30 min past the corral. From the stock trough follow the track as it bears further left (northwest) and becomes narrower and rockier over the subsequent 15 min up to a T-intersection with a much larger jeep track.

The far side presents a welter of possible continuations; the correct choice is a narrow, slightly uphill donkey track just to the left of straight ahead. Within a few moments you should, looking carefully, be able to spy the monastery peeking out from the woods on the opposite side of the Leskaní canyon. From this first glimpse of your destination the rocky trail descends in a leisurely fashion through juniper and holly oak, heading west toward a sizable hilltop meadow with an altitude marker. You arrive here just over 2 hr out of Makrinítsa; beyond the altimeter the route continues down the grassy slope past a dry well. The path subsequently steepens and acquires a steady cobbled surface about halfway down to Leskaní hamlet, which has been visible since before the meadow. The juniper-oak scrub begins to defer to a lush mixture of *valonidhiés* and beech, which carpets much of Pílion.

Close to 3 hr along you change banks of the ravine via a fine stone bridge whose three arches can only be seen by clambering down into the usually dry watercourse. Leskaní is just 10 min further; "downtown" consists of a spring dated 1888 and shaded by the ubiquitous *plátanos*, a single cottage and the nearby chapel of the Panayía. From the chapel proceed right and slightly uphill; the path becomes constricted again in the stream bed between two farmhouses. If uncertain, ask Ksénophon, who seasonally occupies the right-hand cottage just above the creek. According to him, Leskaní was once lived in year-round, but since the civil war the inhabitants have fled, or were forcibly removed, to the lowlands.

The final climb from Leskaní to Sourviás takes 45 min, bringing the total elapsed hiking time from Makrinítsa to just under 4 hr. The path is fairly distinct for the first 35 to 40 min, pending arrival at a large spring flanked by three poplars, which are unusual enough hereabouts to be referred to as landmarks. From the poplars bear left 5 min through trackless walnut groves to reach the monastery. Often herders from Pourí, the northeasternmost village of Pílion, come here to raid for nuts while grazing their flocks in the area; their vigilant dogs will bring them running. After the uproar has subsided you may ask them for advice on the well-hidden trail to Pourí.

Your first thought on arrival at Sourviás is to ask yourself why you've bothered; its crumbling outer walls and ruined cells augur nothing of interest within, and the dry fountain behind the apse of the *katholikón* reinforces the air of desolation. Once inside the sanctuary, and with a moment or two for eyes to adjust to the dimness, opinions improve remarkably. Every square centimeter of the interior is covered with vivid 16th-century frescoes which, with their warmth and humaneness, deviate from the usually austere Byzantine imagery. However, only fragments of what was an intricate *ikonostási* (here, altar screen) remain and many ikons were looted in the 1950s. It's good to bring a powerful flashlight to illuminate the walls, although there are often some tapers on the premises; if you open some of the narrow, creaky windows to admit natural light, please reclose them completely to prevent further deterioration of the frescoes by the elements.

There is a macabre legend associated with the destruction of the monks' quarters which, while taking place during the Second World War, was not attributable to the occupying Axis powers. At some point during the winter of 1943-44, a shepherd described to me only as a Vlach (interesting how these tales acquire racial/ethnic overtones) passed the night in a vacant cell. He lit a fire for warmth and cooking and left the next morning without dousing it properly. An ember found its way into the straw one floor below, igniting it and thus devastating both wings of cells. A year to the day afterward, a hungry wolf appeared out of the snow to prey on the Vlach's flocks which were grazing at Sésklo, near Vólos. The firebug shepherd went out to confront it, and the wolf ate him forthwith. The story is considered by its tellers a striking example of divine justice in action, administered only after a year's reprieve during which the herdsman failed to offer significant restitution to the church.

At the southeast corner of the compound, on the second floor, are two cells which have been recently restored; these offer adequate shelter for the night if the local shepherds have not occupied them. From Sourviás it's possible to continue northeast, within 4 hr, to Pourí, the beach at nearby Horevtó and bus service back to Vólos. Climb past the poplar spring to the ridge behind, keeping the bulk of Pílion summit to your right, and descend down the other side. Also 4 hr beyond Sourviás, to the north, lies the monastery of Flambóuri, to which the trail is so badly deteriorated that once upon the ridge above the spring you'll prefer to make use of a forest road which eventually arrives at the cloister. Flambóuri is tenanted by five monks, so women will have to sleep out. On the positive side, 15 min from the monastery is a quarry from where trucks ply frequently down the hill to Keraséa village.

Sourviás' elevation is about 200 m less than Makrinítsa's, but retracing your steps uphill to Makrinítsa may take as little time as 3½ hr since you're familiar with the route.

Rating/time course: This moderately challenging itinerary makes an ideal full-day hike from April to September. Forays beyond Sourviás toward Flambóuri or Pourí imply possession of overnighting equipment and the willingness to do some exploring in potentially trackless country.

Supplies: Vólos or Makrinítsa.

Map: ESY's Magnisías is probably better than nothing. Most of the tourist-trade maps on sale in Vólos or Makrinítsa fail even to indicate the presence of either Sourviás or Flambóuri.

THE SPORÁDHES ISLANDS AND ÉVVIA

. . . the path skirted some gardens and wound its ways upwards through increasingly abandoned fields . . . and into the first fringes of the pine forest . . . . [it] climbed steeply between high banks where the feet of countless animals had scored the path deep into the earth . . . . Halfway up . . . the path emerged from the pines onto the shallower once-terraced fields . . . where crops had recently been harvested, until finally . . . the presence of the village was heralded by little garden plots . . . and the path itself altered from trampled earth and polished rock to a stone cobbled surface . . . falling away into endless disrepair.

——Juliet Du Boulay

THE SPORÁDHES

This island chain is geologically and climatically a continuation of the shaggy eastern slopes of mainland Pílion; ample winter rainfall (and occasional snow)

The *kalderimi* between Kástro and Hóra, on Skiáthos

nourish a lush cover of forest and orchard on the northern members of the group. Add sandy beaches interspersed with rocky, cave-riddled headlands, lapped by crystal-green water, and you have the archetypical holiday islands so beloved of the travel posters.

The Sporádhes are indeed a boon for those who can't tell a Doric column from an Ionian (and couldn't care less), since with the exception of Skýros they bear few traces of a history before Byzantium; the first inhabitants were more concerned with growing olives and grapes than with leaving lasting monuments. The *hóres* (main villages) of each island are all products of medieval culture that reached a pinnacle of achievement on scrubby Skýros which, by an ironic twist, is both the largest and least hikable island. The entire archipelago is ruggedly hilly and is crowded only in summer, so in principle hiking away from the villages or coasts in any direction should be rewarding; in practice, military and olive-grove service roads tend to disrupt old byways.

25 SKIÁTHOS

That the smallest and most commercialized of the Sporádhes should have perhaps the best hiking may come as a surprise, but good, shaded trail surfaces, a variety of scenery and unique perspectives over Pílion and several islands make a convincing case. The massive influx of tourists may have had the fortunate incidental effect of preserving various footpaths across the island, since foreigners seeking to escape beach-bound crowds seem only too happy to use them. The two itineraries detailed have as their final destination the *kástro*, or fortified old town, at the extreme north tip of Skiáthos, joined to the body of the island by steps replacing a long-vanished drawbridge. The village was abandoned in 1825 after the islanders presumably decided that the nascent Greek state could and would protect them from piracy at the present-day town site.

Getting to Skiáthos: There are two to four ferries daily from Vólos and Skópelos; daily from Áyios Konstantínos (on the mainland) and Alónissos Island, in season;

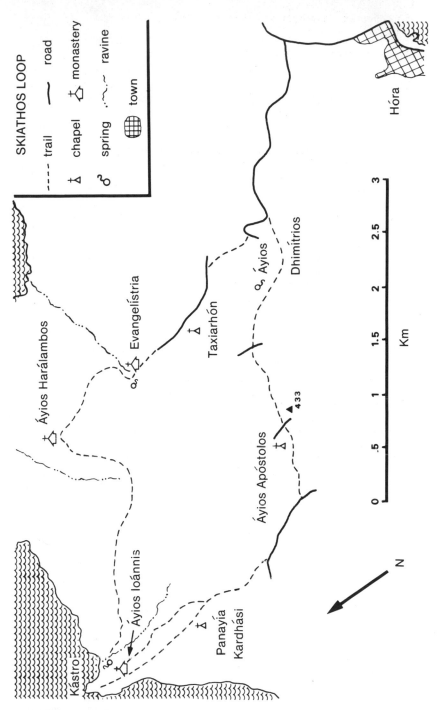

SKIATHOS LOOP

---- trail   ── road

⚐ chapel   ⚑ monastery

♂ spring   ～ ravine

⊕ town

Áyios Harálambos

Evangelístria

Taxiarhón

Áyios Dhimítrios

▲ 433

Áyios Apóstolos

Kástro

Áyios Ioánnis

Panayía Kardhási

Hóra

N

0   .5   1   1.5   2   2.5   3

Km

rarely from Skýros via Kími (on Évvia). Flights from Athens are reasonable; they may exist from Thessaloníki.

Hóra to Kástro via Áyios Apóstolos

Walk north from the dock of Skiáthos' *hóra* on the asphalt road toward the airport. Some 15 min out of town, the road bears sharply right, and you should veer left onto a dirt track prominently signaled by red dots on a tree, a "W" (for German *weg*?) and, most obviously, a blue-white-and-gold sign reading *"Panayía Evangelístria"* (see next section). Climb on this jeep track about another 15 min until a wooden cross and a somewhat shabby white-and-green *ikónisma* mark the actual trailhead (the straight track leads to Evangelístria). Turn left onto the footpath and proceed an occasionally steep 15 min more on a wide, scooped-out surface to another white-and-green *ikonostásis* marking a confusing intersection. Here red dots and a sign seem to indicate a left fork, but the right turning actually works better. About 1 hr from town you'll reach the fountain of Áyios Dhimítrios, labeled as such with a plaque dated 1933. Within another 10 min you'll meet a new lumber road; turn right (north) and walk a few paces to the point where the trail resumes on the opposite side. Soon *kalderími* cobbling appears and a shady glen closes in over the route; some 20 min above the road, ignore an uncobbled fork on the right and pass a usually dry cistern recessed into the hillside left of the path. Just over 1 ½ hr out of Skiáthos town, the *kalderími* is briefly disrupted by another bulldozer track in the vicinity of a red-and-white *ikónisma*. Cross the road-disrupted saddle, aiming for the ochre *ksoklísi* of Áyios Apóstolos, situated at the summit (433 m) of the island, just north of the path's continuation. In the next 15 min the now-revived cobble way dips down to meet another road on its way to Skiáthos' north coast. Turn right and walk a few moments to yet another *ikonostási* on the right shoulder, painted with the legend "KASTRO" and a red arrow pointing to the resumption of the path. Within 15 min of quitting the road, there's a right fork which eventually leads to the *kástro*, but it's preferable to carry on straight toward the chapel of Panayía Kardhási. Here the belfry has been fashioned in the form of a ship's mast with a bosun's nest, and glass fishing floats whimsically stud the roof line. Within another 15 min you reach the well-maintained grounds of Áyios Ioánnis monastery, complete with artesian wells, flower beds and picnic tables. It's another 10 min, or 2 ½ hr from the harbor, to the entrance of the *kástro*.

The town itself is a heap of vine-shrouded ruined foundations; only the bastioned gate (permanently ajar) and three churches remain standing. The most interesting of these, Hristóu, contains some fine frescoes and a massive carved *ikonostási*. Observe the little sign near the entrance: *"Klíste pórta yiatí baínoun pondíkia"* (Close the door, because the mice get in). Behind Hristóu a couple of picnic tables provide a haven for the lunch-minded, and water has been piped down from Áyios Ioánnis. For the energetic, the high points of the *kástro* offer superb views east to Glóssa village on Skópelos, west to Pílion and south back over the island; to the north the open sea stretches uninterruptedly to Halkidhikí. A fine beach in the lee of Kástro Point, to the east, is only crowded with excursion-boat passengers until midafternoon; a potable stream empties onto the shore here for the benefit of a perennial handful of campers.

Hóra to Kástro via Evangelístria and Áyios Harálambos

Upon encountering the *first* green-and-white *ikónisma* described above, continue straight rather than bearing left. After a few minutes take a right off the jeep track onto a prominent path which passes a spring and shortly collides with the cement drive heading toward Evangelístria. Turn left and continue on the road past the chapel of Taxiárhón, which is just before a knoll with a flagpole, an *alóni* (threshing circle) and the road's end. From some chapels near the flagpole a path leads the last few moments down to the gate of Evangelístria, in a total hiking time from town of 1 hr.

The monastery commands the head of a still valley which plunges to the sea, a patch of which is just visible. Most of the cloister dates from 1806, but the beautiful *katholikón* with its intriguing roof lines and carved *ikonostási* is probably three centuries older, judging from its quasi-Byzantine architecture. Evangelístria is a sterling example of the historically close association of Orthodoxy and Greek nationalism, for it was here, in 1807, that the Greek flag in its present form was first raised, and pledged to, by assembled heroes of the Revolution.

To continue to Kástro, duck out the back gate of the monastery and clamber down some steps to a shaded fountain and a picnic area; from here a clear trail proceeds up the opposite side of the stream valley. The locked monastery of Áyios Harálambos, 45 min beyond Evangelístria, was where the Skiathote novelist Alexándhros Moraítis, a contemporary of his more famous fellow islander Alexándhros Papadhiamántis, retired to in 1929. Another hour-plus of walking separates Harálambos from Kástro; this route is about 30 min longer than the one via Áyios Apóstolos, since the trail must curve to avoid various deep canyons in the vicinity of Harálambos. If you use the long way outbound, it's an easy matter to return on the Áyios Apóstolos trail and construct a satisfying loop day hike.

Map: Toumbis' "Skiathos" at 1:25,000 is preferable to others, but none of the tourist maps sold take into account the recent plague of forest and olive-grove roads spreading north from the main Hóra-Koukounariés asphalt. Trails are accurately depicted about half the time—the tough part is knowing which half.

26 SKÓPELOS

After occasionally raucous Skiáthos, the rugged but equally wooded terrain and *two* major towns (a Sporadhean oddity) of Skópelos come as a relief and a surprise to many. With inconspicuous beaches and its farms and orchards inland out of sight, Skópelos is not as immediately alluring as its cosmopolitan neighbor but rewards in direct proportion to any effort expended on walking. The island is distinguished by scores of *ksoklísia*, with peculiar dunce-cap-shaped cupolas, whose slate roofs are fuzzy with flowers in the spring. Prune, apricot and cherry orchards lend Skópelos its well-tended air and surround farmhouses sporting rock shingles and beaked chimneys.

A glance at a map suggests the possibility of an inland walk from Skópelos harbor to Glóssa, via Mt. Dhélfi, but the principal donkey track in use before the south coast asphalt road was built in fact skirts the forested mountain and descends to the coast at Élios, 9 km below Glóssa. A more northerly branching may traverse the Vathiá forest as far as a point above Klíma and Mahalás, two hamlets south of Glóssa. From Glóssa worthwhile foot excursions lead to Perivolioú beach and the monastery of Áyios Ioánnis Kastrí.

Getting to Skópelos: There are the same services and frequencies as for Skiáthos, but some boats do not stop at Glóssa—double check if that's where you wish to disembark.

Élios to Skópelos Hóra or Vice Versa

Get a bus, taxi or a ride to Élios, a rather grim prefabricated village behind a mediocre beach. Such communities are fortunately rare relics of the junta years; one of the colonels' pet social policies was the relocation of villagers displaced by earthquakes into housing projects conducive to surveillance by the authorities. On the inland side of the coast highway, across from the center of Élios, find a two-meter wide mule track intersecting the asphalt at right angles. A few paces toward the Vathiá forest crowding the ridge above, take a right fork and then enter the fringes of

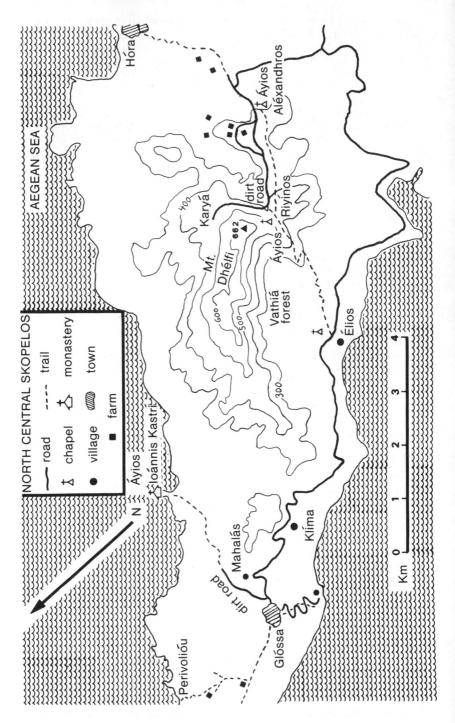

NORTH CENTRAL SKOPELOS

— road
---- trail
⚑ chapel
⚑ monastery
● village
◐ town
■ farm

AEGEAN SEA

Hóra
Áyios Aléxandhros
Karyá
Mt. Dhélfi
Áyios
Ríyinos
Vathiá forest
Élios
Áyios Ioánnis Kastri
Mahalás
Klíma
Glóssa
Perivolióu
dirt road

400
600
500
300
662

0 1 2 3 4
Km

the pine woods. After two more quick right bearings you cross a hillside olive grove, where the trail dwindles. A group of blue beehives above the olives marks (April to October) the spot where the old trail resumes in earnest. Ascend, cross a jeep road and continue climbing steadily through the pines. Soon there is little shade, but this does allow sweeping vistas of Miliá, one of Skópelos' best beaches, to the south and Skiáthos Island to the northwest. Within 1 hr after leaving the road you reach Platanákia with its three enormous plane trees and a spring, unfortunately dry after midsummer. From here on a stone edging buttresses the path, evidence of its former importance. Thirty minutes above Platanákia pass a trail coming up on the right, possibly from Pánormos Bay; a few min later the little *ksoklísi* of Áyios Riyínos,

---

Skópelos Prune Farmer

Stélios (a common name on the island) is one of the last prune farmers on Skópelos. He owns a cottage and four *strémmata* (about an acre) of trees in a district known as Áyios Nikólaos or Ananía, just north of the Áios Riyínos-Áyios Aléxandhros track.

The harvest season, in August and September, involves 20 to 30 nonstop days of working 16-hour shifts. Three thousand kilos of fresh fruit are spread out on wooden racks and then baked repeatedly in an ingenious oven which takes up half the cottage. The oven itself consists of two portions, the fuel chamber and the drying vault. Hot exhaust from the vaulted wood burner at the base of the house is directed through zigzagging flues past the racks before escaping through the roof. However, a domed radiator below the wooden shelves, smeared with prune drippings baked to an enamel consistency, does most of the work.

First there are two bakings of six hours each, at temperatures of 60 to 80 degrees C, and then two more sessions of three hours at higher temperatures (up to 100 degrees C) to drive off the last of the moisture. After each roasting the fruits must be removed and hand-kneaded individually to assist the process and help them maintain an attractive shape. The raw plums bake down to 1000 dry kilos, for which Stélios received 150,000 *dhrachmés* (about $1250) wholesale in 1984.

Because his son is still too young to help and his daughter has married on the mainland, Stélios must hire four extra prune squeezers—usually his parents and in-laws—for about 20,000 *dhrachmés* apiece, thus immediately eliminating half of his gross. The remaining 75,000, when divided by 400 hours of labor, yields 188 *dhrachmés* an hour, which compares poorly to the 2200 *dhrachmés* plus social security Stélios earns in an eight-hour day painting houses in Skópelos. Accordingly, 1984 was Stélios' last year drying his own fruit; in the future he'll sell his fresh crop directly to a big oven in town, if he even bothers to pick it. "California prunes can always undercut the Greek industry," Stélios observed as his wife went to fetch some samples and *oúzo*. "They sprinkle their plums with stuff to draw the water out, but the prunes come out wrinkled and ugly."

Stélios' prunes, when they arrived, were small but smooth, sweet and the best I'd ever tasted. It saddened me to reflect on the demise of the local industry, but I was partly consoled by the pride Stélios obviously still feels in his property; the oven and cottage had just been meticulously repainted, and Stélios will continue to use it as a summer retreat.

Skópelos' patron, huddles just below the summit (662 m) of Mt. Dhélfi. From this high point en route the trail descends out of the Vathiá forest; keep to the right and avoid the bulldozer track soon sighted. Angle down the ridge for 40 min, using power poles as an orienting guide, until meeting the road again near the *ksoklísi* of Áyios Aléxandhros. Continue for 10 min along the road to where it dips down and right; the path picks up again straight ahead. From this junction the red-dotted path descends within 45 min to Skópelos harbor. After passing a tiny *ksoklísi*, continue downhill to the right; ignore jeep tracks going straight on. Total walking time from Élios to the harbor is about 5 hr.

For a reverse itinerary, the trailhead in Hóra is located between the little church and the fountain behind the orange-walled cemetery near the top of Anapavséos St. This thoroughfare begins behind the pagoda shaped four-story apartment building with brown balconies. Once on Áyios Aléxandhros ridge, you need to watch out for the trail ascending to the left under the power poles.

Just north of Áyios Riyínos chapel, a path leads down to the jeep road on its way to the Karyá district, where there's a good spring and some 3000-year-old rock tombs known as the Sendoúkia. From Karyá thoroughfares—probably lumber tracks—continue an undetermined distance along the northeast flank of Mt. Dhelfí, potentially fizzling out close enough to Klíma to make them worth exploring as a way to Glóssa.

Short Walks from Glóssa

Glóssa is a sleepy but beautiful island hill town, minimally prepared for tourism (one *tavérna*, two seasonal inns, two houses for rent) but the preferred base for the two strolls listed below. Don't make the mistake of staying in the characterless port of Loutráki—two of the lodging proprietors there have quarters up the hill, if you insist. Loutráki and Glóssa are linked by a 25-min cobble path.

Set out on the main cart track heading northwest out of Glóssa. After 10 min bear right at a perpendicular intersection marked by a farm; after another few min you reach a hairpin curve on a jeep road. To the right gushes a fountain; bear left for a few hundred meters and then right in the direction of the homestead of Stélios Karvélis, Glóssa's official eccentric and caretaker of Perivolióu beach. You'll know you're on the correct track when you see several crude statues and a reed archway hung with a sign inviting you to stop in. If you do so you'd better not be in any hurry, since Stélios will entertain you and ply you with *oúzo* and olives all afternoon. From the edge of his property, the bottom of a cement walkway, a good trail leads within 40 min to Perivolióu beach, where Stélios and his cousin Dhiamándis have pipe-channeled a spring flowing from the rock and erected a swing set.

Two hr due east of Glóssa, partly on jeep tracks and finally on a serviceable trail, lies the peculiar bouldertop monastery of Áyios Ioánnis Kastrí. The track starts off the asphalt road, between Glóssa and the hamlet of Mahalás.

Map: Stélios Papadhimítriou's "Tourist map," at 1:36,000 is adequate, though many important features seem to have drifted a few hundred meters from their true situation.

ÉVVIA

Separated from the mainland at one point by a mere 30-m strait, Évvia is officially the second largest Greek island, after Crete. However, it's hard to distinguish the attitudes and habits of Evvians from those on the Stereá, and a number of modest peaks with attractively wooded foothills seem lesser versions of the Sterean mountains. The main advantages of excursions on Évvia are the almost instant access from Athens and adaptability to tight schedules.

On the path above Stení; Mt. Dhírfis in background

27 MT. DHÍRFIS

The imposing peak of Mt. Dhírfis, perfectly pyramidal when seen from the southwest, dominates the center of the island and, with its offshoot Ksirovoúni, offers a day or two of surprisingly vigorous climbing. Between the crest joining the two peaks and the north Aegean lies some of the most rugged and deserted terrain on Évvia.

Getting to the trailhead: There are 18 mini-trains daily from Athens to Halkídha, the industrial town at the narrow straits; thence, five daily buses to Stení, the village at the foot of the peak.

Stení is a shady, quaint village built on the south slope of a deep hollow blessed with a number of fountains. Several *exóhika kéndra* and *psistariés* cater to carnivores, but groceries are spotty (get in Halkídha or Athens) and the two hotels are on the expensive side (no singles, $12 double) so bring a friend along.

Route directions: There is a placard in Stení, erected courtesy of the Halkídha EOS, which helps visualize the route, but it's schematic and rather rusty. From the Stení bus stop, walk up the ascending asphalt road, passing the last *psistariá* of the village on the right and a spring and chapel on the left. Just past a *yípedho* (soccer field), the foot trail starts in the stream bed to the right of an abandoned hotel. Initially on the left bank, it crosses to the right side after a few moments and a thick chestnut-fir forest begins almost immediately. About 30 min above the trailhead, you cross a jeep road; the path resumes directly across the track, but from here on it's often littered with fallen branches and boulders. The trail also becomes wide and rather anarchic, with many oxbows, shortcuts and divisions, but always adheres to the spine of the ascending ridge. The cone of Dhírfis is a constant sentinel to your left. Recross the road once again; the path becomes much neater until, 1½ hr above Stení, you reach the saddle connecting Dhírfis with Ksirovoúni to the right. Here is a *kafenéio* and the perpendicular intersection of an auto road (from Stení to Strópones and Metóhi northeast of the ridge) and the track running almost parallel to the ridge that connects the base of Dhírfis to the foot of Ksirovoúni. The latter, a long, low but rugged summit, is perhaps 1 hr walking distance from the crossroads.

A rusty sign points northwest toward the EOS shelter; after 30 min you come to the powerful trough spring of Líri, and then to the refuge 300 m beyond. From this hut a red-dashed mule track continues for 25 min to the base of Dhírfis itself, passing en route some roofless stone huts. At the foot of the peak, a bit to the left, is another trough spring; to the right a path wends down a valley toward the tiny isolated hamlet of Ayía Iríni.

From the second spring it's a 1 ¼-hr climb, following red dots along the southeast spine, to Dhírfis' 1743-m altimeter and a primitive cross. The peak gives an impression of greater elevation due to a low (ca. 1200 m) treeline and all-encompassing panoramas of central Évvia, Skýros and the northeast Aegean. The final ascent is demanding, with a 400-m elevation gain in just over 1 hr; coming down takes about as long, since the trail surface is miserable scree most of the way.

For the return to Stení, it's possible to make a circle trip of sorts. Retrace your steps to the mountain lodge, cross the little ski run just beyond it and begin following red dots painted on the rocks. Almost immediately you'll see red blazes on certain trees ahead, which flank the initially healthy trail that descends through a Cephalonian fir forest. After 15 min, you cross a forest road (not the Stení-Metóhi *dhimósio*) for the first time; after another 15 min the trail meets it again and expires. From here on efforts to find fragments of the trail between switchbacks in the road are not terribly productive, and you've a dusty, traffic-filled 1 ½ hr further to the outskirts of Stení. Not recommended for the ascent.

Rating/time course: The entire outing entails about 8 hr of hiking, with the time divided evenly between uphill and downhill.

THE ARGO-SARONIC GULF ISLANDS

If there is one dream which I like above all others it is that of sailing on land. Coming into Poros gives the illusion of the deep dream. Suddenly the land converges on all sides and the boat is squeezed into a narrow strait from which there seems to be no egress. . . . Hydra is almost a bare rock of an island and . . . the town, which clusters about the harbor in the form of an amphitheatre, is immaculate. The houses are even more cubistically arranged than at Poros.

——Henry Miller

Given the essential poverty of their land, it's not surprising that the islanders of the Argo-Saronic Gulf turned to the sea for a living after most of the archipelago was repopulated in the Middle Ages. It was the fleets of this island group that enabled the Greek revolutionaries to fight the Ottoman Empire to a stalemate in the 1820s, until the balance was tipped in favor of the fledgling Greek state by the famous "accidental" sinking of the Ottoman navy at Navarino by a French and English armada. Éyina, the only Argo-Saronic island to be more or less continually inhabited since antiquity, then served briefly as the capital of Greece.

Nineteenth century bridge at Vlíhos

Of late these quintessential holiday islands southwest of Athens are more evocative of water sports and *la dolce vita*, but at least three of them offer enough hiking to merit inclusion in this book. Ídhra, with its absence of cars and paved roads, is the best bet, though overcrowded and roasting in the summer. Spétses' perimeter road is minimally disruptive, hiking grades are less steep than on Ídhra and the shade-giving pine forest is more consistent. Éyina provides a few paces in the shadow of Mt. Óros, but walking opportunities on overdeveloped Póros are severely limited so the island is not included here. All these islands are small enough to see across along at least one axis, so it's difficult to get badly lost. For detailed information on outings in this archipelago, you can do no better than the excellent coverage in the Lycabettus Press booklets (see Bibliography) and thus this chapter will be limited to a brief overview.

Getting to the islands: Both regular steamers and hydrofoils connect Piráeus with the three islands. Éyina is served up to 12 times daily by each type of craft. The steamers call at Ídhra and Spétses a mere twice a day, once in off-season; there are four to six daily hovercraft crossings.

28 ÉYINA (AEGINA)

Most of the hikes on this island circle or climb the modest (532 m) height of Mt. Óros. From Éyina town take a Pérdhika-bound bus and alight at the halfway village of Marathónas. From there a dirt road leads inland to the hamlet of Pahía Ráhi, and thence a proper trail climbs within 1½ hr to the summit of Óros, site of an ancient

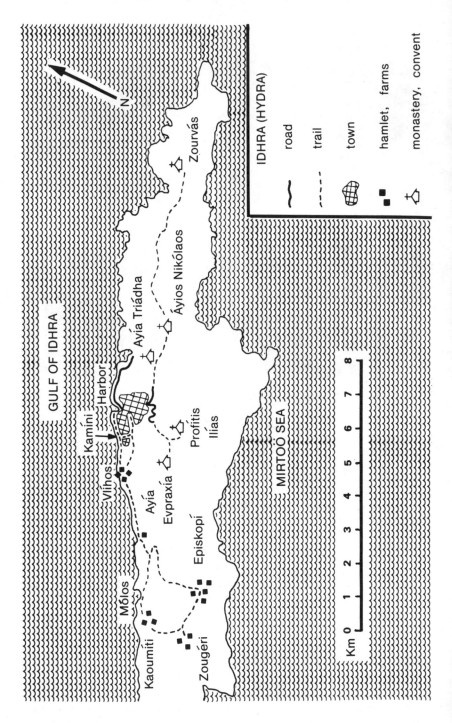

GULF OF IDHRA

MIRTOÖ SEA

Kamíni Harbor

Vlíhos

Mólos

Kaoumíti

Zougéri

Episkopí

Ayía Evpraxía

Profítis Ilías

Ayía Triádha

Áyios Nikólaos

Zourvás

IDHRA (HYDRA)

road

trail

town

hamlet, farms

monastery, convent

Km 0   1   2   3   4   5   6   7   8

shrine to Zeus. This conical peak can be seen from most any unobstructed point in the gulf so, conversely, views from the top, especially to the west, are unrivalled. From the heights you can retrace your steps toward Pahía Ráhi and the nunnery of Hrissoleóndissa a few minutes to the north. Alternatively, you can come down to the east, toward the hamlet of Vlahídhes, and from there bear north toward the settlements of Pórtes, Lazarídhes, and Yannakídhes, finally arriving in Áyia Marína after 3 hr. Lastly, if you stay on the Éyina-Pérdhika bus until the end of the line, you can reach the village of Sfendhoúri, 5 km by dirt road east of Pérdhika, and then proceed on a clear path along the south flank of Óros to Vlahídhes. The Sfendhoúri-Vlahídhes-Pórtes-Lazarídhes-Yannakídhes traverse offers the best glimpses of the roadless, rural face of Éyina, but expect no facilities in any of the tiny hamlets.

29 ÍDHRA (HYDRA)

Although the most heavily touristed island of the chain, Ídhra is conceivably the best for walking (out of peak season) because of its ample size, varied terrain and the prohibition of all automobiles from the island.

The premier excursion is the 2-hr walk to Episkopí, a tiny, usually deserted hamlet in the southwest. Follow the main donkey track which from Kamíni heads west along the island's shore and then, just under 1 hr out, turns inland and heads through some respectable forest. Episkopí is actually a huge plateau devoted to olives and vineyards—oddities on rocky Ídhra—with views of the sea from a house-and-chapel-dotted hillock above the fields. There are perhaps a dozen buildings in all, with no facilities. From Episkopí you can continue another 20 min west toward the ridgetop hamlet of Zougéri and then veer north toward the hamlet of Kaoumíti, perched just above the prominent bay of Mólos. There is reportedly a trail down from Zougéri ridge, but it's hard to find, and even cross-country the descent is only 45 min. Kaoumíti is inhabited only in late summer and early fall; the west end of the island formerly lived off its pine resin and olives, but since World War II most of the villagers have retired to Ídhra harbor and beyond. From Kaoumíti a good trail drops to the often debris-strewn bay of Mólos and continues onward to rejoin the main Kamíni-Episkopi track.

The most popular hike is the stiff 1-hr climb from the main harbor to the monastery of Profítis Ilías and the adjacent convent of Ayía Evpraxía. The tenants of the nunnery seem only too eager to sell their handcrafts, most of which are now imported rather than house specialties. Nonetheless, the view north over Ídhra town justifies the effort and with a little perseverance it's possible to continue on toward the south flank of Ídhra.

Lastly, a 3-hr trek brings you to the isolated monastery of Zourvás (two monks) on the northeast end of the island. The trail begins in the vicinity of Ayía Triádha monastery, above and to the left of the main harbor, and meanders on via the cloister of Áyios Nikólaos. All these structures can be plainly seen from Profítis Ilías and Ayía Evpraxía, so it's helpful to do the short walk first and get oriented.

Map: Kalfakis', sold in Ídhra, is passable; scale approx. 1:50,000.

30 SPÉTSES (SPÉTSAI)

This pine-shrouded island, thinly disguised as "Phraxos" in John Fowles' *The Magus*, has for some years suffered the presence of a perimeter road, but several attractive trails still crisscross the interior, converging at the *ksoklísi* of Panayía Dhaskaláki, near the island's 248-m summit. The easiest path begins near Vrellóu beach; proceed southwest on the Vrelloú-Áyia Paraskeví road and after 500 m make a left at the first fork. This side road quickly dwindles to a wide mule track which reaches the summit chapel within 45 min; there's a cistern and a 360-degree view over Spétses, Ídhra and the Argolid mainland. From the top other tracks lead southwest to the busy resort of Áyii Anáryi and southeast in the direction of Ayiópetres Bay. The most obvious continuation descends within 30 min to the Dápia district of Spétses town.

Map: Drapaniótis' "Tourist Map of Spétses," scale 1:12,000 but of indifferent accuracy, is sold on the island.

THE KYKLÁDHES (CYCLADES) ISLANDS

On leaving the town and ascending the hill, we were as out of the world as if no busy [harbor] existed at our feet. There was scarcely a mule track to guide us, and the rocks and stones by the way called for the exercise of all the ability our mules could display. All the way we never tired of admiring the ever-varying views over island and sea. . . .

——James T. Bent

These 20-odd islands floating southeast of the Attic peninsula conjure stereotypic travel-poster visions in the heads of potential visitors. Gleaming whitewashed villages sprawl like beached starfish on rocky spurs or mimic snow patches in the folds of a hill. Forests of windmills once harnessed the prevailing northwest wind to grind late-summer grain, but today they stand ruined or converted to dwellings. The celebrated cubist architecture hereabouts is not unique—try telling that to an Andalusian or a North African—but much of it has passed beyond that pat classification and into the realm of folk sculpture.

In antiquity the archipelago presented a more wooded and populated profile, but by medieval times the ravages of shipbuilders, earthquakes, wartime massacres and piracy had combined to send most of the islands into decline. Every so often one of them, by virtue of strategic position, fine anchorage or a commodity suddenly in vogue, would enjoy a brief renaissance before subsiding again into obscurity like an exhausted supernova. As modern Greece expanded northward, annexing more arable land, the Kykládhes ceased to play much of a role in the national economy and again served, as they had under the classical Greeks and the Romans, mainly as places of exile for political undesirables. As a result of this neglect these islands became veritable preserves of traditional Greek customs, bloodlines and language. Of course, a recent invasion of nude bathers, discos and boutiques has made inroads on this culture, but not as much or in as many places as you would think. Take the case of monastic, lonely Síkinos, which lies just across a narrow strait from the nonstop party on Íos.

Opposite—top, left: Kostas Mastrókalos, potter of Vathý, Sifnos island (Hike 34); Top, right: The famous Lion of Kea, near Ioulídha (Hike 32); Bottom: Spring plowing at Mésa Vounió (Hike 31)

No two Kykládhes are alike, though the majority, with the exception of Náxos and Ándhros, and to a lesser extent Kéa and Sérifos, are both arid and rocky. More than in any other island group, however, you get the feeling of each island as a microcosm, a recipe concocted from different measures of the stock Greek ingredients of paths, fountains, villages, orchards and beaches.

31   ÁNDHROS

This island, almost due east of Athens, is the second largest of the Kykládhes and one of the more fertile. A half-dozen deep valleys slash perpendicular to Ándhros' long axis, providing havens where well-tended citrus orchards flourish because they can depend on abundant water. In antiquity the island was of some importance; the ancient town site of Paleópoli and the tower of Áyios Pétros are the most substantial relics. Today's Andhriotes are great seafarers, and their villas dot the island, which is also distinguished by its *peristerónes* (dovecotes).

Getting to Ándhros: Daily ferries run from Rafína to Gávrion, and there is frequent service in season from Tínos, Mýkonos and Sýros.

North Ándhros: the Tower of Áyios Pétros

This round watchtower, with its masonry of giant two-meter brown blocks, is one of the largest such preclassical towers remaining in Greece; its estimated age is at least 2600 years. The tower is also beautifully set amid orchards and meadows, and on a clear day you can relive the view its ancient garrison had over islets west of Ándhros.

Route directions: Southeast of Gávrion 1500 m, or 5 ½ km northwest of Batsí on the paved coast road, a dirt road veers inland at a small *ksoklísi* with a blue belfry and a sign facing Gávrion reading *"Bungalows Sofia."* Follow this track about 450 m until coming to a wire-fastened gate. After passing through (and reclosing) it, scramble immediately right down into a walled-in trail that irrupts at this point. Although the tower blends well into its surroundings, you can see it from here on by looking carefully. Follow the enclosed path until it ends at a dirt driveway; some 15 m along this, turn right onto a new footpath and continue another 150 m to a second, unlocked gate at the edge of a meadow. Ahead to the left, about 100 m from the tower, a spring feeds a walled pool, an idyllic lunch spot. From the tower the path continues to Áyios Pétros, a 15-house village with no services; a cement drive beginning behind the church leads up 200 m to a dirt road. Bear left and follow this to where the town of Gávrion and the first walled path on the left come into view. Turn onto this right-of-way, which after various changes in appearance eventually ends in Gávrion.

Rating/time course: This easy hike, starting from a good beach and looping over to Gávrion, requires 2 to 3 hr.

Vourkotí and Áyios Nikólaos Monastery, Extension to Arní

This hike combines fine views over Ándhros *hóra*, the sea and some of the island's many valleys with visits to an inhabited monastery and two unspoiled villages. By press time a bulldozer track from the cloister to the villages of Vourkotí and Arní may have been extended, potentially obliterating much of the trail.

Route directions: Morning and midday buses run from the *hóra* to the village of Apikía. Begin hiking on the stairs climbing past restaurant/cafe O Tassos; at the top of the stairway bear left for 200 m on a path-street, then turn right onto a smaller dirt path. This curls back to the northeast, then runs parallel to a stream. About 30 min along, you pass a *ksoklísi* and from there on red-dotted stones mark the way. Above the chapel is a fork—take the high trail heading toward power poles and more red blazes. Continue uphill past the tiny hamlet of Katokaláyi; after this settlement there's no water until Vourkotí and the stairs dwindle to a narrow path. One hr above Apikía

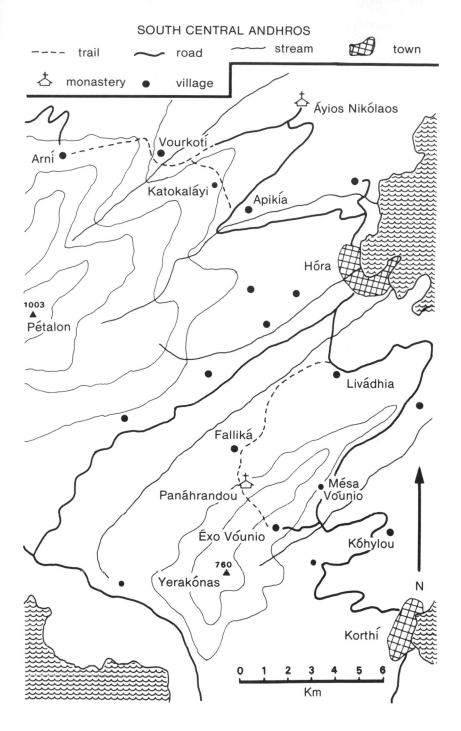

SOUTH CENTRAL ANDHROS

- - - - trail   ⌒ road   ⌒ stream   town

⌂ monastery   ● village

⌂ Áyios Nikólaos

Arní ●

● Vourkotí

Katokaláyi ●

● Apikía

Hóra

1003 ▲
Pétalon

● Livádhia

● Falliká

Panáhrandou

Mésa Voúnio

Éxo Voúnio

Kóhylou

760 ▲
Yerakónas

N

Korthí

0 1 2 3 4 5 6
Km

you'll reach a saddle in a ridge above Katokaláyi; 15 min below the pass the route forks. A right turn takes you to Áyios Nikólaos; a left, after a 15-min walk, to the village of Vourkotí.

In spring the approach to Vourkotí is dramatic, with the village sprinkled across dozens of Asiatically green terraces. It was until recently one of a handful of communities on Ándhros without road access, and it's still an unlikely target for tourist development. One cafe-grill offers basic fare and a good overlook of the valley, watered by a melodious stream.

The path continues beyond Vourkotí another hour to the village of Arní, from where there is bus service down to Batsí (provided you get there early enough in the day). You might be best off retracing your steps from either Arní or Vourkotí to the junction before Vourkotí.

About 1 km along the monastery-bound path—or sooner—you are forced to travel the new road linking the monastery with Vourkotí. Follow it 3 km to the cloister, a blue-and-white rectangular compound with several courtyards and dating from the 16th century. Only one younger monk and an elderly lay couple remain; their hospitality is limited to the traditional *loukoumia* (Turkish delights) and *potó* (spirits, usually *oúzo* or *rakí* but here on Ándhros the local citron liqueur). From Áyios Nikólaos to Apikía it's 1 hr on foot, but you can often beg a ride from parties descending past the monastery.

Rating/time course: Except for one long climb from Apikía to the ridge, this is an easy hike of 3 to 5 hr, depending on whether you visit Arní or not.

Kóhylou to Hóra via Mésa Voúnio and Panáhrandou Monastery

This itinerary, from the hill village of Kóhylou via several hamlets near Mt. Yerakónas to the largest monastery on the island and back to the *hóra*, offers one of the best transects of southern Ándhros. The three weird, bony knobs of Yerakónas, protruding above Mésa Voúnio, contrast sharply with the fertile fields and streams of that village. And nothing heralds the broadside view of Mt. Pétalon and the entire Ménites valley, plus the *hóra* with its twin bays, from the ridge above Panáhrandou.

Route directions: Leave Ándhros *hóra* on the earliest morning bus for the beach town of Korthí. From there arrange wheeled transport up to the village of Kóhylou—otherwise you face a 2-hr road walk with no possible shortcuts. Past Kóhylou the paved road becomes a dirt track, slips over a small pass and drops into a creek valley; Yerakónas' first knob pokes up to the west. Stay on the track until just past the cement bridge over the creek, where you turn left onto a faint uphill path which soon joins an old walled-in right-of-way. These shortcuts to Mésa Voúnio eventually merge with the meandering access road to that village.

Once on this road take the left of the first fork and proceed until it ends at Mésa Voúnio's outskirts. Bear left onto stairs crossing a creek to the left; on the far side more stairs wend through terraced fields before ending at another narrow road. Turn right; after 200 m turn left and take a last look at Yerakónas before topping the pass. The track, now impassable to vehicles, descends to Panáhrandou monastery, the largest and oldest (at least 14th century, some sources say 10th) on the island. The forbidding brown wall that braves the outer world gives no hint of the whitewashed maze of cells and passages within, now tenanted by just three monks; there is room for almost 200.

A red-dotted trail continues steeply downward for 45 min to the village of Fallíka. Turn right at the first street sign, next to a house with a red chimney; after 100 m turn left down a stair-street, then right onto a mule path at the bottom of the steps. Within 1½ hr, this trail, marked by numerous red dots and arrows with 'A's (for Ándhros *hóra*), leads through delightful pastures and meadow to the town. Thirty min out of Fallíka are some troublesome stream crossings, but soon the path widens to a

driveway ending in Livádhia village; from there Hóra is a few min distant.
Those unenthusiastic about bridging the considerable gap between Korthí and Panáhrandou could easily just hike from Ándhros to Panáhrandou and back. Walking in this direction, look for red way-marks labeled "MP" (Monastery Panáhrandou).

Rating/time course: The abbreviated itinerary mentioned just above would be a moderate 4½ hr round trip; the complete traverse from Korthí to Hóra is an all-day (6-plus-hr) affair. Take food—there are no facilities en route.

Supplies: Best selection in Hóra, Gávrion, Batsí and Korthí.

Map: The 1:150,000 map published by Dhimítri Kyriákos, sold on Ándhros, is marginally adequate.

32   KÉA (TZIÁ)

Kéa (or Tziá, as it was called under the Venetians) is even closer to Athens than Ándhros and was graced with no less than four cities in ancient times. During the Middle Ages, before Piráeus or the port of Sýros even existed, Kéa was the entrepôt of the Kykládhes, and consuls to the Ottoman government were stationed here. Following independence the island lapsed into the sleepy backwater status it now enjoys, content to live partly off a commerce in the excellent local almonds and acorns, which serve Kéa in lieu of olives and have allowed the natives to outlast several famines and sieges. Today the valonea oak (*Q. aegilops*) is the unofficial logo of Kéa, and gnarled, century-old specimens surprise and impress visitors to the interior, since they are hardly visible from the sea. The island is amply watered and produces quantities of figs, grapes, citrus and melons according to season, as well as the previously noted staples. The *hóra*, Ioulídha, is named after the ancient township whose site it occupies and is one of the most unusual in the Kykládhes by virtue of its gabled tile roofs, a legacy of the Venetian years.

Getting to Kéa: Daily ferries, once or twice according to season, sail from Lávrion, an industrial port on Attikí's east shore. Hourly buses go from Athens to Lávrion. Once weekly there is a boat to and from Kýthnos Island on the main west Kykladhean ferry route.

Ioulídha to Písses via the Watermill and Ayía Marína

The following 3-hr hike connects Ioulídha with Písses, the largest oasis and beach on Kéa, by way of two historical monuments. Begin by descending the auto road connecting Ioulídha to Korissía harbor. About 1 km along, bear onto a wide path leading away from the hairpin turn nearest the atmospheric 19th-century chapel of Áyios Konstantínos. A marble fountain typical of Kéa and an incomplete baptistry stand near the neoclassical-Byzantine hybrid sanctuary. From this oddly matched ensemble a fine *kalderími*, built in the 1840s on foundations of the ancient way, continues downhill for 30 min through almond groves to the hamlet of Livádhi. Veer left upon reaching the bed of a seasonal wash, then right past a chapel toward an old farmhouse with a quadruple gable at the base of the hill beyond. Behind this dwelling, take a hairpin left onto an ascending, partly cobbled footpath. The *ikónisma* of Áyios Minás beckons after a 25-min climb; just past it the trail is briefly swallowed by a new bulldozer track, but it resumes to the right and below, passing a chapel overlooking the famous *nerómilos* (watermill) of Milopótamos Creek. Just before crossing the stream to visit the mill, 10 min below Áyios Minás, pause to sample some of the excellent watercress growing here.

The mill itself is the last of several once operating in this valley; you can see some of the disused ones downstream. The elderly couple stewarding the sole survivor is pleased to show visitors its interior workings, but since they have no male heirs the mill's future is uncertain. For now, water rushing in the top of a cylindrical tower

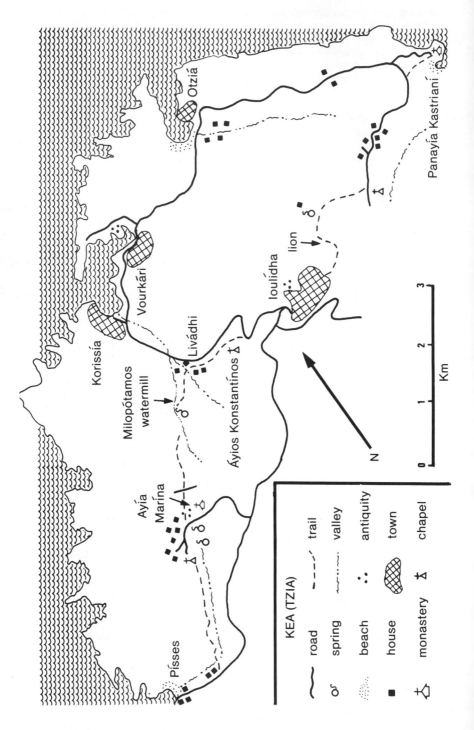

KEA (TZIA)

road
spring
beach
house
monastery

trail
valley
antiquity
town
chapel

Crumbling Hellenistic tower and monastery at Ayía Marína, Kéa

propels an Archimedean screw or similar, invisible device, thus turning an attached millstone against a stationery one. Wheat is the most frequently ground grain.

From the mill, on the west side of the Milopótamos, proceed upstream past the powerful spring feeding the mill sluice. Beyond the fountain the valley bottom is scarred by earthmovers and progress is apt to be muddy, but 15 min beyond the mill you bear right onto a proper trail mounting above this mess. After another 15 min comes the high point of the route, a ridgetop pass marked by a narrow jeep road. Cross it and pick up the trail on the other side, dropping gradually for 15 min more between the high retaining walls of oak groves and corn fields, until arriving at Ayía Marína and another dirt road.

The medieval monastery of Ayía Marína was built on the site of an ancient fort commanding the head of the valley continuing down to Písses. All that remains of the stockade is a four-story, square tower, similar in design and material to the one on Ándhros. The Keote tower is in slightly worse condition, having been used in past centuries for monkish defense but recently pillaged for building material. The roof and one wall are missing, as is a portion of the stairs from the second to the top floors; a century ago it was still possible to climb the whole way.

If you need drinking water, there's a spring 5 min below the tower, along a path directly across the rural road. To continue along the main route from Ayía Marína, move south along the dirt road, passing various farmhouses. Fifteen min later, you'll see a giant irrigation pool in the lush canyon plunging steadily down on your left; this deep (1½-m) cement tank, fed by the Ayía Marína spring, is accessible for a noontime dip. As you leave the pool behind, maintain a level course and keep left—don't take any right forks uphill either on paths or vehicle tracks. A last, tiny farmhouse next to a chapel at the end of a small, left-forking driveway 30 min past Ayía Marína signals the resumption of a proper *kalderími* to Písses. At first the going is flat, still paralleling the wild ravine which is now 200 m below you, but later a sharp, 20-min descent drops you level to the highest almond groves of the *kámbos* (plain) of Písses. Beyond the nut trees, utility tracks lead to the last stretch of the Ioulídha-Písses "highway" and the final 15-min walk to the beach. The most dependable lunch *tavérna* is on the main road, set back some 500 m from the sand.

Ioulídha to Panayía Kastrianí via the Lion

Another trail leads directly out of Ioulídha to the northeast, arriving within 15 min at the ancient lion of Kéa, which has been adopted as the official mascot of the island. This massive (9 m long) recumbent feline is carved from a single piece of granite; its features, best viewed from a distance, include carefully chiseled whiskers and a Mona-Lisa-like smile, as if it were coyly concealing its exact age, which is reckoned at upward of 3500 years.

Unfortunately, the path continues but another 30 min, past a spring and a giant *plátanos*, to a *ksoklísi* on a ridge marred by a new dirt road which has buried most of the onward path. Fifteen min north of the chapel take a right fork and proceed another 35 min to where Panayía Kastrianí, and 20 min of *kalderími* leading down to it, come into sight. The monastery perches on a bluff overlooking the sea, but northern Kéa is largely desolate and windswept and the nearest facilities are at Otziá, a 1-hr road walk further west. Kastrianí shelters one monk and one caretaker family, but only its setting is outstanding.

Seasonal note: Avoid midsummer, when Kéa is swamped with vacationing Athenians. After September 7, almonds and figs ripen and the island is nearly deserted.

Local cuisine: Try *kopanistí*, a fermented cheese appetizer, and *paspalás*, a salt-pork, tomato and egg casserole.

Map: The "Map of Kea," 1:44,000, sold on the island, is not infallible.

33 SÉRIFOS

The third of the western Kykládhes is one of the least visited and has always lain out of the mainstream of history. Just why is mysterious, because Sérifos is blessed with the third highest water table in the archipelago, and her harbors are many and sheltered. Iron and copper were mined here until cheaper African deposits dealt the industry its deathblow. Sérifos' stony and rugged exterior (perhaps a by-product of Perseus' return here with the Gorgon's petrifying head) seems off-putting when seen from an approaching ferry, but this rocky profile belies an interior of numerous streams bubbling through oases of calamus, willows, fig, olives, poplars and the occasional palm tree on their way to various sandy coves. The north and center of the island is a walker's joy, with clear, used trails, plenty of water and well-spaced villages.

Getting to Sérifos: Almost daily ferries link the island with Piráeus, Kýthnos, Sífnos, Kímolos and Mílos. Two to four days a week, depending on the season, ferry lines extend as far afield as Folégandhros, Síkinos, Íos, Thíra and Anáfi.

Island Circuit via Kállitsos, Taxiarhón, Galaní and Panayiá

This 6-hr, mostly road-free itinerary loops through the most beautiful settlements and terrain on Sérifos; every bend in the trail yields another prospect over a fertile valley, hamlet or patch of ocean washing the indented perimeter of the island.

Most visitors stay in Livádhi, the harbor, so first you'll want to transfer to Hóra, the striking village that pours like milk over the rocky hogback overhead. There are several buses daily but the way is simple and brief enough (45 min) to walk; near the power plant, leave the asphalt road in favor of the old stair-path zigzagging up through Káto Hóra to Áno Hóra. From the cafe I Míli, near the bus stop, descend north on another stair-street, and then head out of town on the paved track to the

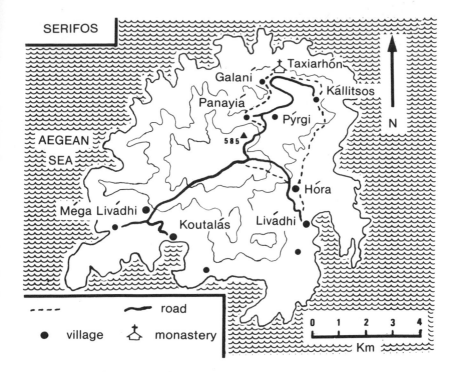

graveyard. Ten min along, veer left off the cement onto a dirt track; two red dots flank the "exit." After another 10 min, you'll cross an old bridge; just upstream is an elaborate, recessed cistern-fed trough where you can fill canteens. Beyond the bridge, the path climbs out of this first stream valley and passes a fork right; red dots point you straight ahead. To your right, notice a small modern bridge over a second creek; you can detour downstream from this bridge to visit the giant rock pools that are the year-round homes of European pond turtles and thousands of the frogs for which Sérifos is famous.

Soon you should pass a lone farmhouse and an adjacent chapel before bottoming out in still a third creek valley. Parallel the stream briefly, then cross it some 45 min out of Hóra on a comparatively modern bridge. After a short claustrophobic stretch between rock walls you ascend slightly, passing a well partly hidden by reeds. Approximately 1 hr from Hóra you'll top a ridge from which the beach hamlet of Áyios Ioánnis is just visible to the right; in front of you spreads yet another rivulet-gully. Keeping all stream-fostered greenery below and to your right, bear left and up toward two white buildings above the vegetation. After a scraggly interval the trail curves above the pair of structures and shortly becomes a well-surfaced *kalderími*. As you attain the high point on the leg to Kállitsos (Kéndarhos) you're treated to comprehensive views over the entire southeast quarter of Sérifos.

From this crest the cobbled way descends toward the attractive village of Kállitsos, poised above its oasis where *korómila* (wild plums) ripen in July. Almost 1 ¾ hr of walking separates the *platía* of Áno Hóra from that of Kállitsos, where there's a shady bench and a fountain. Having torn yourself away from this spot, it's another 20 min to a level zone of terraces and vineyards beyond the last house of the village. As you cross a jeep track off the road to Kállitsos, a prominent *ksoklísi* and Kýthnos Island appear simultaneously. Another driveway leads to this church (nothing of surpassing interest), and you cross it, maintaining a course toward a hamlet visible on the next ridge. Avoid the Kállitsos-bound road above and to the left—it's easy to continue on the path threading its way through a grove of oaks growing 2 ¼ hr out of Hóra. The shoreline to the north is convoluted into a peculiar three-lobed bay; a couple of dovecotes, reed clusters and vegetable patches betray points where water surfaces. Thirty min past the oaks, the trail is ground under the *dhimósio*. A few faint trails cross a new stream canyon in the direction of the hamlet, but it's simplest to take the road for the remaining 15 min to Taxịarhón monastery, the island's largest.

The *katholikón* inside the fortified walls dates from at least the 15th century and is replete with partly damaged frescoes depicting in exquisite detail the tortures of the damned in Hell. Entrance to the cloister is through a Lilliputian door at the top of a short flight of stone steps, but the few remaining monks and their lay retainers lock themselves in from 1 to 4 P.M.

From the fortress-monastery proceed 10 min more along the road until reaching a cement path on the right which leads down within a like period of time to the village of Galaní. This appealing settlement overlooks a sandy bay to the west, and a combination store/*tavérna* provides simple though adequate fare, but buses, taxis or any onward vehicle traffic are scarce.

Without returning to the auto road, leave Galaní on the pedestrian street which is transformed into a trail heading east and up a well-watered valley. Avoid the tempting path crossing the ravine in the direction of a red-roofed chapel. Twenty min beyond Galaní, you'll cross the creek on a damlet; a two-meter pool just a few yards downstream is just large enough to soak two friends on a hot afternoon. From a pair of outbuildings on the opposite bank, the trail, with intermittent cobbling, climbs briskly, double-switchbacking past a chapel and a palm tree. At a prominent knolltop junction 20 min above the stream, take a fork going slightly right, not left and up toward the road and Pýrgi hamlet. Within a few moments you should arrive at a large, cement-improved spring commanding the head of a second valley draining past Galaní, which is seen silhouetted against the Aegean.

One hr above Galaní you'll come out on a ridge in the vicinity of the cemetery for Panayiá, the village visible a few hundred meters to the left. Once across the graveyard access driveway, the trail meanders toward this next community through giant fields of acanthus, and debouches right in front of the village school. Panayiá boasts a handful of *kafenéia* and the 10th-century church of the Virgin from which the settlement takes its name; however, all the frescoes within are obliterated and only several appropriated Roman columns supporting the distinctive dunce-cap cupola remain.

To continue, find a prominent *kalderími* at the top of the village, where a sign announces "*Panayiá.*" The first 15 min are in good repair and provide nice perspectives over both Galaní and Panayiá, but by the time you pass a small chapel and intersect the new road back to Hóra the path is badly mangled. It does in fact persist below and to the left of the road as you head south but is so boulder-strewn and buried that it's safest to stay on the road. At the upcoming junction take the fork toward Méga Livádhi and Koutalás. Ten min past this (40 min above Panayiá) you'll come to a plateau distinguished only by a few low, white buildings and a dry cistern. Turn left into this unpromising landscape and pass the last farm, then locate a white cubic structure ahead in a nest of rocks. A fairly distinct trail progresses toward it. This is the other, most obvious side of Sérifos, lunar and mountainous. Your path merges with another (probably coming up from Koutalás) just before your arrival at the square, belfryless *ksoklísi* of Áyios Yiórgos, which guards a narrow, windy pass 1 hr from Panayiá. Slip through it and take in an unconventional view of Hóra just below, then enjoy the last 20 min on a fine cobble way descending to the highest windmill of Áno Hóra.

Rating/time course: This long but not overly difficult tramp can be done in one or at most two days. No *formal* lodging facilities grace the villages cited, but camping is possible.

Supplies: Livádhi or Hóra to start; replenishments in Galaní.

34 SÍFNOS

Sífnos, the next island south of Sérifos, is large enough (75 km²) to get lost on; most of the population lives on its fertile eastern slopes. In antiquity the island was famous for its gold and silver mines and resultant wealth, but these have long since been abandoned and today Sífnos is celebrated for its good cooks, fine ceramics and popular architecture. If you wish to admire the carved-marshmallow houses and churches that made Mýkonos famous, but without (except June through August) the latter's crowds, come here and also enjoy excellent hiking. The 20-km, long-day loop through the heart of Sífnos connects outstanding Kykladhic churches and monasteries and pre-Christian archeological sites. Vathý, an isolated fishing and pottery settlement on the shores of a funnel-shaped bay, is conveniently situated roughly halfway as a lunch or overnight stop.

Getting to Sífnos: Same schedule as Sérifos; in addition, a twice-weekly *kaïki* connection with Páros in summer.

Island Circuit via Katavatí, Profítis Ilías, Vathý, Taxiarhón, Áyios Andhréas

From Kamáres, Sífnos' harbor, there's bus service up to Apollonía and its extension, Katavatí. On the main street of upper Katavatí, find a small wall sign: "*Pros Vathý.*" Turn off here and descend 200 m, bearing right at the disused monastery of Piyés. (Straight ahead leads to Áyios Andhréas.) Some 100 m further, the trail bears left up a canyon and within 20 min reaches a cement causeway over a dry wash on the right. This is the turnoff for the main path to Profítis Ilías, longer but easier than the alternate route described below. The direct trail to Vathý proceeds straight and soon crosses to the right (northwest) bank of the wash, curves up the valley and passes below the *ksoklísi* of Taxiárhis. This beautiful chapel, surrounded by older medieval fortifications, should not be confused with a namesake monastery between Vathý and Platís Yialós. Twenty minutes above Taxiárhis, the path rises to a pass and almost immediately forks, the right turn being the alternate way to Profítis Ilías. The monastery is 1 hr from the junction—aim between a lone white farmhouse on the right and a white chapel to the left. The last 20 min involve trailless scrambling to the monastery gate; this shorter but steeper route might be best descended, after ascending the gentler trail noted above. Profítis Ilías (680 m) is frequently beset by a nimbus of clouds and howling winds; inside the natural stone boundary wall of the cloister are catacombs and an interesting refectory.

Return to the main route and continue west to the ancient tower of Órnos, just to the right of the path. Several unwanted trails confuse matters here; the correct choice bears left *after* passing the sunken, four-meter stump of the fortification, the only landmark in a thornbush wilderness. In the next 30 min the path descends past a belfryless chapel (on the right) to Mávro Horió, all of two cottages, an *alóni* (threshing cirque) and some classical wall remnants on a bluff. The way to Vathý does not actually enter Mávro Horió but curves gently left some 50 m before and runs across the head of the creek valley just beyond. In the next ¼ hr the path loses altitude, crosses a tiny bridge in a valley bottom, and then passes the only spring en route to

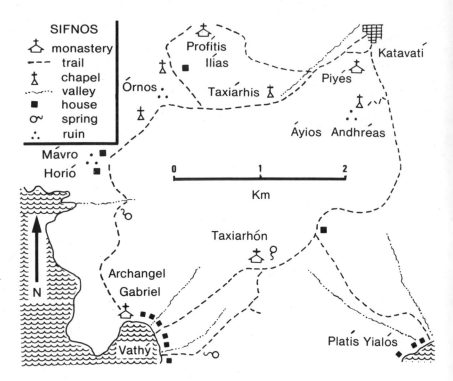

Vathý as you begin to climb out of this canyon. During the subsequent 30 min the trail roller-coasters up and down, passing a giant rock outcropping 500 m to its left—avoid a trail heading down to the base of the pinnacle. As you attain a ridge and round a bend, walls enclose the route; after a few moments' descent between the walls, you'll have your first look at Vathý Bay.

Without a stop at Profítis Ilías, it should take you about 3 hr to reach Vathy. Here the miniscule monastery of the Archangel Gabriel, on its own jetty, guards the tiny fishing harbor; nearby a store triples seasonally as a *tavérna* and "rooms." There are two other *tavérnes* nearer the 200-meter beach, as well as the local pottery studio.

You have a choice of two paths for continuing up to Taxiarhón monastery. A direct one departs from house No. 55, Vathý waterfront, but I describe the other, also the main route to Platís Yialós, which begins in the sandy wash marked by a well opposite house No. 72. Some 20 m inland from the mouth of this gully, look for a second red-dotted well cap on the left; within a few more paces a red arrow on a rock points to the trail climbing up the south (right) bank of the gulch. Waymarks are regular from here on. There's water, after 15 min, from a fern- and frog-laden alcove fountain. As the trail tops a pass, red dots indicate a right turn to Platís Yialós, but even if you've decided to end your walk there, disregard the blazes and bear on to the more interesting left fork, which shortly unites with the previously noted direct trail to Taxiarhón. This monastery lies about 1 hr above Vathý; disestablished, it seasonally hosts travelers who stay in the half-dozen cells. Taxiarhón dominates the head of a creek valley, with a glimpse of the sea; outhouses and waterspouts are permanently accessible.

Soon after Taxiarhón a white house marks a fork in the trail. The right-hand path meanders down to Platís Yialós, first skirting goat pens on the left, plunging through thorns and clay deposits, finally emerging on a wide creek bed. The Panayiá tou Vounóu monastery, most easily reached by a driveway off the Katavatí-Platís Yialós road, peeks through olives and oleanders on the left. Total hiking time for the Vathý-Platís Yialós leg is just under 2 hr; the last bus from there to Katavatí and Appolonía rolls at around sunset. If you miss it, not to worry; Platís Yialós has lodging, good *tavérnes* and its famous beach to keep you occupied.

The main loop trail continues 1½ hr more around the mountain to the detour for Áyios Andhréas. This handsome *ksoklísi* sits amid the hilltop ruins of an extensive pre-Christian settlement surrounded by a double wall. In clear weather you can pick out the islands of (going clockwise) Sýros, Páros, Andíparos, Íos, Síkinos and Folégandhros, plus all the main villages of Sífnos. The 30-min descent from Áyios Andhréas to Katavatí passes again the untenanted but well-maintained monastery of Piyés, which compares favorably with Sífnos' more famous monuments.

Rating/time course: The entire 20-plus-km circuit, including the detour over Profítis Ilías, will occupy a moderately difficult 9 hr, best done near the solstice or apportioned over two days; Vathý is the logical break point. If pressed for time, use the various bailouts or shortcuts.

Seasonal note: This is a better spring or fall itinerary, as it's shadeless and water is oddly spaced. In mid-summer Sífnos is as overrun as any of the more popular islands.

Supplies: Best in Apollonía or Katavatí; limited in Vathý, Platís Yialós.

Map: Greek Tourist Cartography's "Tourist Map of Sífnos," 1:45,000, is reasonably accurate.

35 FOLÉGANDHROS

Seen from an approaching boat, Folégandhros exhibits a forbidding aspect of sheer cliffs unrivaled elsewhere in the Kykládhes except at Amorgós and Thíra. Thus many visitors never venture further than Karavostási harbor, intimidated both by the palisades and the thorny wilderness glimpsed beyond the port. But only the eastern half of the island is semiarid, and a resplendent *hóra* perches out of sight at the brink of the northern palisades. Áno Meriá, the "other" village of Folégandhros, extends for kilometers along an English-style high street which is merely an old wagon track sporadically paved, and not an eyesore roadcut like many of the modern roads linking scattered communities on other elongated islands. The western portion of the island, beyond the tapering that almost pinches Folégandhros in two like a dividing amoeba, is especially beautiful, with striking chapels, barley terraces, *alónia* and adequate wells and springs for the hiker. The best trails have been selected from a myriad, including most of those leading to a succession of beaches at convenient distances from Áno Meriá or Hóra.

Folégandhros was inhabited in ancient days but mostly by political exiles; recent Greek regimes have used it similarly. In the Middle Ages it was depopulated no less than three times by Turks or corsairs. Creto-Venetian refugees were responsible for the most recent repopulation, which accounts for numerous Latinate surnames (Danássi, Gerárdi, Lizárdou) and a heavy Cretan accent in speech.

The island abounds in curious legends, which merit retelling before moving on to the hike descriptions. A valuable silver ikon of the Virgin was among the booty plundered at each sacking and massacre, but three times it came floating back across the waves to Folégandhros. Once it was accompanied by a Christian prisoner (on one of the rare occasions when the raiders took such), who was manacled in a boat with

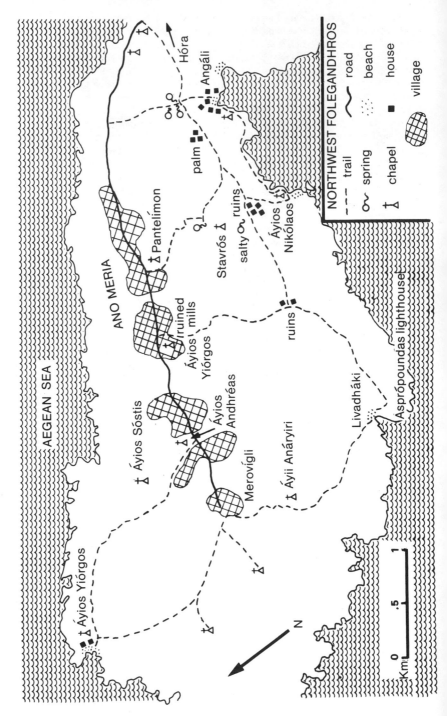

NORTHWEST FOLEGANDHROS

- --- trail
- ∿ spring
- ⌁ chapel
- ﹏ road
- ⫶⫶ beach
- ■ house
- ⬡ village

AEGEAN SEA

ANO MERIA

Hóra
Angáli
palm
⌁ Pantelímon
ruins
salty ∿ ruins
Stavrós ⌁
Áyios Nikólaos
ruined mills
Áyios Yiórgos
Áyios Andhréas
Áyios Sóstis
Merovígli
⌁ Áyii Anáryiri
ruins
Livadháki
Asprópoundas lighthouse
⌁ Áyios Yiórgos

N

0   .5   1
Km

the fleeing ruffians. A great (heaven-sent?) wave capsized the vessel; the prisoner alone was saved by clinging to the ikon, which washed ashore at the base of the cliff on which now stands the gigantic church of the Assumption.

Hrissospiliá, "The Golden Cave," is also below the church and takes its name from another incident during the cycle of depredations. The outgunned islanders had descended from the *kástro* (the fortified heart of the *hóra*) to this cave via a secret staircase, taking with them a large fortune in gold jewelry (the stairs have crumbled away in recent years and the grotto is now accessible only from the sea). The enemy espied the hiding place, plugged the entrance with brush wood and set it ablaze. When the last wave of immigrants came to resettle the island, they found among the ashes the gold of their luckless predecessors.

Getting to Folégrandhros: Two to six weekly ferries, depending on season, run to and from Piráeus, Kýthnos, Sérifos, Sífnos, Kímolos, Mílos, Síkinos, Íos and Thíra; once weekly to and from Sýros, Anáfi and Crete. Four daily buses between Hóra and Áno Meriá get you off to a good start for more remote trailheads—the official bus stops are often the trailheads themselves.

Hóra to Loústria via Petoúsi and Livádhi

This walk cuts through the heart of the semidesertic eastern half of Folégandhros, with good swimming at hike's end.

Beginning in Hóra, find the crossroads just below a sign announcing rooms to rent at Vevis. Turn left onto the cement road leading down to Karavostási; after 100 m bear right onto a wide, walled-in donkey track (the animals or their droppings are usually much in evidence). Twenty min out of town, an enclosed almond grove, the only greenery in a thorn-and-herb-scape, grows to the right; a bit beyond and to the left, a *stérna* provides water appetizing only to livestock. Some 20 min past the almonds you'll emerge onto an elevation from where Síkinos Island appears to the left and the hamlet of Petoúsi dead ahead; off the path to the right huddles the *ksoklísi* of Áyio Pnévma. Shortly after ignore a right fork, to the isolated chapel of Evangelístria, in the neighborhood of some olive trees, the first of many on the relatively fertile agricultural plateau here which supports the hamlet. Within a few more min (ca. 50 min from Hóra), a fork right near some more stunted olives leads up the last 100 m to Petoúsi, a summer hamlet of about 10 inhabitants who engage in the production of barley, grapes, olives and dairy products. They may regale drop-in company with such Folegandhrote specialties as *sourotó*, a soft, sweet cheese; *ksinógalos*, a curdled milk product akin to sour yogurt; and *ksinótiro*, the same substance in the form of a hard cheese.

Upon retracing your steps to the junction, continue down to the east, passing below and to the left of Profítis Ilías chapel on its height some 15 min from Petoúsi. In 25 min, or 1½ hr from Hóra, you approach the outskirts of Livádhi, marginally bigger than Petoúsi. Loústria Bay appears in the distance, so it's impossible to get lost from here on. Below Livádhi the trail widens to a driveway, passing a couple of wells and a trio of *ksoklísia* on the left. Loústria's sand is coarse and pebble-studded, but after 2 hr of walking no one seems to mind, least of all the dozens of campers who frequent the tamarisks and the official campground behind the beach. Karavostási, with its *tavérnes* and bus service up to Hóra, is a mere 20-min walk north along a wide track skirting the coast.

Hóra to Angáli and Áyios Nikólaos

From Hóra walk 30 min along the road to Áno Meriá, then turn left at the blue sign just before two small *ksoklísia*; the half-dozen houses of Angáli soon come into view at the sandy mouth of the canyon extending below. It's 20 min downtrail to a stream

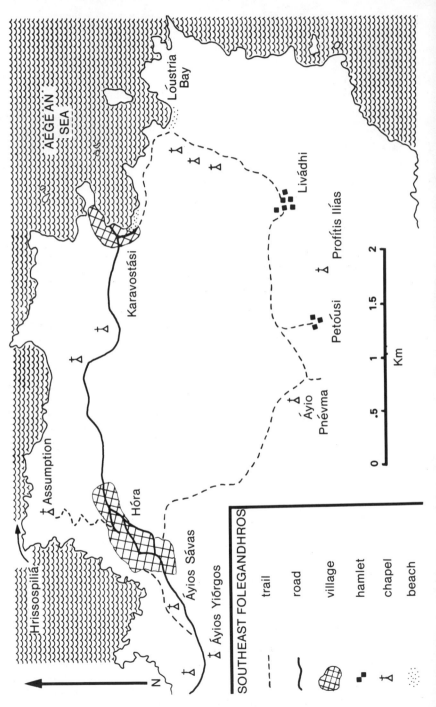

SOUTHEAST FOLEGANDHROS

----- trail

\ road

village

hamlet

chapel

beach

(fed by three sluggish springs) and the left turn onto another path paralleling the watercourse. From the muddy junction walk 15 min seaward to Angáli, a pleasant beach hamlet with two *tavérnes*, "rooms" and a tolerance of camping (though not nude bathing). A faint trail closely hugs the coast for a further 20 min west to Áyios Nikólaos, a waterless but sheltered beach with no dress code. On your way back from Áyios Nikólaos and Angáli, you can continue up the stream valley past the springs and onto a *kalderími* that emerges onto the Hóra-Áno Meriá track just west of the two chapels noted above.

You may also notice that a couple of paths exit the west side of Hóra and pass below and to the north of the cemented drive to Áno Meriá. These shortcuts wind through terraces of wind-distorted olives (scarce on this island) and debouch just between the two chapels of Áyios Savás and Áyios Yiórgos, thus reducing considerably the amount of road-walking for the Angáli-bound.

Pantelímon of Áno Mería to Áyios Nikólaos or Angáli via Stavrós

Turn down (south) from the Áno Meriá "high street" at the Kafepandopoleion I Elpís, passing a venerable church with a brown-and-blue doorway (Pantelímon). A 15- to 20-min descent on a clear flagstone way brings you to a turnout with a spring, just above Stavrós *ksoklísi*. From the fountain you climb slightly and veer east as the trail swoops tantalizingly past Áyios Nikólaos and then appears to forsake it entirely. But 30 min below the store, take a right turn just before a pair of small cottages guarded by a lone palm tree. Within 10 min you come to an abandoned hilltop hamlet, from where it's a brief scramble down to Áyios Nikólaos bay.

Proceeding on the main trail past the palm-tree huts takes you, within 20 min after the junction, to the trio of springs above Angáli.

Áyios Andhréas of Áno Meriá to Áyios Yiórgos Bay

Preferably take a bus to Áyios Andhréas church at the west end of Áno Meriá. Alight when you see the labeled *stégastro* (shelter) built at the bus stop. From this kiosk a distinct path descends, keeping the hilltop *ksoklísi* of Áyios Sóstis to its right, within 1 hr to the bay and chapel of Áyios Yiórgos. The beach is ample but only enjoyable on the rare occasions when a northwest wind is not blowing.

Merovígli of Áno Meriá to Livadháki

The next bus stop beyond Áyios Andhréas, Merovígli, is also the end of the line. From this terminus continue straight along the gravel track, forking left after 5 min (keeping straight on leads past assorted *ksoklísia* to small holdings on the extreme west end of the island). The left-hand path curls down and past the church of Áyii Anáryiri on its knoll, after which the going gets much rougher. The Asprópoundas lighthouse is a good directional marker for Livadháki Bay, a partly sheltered swimming cove (no fresh water) some 45 min below the Merovígli stop.

Livadháki to Áyios Nikólaos

Locate an inconspicuous series of rock stairs at the east wall of Livadháki cove; these lead within 15 min to the grounds of the lighthouse. From there the beginning of the onward trail is difficult to find; start at the phone poles, then veer gradually away to the right, following the general bearing of a prominent stone wall. As the path makes itself more evident, Hóra pops into sight to the east. About 30 min above the lighthouse, you should take a right turn upon meeting some olive trees and two abandoned houses. (Proceeding straight through this junction leads after 30 min to a group of ruined windmills on the Áno Meriá high street, very close to the church of Áyios Yiórgos [not the same as the little chapel near Hóra] and Mimi's *tavérna*.) Descend 20 min from the pair of derelict dwellings to a brackish pond just below

Stavrós chapel, and then climb 5 min to the abandoned hamlet described in "Pantelímon of Áno Meriá. . . ." From the hamlet you've the choice of turning down to the beaches or maintaining a course toward the springs above Angáli.

Seasonal note: Folégandhros gets crowded in midsummer; the spectacle of the barley harvest (see next page) offers some redemption then.

Supplies: Hóra is best, but Áno Meriá has several stores and even one *tavérna*.

Map: "Tourist Map," printed by Toumbis but sold only on the island, is accurate more often than not, at a scale of 1:25,000.

36 SÍKINOS

Sikinotes pride themselves on being one of the most purebred (in the past, inbred) Greek communities in the Aegean; perhaps the only injection of new blood in recent centuries was a share of some of the Cretan refugees who landed on neighboring Folégandhros. Today this isolated, untouristed island offers one superior hike to a unique archaeological treasure.

Getting to Síkinos: Same frequency and schedule as Folégandhros.

Route directions: From the photogenic *hóra*, a 1-hr walk above the port of Allopronía, you can hike in just over another hour to Episkopí, the site of ancient Síkinos. Start heading northward on the *kalderimi* beginning at the school. Thirty min along, take a left turn near a *ksoklísi* overlooking Folégandhros from the seaward side of the path. Within another 15 min a pale church dome, projecting above a dark square base, comes into sight on the ridge ahead.

Upon arrival this proves to be a most improbable conglomerate shrine, an ancient temple to Pythian Apollo later appropriated by the Orthodox Church. (Some authorities maintain that it is instead the family tomb of some wealthy ancient Sikinotes.) The classical outer walls of colossal stone are mostly intact, breached only where the apse protrudes from behind the altar. Two massive Doric columns flank the entrance, but most of the air space that formerly existed around them has been walled up. The addition of a belfry, the dome mentioned and a sort of mezzanine prompted extensive buttressing of the south wall, which accounts for the remarkably well-preserved state of the ancient masonry. The interior of this temple/church is currently in the throes of restoration, and access to the belfry or cupola is not possible until further notice. The actual site of the classical town was on the hill above and to the west of the shrine but is of interest only to the most dedicated archaeologists.

Destination aside, this is a most worthwhile and easy outing through a terraced landscape of olives and arbutus. Weather permitting, you have glorious views of Náxos, Páros, Sífnos and Folégandhros.

37 AMORGÓS

The easternmost of the Kykládhes is shaped like a 33-kilometer-long man with hands clasped in prayer. His spine, the southeast flank, is a row of imposing mountains dropping sharply to the sea in a severe cliffscape. All water flows northwest, reaching the Aegean at numerous secluded bays, some with miniscule beaches; villages and cultivated terraces surround the various springs. But Amorgós is more than a mirror image of Folégándhros, redolent of its own character and possessing remains of three ancient cities near present-day Arkessíni, Katápola and

Opposite—top, left: Taxiárhis chapel glimpsed through an older perimeter wall (Hike 34); Top, right: The senior monk at Hozoviótissa monastery, Amorgos (Hike 37); Bottom: Descending to Vathý Bay (Hike 34)

Threshing barley near Galaní

Kykladhic Barley Growers

The cultivation of barley is probably the single largest economic tie between these islands and the rest of Greece. The grain, harvested in July, is sent to the mainland to be brewed into beer; the rest of the plant is kept as animal fodder. Machinery is useless on the rugged terrain of hillside fields, so reaping is accomplished by hand, as is winnowing. Two- or three-mule teams do the threshing in the *alónia*, which are usually located at the outskirts of villages to facilitate cooperative schedules but may occasionally be found, as in the first photo, in isolated locales. It is common to meet donkey trains, on their way to or from the fields, completely swathed in bundled vegetation, like a portion of Birnam wood on the move against Macbeth. Such a procession of bristly cubes on four legs, silhouetted against the horizon, is a weird, unforgettable sight.

It takes two Folegandhriotes such as Dhimítris Karitinaíos and his cousin Nikítas Marinákis (second photo) about 5 days to gather barley from a seven-*strémmata* (almost two acres) field. In the midsummer heat a sensible working day is from 8 A.M. to noon, and from 4 P.M. until sunset. According to them their field, like many others, is rented from absentee landlords in Athens. But Dhimítris' landlessness has failed to dampen his high spirit or mocking sense of humor, and life is still abundant enough to provide bread and cheese for the three of us among the barley stubble.

July harvest of barley

Eyiáli. More contemporary architecture, as typified by the perfectly preserved *hóra* and one of Greece's most unusual monasteries, is no less compelling, and day hikes to opposite ends of the island visit all of these sites. Though one of the larger Kykládhes, Amorgós is isolated, little developed and (except in summer) untouristed. Only recently has a vehicle track scarred the length of the island, so the old paths used regularly until then are still in good condition.

Getting to Amorgós: Amorgós has the most erratic boat connections of any of the Kykládhes. At certain times of the year twice-weekly ferries link it with Astipálea, Kálymnos, Níssiros and Tílos to the east and various minor islets, Náxos, Páros and Piráeus to the west. In summer these are supplemented by wind-sensitive caiques shuttling to and from Náxos via the small islets in between. Visiting Amorgós at any season, you should plan on an enforced stay of four to five days—either the weather or scheduling will guarantee it.

Katápola to Arkessíni

This route allows sweeping views of Amorgós' north coast and the sierra to the southwest. From Vroútsi you can detour to Kastrí, a wedding-cake-shaped rock banded with medieval walls and the remains of classical Arkessíni. The main trail ends within sight of the *pýrgos* or fort of the ancient Arkessiniotes at Ayía Tríadha. The masonry and lone doorway of the most important pre-Christian ruin on Amorgós are in good condition and make a fitting conclusion to the walk. If you don't get a ride back to Hóra (4 km above Katápola) on the new jeep track, you can overnight in the modern village of Arkessíni.

The itinerary begins on a stairway behind the blue-domed church in Katápola. A steady, 25-min climb brings you to the saddle known locally as Mármara, "marble" (objects), after the remains of ancient Minoa to the right of the trail. Some 100 m

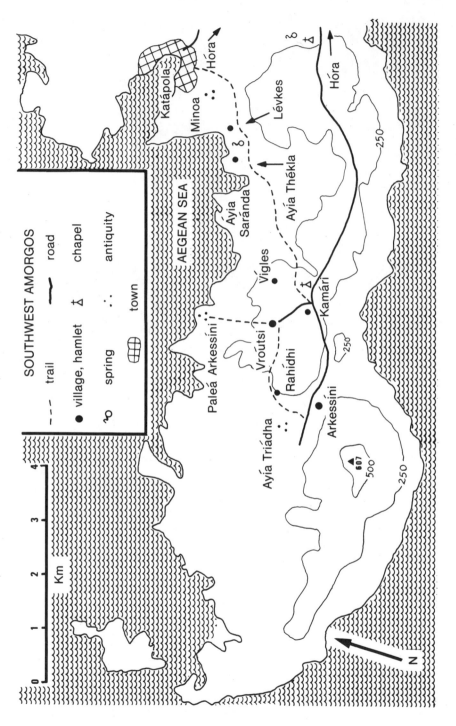

SOUTHWEST AMORGOS

- - - trail   ⌒ road

● village, hamlet   ⚐ chapel

ᕈ○ spring   ∴ antiquity

⊞ town

AEGEAN SEA

Km

N

further, bear right toward the five houses and well of Lévkes hamlet, reached after 25 min more. Once over two bridges, you come to a large oasis; the spring lies below and right from the path. A right fork at Ayía Thékla, a few moments beyond, leads down to Áyia Saránda Bay and its 50-m beach. Soon after, cross the bed of Áyia Saránda Creek and tackle 30 min of uphill switchbacks leading to another crest with one stone cottage. From here you can tick off, going counterclockwise, Cape Kastrí studded with its ruins; a conspicuous modern church on its own hill; the hamlet of Vígles, a handful of houses on still another knoll; and a portion of Kamári village. Thirty min of level hiking separates you from Vígles, with Kamári coming a few moments after. The trail intersects the jeep road next to a lumpy, trilobed, belfryless church, near which a sign reading *"Pros Katápola"* points back the way you've come. Turn right and follow the road 20 min more to Vroútsi. In Vroútsi you'll pass the right turnoff to Kastrí; a sign on a wall reads *"Pros Paliá Arkessíni,"* the ancient town on the promontory. Resuming the main route through Vroútsi, pass a *kafenéio* on the left and then adopt a *kalderími* at the village outskirts. Next pass a pond and wind through the hamlet of Rahídhi; if you look carefully west you may already see the *pýrgos* on a hillock. You arrive at the ancient stockade 30 min after quitting Vroútsi, covering the final stretch on an olive-grove path.

Rating/time course: This easy hike, partly on a cobble surface, takes 3 hr (without the diversion to Kastrí); several springs in the first half of the distance minimize thirst problems.

Hóra to Eyiáli

At some points along this route, Amorgós is so narrow and the path so lofty that you can see both shores of the island at once. Just out of Hóra the trail passes directly under Hozoviótissa monastery; beyond it the itinerary parallels the spine of Amorgós before switching sides of the mountain and descending toward Eyiáli Bay.

Leave Hóra past the *yimnásio* and through the park, a terrace where a solitary bench overlooks the sea. From there a *kalderími* descends 40 min to the cloister of Hozoviótissa, "Our Lady of Hozova," an early Christian village in Asia Minor. With its population dwindled to three monks, rumors of imminent closure persist, a sorry end for the once-powerful institution founded in 1088 by the Byzantine emperor Alexios Komnenos. But nothing can detract from the tremendous setting and architecture of Hozoviótissa, a freakish wedge-shaped structure abutting a reddish cliff 320 m above the sea. The long interior entrance stairway is hewn through living rock; this gallery opens out into the reception room and the balcony, from where you can sometimes see the island of Astipálea 45 km to the southeast. Visiting hours are currently from 8 A.M. to 2 P.M., but they may change if the monastery is disestablished.

To continue from Hozoviótissa, go through a green gate and pass the toilets teetering on the brink to the right. After 1½ hr the trail surmounts the crest of Amorgós and passes the tiny hamlet of Agrilás. Within another 30 min you reach Asfodilítis; the route ends at Pótamos village, just above Eyiáli Bay, some 5 hr after setting out from Hóra. From the sandy shore, dotted with Roman-era relics, you can visit the hill villages of Langádha and Tholária, where there are Roman tombs.

Rating/time course: The surface of this 20-km tramp is largely dirt, rather than cobble, with occasional stretches of road. Unless you arrange transport (either a *kaïki* or wheels) back from Eyiáli, you should plan on overnighting at one of several beach lodgings.

Seasonal note: Amorgós is windy at any time of the year, but especially so in early spring.

Supplies: Only in Katápola or Hóra.

Map: Pseudo-topographical map, German lettering and 1:140,000 scale, compiled by Dr. Georg Perreiter, sold on the island.

SÁMOS

Dash down yon cup of Samian wine!

——Lord Byron

The most verdant island in the Aegean lies just six kilometers off the Turkish mainland; despite its position and fertility Sámos has only sporadically been dominated by outside powers since its days as an important center of ancient Hellenic culture. After imperial Byzantine hegemony lapsed, it was loosely held, more in name than in fact, by various Latin powers; the Ottomans decided in 1453 that pillage and massacre would be simpler than administration, and for about 150 years Sámos was deserted except for two inland villages. After resettlement and the War of Independence, the islanders managed to win a semiautonomous status which persisted until *enósis* (union) with Greece in 1913.

Superficially, Sámos resembles Crete; as on the latter island, the southeast and northeast are arid, scrubby and abandoned to the package tour trade, while the western half is a semiforested wilderness virtually untouched by visitors. Similarly, the best beaches line the northwest and southwest coasts, and two mountains serve as the focus of several days of high-quality hiking.

Getting to Sámos: Four to seven ferries run weekly from Piráeus and neighboring Ikaría; one or two of these pass Sýros and/or Páros en route. Two weekly boats connect with Híos on the north and Pátmos to the south. Daily flights from Athens are relatively economical.

Getting to the trailheads: From Vathý, ten buses roll daily to Kokkári, but only five continue to Áyios Konstantínos and Karlóvassi. The last one returns from Karlóvassi at around 4 P.M., so if you're lazing at Seïtáni or tramping on Ámbelos keep this in mind or be willing to hitch or taxi back.

38   VILLAGES OF MT. ÁMBELOS

A dense network of well-maintained trails links the handful of settlements nestling amid the thick vegetation that blankets the north slope of Mt. Ámbelos, the central peak of Sámos. From nearly every point along the way the sea or Ámbelos crest defines the horizon, and scattered vineyards are often the only sign of man. This scenic region is conveniently close to the north coast towns of Áyios Konstantínos and Kokkári, a fishing village that lately hosts substantial numbers of tourists. Either makes an ideal base for the day hikes described.

Kokkári to Manolátes via Vrondianí and Vourliótes

Next to Disco Kilimantzaro at the outskirts of Kokkári, a dirt track turns inland from the shore highway. Some 5 min up the road is a major fork presided over by three makeshift goat pens.

The leftmost bearing leads to the Vrondianí monastery trailhead. Walk 2 km up this track, then turn right at a red-dotted tree onto another road heading toward a *ksoklísi*, 400 m away on a hillside, which marks the actual start of the footpath. It's about 1 ¼ hr up this clear trail (one spring) to Vrondianí monastery, Sámos' oldest (dating from 1560) and one of its largest. Although the army uses it as a storage depot, most of the building is in good repair. Vourliótes is a 25-min road walk to the west; the way is signposted.

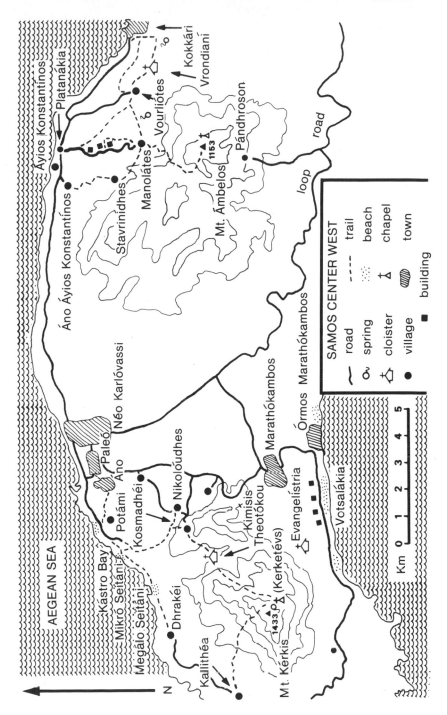

SAMOS CENTER WEST

—— road	- - - - trail
๐ᵥ spring	░░ beach
⇗ cloister	⚲ chapel
● village	● town
■ building	

Km 0 1 2 3 4 5

AEGEAN SEA

N

Manolátes huddles below Ámbelos ridgeline (photo by Martha Degasis)

The most direct Kokkári-Vourliótes route begins with a right fork at the goat pens. This road quickly diminishes to a mule track and after 10 min passes under a unique stone arch; follow red dots on nearby rocks. Twenty min from the junction, the proper trail crosses a stream and continues along the opposite bank. After another 1 ½ hr of walking with no more ambiguities you'll come to Vourliótes, a friendly village with "rooms," *kafenéia* and typical Samiote architecture, which features tile roofs, multi-colored shutters and overhanging upper stories. If you choose not to linger, it's easy to continue on to Manolátes, the next, equally inviting settlement.

The trail to Manolátes starts at the western end of Vourliótes, by the cemetery. Once on it, take the first red-dotted left fork. Soon after make a right turn; 15 min out of Vourliótes, you should pass a small chapel on a hillock. Just beyond the *ksoklísi*, bear left and begin descending along the east flank of an enchantingly wooded and terraced stream valley. You will meet the water about 30 min below the chapel but don't cross the rivulet immediately. Rather, head 50 m upstream, then cut west and uphill; assorted red dots assist you. Coming up this final slope to Manolátes, shun all right forks until a major and unmistakable right fork plunges down into a shady hollow and directly out again. After winding through a few more terraces and sighting consecutive red dots, you arrive rather abruptly on a cement drive at the edge of Manolátes; total walking time from Vourliótes shouldn't exceed 80 min.

Manolátes has a couple of basic *kafenéia* and a store; there is no formal lodging, but arrangements could conceivably be made on the spot.

Manolátes to Platanákia or Vice Versa

Below Manolátes 400 m, a stair-path resumes just to the right of the auto road descending to the coast. The footway takes you through an idyllic landscape burgeoning with olives, sycamores, brambles, citrus, pomegranate, cypress and pine, the result of abundant water heard running on all sides. Unhappily, after 20 min the *kalderími* is swallowed up by the cement road; it's a total 45-min walk down to the bus stop at Platanákia, where there are two *exóhika kéndra* to satisfy appetites whetted by your hike. Aÿios Konstantínos lies only 2 km west along the shore road.

Those who wish to climb Mt. Ámbelos from Kokkári in one day, or reverse the above two sections, are advised to catch a morning bus from Kokkári and alight at Platanákia. The shaded *tavérna* Ta Aïdhónia, some 15 min up the road toward Manolátes, is a major landmark. Just before it, a much-used, dotted path leads left and up, within 1 hr, to the hillock chapel just outside of Vourliótes. Beyond Ta Aïdhónia you veer left onto the equally obvious *kalderími* up to Manolátes—it begins by snaking around two humble cottages. Fifteen min up the mule path you can make a prominent detour left to the abandoned village of Margarítes. All that remains intact here is the church (locked) which contains some respectable frescoes, and a spring. Allow a full hour for the climb from Platanákia to Manolátes.

Up Mt. Ámbelos from Manolátes

Find a fountain in central Manolátes opposite the Kafenéio Yioryídhes; it's dated 1876 and features a marble relief of the Paraclete descending. Climb past it, to the left, until you see a red arrow pointing up Odhós Dexamenís; follow this stair-street out of town to a junction. The right fork leads up Ámbelos.

For the first 1½ hr the path winds through oak, pyracantha, two kinds of pine and vineyards in differing states of upkeep. At times the route is badly overgrown or ambiguous, but there is usually a timely red dot, scrap of rubbish or worn spot to guide you, and always there are dazzling views of the crags of Ámbelos, the lush vegetation or the sea to distract you. From a rocky outcrop—a false summit of Ámbelos—it's 15 min more to a forest road that you cross only once. The next time it appears, bear left along the axis of a long spur until the path resumes clearly (but briefly). Two hr above Manolátes, you reach the watershed itself and the prominent forest road that runs parallel to it. After glimpsing the ocean south of Sámos, turn left;

The author (with stick) and two companions descend Mt. Ámbelos (photo by Martha Degasis)

some red dots on the opposite side of the auto route beckon but the path has been thoroughly plowed under from here on and it's easiest to follow the ugly, dusty new track for about 15 min to where a bonily rocky hogback plummets to meet the road. Just beyond, there's a seep (perhaps a buried spring) on the left and then a low saddle offering easy access to the ridge. Once you leave the road it's another 25 min to the peak; a few red dots assist you the last few moments but mostly you've an easy cross-country scramble.

From Ámbelos summit (1153 m), you look northeast to Kokkári, east toward Vathý (Sámos harbor), Psilí Ámmos Bay and the Turkish coast, dominated by 1200-m Samsun Daǧ, and south over the villages of Pagóndas (inland) and Iréon (shore). Kérkis (Kerketévs, Koumarítis), Sámos' loftiest peak, and the shattered-looking island of Foúrni hover to the west. Ámbelos is adorned by what appear to be military relay antennae and a massive chapel; near the latter some red arrows point toward the 2-hr descent to Pándhroson, Sámos' highest village but 6 km from the loop road that circumnavigates the island.

Retracing your steps to Manolátes takes about 2 hr, a good 45 min less than the ascent.

Manolátes to Áno Áyios Konstantínos via Stavrinídhes

Return to the fountain in Manolátes, walk downhill a few paces and bear left onto a conspicuous path. This dips into and climbs out of two successive canyons, reaching the appealing village of Stavrinídhes in just under 1 hr; here there's a bona fide two-room inn. From the low end of Stavrinídhes, which like Manolátes and Vourliótes sprawls langorously over the flattest portion of a ridge, the route zigzags down— mostly on cobble surface—for 35 min more to Áno Áyios Konstantínos. The trail debouches opposite the highest dwelling in that community. Pause at the fine medieval church in the tiny park on your way down to the coast road.

39 NORTHWEST COAST AND MT. KÉRKIS

All the following itineraries begin from Karlóvassi, either on a bus or on foot. Climbing Mt. Kérkis is moderately challenging but the coastline at its northern base offers splendid and relatively level tramping. West of Karlóvassi a mixture of pine, arbutus, olive and juniper completely swaths a landscape dominated by majestic spurs which plunge down to the aquamarine sea on the right or merge into the folds of Mt. Kérkis to landward. Various paths roller-coaster gently up and down, right and left, narrowing to dirt furrows in olive groves and expanding to natural stairs of polished rock on the saddles. Mikró Seïtáni, a 200-m cove with a sand-gravel bed, and Megálo Seïtáni, a 600-m crescent of finer sand with a few buildings, subdivide the roadless stretch from Potámi to Dhrakéi into manageable intervals. Ikaría or the Turkish coast are your constant companions in the distance.

Áno Karlóvassi to Dhrakéi, via Mikró and Megálo Seïtáni

Cross from Néo Karlóvassi to lower Paleó Karlóvassi by the auto bridge over the river. Head west out of lower Paleó, and take a left onto a cement driveway as soon as the asphalt tends toward the coast. The drive shortly becomes a mule track flanked by an orange dot or two. After 10 min, follow a white arrow and orange dot left onto an uphill *kalderími*; upon arrival in Áno Paleó Karlóvassi, continue up the street to a *platía* with the Mikró Parísi *kafenéio*. Here take the midmost of three possible alternatives, and soon you reach the edge of town. A legitimate path resumes to the left of a little chapel some 40 min beyond the bridge linking Néo and Paleó Karlóvassi. Within 10 min the cobble trail surface mounts to a saddle and an *ikónisma* of Aýios Andónios and then descends fairly sharply toward briefly glimpsed Potámi hamlet. A hideous modern church with an abstract spire lurks below and to the right, drawing attention briefly away from the trail surface which is slippery with pine needles.

Potámi is about a 1¼-hr walk from the Karlóvassi bridge; to pass through it, cross the road encountered at the bottom of the descent from Áyios Andónios and parallel the stream down to the beach. But before leaving Potámi, or on your way back, you may wish to enquire after the exact location of its famous hot springs. They are not overly developed and are in a natural cavelet.

At the far end of Potámi beach, the asphalt road ends and a dirt one replaces it. Twenty min along this track, keep an eye out for a tree with a painted legend "41," a carved arrow pointing right and a cairn of three stones wedged into a cleft in its trunk. (This olive lies about 5 min past Kástro Bay, the first inlet after Potámi, with a ruined square foundation on its shore.) Mikró Seïtáni Bay is 25 min beyond this first turnoff. If you somehow miss it, continue another 10 to 15 min along the road, which ends just after a fork leading up and left (which you ignore). Next, a narrow but well-grooved path passes an abandoned olive ranch before arriving at an obvious, perpendicular crossing.

A 90-degree, down-and-right turn takes you to Mikró Seïtáni within 20 min. However you arrive at Mikró Seïtáni, there's no opportunity for confusion in onward progress; climb the steps on the west side of the cove and follow a good trail some 40 min more to Megálo Seïtani. Until a few years ago, this area was one of the last remaining habitats of the Mediterranean monk seal, and a small colony may still survive. From the larger bay, it's 1-hr-plus to trail's end in the village of Dhrakéi, just out of sight behind the spur above Megálo Seïtáni.

Proceeding straight along the main trail—which soon veers left and uphill—brings you after 1½ hr to the two villages of Nikoloúdhes and Kosmadhéi (shown reversed on most tourist maps); the path clashes repeatedly with a road during the last 25 min of the climb. Kosmadhéi is a rather dismal village, without even a proper spring in its miniscule *platía*, but it is the start for the easiest ascent of Mt. Kérkis (see next section). To reach Nikoloúdhes, simply cross to the far side of the dirt road when it's first met and continue along the descending path.

Climbing Mt. Kérkis

From Kosmadhéi, a good *kalderími* leads within 1 hr to the monastery Kimísis Theotókou, appealingly set at the bottom of a densely forested deep valley. Beyond the cloister a fairly clear trail leads within 3 hr to the vicinity of the 1433-m summit of Kérkis, now frequented only by shepherds but in the past the final refuge of indigenous Samiotes during spells of piracy, and more recently the haunt of World War II guerrilas. The path proper ends near a spring and a chapel 500 and 800 m southeast of the altimeter respectively.

From Dhrakéi, you can walk or bus (twice daily to and from Karlóvassi) the 5 km southwest to Kallithéa village, which has an inn. Here you might stay two nights, sandwiching a full day of ascent and descent. If you've climbed Kérkis from Kosmadhéi, thus missing out on the beautiful coast near the two Seïtánis, consider descending to Kallithéa and hiking Dhrakéi to Potámi.

Votsalákia beach on the south side of the mountain is served by three daily buses from Karlóvassi and provides another possible start or end point for climbs on Kérkis. The accepted route passes Evangelístria, plainly visible on the mountainside northwest of Votsalákia, but the trails are none too easy to locate and this is the steepest, trickiest route up or down the peak.

Supplies: Essentials should be gotten in Kokkári or Karlóvassi; minimal replenishments available in the outlying villages.

Map: ESY Samou and Davaris' tourist map are both studiously inaccurate, at 1:200,000 scale.

THE DHODHEKÁNISOS (DODECANESE) ISLANDS

*As we came closer, we saw waves breaking on the rocky coast ...
Gradually we saw coves and turnings [and] the land cascading sharply
into bottomless blue water .... Halfway up the northern coast, we saw
the first signs of life: the crisscrossing of the dry-stone walls ... then
mills, abandoned and shorn of blades ... at last we saw houses, tiny
white squares on top of a hill, like gravestones.*

———Elias Kulukundis

This archipelago was only recently (1948) incorporated into modern Greece, after 500 years of occupation by the Latin Knights of St. John, Turks, Italians, Germans and British. While not so fertile as the Sporádhes or Ionian groups, the Dhodhekánisos have suffered this fate mostly as a result of lying squarely astride the fast lane of history; it behooved any imperial power with designs on the east Mediterranean to subdue or at least control these islands. Through it all the Dhodhekanisians have maintained their Greek cultural identity, reacting especially strenuously to the repressive Italian sanctions against the Greek language and Orthodox church during the period 1916-1943.

The Dhodhekánisos display a marked geological schizophrenia. Dry limestone outcrops such as Kálymnos, Sými, Hálki and Kastellórizo alternate with the sprawling, sandy giants Rhódhos, Léros and Kos, which are principally agricultural and are crisscrossed with roads. Níssiros is volcanic and Astipálea and Pátmos at the fringes of the group resemble more the Kykládhes. The mountainous and occasionally forested contours of the limestone isles, particularly Kárpathos and Sými, are actually the last stretch of the great alpine arc connecting Crete with Asia Minor. During the Ottoman era the more austere islets were left to the industrious devices of the natives, the Sultan's involvement being often confined to yearly collection of tribute, in exchange for privileges. Today these "minor" Dhodhekánisos are characterized by peaceful (sometimes abandoned) villages and good hiking territory.

40 NÍSSIROS

Nissiros is a quite and relaxating [sic] place for your holiday ...

from an info brochure put out by the municipality

Effects on your system aside, this island, so lush with olives and vineyards, is an anomaly when compared to most of its neighbors in the Dhodhekánisos. The underlying basis of this abundant vegetation is the dormant volcano that forms the core of Níssiros and is probably responsible for the island having risen from the sea in the first place. Lava soils are mineral-rich and moisture-retaining, and the neighboring islet of Yialí is one solid gypsum quarry, so Níssiros supports a year-round

Opposite—top, left: Floor of the main caldera of Lákki, Níssiros (Hike 40); Top, right: Village of Ólymbos, on Karpathos (Hike 42; photo by Ann Cleeland); Bottom: Cyclopean walls of Paleokástro (ancient Níssiros), above Mandhráki (Hike 40)

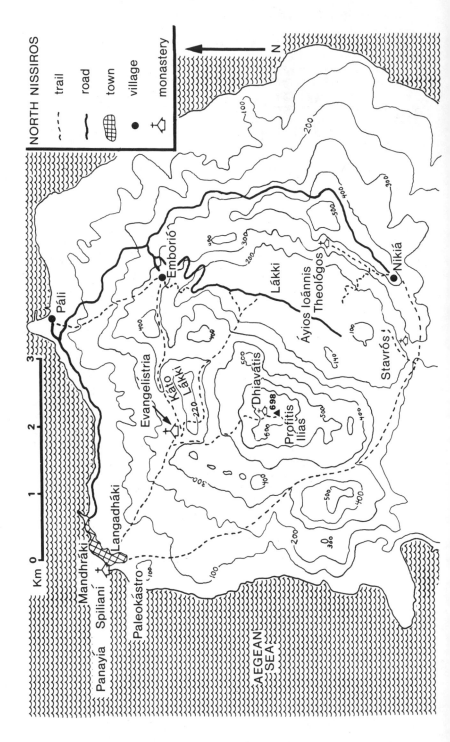

population and isn't deserted and forlorn in winter like so many holiday islands. Day-trippers from Kos come mostly to see the giant (three km²) caldera, and this geological curiosity certainly merits a stop in itself, but you shouldn't overlook the three well-preserved villages of Mandhráki, Emborió and Nikiá, plus the imposing ruins of ancient Níssiros.

Getting to Níssiros: The daily (in season) excursion boats from Kos are more expensive than regular steamers, but more conveniently scheduled; cheapest are those plying Kardhámena-Mandhráki. Car ferries—often the *Nirévs*—sail twice weekly, east and west, connecting Níssiros with Kastellórizo, Rhódhos, Sými, Tílos, Astipálea and Piráeus. The *Panormítis* also calls twice a week, going north or south, on its way to or from Rhódhos, Sými, Tílos, Kos, Kálymnos, Léros, Pátmos and Sámos.

Most visitors are parted from their money by a coterie of crafty taxi drivers who await each tourist boat arriving from Kos, to offer a long ride to and a short look at the volcano for about $15 per car. Skip that and instead walk one or all of the various routes between Mandhráki and the crater.

Volcano Walk via Ancient Níssiros

Leave Mandhráki from its picturesque western neighborhood Langadháki, away from the harbor. Langadháki is crowned by the Panayía Spilianí monastery, adroitly wedged inside the inevitable castle of the Knights of St. John; almost every member of the Dhodhekánisos has one. Follow signs with the legend "*Pros kastro*—to ancient wall", and 15 min out of town you'll cross a dirt jeep track. Here you should detour right to visit the Paleokástro citadel, dating back to at least 500 B.C. With its massive, perfectly masoned walls and stunning views over Mandhráki and Kos to the north, it's vastly more intriguing than the Knight's castle. Return to the main route and continue, with a left fork after 100 m, on the clear, lava-dressed *kalderími* conducting you through a green countryside of arbutus, oaks and orchards and views over islets to the west. About 45 min past the ancient fort, pass a white *ksoklísi* on your right, at the base of the long valley leading up to the caldera lip. There's a well here, capped by piled stones, just off the trail. After another 30 min the path attains a pass and within a few moments acquires a pumice-sand surface. You now have a grandstand view of Níssiros' south coastal plain and Tílos Island. Ignore in this vicinity all forks bearing right and down to the sea; if the wind is right you may catch a first whiff of sulfur admixed with windborne herbal smells. About 1½ hr above Mandhráki you should reach a fork presided over by a corral and a well (left) and a chapel (right); take a left through a prominent gap in the foliage (keeping straight leads to Nikiá). Almost immediately parts of the crater come into sight and within 15 min this trail broadens into a track of lava clinkers. The small monastery of Stavrós perches on the slope to your right; Emborió and the secondary crater should be well to your left, while the main caldera sprawls at your feet with Nikiá clinging to the palisades above it. Another 30 min on the track, or 2¼ hr from Mandhráki, should bring you to the volcano floor.

The volcano of Níssiros—known locally as Lákki—is actually the magma chamber floor of a much larger volcano that collapsed, Crater Lake style, in 1522. Today two craters slump still deeper below the level of the high, 3-km² plateau. The primary, eastern round caldera is obvious and noisy: hissing fumaroles are encrusted with sulfur crystals, scalding water trickles out in spots and everywhere there's the oatmealish sound of mud boiling a few inches below your shoes. Halfway up the western lip of the volcanic desert lies the secondary crater, quieter but more visually dramatic and too deep to get into. A drink stand about midway between the two operates seasonally.

Crater Floor to Nikiá

Walk to the northeast corner of the volcanic zone, some 400 m north of the main caldera itself. The trail begins zigzagging upslope from the vicinity of a small chapel and a red metal wellhead—the start is inconspicuous but there are some red dots. About 25 min up the path a *dexamení* (water tank) with a tap offers refreshment; 45 min from the volcano floor you'll have the option of forking left to visit the attractive monastery of Áyios Ioánnis Theológos, 300 m distant. Otherwise it's 5 min more, and a total of just under 1 hr, to the bus plaza of Nikiá. Hikers reversing the above instructions will look for a small metal sign near the bus stop pointing toward the crater and the trailhead.

The highest of Níssiros' villages is perched between the devil and the deep blue sea, as it were, with incomparable views of both. Unfortunately no short-term lodgings are rented and refreshment is limited to the stock of the lone cafe. This shouldn't put you off, as Nikiá is architecturally pristine, the inhabitants friendly, and visual stimulation, especially from the round main *platía*, unparalleled. Ask at the *kafenéio*, especially in the fall, for the local specialty *soumádha*—it's an almond-extract drink guaranteed to banish the hot-lava blues. Major local festivals take place September 26 and November 21. If you arrive in Nikiá by 2:30 P.M. on the right day of the week (usually Mon, Wed, Fri), you can catch the bus for its return journey to Mandhráki.

Mandhráki to Evangelístria Monastery

Leave Mandhráki via the stair-streets leading up from the neighborhood of Zervo's pastry shop and the public library. Once you're clear of the houses, bear onto the cement drive that snakes uphill, passing a giant municipal cistern system on your left. Soon the paved road splits; right in the groin of the fork a red-dotted path begins between two stone drywalls. This old donkey trail collides repeatedly with the soon-dirt road, submitting after 30 min to the bulldozer until you reach Evangelístria some 45 min out of Mandhráki. Inside the monastery there's a well with a bucket; you may prefer to rest in the shade of a giant pepper tree, girded by a cement apron, which lies just outside the monastery gate and marks the end of the road.

Evangelístria to Profítis Ilías via Dhiavátis

Backtrack about 150 m from the pepper-tree roundabout and find a path bearing south uphill; "*Pros Dhiavátis*" is sloppily splashed with white paint on a rock. Fifteen min up the trail you'll pass a cistern and a small hut. Immediately after, fork left, following a faint white arrow. From this junction it's a 1-hr climb along an occasionally messy but always traceable path to the farmlike monastery of Dhiavátis. The trail ends there; scramble another 15 min, by line of sight, to the chapel of Profítis Ilías on the island's summit (698 m). Note that there is no safe, easy, direct way down to the crater floor from the mountain, nor do you really have the best view of it possible. Rather, Profítis Ilías offers panoramas of the following, going clockwise from due south: the islet of Sýrna (southwest), Astipálea (west), Kos (northwest to northeast), Kálymnos and Psérimos (partial, to the north), Turkish Resadiye peninsula (northwest to northeast), Symi (east), and Tílos and Rhódhos (southeast).

Evangelístria to the Crater or Emborió via Káto Lákki

Locate, on the east edge of the pepper-tree roundabout, the start of the footpath continuing toward the volcano. You will almost instantly dip into, cross and climb out of the volcanic gulch known as Káto Lákki. Inching up its far side, roughly 30 min beyond Evangelístria, you can turn around and take in the *lákkos*, Yialí islet, Kos (especially Cape Kríkelos) and Kálymnos. Soon the path levels off and slips through a pass in a volcanic moonscape; if you're alert you'll spot a stray steam vent on the high side of the trail. The descent from the saddle is marred somewhat by a loose, pumice trail surface and 45 min beyond the monastery the route becomes haphazard. Bearing right will bring you within 20 min to the crater's edge; descending 15 min to the left puts you onto the asphalt road which, if followed north for a few moments, meets the start of the mule path up to Emborió which is just visible on the cliff overhead. Twenty-five min of huffing and puffing along this *kalderími* separates you from the roadway and the largely desolate and abandoned village; most of the Emboriotes have decamped to Páli or Mandhráki. A single *kafenéio* serves cold drinks and ice cream.

A highly visible stairpath shortcuts the road hairpins below Emborió to the north; by following it you'll arrive in Páli, a pleasant fishing port, in about 1 hr. Considerably more difficult to find is the abandoned, overgrown trail leading direct from Emborió to Evangelístria. Climb to the top of Emborió and fork left before reaching the cemetery. The first 20 min are ordinary enough, but once over the pass and within sight of Káto Lákki the trail fizzles out and you spend the next 25 min shuffling along the north boundary ridge of the gulch. The path—what's left of it—finally debouches onto the main Evangelístria-crater trail about 50 m shy of the pepper-tree roundabout.

Rating/time course: Novices may want to take advantage of a taxi or morning bus up to Nikiá (regularly scheduled Mon, Wed, Fri, otherwise according to demand) and do a downhill hike via the crater and Paleokástro; this will take no more than 3 hr. If you walk uphill via the points listed you can take the bus down from Nikiá at midafternoon, but if you pick a day without bus service note that private cars in Nikiá are rare and taxis are expensive. A grand tour, Langadháki-Paleokástro-Stavrós-Crater-Káto Lákki-Evangelístria-Mandhráki, is a serious undertaking of about 5 hr, not counting rests; if you append a visit to Nikiá, this becomes a 7-hr marathon. Exiting the volcano to Páli, via Emborió, only cuts your elapsed walking time by 30 min. By mixing and matching the available trail sections you can construct an itinerary to suit any taste. There are few killer grades on Nissirian paths, with the exception of the Evangelístria-Dhiavátis leg; however, the looseness and high reflectivity of volcanic hiking surfaces will exact their toll on both you and your water bottle. In the hot months you risk simultaneous grilling from above and below in the caldera—the *kafenéia* refrigerators of Nikiá, Emborió and the crater kiosk await you.

41   SÝMI

Closer to Turkish Asia Minor than Greek Rhódhos, and possessing a jagged outline correctly implying rocky terrain, Sými would not at first strike the map browser as a good hunting ground for day hikes. But along with Kárpathos and Rhódhos, it is the only Dhodhekánisos to have retained a substantial portion of its ancient forests and is crisscrossed by an excellent trail network. The road system is and probably always will be stalled at a vestigial, nonasphalt stage; some Chicago Symiotes took up a collection about 30 years ago for the paving of various rights-of-way and the purchase of a bus, but happily for walkers the locals cannibalized the vehicle for spare parts and embezzled the balance of the funds after completing a single driveway down to Pédhi Bay.

Visits begin auspiciously at Yialós harbor, whose gracious villas and waterfront attest the wealth of the 19th-century sponge fleets and merchant marine. After the First World War nearby Kálymnos outranked Sými as the Aegean's premier sponging center, and German-British bombardment during the next war gutted many of the houses, so it's a slightly sad and faded tableau of past glories that meets the eye. Yialós blends without demarcation into Horió, which covers the high ridges to the south, and the two communities are known collectively as Sými.

Forays beyond the port reveal a striking, unspoiled and deeply indented isle with numerous protected bays. Sandy stretches are few but swimming is unsurpassed on calm days. In the south and west particularly extensive stands of juniper and pine enliven the bare rocks. You're unlikely to meet anyone away from the town, and the silence is broken only by the occasional bleat of a goat or the hum of bees in the herb bushes.

Sými rivals Pátmos and certain of the Kykládhes in the sheer number—close to 100—of churches and small convents scattered uniformly over the island. Sými is as poor in natural ground water as it is rich in shrines, but almost all of the latter have rain cisterns, so *if* someone hasn't absconded with the necessary *sikláki* (bucket)-on-a-string, you need never go thirsty.

Getting to Sými: Sými is on the same lines as Níssiros, served by the *Panormítis* on north-south routes and the *Nirévs* or similar boat on east-west runs. The daily tourist ferry from Rhódhos is more expensive than either.

Sými (Yialós) to Áyios Emilianós via Mihaél and Áyios Ioánnis Theológos

This delightful walk heads west-southwest past the island's second largest monastery, continues through fine woods and ends at one of the most peculiar spots on Sými.

Leave the *platía* by the highest, most inland road, then bear up and left at Villa Skiathítis (a Budget Tours lodge). Follow the main stair-street as it zigzags up and out of town; incorrect turnings dead-end. When confirming directions remember that your first destination is known popularly as Mihaél, not by its full map name, Taxiárhis Mihaél Roukouniótis. Avoid, 20 min out, a tempting straight continuation to the conspicuous *ksoklísi* of Áyios Fanoúrios; instead hairpin left to stay with the flagstone-bordered principal trail. Within 10 min you attain the first ridge; here there's a junction of two jeep tracks (not on the tourist map), a clump of eucalyptus and a pair of footpaths. The monastery can be seen ahead; so can the resumption of the trail, a narrow, uncobbled but well-worn path which bears left past an army camp directly to the small convent of Áyii Anáryiri. Or you can follow the *kalderími* that continues briefly to the right before being swallowed up by the jeep road, which brings you to the enormous cypress at the gate of Mihaél 1 hr after leaving the harbor. The monastery is said to contain many fine treasures but was locked the day of my visit.

To rejoin the through trail to Áyios Emilianós, go south through the monastery grounds to a gate opening onto a small path, cross the ravine and head up to Áyii Anáryiri. The path appears to die at the front door of this tiny cloister, but you can pick it up again just on the left side of the compound. Beyond Áyii Anáryiri, continue straight; many animal pens and junipers should be to your right, but few if any trees will be growing to the left of the route. Aim now for the low saddle, marked by a neat clump of juniper, in the hills ahead. At this next (and last) high point of the walk is a complex of half-ruined stone huts and pastures. Keep all these well to your right and take a 40-degree left turn onto a clear trail skirting the base of an increasingly well-forested hillside. Two hr from Yialós, you'll arrive at Áyios Ioánnis Theológos, a small monastery with a water spigot (only semireliable); from the terrace you can see Áyios Filímonos, Áyios Emilianós and Skoumíssa Bay.

Shortly after Áyios Ioánnis the path forks; bear right for 1 hr of steady descent through junipers, past Maróni Bay, before the trail frays into aimless goat traces. Proceed by line of sight to the monastery of Filímonos, where there's a well-with-bucket left of the main gate (which is unlocked for a peek inside). To the right of the gate a cemented path leads down to Skoumíssa Bay and a small dock—good swimming off it if there's no wind. Only faint tracks exist for the last 500-m push to Emilianós, 20 min away.

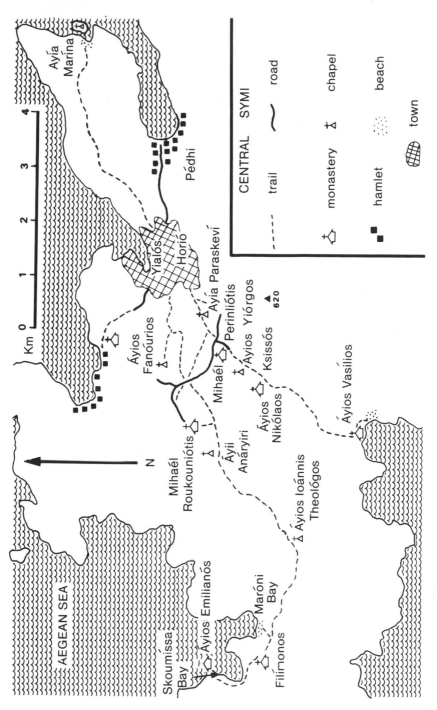

CENTRAL   SYMI

- - - - -   trail

—————   road

⚑   monastery

⚑   chapel

■   hamlet

∴   town

⊞   beach

Kéfala headland and Áyios Emilianós seen from Áyios Ioánnis Theologos

Áyios Emilianós is joined by a long, wave-lashed causeway to the headland of Kéfala. The monastery is not architecturally or historically exceptional, merely remarkable for its setting. Overnighting is convenient, whether by contingency or choice; the "kitchen" (first interior door on the right) has a *stérna*, a fireplace and a sleeping platform. Outhouses are exiled to the edge of the little islet on which the cloister sits. You can also swim on the lee (south, usually) side of the islet, but beware of sea urchins.

On your way back you may wish to stop in at Maróni Bay—the water's on a par with Skoumíssa's but the pebble shore may be tar or garbage fouled. More importantly, there are two wells with buckets behind a modern cottage, occupied in summer.

Rating/time course: This moderate, 7-hr transect of Sými is an ideal full-day excursion; almost half the route is shaded.

Alternate return: At the eucalyptus-tufted ridge, veer right instead of descending directly to Yialós via the *kalderími*. This return via Horió is 30 roundabout min longer but offers late-afternoon perspectives on the harbor from yet another angle. Ten min before the edge of Horió lies the chapel of Ayía Paraskeví, with a much-needed cistern-and-bucket.

Sými to Ayía Marína

Once again a small church graces an islet, but this time there's no causeway—you must swim out to visit! Unfortunately the bucket for the cistern was missing in 1984, and there's no water along the way, so come prepared. The hiking route itself is not particularly memorable, nor is it long.

Climb up to Horió and find the highest windmills on the ridge to the northeast; the trail begins to the left of the row of five. Almost instantly you should pass the circular foundation of an ancient watchtower. The trail, faint though traceable, hugs the left flank of the hillside and is sporadically marked by the legend *"BK"* and piled-rock cairns. One hr along you'll reach a large, fenced-off meadow at the base of a large hill. The path, except for products of wishful thinking, ends here; skirt the enclosed pasture to its right and climb the saddle lying to the right of the rocky knob looming beyond the plain. Ayía Marína island and its baby monastery are plainly visible from the saddle, which has some rudimentary terraces and pastures on top. A followable trail does resume through the exact middle of the valley dropping sharply down to the shore opposite Ayía Marína. Despite an absence of fresh water it's a favored spot, with fine swimming in the shallow, sandy-bottomed cove.

Sými to Áyios Vasílios

This fairly demanding hike leads to one of the best Symiote beaches accessible on foot, as well as yet another improbably situated chapel-monastery.

Ascend from the *platía* of Yialós to Horió via the stairway called Kataráktis, after an adjacent drainage system. Find the uppermost right-hand (westerly) street in Horió, distinguished by three consecutive belfries, on the hillside south of the castle. Follow this thoroughfare out of Horió; very soon after leaving the last habitation behind, ignore a left fork; do take a left fork almost immediately after passing the *ksoklísi* of Ayía Paraskeví with its giant oak. Some 20 min after clearing town the path will intersect a new army road; just the other side are the sprawling (but locked) grounds of the monastery Mihaél Perinliótis. To relocate the trail follow the new bulldozer track that scars the ground just to the left of Perinliótis' outer walls. Soon the original trail surfaces on the right, near the chapel of Áyios Yiórgos; bear straight ahead, through the relatively green agricultural plateau of Ksissós, toward a cleft in the landscape.

About 50 min out of Horió, trail and bulldozer track both expire at the door of Áyios Nikólaos monastery, where there's a cistern, a quaint sanctuary of recent origin and a patriotic sexton who spent the best years of his youth interned near Civitavecchia for refusing to cooperate with the Italian occupation authorities. Leave the grounds of the cloister to its lower left, through a lone gate; the above-noted cleft resolves into a canyon yawning below the last oak trees of Ksissós. The path resumes, passing a small white building and a barb-wired goat pen. Now you zigzag over to the right (west) bank of the rapidly plunging ravine; you should pass a yellow "*NT*" painted on the rock as you cross the split upper reach. The trail parallels the gully for some 20 min before the sea, in the form of Ayíou Vasilíou Bay, appears. The route crosses another gulch 1½ hr from town, is briefly shaded by tufts of junipers and then levels out on a plateau dense with thyme and oregano. Keep to the center of this landscape poised directly above the Aegean and locate cairns leading down toward the water. A bit less than 2 hr along, the path halts at a natural "balcony" from where you can first glimpse Áyios Vasílios, 30 m downhill; a few paces to the left an improvised stairway drops down to the tiny monastery.

The chapel boasts unexpected frescoes and a pebble mosaic floor; a water cistern, cooking area and a sleeping platform may be found in the building to one side. If the blinding light or heat is not too debilitating, you can laze on the terrace between the two buildings and take in the cobalt-colored bay 100 m below. For most, its blandishment is irresistible; turn right at the top of the stairs and carefully pick your way down a stable rock pile to Lápathos, a clean sand-and-pebble beach. Wooded slopes plummet down on all sides to shelter the bay and any human visitors from the wind; outside of summer you'll probably have the premises to yourself.

Rating/time course: Though only 2½ hr one way, the grade is often steep and the surface potentially ankle-turning.

Seasonal note: From June to September Sými is one of the hottest, if not the most torrid, of the Greek islands. Rainstorms occur anytime between mid-November and mid-March.

Map: "Symi Tourist Map," by I. Koza, is reasonably accurate at an approximate scale of 1:43,000.

42   KÁRPATHOS

While most of the Dhodhekánisos are either mainly limestone or principally sandy, this long, skinny finger of an island pointing up between Rhódhos and Crete is a hybrid. Forests soften Kárpathos' northern, sedimentary contours, and a half-dozen "pocket" beaches 100 to 200 m long, and accessible in some cases only by sea, grace the east coast, but in the south little save thornbush grows on acres of karst. Kárpathos is the second largest island of the archipelago but despite its size has always been a backwater. Its pre-Christian towns were of minor importance, and because of its relative poverty medieval depredations and interference by foreign overlords were token. A happy consequence of this neglect is the persistence on Kárpathos of a couple of communities living much as they did in Byzantine times.

The two hikes detailed pass through what remains of the pine forests that once covered the northern end of the island. A major fire in 1983 devastated most of northern Kárpathos' woodlands, so you should enquire as to the condition of the trail between Ólymbos and Spóa especially—it may have been destroyed by rain-promoted erosion.

The main interest for hikers, conflagration or no, is the stopover in Ólymbos village, where the inhabitants wear traditional dress and follow daily routines dating back 700 years. The recent construction of two taxi roads, the introduction of electricity and swelling numbers of tourists will undoubtedly accelerate change in Ólymbos, but for the near future the community should remain a living museum of medieval Greek folk culture.

Getting to Kárpathos and the trailheads: The *Panormítis* connects Rhódhos, Hálki, Kárpathos and Kássos once a week going west, then east; a car ferry duplicates this service, with Crete and a few of the Kykládhes thrown in, on another day of the week; and once a week (in season) the ferryboat *Kykládhes* serves Kárpathos on a far-flung route that includes Kaválla, Límnos, Lésvos, Híos, Ikaría/Sámos, various Dhodhekánisos, Crete and such Kykládhes as whim, time and engine health permit. Note that most ferries stop at both ports, Dhiafáni in the north (weather permitting) and Pigádhia in the south. It's preferable to disembark at Dhiafáni and do the hikes as described. If you choose to reverse the directions, there is only one daily bus (in the morning) from Pigádhia to Spóa, often prebooked (see note on Spóa below); it may be easier to find a *kaïki* from Pigádhia to Áyios Nikólaos, the bay below Spóa. There are also seasonal flights from Rhódhos to Pigádhia.

Dhiafáni to Ólymbos

Leave Dhiafáni by the right-hand (northmost) track; after some 200 m this becomes a path paralleling the new taxi road (the more southerly right-of-way). Not surprisingly, the trail is shorter and more scenic, and may have escaped the worst effects of the 1983 blaze. Pass a fountain 30 min along on your right; to the left a red rock-dot indicates a turn toward a line of power poles. The path climbs through a ravine, following a stream, and within 20 min more reaches a shady pine grove with another fountain. After another 30 min of walking you leave the stream bed, use the taxi road for 100 m and then veer left along a ridge to bypass a series of switchbacks in the road ahead. You're out of such forest as remains and among thorny scrub by now.

Opposite—top: Women of Ólymbos make doll clothes for fun (Hike 42); Bottom, left: Baking bread at Ólymbos (Hike 42); Bottom, right: Woman of Ólymbos (Hike 42; photo by Ann Cleeland)

The trail soon rejoins the road, which within 5 min forks; bear left. Three hundred m beyond the junction a footpath appears faintly in a gully to the right. Ólymbos comes into view shortly thereafter; its pastel cubic houses and a few windmills extend along a ridge for a full kilometer. A further 30-min walk brings you to the lower fields and outermost *ksoklísia* of the village, and you'll finish the climb to central Ólymbos no more than 2½ hr after quitting Dhiafáni.

Life in and around Ólymbos

Both Dhiafáni and Ólymbos are famous for the distinctive garb of their women. Young girls wear a variety of colored hose, gowns and embroidered vests, but for grown women the outfit is more uniform. Women wear white smocks covered by either black embroidered skirts and gray or navy vests or by dark, full-length dresses. Each wears a plain or embroidered black kerchief wrapped around her head, and tan leather boots complete the outfit.

You may happen upon embroidered clothing elsewhere, but "embroidered" houses as found at Ólymbos aren't so common. Most bannisters, lintels and eaves sport molded plaster reliefs painted in a dozen colors. Floral, animal, mythical or geometrical designs are all represented, but the most popular motif is the double-headed eagle of the Paleologi, the last Orthodox dynasty to rule at Constantinople.

The *salónia* (front rooms) of many dwellings are decorated with bolts of embroidered cloth, multicolored dishes and tapestries. These dowries and festival linens woven by the women of the families are not for sale; incidentally, Ólymbos is one of the few surviving matrilineal communities in modern Greece, with property and real estate inherited from one's mother.

Several *pensions* have sprung up in Ólymbos to accommodate the tourist trade, but there are only two small *tavérnes* as such and you'll find it expedient to arrange for bed *and* board with your host(ess). Neither are there any bakeries in Ólymbos; the women bake their own bread at four or five communal ovens several days a week (except, of course, Sunday). If you want bread, you may be offered some by the bakers or you save it from the dinner table. The product is faintly sourdough and often sprinkled with sesame seeds. Around Eastertime you'll see hand-size *kouloúria* and the larger, twisted *tsouréki*, bread baked with a whole red-dyed egg stuck in the middle. Spinach turnovers are another spring delicacy.

Olymbiotes of necessity hunt and gather in addition to tending their fields down in the creek valley. Everyone departs in the early morning with goats and farming implements but returns at dusk with an additional cargo of herbs, firewood and other foraged items. *Petalídhes* (limpets) and *myrgouátana*, a local seashore alga, are consumed in large quantities; one cafe in town even serves fried *myrgouátana*-and-flour cakes as *mezédhes* (appetizers).

Easter and the week after, plus the Assumption of the Virgin (August 15) are the most devoutly celebrated festivals at Ólymbos; weddings, live music and sundry bacchanalia are for all to enjoy at these times. Unfortunately, lodging can be impossible to secure during these two holiday seasons, since hundreds of Europeans (especially Germans) descend on Ólymbos, with the overflow even sleeping in the streets. Lent, on the other hand, is strictly observed, so that's a dull time to visit.

Ólymbos to Spóa

Leave Ólymbos from its westernmost or seaward neighborhood; a small rusty sign points toward the Spóa path. The first hour is taken up by a steady climb on a *kalderími* looping around Profítis Ilías (718 m). There are eagle-eye views of the sea, cliffs and terraces in this stretch, but no water. The second hour begins with a descent through hedges of rock rose and (formerly) a pine grove. After 30 min the path proceeds levelly through terraced meadows and passes a spring on your left in one of the first such pastures. Follow red-dotted rocks to an abandoned settlement of three dwellings; here the trail triple forks right, center and hairpin left.

Continuing straight ahead along an old, apparently abandoned mule track *may* be productive, but I was strongly dissuaded from attempting it by the Olymbiotes and I never found the other end of the trail in Spóa; conceivably it winds up in Messohóri, a few kilometers west of Spóa. If you do attempt this central route, be prepared to spend the night in the (before 1983 anyway) pine-choked gullies further along.

The hairpin left path rises to join the Ólymbos-Spóa dirt road, which for the next 45 min parallels Kárpathos' north-south crest, offering tremendous views east and west before reaching the base of Mt. Kymáres. Next you descend 30 min along the east flank of this mountain to a large spring or stream at a bend in the road; from here it's another 2 hr to Spóa. You should budget more than 6 hr for the full trek from Ólymbos because fire damage may have made the route slower going than described.

The bus that plies the Spóa-Pigádhia route only carries 14 passengers, advance seat reservations must be made and priority is given to villagers—outsiders are boarded on a space-available basis. Taxis are rare and expensive; private cars are equally scarce. Spóa has spartan lodgings for five persons while you await your ride. Alternatively you can walk 1 hr west to Messohóri, where transport is slightly more likely, or descend to the bay of Áyios Nikólaos for a *kaïki*.

Rating/time course: These are two easy-to-moderate day jaunts; I throw in the latter qualification partly because the Ólymbos-Spóa leg is long (ca. 17 km) though not particularly arduous unless fire damage has turned it into a cross-country trek.

Supplies: Haphazard in Dhiafáni and Ólymbos; come prepared.

CRETE (KRÍTI)

*The island has always abounded with marvels and portents and the
exaggeration of the mountains casts an overpowering spell . . . the
metamorphic limestone mass, especially where it soars above the
treeline in a wilderness where nothing can grow, (shines) like silver and
lends to the great peaks, even in August, an illusion of eternal snow . . . .*

——Patrick Leigh Fermor

The southernmost island of Europe suffers even more than the rest of Greece from a popular misconception that it is merely the seat of distantly past, and vanished, glories. This view ignores a rich Greco-Venetian culture that flourished in three post-Byzantine centuries, followed by a bizarre, brutal Ottoman interlude of almost equal duration. Independence in 1898 was a prelude to union with the mainland 15 years later.

It's equally little-known that Crete possesses some of the most striking wilderness areas in Greece, with rough-and-ready mountaineers, never completely subdued by occupying powers, to go with them. As you proceed west and south along the length of the island, past the isolated knobs of Mts. Dhíkti and Psilorítis to the imposing, many-peaked Levká Óri (White Mountains), both terrain and inhabitants assume legendary, larger-than-life proportions. A Cretan patriarch all got up in *tsalvária* (baggy pants), high boots, vest, leather apron and *sariki* (headband) invites you onto his porch for a *raki*, and soon it's clear that, for him at least, the heroic age is not over. Memories of the fierce resistance against the Germans 45 years ago are still fresh. An

Chapel at Ayía Roúmeli (Photo by Ann Cleeland)

enormous oral tradition keeps alive memories of Crete's struggle for independence against invaders from Byzantine to modern times.

Other Greeks regard Cretans with a mixture of amusement, fear and respect, much as southern British consider Scots, and Americans those hailing from the Deep South. For Greeks, Crete is stereotypically the first and last bastion of freedom and a repository of practices and follies long since disappeared elsewhere in the nation. To foreigners, as well, Cretans (with a long 'e', as opposed to "cretin") may seem to embody all of the Greek virtues and vices but in fourfold measure. Moderation is scorned; rustling, blood feuds, marriage by abduction, three-day festivals, courageous resistance against hopeless odds, and self-abnegating generosity were until very recently staples of a life that contributed to the legend of the *Kritikí* (Greek for Cretans) as Super-Greeks, a reputation that the islanders themselves seem loath to counter or gainsay. *Levendiá*—an expression difficult to translate but implying grace, eloquent wit, physical agility, musicality, high spirits in the face of adversity, and pride in self-sufficiency—is still a quality prized in men and women.

The Cretan has faced armed enemies and hordes of tourists with the same security born of a feeling of superiority which led the Sicilian Don Fabrizio to exclaim in *The Leopard*: "They have come to teach us good manners! But they won't succeed, because we are gods."

Getting to Crete: There is daily ferry service between Piráeus and the ports of Haniá and Iráklion and twice-weekly service from neighboring Kykládhes and Dhodhekánisos (see Hikes 35, 36 and 42); these call at Áyios Nikólaos and Sitía. Seasonal ferries run, from one to six times a week, between Iráklion and Thíra. Planes fly daily from Athens to Haniá or Iráklion.

Map: Nelles Verlag, 'Creta,' 1:200,000, or Geobuch product of same scale; try to get before arrival.

43   MT. PSILORÍTIS (ÍDHI)

At 2456 m, this is the highest peak in Crete though by no means as interesting as the White Mountains. There are at least two different ascent routes. The most conservative involves a 3- to 4-hr climb by trail from the village of Kamáres (bus from Iráklion twice daily), on the south side of the mountain, as far as the archaeologically important grotto of Kamáres at 1600 m. From here it's another 4 hr to the Idhéon Ándron (1700 m), the cave which in rivalry with a similar one near Mt. Dhíkti is claimed to be the birth chamber of Zeus. From this second grotto a trail leads, within another 5 hr, to the summit.

Upon return from the top you can descend from the cave in 4 hr, by trail and/or jeep track serving the EOS hut at Prínos, to the important village of Anóyia, north of Psilorítis. From Anóyia up to Idhéon Ándron it's about a 6-hr climb, via the beautiful Nídha plain. Except for possibly a spring at Prínos, there is no dependable running water on the mountain, although the summit chapel formerly contained a cistern.

Map: ESY, Réthimnou.

44   COASTAL VILLAGES OF SFAKIÁ AND THE SAMARIAN GORGE

A line drawn from Soúyia to Frangokástello may be considered the diameter of Sfakiá, a roughly semicircular district in Haniá province, and some of the most rugged, inaccessible and fascinating areas of Crete lie entirely within its limits. Until a couple of decades ago most of its villages had no road connections, and there are still a half-dozen communities that will never see an automobile. This exclusion of vehicles is due mostly to a series of deep and dramatic canyons which furrow the south coast of the island across the diameter described. The gorge of Samariá is merely the largest and most renowned of more than a dozen such clefts.

Even if you have only three days to spend in Crete, it's possible to assemble an itinerary connecting the most isolated settlements of Sfakiá with its most impressive natural treasure, the gorge. A less cramped schedule allows for dallying at various archaeological sites, beaches and watering holes.

Getting to the trailheads: From Réthimno, take a morning bus to Vrýsses and wait there for the Haniá bus to Anópoli (see below). From the beaches at Frangokástello, Plakiás or Préveli—all east of Anópoli—there are one or two buses daily toward Hóra Sfakíon. Anópoli is 12 km above and beyond this town, and it's not a particularly pleasant road walk, so you're best off waiting in Hóra for the afternoon bus to Anópoli. The trailhead for "Freshwater Beach" and Loutró is only 40 min up the road though. As of 1984 there was but one direct bus a day from Haniá to Anópoli via Vrýsses, at 1 P.M.; it returned at 6:30 the next morning.

From Haniá there is bus service (May to October) at 6, 8:30 and 9:30 A.M. and 4:30 P.M. to Ksilóskala (top of the Samarian gorge), with usual immediate turnaround upon arrival 1½ hr later. Service to Hóra Sfakíon, from Haniá is approximately 8:30 A.M., 11:30 A.M., 2 and 3:30 P.M. outbound, and 7 A.M., 11 A.M., 3:30 and 6 P.M. back to Haniá. In peak season there *may* be an extra evening bus to accommodate passengers from the extra evening caique(s) from Ayía Roúmeli.

Kaíkia sail (or motor, to be precise) from Ayía Roúmeli to Hóra Sfakíon, with a stop at Loutró, at 9 A.M. (sometimes), 2 and 5 P.M.. It's 45 min to Loutró from Ayía Roúmeli and another 20 min to Hóra. There is also daily (sometimes twice) service from Ayía Roúmeli to Paleohóra some 2 hr west along the Sfakian coast, with a stop at Soúyia. Note that these are sample schedules for the periods June through September; departures are sharply reduced in April, May and October and are almost nonexistent

Church at Arádhena and the White Mountains

November through March (when the gorge is closed anyway). Confirm schedules at the Haniá port police or tourist office.

Anópoli to Ayía Roúmeli

The bus leaves passengers at the large round *platía* of Anópoli, a sleepy farming village in a high valley at the foot of Levká Óri. There are some "rooms" at the east end of the plateau and two *kafenéia* on the roundabout. Next to the left-hand or southerly cafe, a trail begins to Loutró (see "Anópoli to Loutro"), while the track proceeding straight ahead (west) leads to Arádhena. Within 10 min this ends at a second, smaller round *platía*; from its southwest corner a footpath takes off between several houses. Over the next 30 min the trail rounds a ridge and then continues straight along a *kalderími* to the edge of the Arádhena gorge. The cobbled route zigzags into and out of this small cousin of the Samarian canyon, leveling out in the dying village of Arádhena (population 8). A singularly attractive white church on the brink of the gorge marks Arádhena's highest point, from where you may gaze on the gleaming west face of Levká Óri. About 70 m past the turnoff to the church a faint path heads right for 200 m to a group of three wells with a bucket, where you can camp.

From Arádhena the trail continues another 1¼ hr, passing the faint path coming up on the left from Loutró via Livanianá (see "Livanianá to the Arádhena-Áyios Ioánnis route"). Áyios Ioánnis is a friendly village of about 100 people and one *kafenéio* owned by an old woman; if you lunch or stay the night there, her menu is limited to bread and cheese. Note also that the many water spigots visible in the village streets tend to run dry after July, so you must ask householders for water, or better, fill up in Arádhena.

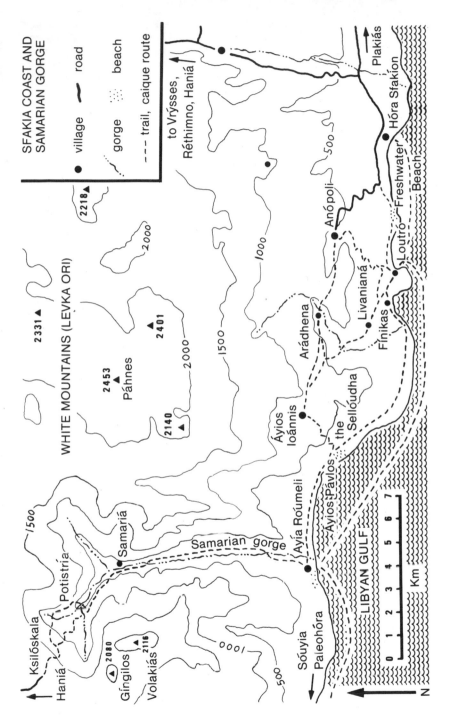

SFAKIA COAST AND
SAMARIAN GORGE

● village   ⌒ road

gorge   ⋮⋮⋮ beach

– – – trail, caique route

to Vrýsses,
Réthimno, Haniá

Plakiás

Hóra Sfakíon

2218▲

'Freshwater'

Anópoli

500

Beach

WHITE MOUNTAINS (LEVKA ORI)

2331▲

2453
▲
Páhnes

2401
▲

2140
▲

Loutró

Livaniana

2000

Fínikas

1000

Arádhena

1500

Selloúdha

the

2000

Áyios
Ioánnis

1500

Samariá

Ayía Roúmeli

Áyios Pávlos

Potistría

Samarian gorge

LIBYAN GULF

Ksilóskala

Haniá

Gíngilos ▲ 2080

Volakiás ▲ 2116

Sóuyia

Paleohóra

1500

1000

500

0   1   2   3   4   5   6   7
|___|___|___|___|___|___|___|
Km

N ◀

To proceed to Ayía Roúmeli you needn't actually enter Áyios Ioánnis. Take a left fork at the village outskirts, just before the gate and the school; the trail descends between two chapels, a small white one and a large tiled *ksoklísi*. In the next 15 min you pass a first livestock pen on your right and then approach a second one, but rather than pass it, turn right across a small, dry wash. The faint trail becomes an obvious right-of-way as you climb out of the wash and head for the brink of a 600-m coastal cliff. From the edge Ayía Roúmeli is just visible to the west as part of a sweeping vista over 20 km of coastline. An extremely rocky *kalderími*, the Selloúdha, zigzags 1 hr down to the shore, merging, as it levels out, with the coastal trail coming over from Loutró (see "Ayía Roúmeli to Loutró via the Coast"). About 15 min past the junction the path peters out directly in front of the 15th century basilica of Áyios Pávlos; on this site the Apostle Paul is said to have made his first landfall on Crete to preach the gospel. The little *ksoklísi* rests on a pebbly shore with sand dunes on all sides, looking out of place as if it had been shipwrecked on this lonely coast (as indeed Paul himself was). The *ksoklísi* may be open, but only fragments of frescoes remain to be seen. The water is cool before May, but if you fancy going in anyway, just sit on a noon-time dune for a moment to warm up.

The trail resumes, beneath nearby power lines, over a surface varying between sand, pebbles and packed dirt for the sloggy hour-long walk to Ayía Roúmeli. There are good campsites east of that village, where the river flows out of the Samarian gorge; old Ayía Roúmeli, 1 km inland, is largely abandoned. The new settlement on the shore is strictly a tourist facility with mostly overpriced restaurants, "rooms" and even a disco. Beyond the small harbor, docking point for east- and westbound caiques, stretches an enormous beach which serves as a fitting end to any and all treks to Ayía Roúmeli. Many people camp on this beach; if you patronize the restaurant at the Tzatzimáki family's hotel, they'll let you use their outdoor shower.

Anópoli to Loutró

Walk south from the *platía* with the two *kafenéia*. The auto track dwindles to a footpath among the southernmost houses of Anópoli, with a splendid overlook of the fertile basin and the flanks of Levká Óri to the north. The landmarks to aim for, which you pass some 25 min out of "city center," are power lines marching over the ridge and a chapel perched on a bluff above the wires. Twenty min past the crest separating Anópoli plain from the sea, take the right of a fork; there's little possibility of confusion, since your goal lies before you (albeit in toylike dimensions) and the steep palisade is as bare and grim as could be imagined. Thirty min further down the limestone slope, the direct trail to Livanianá forks right (west); pass it. Stray vegetation begins and soon you meet the Hóra Sfakíon-Loutró trail, between a white *ikónisma* and the ruined, eastmost house of Loutró. A few moment's more walking into the hamlet itself brings the elapsed time from Anópoli to 1¾ hr.

Loutró

There are still a few fisher-families at the sleepy port of Loutró, but the place has been discovered of late by a young and slightly penurious crowd, which on the bright side keeps prices lower than in Ayía Roúmeli. There are plenty of "rooms"—except in midsummer—and a handful of *tavérnes*. Scores of individuals camp on the headland past the cemetery, but it's dusty and unsanitary. Wind surfing and kayaking are big here—both types of craft are rented.

Loutró to Anópoli

Categorically unrecommended in the hot months. The trail, conspicuous from Loutró, zigzags staggeringly up the sheer cliff face: easily, but not an easy 2½ hr up—for mad dogs and Englishmen only.

Loutró to Hóra Sfakíon

This route is heavily traveled and hemmed in between the sea and vertical rock faces most of the way, so trail description will not be meticulous. Instead, it's a freak of nature halfway to Hóra that merits attention. The famed "Freshwater Beach" lies a bit over 1 hr east of Loutró, just past a white chapel on a promontory. Sweet water percolates down from the cliffs above into several potholes in the 700-m span of pebbles; drink only from the one(s) labeled with blue paint—the others are for washing. Although a long-term residence for numerous nudists, the beach and water here are perhaps the cleanest in Crete so help keep it that way. Lack of litter also usually means an absence of police harrassment or "no camping or nudism" signs.

To the east, 15 min above the beach, the trail is briefly muddled by a rockslide, but good cobbling resumes until you intersect the Hóra-Anópoli blacktop as it swerves inland. Walking 40 min downroad brings you to Hóra Sfakíon, some 2¼ hr after leaving Loutró. (If you're coming up from Hóra, you can easily recognize the trailhead by the dirt turnout where autos are invariably parked; "Freshwater" is in sight to the west.)

Loutró to Livanianá

Going west from Loutró, the path begins from the last (southwesternmost) *tavérna* on the waterfront. From here take a sharp uphill toward the castle; don't follow the coastline trail, which merely ends at the south tip of Fínikas cape (among the ruins of the Biblical Phoenice). Once on the crest of the hill, beyond the castle, that divides the Fínikas littoral into two zones (one *tavérna*/rooms each), the trail splits. The left yellow-arrowed fork proceeds to the westernmost *tavérna* and on to Ayía Roúmeli (see "Ayía Roúmeli to Loutró . . ."); the unmarked but prominent path on the right climbs to Livanianá, the inviting village crouched on the hillside before you. The trail is easy to miss at first—you must veer hard right to pick it up as it crosses the base of the hillside, above all old terraces. Within a few moments the surface is that of a good *kalderími*; phone wires and olive trees should be kept well to your left, though the AC power lines do pass over the start of the trail, at the turnoff. Some 30 min above the junction, enter Livanianá on its east side, behind most of the houses and well to the right of the gully draining from them. Once "in town," pass the well (the only dependable water during the dry months) and head for the church atop the village. Once on the ridge, behind and to the right of the chapel, you can peer down into the lower reaches of the Arádhena gorge; the viewpoint is also the start of the path up to Áyios Ioánnis.

Livanianá enjoys a marvelous setting on its ridge between the gorge and the Libyan Sea, its amphitheatrical layout partly obscured by the olive groves today tended by only 40 inhabitants. No *kafenéio* (the closest is in west Fínikas), no accommodation, but Bárba Andhréas, if he's still alive, is happy to offer traditional Cretan hospitality in the form of a *tsikoudhiá* (firewater) and a good talk (in Greek).

If you're coming down from Áyios Ioánnis, red dots mark the way out of Livanianá from the all-important well; the medieval Finikás castle and a watchtower behind it orient you.

Livanianá to the Arádhena-Áyios Ioánnis Route

This trail is so decrepit in places that you may have trouble believing that the Sfakiá mailman uses this route twice a week! In a large measure it is thanks to him that the path stays open at all; fortunately for the average hiker the route is minimally red-dotted.

From the highest church of Livanianá (next to an unreliable *sterna*) proceed northwest toward another *ksoklisi* visible on a knoll overlooking the Arádhena gorge.

Near Sidheresportes of the Samarian gorge (Photo by Ann Cleeland)

Just before the shrine, some 20 min along, find a well equipped with a stock trough and a bucket—this is the only water until Arádhena or Áyios Ioánnis. Once at the chapel itself, point straight from the front door, over thornbush terraces, to a cluster of wild pear trees below. This gives you the correct general bearing of the trail as it continues toward Áyios Ioánnis; the path is just visible to the sharp-eyed as a break in the rock face as it ascends the far side of the canyon. You reach the bed of the gorge 40 min past Livanianá; next there are some 20 min of rock-strewn switchbacks climbing out of the ravine to the edge of some much-appreciated pine woods. After crossing a small gully, the grade lessens and the faint trail becomes straight. Ninety minutes out of Livanianá, a larger trail from the piney slope on the left crosses your path (ignore this fork if descending—it dead-ends on a sheer-sided bluff). Continue straight without bearing right until reaching a goat pen about 5 min beyond the junction. If you're headed for Arádhena bear right on the trail just behind it; turn left if bound for Áyios Ioánnis. This is not the main Arádhena-Áyios Ioánnis *kalderími*, which is 20 min in either direction along this subsidiary path. If frustrated or lost, move uphill through the weedy plateau before you and you'll eventually run perpendicular to the main Sfakian "highway."

Áyios Ioánnis to Livanianá

This is essentially the reverse of the above, with a few twists. Thirty min toward Arádhena on the Áyios Ioánnis-Anópoli *kalderími*, bear right onto a prominent side trail. Just before it appears to curve back up to the main artery, plunge downhill on goat traces to a flat area with olive trees and the above-noted goat pen. Heading downhill from the knolltop chapel to Livanianá, you may pass the well-and-bucket without seeing it, so take on plenty of water in Áyios Ioánnis.

Up the Samarian Gorge: Ayía Roúmeli to Ksilóskala (Omalós)

Contrary to almost unanimous popular belief, this is not that difficult an exercise; the only severe altitude change occurs in the highest 5 km, generally in cool alpine conditions. It's certainly not in the same league as the torturous 600-m ascent from sea level to Áyios Ioánnis via the Selloúdha, over scarcely 3 horizontal kilometers.

As you leave Ayía Roúmeli, the trail keeps to the left (west) bank of the gorge which narrows drastically about 500 m inland from the last vestiges of the old village. Near the boundary of the Samarian National Park a large placard-map summarizes the botanical biomes of the reserve and pinpoints shelter and fire-fighting post locations. Another sign lists prohibitions against flower gathering, littering, fires, radios, leaving the main trail and camping. It used to be a simple matter to camp discreetly for one night; but now free, dated tickets are issued at both upper and lower park entry posts, and showing up at the opposite trail terminus with a day-old chit could prove embarrassing. In addition to this human inventory control, mule rescue teams and a burly warden based in Samariá hamlet patrol constantly.

Much of the way through the gorge is studded with kilometer signposts, but keep in mind that while the entire hike is actually over 16 km, only the distance contained within the national park boundaries—13 or 14 km— is marked. So, for example, Samariá, at "6" ascending or "7" descending, is really 9 to 10 km from the shore. This is a somewhat cruel deception which can cause no end of bafflement or even disputes unless recognized. In discussing the trail, the signed distance will be given in quotes, with the true distance in parentheses.

Shortly after "3" km (6), the gorge narrows to a mere 2 m at the famed Sidherespórtes, or "iron gates," which are almost impossible to photograph satisfactorily except at noon. In spring you don't hike this portion of the route so much as wade it; there may be up to a dozen water crossings on either side of the narrows. Once through this towering bottleneck the path, often little more than a slight disturbance in assorted rock piles, climbs gradually to some pine and cedar groves and passes a point, 8 to 9 km inland, where the river gushes forth from an underground channel in the canyon bottom.

The empty village of Samariá (natives relocated in 1964), with its burbling fountains, ranger's station and picnic tables, lies on the east bank of the gorge and is reached by a foot bridge between the "6" and "7" km markers. Beyond Samariá the trail grade stiffens en route to the chapel of Áyios Nikólaos, roughly "10" (13 ½) km beyond Ayía Roúmeli. To the west and east respectively Gíngilos and Melidaóu peaks loom overhead, catching the sun's rays at dawn and dusk. Both above and below Áyios Nikólaos are delightful pools in the now-resurfaced river which are fine for a dip in the heat of the Cretan summer. When the stream is in full spate you may again, as at Sidherespórtes, be repeatedly donning and shedding your boots. From the last river crossing at "11" km (14) the trail switchbacks steeply up to Ksilóskala (wooden stair) and the head of the gorge. Except for one fountain at "12" (15) km, there is no more water along the way.

Most hikers reach Ksilóskala, "14" (17) km, roughly 6 hr after setting out from Ayía Roúmeli. Here a large tourist pavilion with a view off the rear balcony offers slightly overpriced meals and beds. More conventional lodging can be found 2 km downhill at Omalós hamlet.

Down the Gorge: Omalós to the Sea

Using the main, most heavily traveled trail, it's 2 ½ hr or so from Ksilóskala to the abandoned village of Samariá. Thirty min along the way you may wish to consider the alternate route passing through Potistría. This path, clear but nowhere as wide as the gorge-floor route, crawls high up the flanks of Melidaóu peak before looping down to rejoin the main trail within sight of Áyios Nikólaos chapel. The Potistría detour is not as shaded as the principal track but ample compensation is provided in the form of sweeping vistas over Gíngilos and Volakiás peaks and a sense of wilderness and solitude at times completely lacking on the conventional tourist route. There are two springs along the way, which is at most 30 min longer than the main path to Áyios Nikólaos. Once in Samariá, you've another 2-hr march down to Ayía Roúmeli, bringing the downhill elapsed time to just under 5 hr.

Incidentally, the name Samariá has nothing to do with either the Biblical kingdom or St. Mary, but is a contraction of Ossía María, "Mary the Beatified" (but not canonized), an Egyptian courtesan who, repenting of her ways, became an ascetic in the desert.

Ayía Roúmeli to Loutró via the Coast

In recent years this trail has been red- and yellow-blazed, to the relief of many. Once on the outskirts of Ayía Roúmeli, cross the mouth of the Samarian River and find the small blazed gap in the opposite bank where the trail proper begins. The *ksoklísi* of Áyios Pávlos lies just over 1 hr ahead. Twenty min uphill from the chapel is the well-marked fork; left leads up the Selloúdha to Áyios Ioánnis, right takes you to Loutró, the present goal. Walking along the right option for 45 min brings you through the last of the coastal pine forest to a single cottage and stock trough by a well, the only signs of refreshment in a landscape that fairly shimmers with heat seven months of the year. Ninety minutes beyond the junction, you'll top a hillock and have your first look at the tiny port of Fínikas and the Venetian castle on the long tongue of land hiding Loutró. Within another 30 min the trail dips down to the exit of the Arádhena gorge and a small pebbly cove. After another 20 min on a ledge just above the water, the route dips to sea level just before the first cafe of Fínikas, where you'll probably guzzle a full 750-ml can of grapefruit juice if you haven't already flung your shriveled self into the tantalizing ocean. On course once more, you should pass right by a

View from the top of the Selloúdha; Ayía Roúmeli at extreme left

medieval cistern atop the headland, then the castle (more appealing from outside than in), and just under 3 hr past the fork, you descend triumphantly into Loutró.

Itinerary recommendations: Given the complexity of the Sfakian trail network, it's difficult to give general advice. Some won't want to miss the seashore life at Loutró and "Freshwater," others will prefer to immerse themselves in the village rhythms further inland. The only stretch I personally would not repeat is the coast between Fínikas and the base of the Selloúdha, and I never intend to essay the pleasures of an ascent from Loutró to Anópoli. Also, ascents of the Selloúdha are inadvisable in hot weather.

Rating/time course: This is a demanding trek, with or without side trips, because of its 35- to 40-km length, altitude changes totaling over 2000 m in that distance, and uneven trail conditions. A leisurely paced hike from Anópoli to Ksilóskala via Ayía Roúmeli, or vice versa, will take two full days. Allow the same time if you detour from Anópoli down to Loutró and proceed along the coast to Ayía Roúmeli. Budget an additional half-day for a meander up through Áyios Ioánnis via Livaniana and a return to the coast at Áyios Pávlos. Add an extra day for a start from Hóra Sfakión, with time to linger at "Freshwater Beach" or Loutró.

Seasonal note: The gorge itself is officially closed from November through April; during winter rains and snowmelt, Samariá is subject to severe flooding and several hikers have perished here in roiling, man-high water. Late-April to mid-May offers snow-White Mountains, wildflowers and tolerable coastal temperatures; September and October mean the best swimming.

Supplies: Get in Réthimno or Haniá; Hóra Sfakión is expensive.

45   BEYOND SFAKIÁ: SOÚYIA TO PALEOHÓRA VIA ANCIENT LISSÓS

The forbidding coastline between Ayía Roúmeli and Soúyia constitutes the "missing link" in the trail system of western Crete. The countryside is steep and rugged, and any thoroughfares that may once have existed have been forgotten since the last world war. Onward trekkers are accordingly advised to take a *kaïki* from Ayía

Roúmeli to Soúyia, or one of two daily buses (morning and early afternoon) from Haniá.

Soúyia is a tiny hamlet which before World War II was merely the harbor annex of the mountain village of Koustoyérako. Today it boasts a modern olive press (just follow your nose) hard by a church built on foundations of an earlier 6th century one; there are brilliant mosaics both inside and outside it, and you can see quite a bit through the windows if the keys are unavailable. Most visitors are primarily interested in the beach (better than Ayía Roúmeli's), sea caves and a handful of snack bars, conventional *tavérnes* and "rooms."

To proceed to Lissós or beyond, start from the new harbor, where a rusty, barely legible sign ("*Lissos*") points up a ravine beyond the dock. It's a fine *harádhra* with pines, oleander, carob and overhanging, tawny walls strongly evocative of the American southwest or the Australian outback. The path is marked with green and red dots and elaborate cairns but most of the way is clear. After 25 min there's a definite veering up the left (south) side of the canyon, and a climb up to a sparsely wooded plateau for views of the sea, the ground covered thus far and the western buttresses of Levká Óri. Beyond the overlook 15 to 20 min, the plateau, now completely treeless, drops sharply into the valley containing ancient Lissós. From the edge you can spy two *ksoklísia*, a beachlet and the gaping tombs of a plundered Roman-era necropolis on the opposite (west) slope of the vale; Hellenistic Lissós is not immediately obvious. The trail switchbacks 20 min further down the bluff face, through some olives and past some signs until, 1 hr from Soúyia, you come upon the fenced-in focal point of Lissós, a shrine of Asklipiós which was only discovered in 1957. A spring issues from among maidenhair and mint within the sacred precincts and pours from a foundation just below the massive walls of the sanctuary. Inside are some floor mosaic fragments, and on the outer walls are numerous Greek inscriptions; beyond are traces of the baths used by the sick, a priest's residence and a *katagoyéio* or pilgrim's quarters. To gain admission to the grounds, visit the guard's hut 100 m ahead—he has the keys. Siesta is from noon to 4 P.M., and no amount of pleading will induce the keeper to interrupt his nap.

Just above the guardhouse is a perennially open chapel, dating to the 13th or 14th century and of uncertain dedication, with a number of faded frescoes; only those of "St. George and the Dragon" and "The Presentation" are recognizable. In the opposite direction many pathlets thread their way through vegetable patches and the Roman graves on their way to the beach. Just 10 min above the pebble cove, a Byzantine chapel, patron saint unknown, bodily incorporates ancient columns, pediments and *stelae* to form a gingerbread exterior. The Asklipian shrine must have supported a sizable village, and well into Byzantine times, because ancient foundations poke up through the weeds everywhere, leading down to the presumed site of the old dock and up inside the fenced boundaries of the Asklipíon.

Beyond the keeper's house, the trail continues, yellow- and green-marked, for 5 hr to Paleohóra (Selinó), a bare, dusty town, with banks, a post office and four daily buses to Hanía. The route passes well to seaward of any settlements, threading uphill and downdale like the Ayía Roúmeli-Loutró path; the spring of the Asklipíon is the last dependable fresh water.

APPENDICES

APPENDIX A: EQUIPMENT LIST

Trail conditions encountered in Greece are not nearly so rigorous as those in Africa, Asia or other parts of the Third World. Still, you'd be well advised to have the following items in your luggage before departure.

Clothing

2 pair lightweight, loose, 100 percent or mostly cotton pants—avoid polyester, spandex or corduroy.

1 pair shorts or cutoffs—a must for warm-weather walking

1 long-sleeve cotton turtleneck or fishnet thermal top

1 acrylic or other synthetic ski top

1 button-down wool shirt

1 shell windbreaker, warm-up jacket, *lightweight* Gore Tex, or similar jacket—the "layer method" should protect you in every condition encountered from March to late October. High-tech parkas are unnecessary unless you're planning on winter mountaineering, which is beyond the scope of this guide.

socks—assortment of cotton, synthetic, synthetic/wool blends

boots—Vibram-soled, over-the-ankle *de rigueur*; uneven and treacherous trail surfaces turn the ankles of walkers in running shoes or tennies with depressing frequency.

leather conditioner—nonsilicone based

hats—lightweight, symmetrically brimmed, reflective for warm conditions; wool or corduroy cap, or ski pull-on, for blustery summits.

Camping gear

backpack (choice of)—whether you choose soft, internal frame or external frame, traditional or convertible pack, you'll want a minimum capacity of 3500 cubic inches and a design that will effectively carry up to 30 pounds on long treks. Soft or ski-touring packs are not advised because with one your back will shortly be sweat-drenched in the mild conditions usually encountered. Packs should have some gismos—leather grommets, projecting struts or Kletter clamps—on which to hang unused day pack, water container, etc.

day pack—just the thing for day hikes, as you'd suppose. Should hold food, map, extra clothes, notebook *and* prevent contents from digging into your spine—a common failing of cheapo models.

foam pad—medium-density cell types best

sleeping bag—three-season

Above two items are for camping *and* boat trips where cushionless decks and seats get damp at night; sleeper cabins not always available.

poncho—to fit over you *and* your pack. Can double as a groundcloth and be rigged as a tube tent.

campstove—if you don't yet own one, purchase a butane stove upon arrival in Greece; they can be had for as little as $7 and the fuel is ubiquitous. Kerosene stoves can be provided for in Greece, but white-gas stove partisans should bring sufficient fuel with them—the solvent benzene usually substituted for it in Greece gums up the valves (see Stove Fuel under "Services") mess kit and cutlery—a wide tongue depressor makes an excellent, nonabrasive spatula, and a tiny Nalgene bottle of olive oil has several uses besides frying lubrication (see "Dog Days and Other Health Hazards.")

egg case—for six eggs

water container—Spanish-style wine *botas* are best. Greek water is invariably delicious and pure, so iodine tabs are as likely as not to stay in the bottom of your pack.

camera belt pack—several companies make serviceable carriers for up to two bodies and most size lenses. Will pay for itself within a month in terms of falls cushioned, and repairs avoided.

Odds and Ends

nylon stuff sacks with drawstrings, assorted—make great shopping bags, laundry hampers, gear protectors

plastic bags, especially Zip-lok or bread bags—ideal for isolating drippy or messy items

swimsuit—the recent "legalization" of nude bathing applies to *designated beaches* only; elsewhere it is tolerated only in the most secluded coves. By swimming in the buff at exposed coves you will merely be offending the sensibilities of the Greek country folk, not "liberating" them.

swim goggles or dive masks—the Aegean is extremely salty and eye-burning; it also abounds in jellyfish and sea urchins which are much better seen than felt. Friendly colorful fish are, alas, less abundant.

sunglasses—the glare can be equally murderous in the whitewashed islands and in the mountains.

binoculars, monocular, camera telephoto—see what's happening at a distance; e.g., spot hiking landmarks.

compass—rarely used, but when the mists descend on Mt. Ólymbos or the Píndhos all landmarks disappear.

compact flashlight—bring spare bulbs; batteries easy to find in Greece.

candle lantern, camp mirror—great morale boosters in the mountains; read after dinner and shave before breakfast.

parachute cord, 3 m—for rigging your poncho up as a tent; also becomes a clothesline.

Nalgene or polyurethane bottles, assorted—large for laundry soap; medium for mixing powdered milk; smalls have variety of uses

tape—strong, lightweight, sheer tape such as Micropore, in addition to securing bandages, mends torn money, book bindings and maps.

lip balm—a must for low-humidity areas (that is, most everywhere)

insect repellent

sewing kit—assorted needle sizes, thread gauges, patching materials (Patches are almost impossible to find in Greece.)

spares—eyeglasses, backpack clevis-pin-and-ring sets, photo copy of passport personal data page, bootlaces, bota flask: i.e., anything that could conceivably be tedious or impossible to replace overseas and doesn't take up much room.

moleskin—you may *think* your new boots are broken in before leaving home but that's often not the case.

walking stick—protect knees on downhills; also good safety measure. Some hikers use ski poles; others prefer fancy items from mail-order houses. You can improvise on the spot in the beech woods of northern Greece; discarded staves near logging sites are easily whittled to size. Beech cracks as it dries but remains phenomenally strong. In Hania, Crete, you can get a good, knobby walking stick (*bastouni* in Greek) made from *abelitsia,* a local wood.

loud whistle or distress flare—especially if you hike alone

Swiss army or similar knife—I have used every attachment on mine, including the sawlet to trim aforementioned walking stick. Should also have can opener, bottle opener, corkscrew as a minimum.

paperbacks—just a couple, English reading material is easily available in Greece.

waterproof magic marker—great for addressing packages at the post office, and serially labeling film rolls as exposed—in conjunction with a logbook, this enables you to know which shot is on what roll.

sunburn lotion—this is a personal decision. I find Nosekote useful for the intended part but am skeptical of the effectiveness of whole-body creams. Nothing beats judicious use of protective clothing (hats pulled over face while sunbathing, martial arts trousers on beach, swimming with white T-shirt, etc.).

timepiece with alarm (loud)—for making that early bus, boat, plane. I use a small quartz clock powered by a AA battery, kept in a leather belt pouch. Such clocks are not much bigger than a watch and run about $11-$22, depending on country of purchase.

dental floss—meat and crunchy foods stick painfully between teeth.

cuticle scissors—in conjunction with the blunt end of a sewing needle, deals with ingrown big toenails.

money belt—in Greece, where most rural people are scrupulously honest, more for convenience than for safety. Can be stowed in pack when tramping, worn at discretion at other times.

photo film—bring an ample supply.

APPENDIX B: FESTIVAL CALENDAR

The major festivals in Greece come in bunches, with the principal concentrations in late winter, spring and midsummer. This doesn't mean that the country is dead-silent otherwise; every locale has its patron saint, whose day is the occasion for festivities that may catch you by surprise. The most important, nationwide *paneyíria* (festivals) guarantee spectacles of some sort. The following festivals have particularly fervent celebrations or are in good locations for trekkers.

Áyios Vasílios (New Year's) January 1—An indoor, family holiday. Parades on the seafaring islands of Híos and Ándhros; some mummery in Makedhonian towns, through January 6.

Epifánia (Blessing of the Waters) January 6—At sea or lakeshore locations, consecration of the waters: Priest or bishop hurls crucifix over the water and young men swim for the honor of recovering it.

Apókries or Karnaváli (Carnival) February to March—Especially on the seventh weekend before Easter, many mainland towns celebrate Carnival with parades, masking and mischief. Premier Aegean observance is on Skýros Island, where the "Goat Dance" is enacted.

Katharí Dhevtéra ("Clean Monday") First day of Lent, seventh Monday before Easter—Mass exodus to the country for picnics and kite-flying. Last convulsion of mummery, music and meat-eating before Lenten austerities.

Megáli Sarakostí (Lent) Seven weeks before Easter—Not observed rigorously in urban areas, but even there seafood and greens dominate menus. Observance in rural areas can be strict and it may be difficult to find animal protein. Weddings are not conducted and music is not played in the villages.

National Day (March 25)—A mixed secular/religious festival commemorating both the beginning of the Greek Revolution and the Annunciation of the Virgin. In any sizable town there will be parades and evening folk dancing. Most famous observance is on Tínos Island, where a healing ikon of the *Panayía* (Virgin) is carried in procession over the sick, who kneel before it.

Páskha (Easter) Variable, usually mid-April—Easter is the grandest holiday in Greece, though observance varies from place to place. In big towns the crowds and candlelight processions on Good Friday Eve are impressive but a bit intimidating. In the rural areas the *Epitáfios* or recreation of Christ's funeral on Good Friday is more poignant. At Ólymbos (Kárpathos) women wail the traditional *myrolóyia* (laments for the dead) and tear their hair and garments. The candlelight *Anástasi* (Resurrection) ceremony on Saturday midnight is arguably the most beautiful rite of Christianity. On Easter Sunday, in the wee hours after the midnight service, the Lenten fast is broken with a meal of *mayerítsa* (lamb tripe and dill soup). Lambs slaughtered the day before are put to the spit Sunday afternoon and you may be invited to a festival that lasts well into Monday.

Áyios Yiórgos Day April 23, or Monday after Easter if Easter is later—The dragon-slaying saint is the patron of the Greek army and of shepherds. Barbecues, dancing and games in Aráhova at the base of Mt. Parnassós. Start of the pastoral year; grazing leases finalized and flocks head up the mountains.

Protomáyia (May Day)—Most visible signs of the holiday are the wreaths hung on front doors and automobiles. The garlands are credited with various magical properties and are saved until summer.

The close spacing of the following four holidays brings Greece to a midsummer standstill that persists through the end of August—best not to have any plans other than enjoying yourself.

Profítis Ilías July 18-20—Observances at any hilltop chapel dedicated to this patron of the weather.

Ayía Paraskeví July 26—An important bacchanale in rural areas, where the saint's chapels are everywhere.

Metamórfosi (Transfiguration) August 6—Another big rural festival, with more dances and banquets.

Apokimísis tis Panayías (Assumption of the Virgin) August 15—Probably the most important feast after Easter. Celebrated with special fervor at Tínos (procession as in March), Páros, and any mountain village.

Áyios Dhimítrios October 26—First wine traditionally tapped today. Big cultural festival the weeks before and after in Thessaloníki. Pastoral year ends.

Óhi ("No") Day October 28—Civil holiday commemorating Metaxa's apocryphal one-word answer to Mussolini's ultimatum in 1940. Parades, folk dancing, etc.

Hristoúyenna (Christmas) December 25-26—This, like New Year's, is a private, indoor festival.

Other events

You may be invited to weddings or baptisms, which are quite similar to non-Orthodox rites, but some Greek funerary customs may take getting used to. Do not be alarmed if you see people tucking bones into metal ossuaries in country church-yards—it is customary to unearth the dead after three years and make room for the newly deceased. Similarly, you may be approached by the bereaved and offered *kóllyva*, a mixture of sugar, cinnamon, barley, rice, pomegranate seeds and other ingredients. This is offered to everyone met on various anniversaries of the death date and you should politely accept your handful.

APPENDIX C: GREEK MOUNTAINEERING CLUB BRANCHES

Club branches are listed by geographical location. EOS denotes branch of Greek Alpine Club; SEO denotes branch of the Association of Greek Climbers; other organizations are spelled out in full.

Aharnés: (EOS) Platía Ayíou Vlasíou 16, tel. (01) 246-1528. Also the offices of *Korfés* Magazine. Information on Párnitha especially.

Amfíklia: (eparch of Parnassidhos) tel. (0234) 22-640. (EOS) Information on Parnassós.

Áspra Spitia: (EOS) (Paralía Dhístomou, Viotías) tel. (0267) 41-552.

Athens: (EOS) Ermóu 52, tel. (01) 321-2429. Greek Federation of Mountaineering and Skiing (EOHO), Karayióryi Servías 7, tel. (01) 323-4555. Athens Hiking Club, Kánningos 12, tel. (01) 643-5078.

Dhráma: (EOS) Ethnikís Amínis 25, tel. (0521) 23-049, 23-054. Closest club to Falakró.

Égion: (EOS) corner S. Londóu and Aratóu, tel. (0691) 25-285.

Elevsína: (EOS) Thivón 23, tel. (01) 554-6572.

Florína: (EOS) Dhragoúmi 50, tel. (0385) 28-008, 22-354. Information for Vítsi, Varnóus, Kaïmaktsalán.

Grevená: (EOS) Platía Aimilianóu, tel. (0462) 28-602, 28-352.

Halkídha: (EOS) Tsirigóti 10, tel. (0221) 25-230. Closest club to Dhírfis.

Haniá: (EOS) Tzanakáki 90, tel. (0821) 24-647. Information on the White Mountains (Levká Óri).

Ioánnina: (EOS) Moulaïmídhou 6, tel. (0651) 22-138. Information on the Píndhos in general.

Iráklion: (EOS) Dikaiossínis 53, tel. (081) 287-110. Information on Psilorítis.

Kalávryta: (EOS) *Zaharoplastéio Eremídhis,* 25 Martíou St. tel. (0692) 22-611, 22-346. Information on Helmós.

Karpeníssi: (EOS) Zinopoúlou 2, tel. (0237) 22-394. Information on Tímvristós, Panetolikó, Helidhóna, Kaliakoúdha, Ágrafa.

Kateríni: (EOS) Ayías Lávras 13, tel. (0351) 23-102. Closest branch to Piéria. (SEO) tel. (0351) 31-311, 29-712.

Kaválla: (EOS) Omónia 90, tel. (051) 23-464. Information on Pangéo.

Kórinthos: (EOS) Vassiléos Yiorghíou 39, tel. (0741) 24-335. Closest club to Yeránia.

Kozáni: (EOS) Fon Kozáni 13, tel. (0461) 25-600. (SEO) tel. (0461) 25-909. Nearest clubs to Áskio, Voúrinos.

Ksánthi: (EOS) 28 Oktovríou 284, tel. (0541) 26-939.

Lamía: (EOS) Ipsilándou 25, tel. (0231) 26-786. Information on Oíti, Vardhoússia, Oxiá, Órthris.

Lárissa: (EOS) Vassilíssis Sofías 6, tel. (041) 220-097. Closest club to Kissávos (Ossa).

Litóhoro: (EOS) Kendrikí Platía, tel. (0352) 81-944. Booth with Ólymbos information. (SEO) Few meters from bus station, tel. (0352) 82-300. Storefront with Ólymbos information.

Livádhia: (EOS) Filonos 6, tel. (0261) 29-232. Information on Elikónas.

Métsovo: (EOS) Níkou Gátsou 2, tel. (0656) 41-249. Nearest branch to Peristéri (Lákmos).

Náoussa: (EOS) Platía Karatássou, tel. (0332) 28-567. Information on Vérmio.

Pátras: (EOS) Pantanassi 29, tel. (061) 273-912. Information on Panahaïkó, Erýmanthos.

Réthimno: (EOS) Arkadhíou 143, tel. (0831) 22-710. Closest club to Psilorítis.

Sérres: (EOS) Tsalopoúlou 12, tel. (0321) 23-724. Information on Vrondoús.

Spárti: (EOS) *Dhimarhéio* (town hall), Kendrikí Platía; tel. (0731) 22-574, 22-444. Information on Táyettos and Párnon.

Thessaloníki: (EOS) Karólou Diéhl, tel. (031) 278-288.
(SEO) Platía Aristotélous, tel. (031) 224-719.

Tithoréa: (EOS) Káto Tithoréa, tel. (0234) 49-563, 49-279. Nearest to Parnassós.

Tríkala: Mountaineering Club, Asklipíou 17, tel. (0431) 27-456. Information on Kóziakas, Tringía, Avgó, Central Ágrafa.

Trípoli: (EOS) Ayíou Konstantínou 50, tel. (071) 222-101. Nearest branch to Ménalo.

Véria: (EOS) Vikéla 15, tel. (0331) 26-970.

Vólos: (EOS) Dhimitriádhos 92, tel. (0421) 25-696. Closest branch to Pílion.

Readers are cautioned that Greek mountaineering club branches can move or change phone numbers just like any storefront business, though perhaps not with the same frequency. This list may have inadvertently omitted small excursion clubs particular to one area or town—I apologize both to them and to hikers who run across them.

APPENDIX D: GREEK MOUNTAIN SHELTERS

The following list of shelters is arranged by region. After the name of the mountain or massif and its elevation (in bold type) is a brief description of the site, the altitude of the shelter and other pertinent information. The last entry (in italics) is the name of the controlling organization or the person with the key to the shelter. EOS denotes branch of Greek Alpine Club.

Note that the presence or absence of a mountain hut is not an infallible indicator of a mountain range's hike worthiness or lack of it. You may in fact choose to avoid those shelters that are primarily road accessible, as opposed to hike-ins, and those that are obviously ski resorts. "Spring" means that there is supposed to be an outside water source available even if the hut is locked, but springs can (especially in Crete and the Pelopónnisos) run dry in summer.

PELOPÓNNISOS

Párnon (1935 m)—35-bunk hostel at Arnómoussa; 1450 m. 1 spring near hut. *EOS Spárti.*

Taïyettos (2407 m)—26-bunk hostel at Ayía Varvára; 1600 m. 2 springs near hut. *EOS Spárti or Kannélo family in Anóyia, (0731) 26-043.*

Helmós (Aroánia) (2355 m)—12-bunk hostel built in 1931 at Poulioú toú Vrýssi; 2100 m. Namesake spring unreliable. *EOS Kalávryta (start at Zaharoplasteio Eremídhis, 25 Martíou Street); EOS Égion.*

Panahaïkó (1926 m)—40-bunk refuge at Psárthi, 1500 m. 2½-hr walk from Pournarókastro village. 10-bunk shelter near summit, 45 min above Psárthi, at Prassoúdhi, 1900 m. Springs reported at both huts. *EOS Pátras.*

Zíria (Kyllíni) (2376 m)—50-bunk hostel, new, at Megáli Vrýssi, 1650 m (2376). 1 spring. 2½-hr walk from Áno Tríkala village; car road allows access in 30 min. 20-bunk shelter at Pórtes (1750 m), 45 min above first hostel. No spring. *EOHO, Karayióryi Servías Street, Athens.*

Ménalo (Two summits: 1730 m, 1980 m)—20-bunk hostel, important mostly as a winter sports facility; at 1540 m on Oropédhio Ostrakína. Road access; phone (0756) 21-227. *EOS Trípoli.*

STEREÁ

Párnitha (1413 m)—50-bunk refuge at Báfi, 1160 m. Road-accessible, or by 3-hr trail from Thrakomakedhónes. Open year-round, resident warden; phone (01) 246-9111. *EOS Athens.*

Refuge at Flamboúri, 1100 m. Road-accessible, trail from Thrakomakedhónes. (01) 246-4666. *EOS Aharnés.*

Parnassós (2457 m)—20-bunk hut at Sarandári ridge; 1900 m. No spring. Road-accessible. Nearly 4-hr walk from summit. *EOS Athens; or Níkos Yiorgákos, Aráhova (0267)* 31-391.

Oíti (2152 m)—28-bunk refuge at Trapezítsa, 1800 m. Beautiful site with spring. 3½- to 4-hr walk from Ypáti village; road accessible. *EOS Lamía.*

Gkióna (2510 m)—25(?)-bunk refuge at Lákka Karvoúni, 1700 m. 1 spring above hostel. Side room open for shepherds. *Athens Hiking Club.*

Vardhoússia (2495 m)—18-bunk hostel at Lower Pitimáliko; 1750 m. *EOS Lamía.*

18-bunk hostel at Upper Pitimáliko; 1850 m. *Athens Hiking Club.*

Both hostels near a spring; both appox. 3-hr walk from Áno Moussounítsa village; dirt road as far as Stavrós, 1 hr below huts.

Oxía (small peak between Vardhoússia and Timvristós) (1926 m)—40-bed refuge at 1700 m, near Kríkello and Gardhíki villages. Spring. May be road accessible? *EOS Lamía.*

Timvristós (Veloúhi) (2315 m)—44-bed shelter at Seïtáni; 1840 m. No spring; road and path accessible from Karpeníssi. Primarily a winter sports center. Phone (0237) 22-002. *EOS Karpeníssi.*

ÍPIROS

Astrákas (2436 m)—28-bed hostel at Astrákas col; 1950 m. Two springs nearby; often in use. 3 hr above Pápingo, 7-hr walk from Tsepélovo. *Koúlis Hristodhoúlos in Pápingo; Alékos Góuris in Tsepélovo; EOS Ioánnina.*

Vassilítsa (2249 m)—11-bunk public shelter at 1800 m; water tap, permanently open. Adjacent: locked, modern ski lodge (28 bunks?). *EOS Grevená.*

Mitsikéli (1810 m)—28-bunk hostel at Výssi Paliohóri; 1400 m. Spring, road and trail (3-hr) access from Ioánnina. *EOS Ioánnina.*

Tsoúka Aróssia (near Flambourári village, *not* spur of Gamíla) (1987 m)—Undescribed shelter at Vakarátsa; 1487 m. *EOS Ioánnina.*

Kóziakas (1901 m)— Undocumented shelter at approx. 1700 m; spring. 40 road km via Píli-Eláti, plus hike, from Tríkala. *Mountaineering Club, Tríkala.*

MAKEDHONÍA

Falakró (2232 m)—40-person lodge at Áyio Pnévma plateau; 1700 m; near completion. Primarily for winter sports. *EOS Dhráma.*

18-person hut at Horós; 1700 m, 30 min west of Áyio Pnévma plateau. No spring; 3 hr from Vólakas. *EOS Dhráma.*

20-person hut at Kourí ridge; 1400 m. No spring. 1½ hr above Vólakas, and road accessible. *EOS Dhráma.*

Pangéo (1926 m)—20-bunk refuge at Aryíris Petalóudhas (a.k.a. Vláhika Kalívia); 1550 m. Spring water; 3 ½ hr by foot from Avlí village, or 1 ½ hr from Kaválla by road. *EOS Kaválla.*

Vroundoús (1849 m)—60-bed hostel at 1500 m, near the village of Laïliás. Spring, road-accessible. Ski-oriented. *EOS Sérres.*

Vérmio (2052 m)—Two huts, capacity 35 and 60 persons, at Tría Pigádhia, 1450 m. Spring. *EOS Náoussa.*

Various lodges at the village of Káto Vérmio. Joint capacities 180 persons. Primarily a winter sports complex; phone (0332) 71-208. *EOS Thessaloníki, Véria, Náoussa.*

Piéria (2190 m)—Sumptuous 50-bunk lodge at Áno Miliá; 1000 m. Spring. 5 ½ road km above village of Messáia Miliá. Also reachable from Katafígio village, via the peak (all-day hike). Phone (0351) 21-284. *EOS Kateríni.*

Vítsi (Vérnon) (2128 m)—70-bed lodge at Vígla Pissodheríou, 3 km above Pissodhéri village; 1600 m; spring. Primarily a ski lodge; phone (0385) 22-354. *EOS Florína.*

THESSALÍA AND MAGNISÍA

Ólymbos (2917 m)—90-bed lodge at Spílios Agapitós; 2100 m. Meal service, open daily from 6 A.M. to 10 P.M. from mid-May to mid-October. 3 hr from Priónia trailhead; phone (0352) 81-800. *Call hostel number during work hours; otherwise Kóstas Zolótas at 81-329.*

80-bunk shelter Yióssos Apostolídhis, on Oropédhio Musón; 2750 m. Open mid-June to August; otherwise access to front porch and water spigot. 6 hr from Dhiakládhosi trailhead, 1¾ hr from Spílios Agapitós. *SEO branches in Litóhoro (82-300) and Thessaloníki.*

18-bunk shelter at 2650 m on the Oropédhio Musón. No spring; 1½ hr from Spílios Agapitós, 6 hr from Dhiakládhosi trailhead. *By arrangement with EOS Litóhoro, Kóstas Zolótas, or EOS Kateríni.*

15-bunk shelter at Stavrós; 1000 m; 10-km drive from Litóhoro. Open, with meal service, much of the year. *EOS Thessaloníki.*

50-bed refuge at Vryssopóules; 1900 m, on mountain's SW flank. Primarily a soldiers' ski lodge. *(0493) 22-261, Ellasóna; (041) 228-915, Lárissa.*

Kissávos (Óssa) (1978 m)—35-bunk hostel at Kánalos; 1604 m. Well-appointed, spring. Trail (from various points) and road accessible. Phone (0495) 51-485. *EOS Lárissa.*

Pílion (1651 m)—80-bed lodge at Agriólevkes; 1350 m, 27 road km from Vólos. This is a ski resort, not a hikers' hut. Phone (0421) 91-136. *EOS Vólos.*

Two more hostels with a combined capacity of about 70 persons, in Hánia village; phone (0421) 91-155. Again, intended for skiers. *EOS Vólos.*

EVVIA

Dhírfis (1743 m)—30-bunk lodge at Líri; 1150 m. Spring. Road- and trail-accessible from Stení. Ski-oriented; phone (0228) 51-285. *EOS Halkídha; in Stení, (0228) 51-248.*

Óhi (1398 m)—Description uncertain for refuge at Kastanólongos; 1100 m. 4 hr by track and path from Káristos. *Dhimarhéio (town hall), Káristos.*

CRETE

Psilorítis (Ídhi) (2456 m)—16-bunk hut at Prínos, 1100 m. Spring; road & trail accessible from Anóyia. *EOS Iráklion.*

Levká Óri (White Mountains) (2453 m)—35-bunk refuge at Vólikas; 1480 m. Spring; reported 3-hr walk from Kámbi village. *EOS Haniá.*

50-bed shelter at Kallérgi; 1680 m. Spring. Accessible by road from Omalós hamlet or by foot (1 ½ hr) from a path beginning at Ksilóskala. *EOS Haniá.*

BIBLIOGRAPHY

"O.P." means out of print—consult a major library or used book store.

Ethnology, Sociology, Anthropology

Bent, James T. *The Cyclades, or Life Among the Insular Greeks.* Chicago: Argonaut Press, 1965 reprint of 1885 British edition. O.P. Bent and spouse spent a year in the archipelago back when it took a year to visit them all. Still *the* English-language monograph for anyone interested in island folklore, archaeology.

Blum, Richard and Eva. *The Dangerous Hour: The Lore of Crisis and Mystery in Rural Greece.* New York: Scribners, 1970. O.P. Narratives on the supernatural, afflictions and cures; overnice analysis and a useful comparison with belief systems in other eras and Mediterranean cultures.

Campbell, John. *Honor, Family, Patronage: A Study of a Greek Mountain Community.* Oxford: Oxford Univ. Press, 1964. More precisely, a study of Sarakatsani transhumants in West Zagória during the late 1950s. Not entirely outdated.

DuBoulay, Juliet. *Portrait of a Greek Mountain Village.* Oxford: Clarendon Press, 1974. One of John Campbell's students lived in a remote Evvian hamlet. Indispensable for understanding the interior landscape and daily life of rural Greeks.

Holst, Gail. *Road to Rembetika: Music of a Greek Subculture—Songs of Love, Sorrow and Hashish.* Athens: Denise Harvey & Co., 1983. The predominant urban musical style of 20th-century Greece as depicted by a Cornell University musicologist.

La Carriere, Jacques. *L'été Grec, une Grèce quotidienne de 4,000 ans.* Paris: Plon, 1976. A sensitive, subjective journal (in French) of the author's several journeys to Greece, in the tradition of the great French anthropologists. Focus on folklore, handcrafts, and traditional communities.

Lawson, John Cuthbert. *Modern Greek Folklore & Ancient Greek Religion: A Study in Survivals.* New York: University Books, 1964. O.P. To Greece what *The Golden Bough* is to the world—and Lawson's conclusions have stood the test of subsequent scholarship better than Frazer's.

Megas, George. *Greek Calendar Customs.* Athens: The author, through University of Athens, 1982. Chronological compendium of holiday observances throughout the country. Sadly, many customs have vanished since the first, 1953 edition.

Sanders, Irwin T. *Rainbow in the Rock: The People of Rural Greece.* Cambridge: Harvard University Press, 1962. O.P. Outstanding, moderately analytic introduction to Greek geography, demography, sociology and folklore that confirms surface impressions of life in the hills.

General History and Political Science

Clogg, Richard. *A Short History of Modern Greece* (1979) and *Greece in the 80s* (1983). Cambridge: Cambridge University Press. If you haven't the time for both, pick the short history, a 200-page distillation of salient events since 1454.

Heurtley, W. A., et al. *A Short History of Greece.* Cambridge: Cambridge University Press, 1965. More middle-of-road than Clogg, less emphasis on postindependence events and more on pre-Byzantine, *but* slightly out of date. Good maps show shifts in ethnic and linguistic groups during this century.

World War II and its Aftermath (1940-49)

Eudes, Dominique. *The Kapetanios: Partisans and Civil War in Greece, 1943-1949.* New York: Monthly Review Press, 1972. French Maoist's perspective on how/why Stalinists of the Greek Communist Party bungled the victory won by the popular resistance army.

Gage, Nicholas. *Eleni*. New York: Random House, 1983. Controversial account of a Greek-American journalist who returns to Ípiros to avenge the death of his mother, condemned by a communist tribunal in 1948.

Sarafis, Marion. *Greece: From Resistance to Civil War*. Nottingham: Spokesman, 1980. Former military adversaries confront each other in the halls of academe, in these never-dull proceedings of a 1978 conference on the Greek 1940s.

The Junta Years (1967-74)

Andrews, Kevin. *Greece in the Dark*. Amsterdam: Adolf Hakkert, 1980. The experiences of the author and his acquaintances living under the dictatorship, liberally interspersed with footnotes and citations from public documents.

Clogg, Richard and G. Yannopoulos, eds. *Greece Under Military Rule*. New York: Basic Books, 1972. O.P. Dated but still useful analysis of the junta "program," its antecedents and backers.

Falacci, Oriana. *A Man*. New York: Pocket Books, 1981. The famous interviewer turns participant when she becomes involved with Alekos Panagoulis, the political activist who attempted to assassinate Colonel Papadhopoulos in 1968. Gripping, by turns depressing and inadvertently humorous.

Holden, David. *Greece Without Columns*. London: Faber & Faber, 1972. O.P. Pessimistic interpretive history and Greek national character analysis which clarifies more than it glosses over despite a mild projunta bias.

Byzantine & Athonite Studies

Byron, Robert. *The Station*. London: Century Books, 1984. The author of the classic *Road to Oxiana* actually made his debut, at the age of 24, with this account of a season on Áthos.

Cavarnos, Constantine. *Anchored in God*. Belmont: Institute for Byzantine and Modern Greek Studies, 1975. As the subtitle says, "an inside account of life, art, and thought on the Holy Mountain." Plain, almost catechismic style makes it a good introduction to Áthos.

Loch, Sidney. *Áthos: The Holy Mountain*. London: Lutterworth, 1957, or Thessaloníki: Librairie Molho, 1971. The male half of a missionary couple which dwelt in Ouranopóli tower from 1928 onward recounts his hikes on the mountain. Good source for recent Athonite history and the legends surrounding various ikons and monasteries; uneven style because edited posthumously.

Sherrard, Philip. *Byzantium*. New York: Time-Life Books, 1966. Well-written overview, part of the "Great Ages of Man" series, features Constantine Manos' noted photo-essay on Ólymbos, Kárpathos and plates of surviving Byzantine mosaics.

Belles Lettres, Memoirs, Travelogs, Mountaineering, Exploration

Andrews, Kevin. *The Flight of Ikaros*. New York: Penguin Books, 1984 (reissue of London: Weidenfeld & Nicholson, 1959). Conceivably the best book written about Greece in English. Whether breaking bread with a royalist death-squad member, officiating as a godfather, or laid up in a sanitarium, Andrews as "Ikaros" is shattering, unsentimental and unforgettable. Generous hiking accounts, including a harrowing ascent of Ólymbos.

Fermor, Patrick Leigh. *Mani* and *Roumeli*. New York: Penguin, 1984 (reissues of New York: Harper, 1958 and London: John Murray, 1966 respectively). This comrade-in-arms of Fielding's (see below) is an aficionado of the vanishing minorities, relict communities and disappearing customs of rural Greece. Good scholarship interspersed with strange yarns.

Fielding, Xan. *The Stronghold.* London: Secker & Warburg, 1953. O.P. British ex-commando revisits World War II haunts in Sfakiá, Crete; hearty reunions and some hikes retraced in the Crete section of this book.

Greenhalgh, Peter, and Edward Eliopoulos. *Deep into Mani.* London: Faber & Faber, 1985. Two wartime resistance members return to the Mani 25 years after Fermor's research and find village life, as well as many monuments, disintegrating.

Hunt, Sir John, and D. E. Sugden. *A Journey Through the Pindus Mountains in 1963.* Journal of the Royal (British) Geographical Society, 130 (1964) 3:355-364. A veteran of Arctic and Everest expeditions leads one from Ámfissa to Grevená in spring conditions and finds it's no picnic—not surprising to anyone with Greek hiking experience. Sugden contributes a technical section on the geomorphology of the Ágrafa.

Kazantzakis, Nikos. *Travels in the Morea.* New York: Simon and Schuster, 1965. The people and antiquities of the Pelopónnisos speak through a gifted intermediary chronicling his wanderings there in the 1930s.

Kitto, H. D. F. *In the Mountains of Greece.* London: Methuen, 1933. O.P.; rare. Jolly little jaunt through Óiti, Vardhoússia, Karpeníssi, Proussós and central and southern Pelopónnisos. Quaint but neither terribly insightful nor practical.

Kulukundis, Elias. *Journey to a Greek Island.* London: Cassell, 1968. O.P. And a journey back through time and genealogy by a Greek-American two generations removed from Kássos, poorest of the Dhodhekánisos. A delightful exploration that reads like nonfiction García Márquez.

Levi, Peter. *The Hill of Kronos.* New York: Penguin, 1984 (reissue of original New York: Dutton, 1981). A Jesuit priest comes to Greece in 1963 as an archaeologist and translator of Pausanias and is transformed by the people, the landscape, marriage and ultimately resistance to the junta. He's also an indefatigable walker who made it to the Nédhas gorge, Párnitha and Lissós, among other places.

Miller, Henry. *The Colossus of Maroussi.* New York: New Directions, 1958. The famous expatriate moves from Paris to Greece in 1939 and finds his true element. A bohemian counterpoise to Levi.

Trevor-Battye, Aubyn. *Camping in Crete.* London: Witherby & Co., 1913. O.P.; rare. Plus tramping, monasterying, collecting, etc. Though much of the landscape has been rendered unrecognizable by roads, the book is still valuable for its outstanding natural-history appendices. Speaking of which . . .

Botanical Field Guides

Huxley, Anthony and William Taylor. *Flowers of Greece and the Aegean.* London: Chatto & Windus, 1977. The leading English-language field guide.

Polunin, Oleg. *Flowers of Greece and the Balkans.* Oxford University Press, 1987.

Sfikas, George. *Wildflowers of Greece, Trees & Shrubs of Greece, Medicinal Plants of Greece, Wildflowers of Mt. Olympos.* Athens: Evstathiadhis Group, 1976-1980. Available in U.K., Greece only.

General & Regional Guidebooks

Ellingham, Mark, et al. *Rough Guide to Greece.* London: Harrap-Columbus, 1988, 3rd ed. Despite the title, a sophisticated guide for independent travelers of modest means; sympathetic to hikers, with some walking directions.

Haag, Michael and Neville Lewis. *Guide to Greece.* London: Travelaid, 1986, 3rd ed. Good compromise between the budget guides and stuffy mainstream volumes, authored by two who've walked, sailed, eaten, worked and lived in Greece more than most.

Hachette World Guides. *Greece.* Paris, 1964 (never updated). I favor this volume because it's compact, has excellent listings of Byzantine and medieval castles and churches (often lost in the shuffle to older antiquities), and details a surprising number of trails (some paved over in the interim).

Harvard Student Agencies. *Let's Go Greece.* New York: St. Martins, updated yearly. That doesn't stop laughable errors, and collegiate attitudes, from persisting edition after edition, but it *is* thorough, with token walker's information.

Lycabettus Press Publications (various authors). *Aegina, Poros, Hydra, Spetsai, Paros, Naxos* and *Patmos.* Athens, 1975-1984. Not the complete inventory, merely those volumes of most interest to hikers. The first four Argo-Saronic titles are especially recommended as an elaboration of this book's slim chapter; all have adequate maps and excursion descriptions.

Von Bolzano, Klaus and Yvonne. *Karpathos.* Salzburg: The authors, 1980. English-German pamphlet available on Kárpathos.

Greek Literature in English

FICTION

Haviaras, Stratis. *When the Tree Sings.* New York: Simon & Schuster, 1979; reissued in paperback, New York: Ballantine, 1981; Picador, London: 1982. Impressionistic semiautobiography, seen through the eyes of a boy growing up in a 1940s Greece ruled by the occupiers but attuned to the resistance. A successful foray into prose by an emigre to the U.S. who had previously published four volumes of poetry.

———. *The Heroic Age.* New York: Penguin, 1985.

Kazantzakis, Nikos. *The Last Temptation.* New York: Simon & Schuster/Touchstone, 1961.

———. *Freedom or Death (Captain Mihalis).* New York: Simon & Schuster/Touchstone, 1971.

———. *Zorba the Greek.* New York: Simon & Schuster/Touchstone, 1971.

———. *Christ Recrucified (The Greek Passion).* New York: Simon & Schuster/Touchstone, 1981. Many editions. The most accessible works of Greece's most famous novelist—who was probably a better journalist and whose work does not translate well into English.

Myrivilis, Stratis. *The Schoolmistress with the Golden Eyes* and *The Mermaid Madonna.* Athens: Evstathíadhis Group, 1981. Two tempestuous novels set in the villages of Lesvos' north shore, Myrivilis' homeland. Available in Greece and U.K. only.

Papadhiamantis, Alexandhros. *The Murderess.* London: Writers and Readers, 1983. Turn-of-the-century novel by a Skiathote often dubbed "the Greek Thomas Hardy."

Tsirkas, Stratis (Ioannis). *Drifting Cities.* New York: Knopf, 1974. O.P. Tsirkas makes Malraux and Durrell look amateurish with this epic tapestry of Communist and rightist intrigue within the Greek army-in-exile, set in wartime Jerusalem, Alexandria and Cairo.

Venezis, Ilias. *Beyond the Aegean (Aeolia).* New York: Vanguard Press, 1956? O.P. Dreamlike symbolic novel set in Greek villages of Asia Minor before the 1922 military debacle and subsequent exodus.

POETRY

With two Nobel laureates in recent years—George Seferis in 1963 and Odysseus Elytis in 1978—modern Greece dynamically carries on a poetic tradition established in antiquity. Many excellent bilingual text collections of the best modern Greek poets, most of them translated by Edmund Keeley and Philip Sherrard, are available from Princeton University Press. British co-publisher is cited when known.

Elytis, Odysseus. *Axion Esti*. Pittsburgh: Univ. of Pittsburgh Press, 1974 and London: Anvil, 1980. English version by E. Keeley & G. Savidis.

———. *Selected Poems*. London and New York: Viking Penguin, 1981. English renderings only, by E. Keeley and P. Sherrard.

———. *Sovereign Sun*. Philadelphia: Temple Univ. Press, 1974. English translations by Kimon Friar.

Kavafy (Cavafy), Constantine. *Selected Poems*. Princeton: PUP (1972) and the more complete *Collected Poems* London: Chatto, 1978; Princeton: PUP, 1975. Paperback editions have English text only.

Pavlopoulos, George. *The Cellar*. London: Anvil Press, 1977. The work of a lesser-known poet from Peloponnesian Pýrgos, translated by Peter Levi.

Ritsos, Ioannis. *Ritsos in Parentheses*. Princeton: PUP, 1979. Representative gleaning of Europe's foremost leftist poet. Both cloth and paper editions have bilingual text.

Seferis, George. *Collected Poems, 1924-1955*. Princeton: PUP, 1981. 3rd edition. London: Anvil Press, 1982. Both hardback and paperback editions have bilingual text. Virtually the complete works of the Nobel laureate.

Sikelianos, Angelos. *Selected Poems*. Princeton: PUP, 1979; London: Allen & Unwin, 1980. A small collection by a poet often termed "the Greek Dylan Thomas." Unfortunately, he suffers in translation more than the poets listed above, but readers of Greek can enjoy a bilingual paperback edition.

Greek Language Learning Materials

Farmakidhes, Anne. *A Manual of Modern Greek*. New Haven: Yale Univ. Press, 1983, 2d ed. The best crash course; there's an intermediate sequel and two reading primers for those who master the basics. The entire series costs $65 but is worth it.

Rassias, John and Peter and Chrysanthi Bien. *Demotic Greek*. Hanover, N. Hamp. and London: University Press of New England, 1983. Passable second choice to first listing.

Sofroniou, S. A. *Modern Greek*. New York: David McKay and London: Hodder & Stoughton, 1983. Most useful as a quick brushup for those who've already studied Greek.

Stone, Tom. *Greek Handbook*. Athens: Lycabettus Press, 1982. The best emergency manual—light years ahead of any Berlitz or Hamlyn phrase book. "An A-Z phrasal guide of almost everything you want to know about Greece (and are sometimes afraid to ask)" is the well-put subtitle.

Collins Contemporary Greek Dictionary. London and Glasgow: Collins, 1977. Reprinted in an enlarged plastic binding for the U.S. market in 1982.

Divry's New Handy English-Greek and Greek-English Dictionary. New York: Divry, 1983. Very compact and cheap but slanted toward *katharévousa* Greek. This and *Collins* should together handle most questions.

Pring, Julian. *Oxford Dictionary of Modern Greek*. Oxford and New York: Oxford Univ. Press, 1985. Indisputably the most thorough and current—and finally available as an inexpensive, compact, bilingual paperback.

GREEK FOR HIKERS

Simple accents are indicated over the stressed syllables. Accentuation is critical in Greek, occasionally counterintuitive and often the only difference between two otherwise identical words. *Mílo*, "apple," vs. *miló*, "I speak," is one of numerous examples. To ensure comprehensible pronunciation, these transliterations are phonetic and do not parallel, letter-for-letter, the word spelling in the Greek alphabet. Nouns are given in the nominative singular case, unless otherwise noted; adjectives, except for numbers and nationalities, appear in the neuter gender.

Greetings, Partings, Courtesies, Basic Expressions

In most areas the approaching individual is expected to address first the seated or stationary person(s), but this rule is not hard and fast.

Kalí méra, spéra, níhta   Good day, evening, night—all-purpose but somewhat colorless.

Ya sou (sas, plural or formal)   "Health to you"—standard greeting, parting and toast.

Hériteh   "Rejoice"—still common with older people in rural areas. The greeting of the early Christian fathers.

Kalóston!   Very friendly greeting uttered by those in the community being approached—a contraction of the two greetings below.

Kalós ílthateh!   Welcome! Literally, "It is well that you have come." To which the response is:

Kalós sas vréekameh!   Literally, "We have found you well!" Very formal usage.

Adíou   Good-bye—a Venetian loan-word similar to Spanish *adios*.

Ya hará   "Health and joy"—very casual parting equivalent to "bye."

Kaló taxídhi   Bon voyage.

Na pas sto kaló   "May you go towards the good"—formal farewell uttered by the staying party.

Kalí óra sou   The good hour to you.

Pos eésay (eéstay)?   Formal "how are you," singular and (plural) second person.

Ti káneis (káneteh)?   More casual "how are you," singular and (plural) second person. The response is:

Kalá, kai esée (eseés)?   Fine, and you?—singular/familiar (plural/formal).

Parakaló   Please.

Efharistó (polí)   Thank you (very much).

Kai egó   You're welcome (literally, "I also" [thank you]). Occasionally you'll hear *típota*, "(it was) nothing."

Signómi   Excuse (me).

Málista   Certainly.

En dáxi   O.K.—used exactly as in English.

Neh   Yes.

Óhi   No.

Greeks' Questions

Apo pou eésay (eestay)?   Where are you from—(singular [pl])?

Pandremén(os)(i) eésay?   Are you married?—'os' and 'i' are masculine and feminine endings, respectively.

Ya pou pas (páteh)?   To where are you going (again, singular/familiar and [plural/formal] second person)?

Na se keráso káti?   Can I treat you to something?

Nationalities

First parenthetical ending is masculine, second is feminine.
Amerikan(ós)(ídha) American
Kanadh(ós)(éza) Canadian
Ángl(os)(ídha) English
Avstral(ós)(ídha) Australian
Nea Zilandh(ós)(í) New Zealander
Olandhés(os)(a) Dutch
Irlandh(ós)(í) Irish
Yerman(ós)(ídha) German
Gáll(os)(ídha) French
Elvet(ós)(ídha) Swiss
Souidh(ós)(éza) Swedish
Dhan(ós)(éza) Danish
Finlandh(ós)(í) Finnish
Norveg(ós)(í) Norwegian
Israilin(ós)(í) Israeli

Apologies to any reader from an omitted country. In all cases, you can make a complete sentence with the verb . . . *eémay* (I am).

Common Requests

Boró na kataskinóso edhó? Can I camp here?
Boró na afíso toúto edhó? Can I leave this here?
Póso makriá eénay ya———? How far is it to ———?
Zitó to monopáti ya———. I'm looking for the path to ———.
Pou eénay i toualéta? Where is the toilet?
Éhi ———? Is there ——— (a bus, a beach, a trail)?
Éhoun ———? Are there (any) ——— (tickets, apples, etc.)?
  Answer
Éhi/ehoun There is/are.
Dhen éhi/ehoun There isn't/aren't any.

The verb *ipárhi/ipárhoun*, with similar meaning to *éhi/éhoun,* is also common.

Other Useful Verbs

Given in the first-person, present form, as in dictionaries. Most verbs have a different basic stem for continuous and simple tenses—both must be understood.
Ého I have
Piyáino, páo I go
Eémasteh we are; other forms of "to be" given above
Vrísko, vro I find
Mayerévo, mayerépso I cook
Thélo I want
Perimáino I wait (for)
Vlépo, dho I see
Katalaváino, katalávo I understand
Pliróno, pliróso I pay

Staying

Méno edhó ——— méres. I'm staying here ——— days.
Dous meh zestó neró Shower with hot water
Dhomátio meh paráthiro Room with a window
Skliró kreváti Hard bed (for the particular)

Boró na plíno roúha? Can I wash clothes?
Klidhí Key
Lámba, fanári Oil lamp, lantern
Fós, kerí Electric light, candle
Monóklino, dhíklino, tríklino Single, double, triple (room)
Sendhónia Sheets
Kouvérta Blanket
Maxilári Pillow

Numbers

Counting is made somewhat challenging by the fact that some, but not all, numerals are declined according to the three genders, masculine, feminine and neuter.

énas, mía, éna m, f, and n, respectively, for "a," "one"
dhío 2 (invariable)
tréis, tría 3 (m/f, n)
tésseres, téssera 4 (m/f, n)
pénde 5
éxi 6
eftá 7
októ 8
ennéa, enyá 9
dhéka 10
éndheka 11
dhódheka 12
dheka-tréis (tría) 13
dhéka-eftá 17
eékosi 20
eékosi-pénde 25 (pattern for numbers 20-99)
triánda 30

saránda 40
penéeda 50
exeénda 60
evdomeénda 70
ogdhónda 80
eneneénda 90
ekató(n) 100
ekató(n) dhéka-októ 118 (pattern for numbers 100-999)
dhiakósia (n) 200
trakósia (n) 300
tetrakósia (n) 400
pendakósia (n) 500
exakósia (n) 600
eftakósia (n) 700
oktakósia (n) 800
oktakósia triánda éxi 836
enniakósia (n) 900

Proper Greek uses masculine and feminine endings for the multiples of hundred, i.e., *enniakósii* (m) and *enniakósies* (f), since the numerals are grammatically adjectives defining the item counted.

Hílii (m), hílies (f), hília (n) 1000
dhío hiliádhes (invariable) 2000
tésseres hiliádhes tetrakósies tréis 4,403 feminine objects
pénde hiliádhes exakósia dhéka-téssera 5,613 neuter items

Time

anatolí ilíou sunrise
vradhiázi it gets dark
iliovasílema sunset
mía óra one hour
misí óra half-hour
dhío óres two hours
dhío (kai) misí óres two-and-a-half hours; "and" optional in Greek
éna tétarto a quarter (hour)
dekapénde leptá 15 minutes

éna leptó one minute—extremely elastic unit of time, beloved of waiters
stís ——— óres at ——— o'clock
eénay ——— óres it's ——— o'clock
Póte? When?
Poté. (note accent) Never.
tóra now
tóte then
seémera today

kthés yesterday
prokthés day before yesterday

ávrio tomorrow
metávrio day after tomorrow

Weather

sýnefa, synefiázi clouds, it clouds over
vrohí, vréhi rain, it rains

kane krío it's cold (literally, "it makes cold")
hióni, hionízi snow, it snows
omihlí mist, fog

Equipment

sakídhio backpack
bótes boots
pagoúri canteen
gaziéra compact stove
(poupoulénio) ipnosákko (down) sleeping bag
stromáki foam pad

boutília, fiáles butane cartridges
fotístiki parafíni kerosene
spírta matches
souyás pocketknife
skiní tent
bastoúni walking stick

Receiving Directions

katefthía, ísia straight ahead
lígo akóma a bit more, further
kondá/makriá near/far
dhexiá/aristerá right/left
aníforo/katíforo uphill/downhill
platí/apótomo flat/sheer
omaló/anómalo level/uneven
fardhí/stenó wide/narrow
kaló/kakó good/bad
oréo/áskimo nice, pretty/unpleasant, ugly

megálo/mikró big/small
edhó/ekéi here/there
apó from
méhri, os until, up to
prin/metá before/after
péra beyond, other side
apénandi across from
dhípla adjacent
pros toward
(e)páno apó above
káto apó below

Describing Trails

dhrómos road, way (general term)
ohimátikos dhrómos auto road
dhasikí odhós forest or lumbering road
dhimósio literally, "public"—any government-maintained road other than a *dhasiki*, usually between villages
monopáti footpath

kalderími cobbled or flagstone path
skála stairway
mouláriko mule track
katsikódhromos livestock trace
stavrodhrómi, dhiastávrosi, dhiakládhosi crossroads, forking
simádhi(a) mark(s), trail blaze(s)
métra, hiliómetra meters, kilometers

Landmarks

voun(ó)(á) mountain(s)
korfí peak
loúki couloir, summit incline
loútsa cirque, often pond
pérazma, dhiáselo, avhénas pass, saddle
oropédhio high plateau
lófos hill, knoll
pláya slope, hillside
meriá side, as in *álli meriá*, "other side"
ráhi ridge

pétra rock (substance, singular)
vráhos, vráhi is generally understood to be cliff, cliffs (s, pl); sometimes rock (object)
lithári boulder
farángi gorge
langádhi, harádhra ravine, canyon
kiládha valley
lakka gulch, hollow, clearing (in forest)
spílio, spiliá cave
dhéndhro tree

233

pèvko pine
róbolo Balkan pine
élato fir tree
oxiá beech
lévka poplar
flamoúri linden
koromiliá wild plum
kastaniá chestnut tree
karidhiá wild walnut tree
valanidhiá valonea oak
pournári holly oak
kédhros juniper, cedar
kiparíssi cypress tree
plátanos plane tree
itéa willow
eliá olive tree
pikrodháfni oleander
fínikas palm tree
dhássos forest
livádhi meadow
báltos marsh, swamp
horáfi field
kámbos clearing, high pasture or field
amoudhiá, paralía sandy beach
yialós shore
thálassa sea
límni lake
potámi river
idhragoyéio aqueduct, irrigation canal
ksiropótamos dry wash
révma stream; also electric current
vrýssi fountain; also faucet
piyí spring
pigádhi well
stérna rain cistern
sikláki can-on-a-string to fetch water from above two constructions

dexamení capped (sealed) reservoir
spíti house
kalívi hut, cottage
stáni shepherd's colony
mandhra, stróunga sheep pen, corral
katafýgio alpine refuge
eklisía church
ksoklísi isolated rural chapel
ikonostási, ikónisma wayside shrine; the former, also "altar screen"
nekrotafío cemetery
alóni threshing circle
yéepedho soccer field
latomeío quarry
yefíri, yéfira bridge
froúrio, kástro castle, fortified elevation
pýrgos tower
monastíri, moní monastery or nunnery
arhaiótites, arháia antiquities, ruins
pinakidha, tabéla sign, placard
áyios, ayía, áyii saint (m, f, plural)
pólis city, large town
horió village
hóra main town of an island, usually called by the same name as the island
platía plaza, village square
kafenéio cafe
tavérna most common kind of Greek eatery
psistariá grill-restaurant
exohikó kéndro roadhouse, isolated *tavérna*

Sorts of People

kalóyeros, monahós monk
kalógria, monahí nun
igóumenos abbot
igouménissa abbess
arhondáris monastery guestmaster
fílakas guard
horofílakas gendarme, soon to be phased out in favor of:
(éthnikos) astinómos (national) policeman

tsombánis, voskós,
  ktinotrófos shepherd
kinigós hunter
tsangáris cobbler, leather worker
ráptis tailor
ksénos, kséni foreigner, also guest. What you should hope to be called.
tourísta exactly what it sounds like. Your demeanor determines whether you get called *ksénos* or this.

Beasts, Birds, Bugs

arkoúdha bear
lýkos wolf
eláfi deer
agriaíga chamois
katsíka, gídha goat
próvato sheep
álogo horse
mulári mule
gaïdhoúri donkey
alepoú fox
asvós badger
skanzóhiros hedgehog
kounávi weasel
arouraíos rat
pondíki mouse
aetós eagle
pérdhika partridge
yeráki hawk
órnio vulture
trigóni turtle dove
pelargós stork
peristéri pigeon
koukováyia little owl

boúfos eagle (horned) owl
mikróboufos long-eared owl
aïdhóni nightingale
helóna tortoise
vátrahos frog
sávra lizard
trítona newt
fídhi snake
ohiá viper, adder
skorpiós scorpion
kounoúpi mosquito
mïga fly
aráhni spider
mélissa bee
sfíka wasp, hornet
petaloúdha butterfly
psílos flea
pseíra louse
tsimbóúri tick
tsoúktra, médhousa jellyfish
ahinós sea urchin

and last, but not least

mandhróskilo sheep guard-dog

INDEX

SUBJECT INDEX

GEOGRAPHICAL INDEX

Places included in the Table of Contents are not listed below. Places with identical or similar names are identified by a parenthetical qualifier; e.g. (mountain range, province, or island). Important alternative names are also set off in parentheses.

Martha Degasis photo

About the author:

MARC S. DUBIN has spent much of the last six years hiking and traveling in Greece. He has led organized hiking expeditions in the Pindhos ranges, the Peloponnisos, and on the island of Crete for both British and American travel firms. He's also led yacht tours in the islands and along the Turkish Aegean coast.

An inveterate traveler, Dubin has trekked in the Himalaya and the Peruvian Andes, and toured South America, southern Asia and the entire Mediterranean basin. He speaks four languages in addition to near-fluency in Greek.

Dubin is a major contributor to *The Rough Guide to Greece* and *The Rough Guide to Yugoslavia* (Routledge & Kegan Paul), and has written many travel-magazine articles as well as an earlier book on backpacking in Greece. His color photos were selected for a recent engagement calendar, "Images of the Greek Islands" (Pomegranate Art Books). When not ranging across the globe, Dubin resides in California.